Psychology Statistics
FOR
DUMMIES®

by Donncha Hanna and Martin Dempster

WILEY

A John Wiley and Sons, Ltd, Publication

Psychology Statistics For Dummies®

Published by
John Wiley & Sons, Ltd
The Atrium
Southern Gate
Chichester
West Sussex
PO19 8SQ
England
www.wiley.com

For general information on our other products and services, please contact our Customer Care Department within the U.S. at 877-762-2974, outside the U.S. at 317-572-3993, or fax 317-572-4002.

For technical support, please visit www.wiley.com/techsupport.

Wiley publishes in a variety of print and electronic formats and by print-on-demand. Some material included with standard print versions of this book may not be included in e-books or in print-on-demand. If this book refers to media such as a CD or DVD that is not included in the version you purchased, you may download this material at http://booksupport.wiley.com. For more information about Wiley products, visit www.wiley.com.

British Library Cataloguing in Publication Data: A catalogue record for this book is available from the British Library

ISBN 978-1-119-95287-9 (pbk); ISBN 978-1-119-95393-7 (ebk); ISBN 978-1-119-95394-4 (ebk); ISBN 978-1-119-95395-1 (ebk)

Printed and bound in Great Britain by TJ International, Padstow, Cornwall.

10 9 8 7 6 5 4 3 2 1

WILEY

About the Authors

Donncha Hanna is, among other more interesting things, a lecturer at the School of Psychology, Queen's University Belfast.

He has been teaching statistics to undergraduate students, postgraduate students and real professional people for over 10 years (he is not as old as Martin). His research focuses on mental health and the reasons why students do not like statistics; these topics are not necessarily related. He attempts to teach statistics in an accessible and easy to understand way without dumbing down the content; maybe one day he will succeed.

Donncha lives in Belfast with two fruit bats, a hedgehog and a human named Pamela.

Martin Dempster is a Senior Lecturer in the School of Psychology, Queen's University Belfast. He is a Health Psychologist and Chartered Statistician who has also authored *A Research Guide for Health & Clinical Psychology*.

He has been teaching statistics to undergraduate psychology students for over 20 years. As a psychologist he is interested in the adverse reaction that psychology students often have to learning statistics and endeavours to work out what causes this (hopefully not him) and how it can be alleviated. He tries to teach statistics in an accessible manner (which isn't always easy).

Martin lives in Whitehead, a seaside village in Co. Antrim, Northern Ireland, which isn't very well-known, which is why he lives there.

Dedication

From Donncha: For my mother and father. Thank you for everything.

From Martin: For Tom, who joined the world half way through the development of this book and has been a glorious distraction ever since.

Author's Acknowledgments

From Donncha: I'm very grateful to the team at Dummies Towers for their work and guidance in getting this book to print – particularly our editors Simon Bell and Mike Baker.

I would like to thank all the students, colleagues and teachers who have helped shape my thinking and knowledge about statistics (and apologise if I have stolen any of their ideas!). I must also acknowledge Pamela (who didn't complain when I used the excuse of writing this book to avoid doing the dishes) and my sister, Aideen, who offered practical help as always. Thanks to my friend and colleague Martin Dorahy who put up with me in New Zealand where half of this book was written. And of course to Martin Dempster, without whom there would be no book.

From Martin: This book is the product of at least 20 years of interaction with colleagues and students; picking up their ideas; answering their questions; and being stimulated into thinking about different ways of explaining statistical concepts. Therefore, there are many people to thank – too many too list and certainly too many for me to remember (any more).

However, there are a few people who made contributions to the actual content of this book. My brother, Bob, who has a much better sense of humour than me, helped with some of the examples in the book. Noleen helped me to better formulate my thinking when I was having some difficulty and supported my decision to undertake this project in the first place. My mum and dad spurred me on with their ever-present encouragement. Finally, thanks to my colleague Donncha, who floated the idea of writing this book and asked me to collaborate with him on its development.

Publisher's Acknowledgments

We're proud of this book; please send us your comments at `http://dummies.custhelp.com`. For other comments, please contact our Customer Care Department within the U.S. at 877-762-2974, outside the U.S. at 317-572-3993, or fax 317-572-4002.

Some of the people who helped bring this book to market include the following:

Acquisitions, Editorial, and Vertical Websites

Project Editor: Simon Bell

Commissioning Editor: Mike Baker

Assistant Editor: Ben Kemble

Development Editor: Charlie Wilson

Copy Editor: Mary White

Technical Editor: Alix Godfrey

Special Advisor: Vince Kwasnica

Proofreader: Kim Vernon

Production Manager: Daniel Mersey

Publisher: David Palmer

Cover Photos: © iStock / Blackie

Cartoons: Ed McLachlan

Composition Services

Project Coordinator: Kristie Rees

Layout and Graphics: Carrie A. Cesavice, Joyce Haughey, Christin Swinford

Proofreader: Melissa Cossell

Indexer: Potomac Indexing, LLC

Publishing and Editorial for Consumer Dummies

    Kathleen Nebenhaus, Vice President and Executive Publisher

    Kristin Ferguson-Wagstaffe, Product Development Director

    Ensley Eikenburg, Associate Publisher, Travel

    Kelly Regan, Editorial Director, Travel

Publishing for Technology Dummies

    Andy Cummings, Vice President and Publisher

Composition Services

    Debbie Stailey, Director of Composition Services

Contents at a Glance

Table of Contents

Introduction

We recently collected data from psychology students across 31 universities regarding their attitudes towards statistics; 51 per cent of the students did not realise statistics would be a substantial component of their course and the majority had negative attitudes or anxiety towards the subject. So if this sounds familiar take comfort in the fact you are not alone!

Let's get one thing out of the way right now. The statistics component you have to complete for your degree is not impossible and it shouldn't be gruelling. If you can cope with cognitive psychology theories and understand psycho-biological models you should have no difficulty. Remember this isn't mathematics; the computer will run all the complex number crunching for you. This book has been written in a clear and concise manner that will help you through the course. We don't assume any previous knowledge of statistics and in return we ask you relinquish any negative attitudes you may have!

The second point we need to address is why, when you have enrolled for psychology, are you being forced to study statistics? You need to know that statistics is an important and necessary part of all psychology courses. Psychology is an empirical discipline, which means we use evidence to decide between competing theories and approaches. Collecting quantitative information allows us to represent this data in an objective and easily comparable format. This information must be summarised and analysed (after all, pages of numbers aren't that meaningful) and this allows us to infer conclusions and make decisions. Understanding statistics not only allows you to conduct and analyse your own research, but importantly it allows you to read and critically evaluate previous research.

Also, statistics are important in psychology because psychologists use their statistical knowledge in their day-to-day work. Consider a psychologist who is working with clients exhibiting depression, anxiety and self-harm. They must decide which therapy is most useful for particular conditions, whether anxiety is related to (or can predict) self harm, or whether clients who self harm differ in their levels of depression. Statistical knowledge is a crucial tool in any psychologist's job.

About This Book

The aim of this book is to provide an easily accessible reference guide, written in plain English, that will allow students to readily understand, carry out, interpret and report all types of statistical procedures required for their course. While we have targeted this book at psychology undergraduate students we hope it will be useful to all social science and health science students.

The book is structured in a relatively linear way; starting with the more basic concepts and progressing through to more complex techniques. This is the order in which the statistics component of the psychology degree is normally taught. Note, though, that this doesn't mean you are expected to start from page one and read the book from cover to cover. Instead each chapter (and each statistical technique) is designed to be self-contained and does not necessarily require any previous knowledge. For example, if you were to look up the technique 'partial correlation' you will find a clear, jargon-free explanation of the technique followed by an example (with step-by-step instructions demonstrating how to perform the technique on SPSS, how to interpret the output and, importantly, how to report the results appropriately). Each statistical procedure in the book follows this same framework enabling you to quickly find the technique of interest, run the required analysis and write it up in an appropriate way.

As we know (both from research we have conducted and subjective experience of teaching courses) statistics tends to be a psychology student's least favourite subject and causes anxiety in the majority of psychology students. We therefore deliberately steer clear of complex mathematical formulae as well as superfluous and rarely-used techniques. Instead we have concentrated on producing a clear and concise guide illustrated with visual aids and practical examples.

What You're Not to Read

We have deliberately tried to keep our explanations concise but there is still a lot of information contained in this book. Occasionally you will see the technical stuff icon; this, as the icon suggests, contains more technical information which we regard as valuable in understanding the technique but not crucial to conducting the analysis. You can skip these sections and still understand the topic in question.

Likewise you may come across sidebars where we have elaborated on a topic. We think they are interesting, but we are biased! If you are in a hurry you can skip these sections.

Foolish Assumptions

Rightly or wrongly we have made some assumptions when writing this book. We assume that:

- You have SPSS installed and you are familiar with using a computer. We do not outline how to install SPSS and we are assuming that you are familiar with using the mouse (pointing, clicking, etc.) and the keyboard to enter or manipulate information. We do not assume that you have used SPSS before; Chapter 3 gives an introduction to this programme and we provide you with step-by-step instructions for each procedure.

- You are not a mathematical genius but you do have some basic understanding of using numbers. If you know what we mean by squaring a number (multiplying a number by itself; if we square 5 we get 25) or taking a square root – the opposite of squaring a number (the square root of a number is that value when squared gives the original number; the square root of 25 is 5) you will be fine. Remember the computer will be doing the calculations for you.

- You do not need to conduct complex multivariate statistics. This is an introductory book and we limit out discussion to the type of analyses commonly required by undergraduate syllabuses.

How this Book is Organised

This book has been organised into six parts:

- Part I of the book deals with describing and summarising data. It starts by explaining, with examples, the types of variables commonly used and level of measurement. These concepts are key in deciding how to treat your data and which statistics are most appropriate to analyse your data. We deal with the SPSS environment, so if you haven't used SPSS before, or need a refresher, this a good place to start. We also cover the first descriptive statistics: the mean, mode and median. From there we go on to key ideas such as measures of dispersion and interpreting and producing the most commonly used graphs for displaying data.

✔ Part II of the book focuses on some of the concepts which are fundamental for an understanding of statistics. If you don't know the difference between a null and alternative hypothesis, unsure why you have to report the *p*-value and an effect size or have never really been confident of what statistical inference actually means, then this part of the book is for you!

✔ Part III of the book deals with inferential statistics, the ones that examine relationships or associations between variables, including correlations, regression and tests for categorical data. We explain each technique clearly – what it is used for and when you should use it, followed by instructions on how to perform the analysis in SPSS, how to interpret the subsequent output and how to write up the results in both the correct statistical format and in plain English.

✔ Part IV of the book deals with the inferential statistics that examine differences between two or more independent groups of data. In particular we address the Independent *t*-test, Mann-Whitney test and Analysis of Variance (ANOVA). For each technique we offer a clear explanation, show you how it works in SPSS, and how to interpret and write up the results.

✔ Part V of the book deals with the inferential statistics that examine differences between two or more repeated measurements. Here we cover the Paired *t*-test, the Wilcoxon test and Analysis of Variance (ANOVA). We also focus on analysis of research designs that include both independent groups and repeated measurements: the Mixed ANOVA.

✔ Part VI, the final part of the book, provides you with hints and tips on how to avoid mistakes and write up your results in the most appropriate way. We hope these pointers can save you from the pitfalls often made by inexperienced researchers and can contribute to you producing a better results section. We outline some of the common mistakes and misunderstandings students make when performing statistical analyses and how you can avoid them, and we provide quick and useful tips for writing your results section.

Icons Used in This Book

As with all *For Dummies* books, you will notice icons in the margin that signify there is something special about that piece of information.

This points out a helpful hint designed to save you time or from thinking harder than you have to.

 This one is important! It indicates a piece of information that you should bear in mind even after the book has been closed.

 This icon highlights a common misunderstanding or error that we don't want you to make.

 This contains a more detailed discussion or explanation of a topic; you can skip this material if you are in a rush.

Where to Go from Here

You could read this book cover to cover but we have designed it so you can easily find the topics you are interested in and get the information you want without having to read pages of mathematical formulae or find out what every single option in SPSS does. If you are completely new to this area we suggest you start with Chapter 1. Need some help navigating SPSS for the first time? Turn to Chapter 3. If you are not quite sure what a *p*-value or an effect size is, you'll need to refer to Part II of the book. For any of the other techniques we suggest you use the table of contents or index to guide you to the right place.

Remember you can't make the computer (or your head) explode so, with book in hand, it's time to start analysing that data!

Part I
Describing Data

In this part . . .

We know: you're studying psychology, not statistics. You're not a mathematician and never wanted to be. Never fear, help is near. This part of the book covers the key concepts you need to grasp to describe statistical data accurately and successfully. We talk about the simplest descriptive statistics – mean, mode and median – and important ideas such as measures of dispersion and how to interpret and produce the graphs for displaying data.

We also introduce you to SPSS (Statistical Package for Social Sciences, to give it its full name) and walk you through the basics of using the program to produce straightforward statistics.

Chapter 1

Statistics? I Thought This Was Psychology!

In This Chapter

▶ Understanding variables

▶ Introducing SPSS

▶ Outlining descriptive and inferential statistics

▶ Differentiating between parametric and non-parametric statistics

▶ Explaining research designs

*W*hen we tell our initially fresh-faced and enthusiastic first year students that statistics is a substantial component of their course approximately half of them are genuinely shocked. 'We came to study psychology, not statistics', they shout. Presumably they thought they would be spending the next three years ordering troubled individuals to 'lie down on the couch and tell me about your mother'. We tell them there is no point running for the exits as they will quickly learn that statistics is part of all undergraduate psychology courses, and that if they plan to undertake post-graduate studies or work in this area they will be using these techniques for a long time to come (besides, we were expecting this reaction and have locked the exits). Then we hear the cry 'But I'm not a mathematician. I am interested in people and behaviour'. We don't expect students to be mathematicians. If you have a quick scan through this book you won't be confronted with pages of scary looking equations. These days we use computer-based software packages such as SPSS to do all the complex calculations for us. We tell them that psychology is a scientific discipline. If they want to learn about people they have to objectively collect information, summarise it and analyse it. Summarising and analysing allows you to interpret the information and give it meaning in terms of theories and real world problems. Summarising and analysing information is statistics; it is a fundamental and integrated component of psychology.

The aim of this chapter is to give you a roadmap of the main statistical concepts you will encounter during your undergraduate psychology studies and to signpost you to relevant chapters on topics where you can learn how to become a statistics superhero (or at least scrape by).

Know Your Variables

All quantitative research in psychology involves collecting information (called *data*) that can be represented by numbers. For example, levels of depression can be represented by depression scores obtained from a questionnaire, or a person's gender can be represented by a number (1 for male and 2 for female). The characteristics you are measuring are known as *variables* because they vary! They can vary over time within the same person (depression scores can vary over a person's life time) or vary between different individuals (individuals can be classified as male or female, but once a person is classified this variable doesn't tend to change!).

Several names and properties exist, associated with variables in any data set, which you must become familiar with. Variables can be continuous or discrete, have different levels of measurement and can be independent or dependent. We cover all this information in Chapter 2. Initially these terms may seem a little bamboozling, but it is important you ensure you have a good understanding of them, as they dictate the statistical analyses that are available and appropriate for your data. For example, it helps to report a mean depression score of 32.4 for a particular group of participants, but a mean gender score of 1.6 for the same group doesn't much make sense (we discuss the mean in Chapter 4)!

Variables can be classified as *discrete*, where you specify discrete categories (for example, male and female), or *continuous,* where scores can lie anywhere along a continuum (for example, depression scores may lie anywhere between 0 and 63 if measured by the Beck Depression Inventory).

Variables also differ in their measurement properties. Four levels of measurement exist:

- **Nominal**: This contains the least amount of information of the levels. At the nominal level, a numerical value is applied arbitrarily. Gender is an example of *nominal* level of measurement (for example, 1 for male and 2 for female), and it makes no sense to say one is greater or less than the other.

- **Ordinal**: Rankings on a class test are an example of an *ordinal* level of measurement; we can order participants from the highest to the lowest score but we don't how much better the first person did compared to the second person (it could be 1 mark or it could be 20 marks!).

- **Interval**: IQ scores are measured at the *interval* level, which means we can order the scores but the difference between each point is equal. That is, the difference between 95 and 100 is the same as the difference between 115 and 120.

✔ **Ratio**: In a ratio level of measurement, the scores can be ordered, the difference between each point on the scale is equal and the scale also has a true absolute zero. Weight, for example, is measured at the *ratio* level; having a true zero means a weight of zero signifies an absence of any weight and it also allows you to make proportional statements, such as '10 kg is half the weight of 20 kg'.

You will also need to classify the variables in your data as *independent* or *dependent* and the classification will depend on the research question you are asking. For example, if you are investigating the difference in depression scores between males and females, the independent variable is gender (this is the variable you think that is predicting a change), and depression scores are the dependent variable (this is the outcome variable where the scores depend on the independent variable).

What is SPSS?

The initials SPSS stand for Statistical Package for the Social Sciences and it provides you with a program capable of storing, manipulating and analysing your data. This book assumes you will be using SPSS to analyse your data. SPSS is probably the most commonly used statistics package in the social sciences, but of course other similar packages exist as well as those designed to conduct more specialised analysis.

There are three main 'views' or windows you will be using in SPSS. The first is the 'variable view' and this is where you label and code the variables you are working with, for example, if you wanted to specify the two variables 'gender' and 'depression'. The 'data view' is the spreadsheet where you enter all your data. The normal format when entering data is that each column will represent a variable (for example, gender or depression) and each row will represent one individual or participant. Therefore if you collected and entered information on the gender and depression scores of 10 participants you would have 2 columns and 10 rows in your SPSS data view. SPSS allows you to enter numeric data, string data (which is non-numeric information such as names) and also assign codes (for example, 1 for male and 2 for female).

Unlike other programs you may have used (for example, Microsoft Office Excel) cells do not contain formulae or equations.

Once your data is entered, SPSS allows you to run a wide variety of analyses by using drop down menus. There are literally hundreds of different analyses and options you can choose; in this book we will only explain the statistical procedures necessary for your course. When you have selected the analyses you want to conduct, your results will appear in a separate 'output window'; your job then is to read and interpret the relevant information.

In addition to using the pull-down menus you can also program SPSS by using a simple syntax language. This can be useful if you need to repeat the same analyses on many different data sets, but explaining how to use it is beyond the scope of an introductory text.

SPSS was first released in 1968 and has been through many versions and upgrades; at the time of writing this chapter, the most recent version was SPSS 20.0 which was released in August 2011. Between 2009 and 2010 SPSS briefly was known as Predictive Analytics SoftWare and could be found on your computer under the name *PASW*. In 2010 it was purchased by IBM and now appears in your computer's menu under the name *IBM SPSS statistics* (and no, we don't know why the last 'statistics' is necessary either!).

Descriptive Statistics

When you collect your data you need to communicate your findings to other people (tutor, boss, colleagues or whoever it may be). Let's imagine you collect data from 100 people on their levels of coulrophobia (fear of clowns); if you simply produce a list of 100 scores in SPSS this won't be very useful or easy to comprehend for your audience. Instead you need a way to describe your data set in a concise and repeatable format. The standard way to do this is to present two pieces of information, a measure of central tendency and a measure of dispersion.

Central tendency

There are several different types of central tendency, but they all attempt to give a single number that represents your variable. The most common measure is sometimes known as *average* but it is more correctly called the *arithmetic mean,* and you are probably familiar with it. To obtain the mean you simply add all the scores on a variable and divide by the number of participants or cases you had. One of the strengths of the mean as a measure of central tendency is that it represents all your data; however, this means it has a weakness in that it can be influenced by extreme scores. The mean isn't always an appropriate number to represent your data. The *median* (the middle value when the scores are ranked) is more appropriate when your variable is measured at the ordinal level of measurement and the *mode* (the most frequently occurring value) is appropriate when your variable is measured at the nominal level. Measures of central tendency are covered in Chapter 4.

Dispersion

There are also several measures of dispersion, and each aims to give a single number that represents the spread or variability of your variable. The larger the dispersion value for your variable, the larger its variability (participants vary on the scores they obtain), whereas a small value of dispersion indicates that the scores vary less (participants tend to score similarly). The most common measure of is the standard deviation, an estimate of the average variability of spread of your variable. Chapter 5 describes the standard deviation along with the other important measures of dispersion which include the variance, range and interquartile range.

Graphs

Another way of displaying your data is to provide a visual representation in the form of a graph. Graphs are important for another reason; the type of statistical analysis you can conduct with variables will depend on the distribution of your variables, which you will need to assess by using graphs. Chapter 6 outlines the common types of graphs used in psychology (the histogram, bar chart, cumulative frequency plot, and box and whisker plot) and how to generate each of them in SPSS.

Standardised scores

Imagine you measured a friend's extraversion level with the Revised NEO Personality Inventory and told them they obtained a score of 164; it is likely they will want to know how this score compares to other people's scores. Is it high or low? They also might want to know how it compares to the psychoticism score of 34 you gave them last week from the Eysenck Personality Questionnaire. Simply reporting raw scores often isn't that informative. You need to be able to compare these scores to other people's scores and importantly you'll need to compare scores that are measured on different scales. The good news is that it is quite easy to convert your raw score into a standardised score, which means it is possible to make these comparisons. A standardised score is measured in terms of standard deviations (so it can be compared against standardised scores from different variables) and allows instant comparisons to the mean score on a variable (which means you can tell if an individual's score is greater or less than the mean). We cover standardisation in more detail in Chapter 10.

Inferential Statistics

Descriptive statistics are useful in illustrating the properties of your sample (that is, the participants you have collected data from), but the majority of the time you will be more interested in the properties of the population (that is, all possible participants of interest). For example, if you are interested in differences in attitudes to sectarianism between boys and girls enrolled in schools in Northern Ireland, then your population is all Northern Irish school children. As it is unrealistic to recruit all the children in Northern Ireland (in terms of time, money and consent) you would measure sectarianism in a small subset or *sample* of the children (we examine the differences between samples and populations in Chapter 7).

Inferential statistics allows you to make inferences from your sample about the larger population. For example, if you found a difference in sectarianism between boys and girls in your sample you could infer this difference to all schoolchildren in Northern Ireland (inferential statistics are explained in Chapter 7). You can't be completely sure this difference exists in the population as you haven't tested every child in the population, but you should be 95 per cent confident that the difference you found in your sample exists in the population (under certain conditions), and this is what an inferential statistic assesses (this is discussed in more detail in Chapter 7).

The inferential statistic you conduct will tell you about the probability of your result occurring in the population (that is, whether the difference in your sample really exists in the population, or whether you obtained this result by chance) but it does not tell you anything about the size of the difference. For instance, you may find that males are more likely to show sectarian attitudes than females, but this isn't very interesting if the difference between the attitudes is really tiny. *Effect sizes* indicate the strength of the relationship between your variables (we cover effect sizes in Chapter 11) and should always be reported in conjunction with the probability level associated with any inferential statistic.

Hypotheses

Before you commence any study it is important to have a hypothesis or a specific testable statement that reflects the aim of your study. In the example above you would specify the hypothesis: 'there is no difference between levels of sectarianism between boys and girls enrolled in Northern Ireland schools.' We outline hypothesis testing in Chapter 8 and explain why we always start with the assumption that your data demonstrates no effect, difference or relationship.

Parametric and non-parametric variables

When you are addressing a hypothesis there are two main types of statistical analysis you can conduct; a *parametric* test or the *non-parametric* equivalent. Parametric statistics assume that the data approximates a certain distribution, such as the normal distribution explained in Chapter 9. This allows us to make inferences which make these types of statistics powerful (see Chapter 11 for a discussion of power) and capable of producing accurate results.

However, because parametric statistics are based on certain assumptions, you must check your data to ensure it adheres to these assumptions (we explain how to do this for each individual statistic in the book). Failure to check the assumptions means you run the risk of performing inappropriate analyses which means your results, and therefore conclusions, may be incorrect.

By comparison, non-parametric statistics make fewer assumptions about your data, which mean they can be used to analyse a more diverse range of data. Non-parametric tests tend to be less powerful than their parametric equivalents, so you should always attempt to use the parametric version unless the data violates the assumptions of that test.

Research Designs

The type of statistical analyses you should conduct depends on several things, but to decide on the correct 'family' of tests, you must first decide on the design of your study. The choice of design is influenced by the question you want answered or your hypothesis. Research design can be broadly classified into *correlational design* and *experimental design*.

Correlational design

Correlational design is when you are interested in the relationships or associations between two or more variables. Correlational design is distinguished from experimental design as there is no attempt to manipulate the variables; instead you are investigating existing relationships between the variables. For example, you may be conducting a study to look at the relationship between the use of illegal recreational drugs and visual hallucinations; in this case you need to recruit participants with varying levels of existing drug use and measure their experience of hallucinations. The ethics panel of your department may have some serious misgivings if you try to conduct an experimental study in this area, manipulating your variables by handing out various amounts of illegal drugs or attempting to induce hallucinations in your participants. Part III of the book deals with inferential statistics that assess relationships or associations between variables which normally relate to correlational designs (please note our use of normally! There are always exceptions!).

Correlation coefficients provide you with a number that represents the strength of a linear (straight line) relationship and also its direction; if there is a strong positive correlation, high scores on one variable tend to be correlated with high scores on the other variable (for example, participants who report high drug use tend to report high levels of hallucinations) and a strong negative correlation indicates that high scores on one variable tend to be correlated with low scores on the other variable (for example participants who report high drug use tend to report low levels of hallucinations). There are several different types of correlation coefficients and you will need to decide which one is appropriate for your data. We explain how to do this, as well as obtaining and interpreting correlation coefficients, in Chapter 12.

Regression takes the concept of looking at relationships further, as it allows you to test whether one or more variables can predict an outcome variable or criterion. For example, you could use regression to test whether use of illegal drugs, neuroticism and age can predict visual hallucinations. In comparison to the correlation, this technique gives you more information, such as which variables are significant predictors of hallucinations and the relative strength of each predicting variable. Liner regression is covered in Chapter 13 of this book.

There may be times where you want to examine the association between two discrete variables, for example, if whether or not someone ever took illegal drugs was associated with whether or not they ever experienced a visual hallucination. This type of data is examined in a specific way and in Chapter 14 we outline how to use contingency tables and inferential statistics (for example, the chi-square test and the McNemar test) to analyse discrete data.

Experimental design

Experimental designs differ from correlational designs as they may involve manipulating the independent variable (see Chapter 2 for a discussion of independent variables). Correlational studies focus on the relationship between existing variables, whereas in experimental designs a variable is changed (directly or indirectly) and you assess whether this has an effect on your outcome variable. For example, you may hypothesise that ergophobia (fear of work) in psychology students increases throughout their courses. There are two experimental designs you could use to test this hypothesis.

In the first design, you could test levels of ergophobia in students at different stages of their courses. This example, where you are comparing separate independent groups of people, is known as *independent groups design* (the statistical analyses relevant for this design is covered in Part IV of the book). The second design involves measuring the ergophobia levels of all the students in their first year and then measuring the same participants several times throughout their course. This type of study, where you are interested in changes within the same group of participants, is known as *repeated measures design* (the statistical analyses relevant for this design is covered in Part V of the book).

Independent groups design

When you employ an independent groups design you are looking for differences on a variable between separate groups of people. If you are investigating differences between two separate groups on a variable (for example, first year and second year psychology students on ergophobia levels) it is likely the two sets of scores will differ to some extent. Using an inferential statistic estimates whether this difference is likely to exist in the population or if you could have obtained the result by chance (assuming certain conditions). In this scenario you can employ either the parametric independent *t*-test or non-parametric Mann–Whitney test. We explain these tests in Chapter 15.

If you want to investigate the difference between more than two groups (for example, first, second and third year psychology students on ergophobia levels) the parametric between-groups ANOVA is most appropriate. (The non-parametric equivalent is the Kruskal–Wallis test). These analyses are covered in Chapter 16. If you find there is a statistically significant difference in ergophobia levels between the first, second and third year psychology students you will need to find out where these differences exist (is it between first years and second years, between first years and third years, and so on). The post-hoc tests and planned comparisons you need to do this are covered in Chapter 17. You could employ a slightly more sophisticated design where you examine the effect of two independent variables on a dependent variable. For example, does year of study and gender affect ergophobia levels? The benefit of this design is that you can examine the interaction between your two independent variables, for example, females' ergophobia levels may remain constant, but male scores increase in the three year groups. This two-way between-groups ANOVA design is covered in Chapter 16.

Repeated measures design

When you employ a repeated measures design you are looking for differences on a variable within the same group of people. For example, you could measure ergophobia levels when the students first start their psychology course and then 12 months later test the same group to see if the scores have changed. If you have tested your participants twice (that is, the independent variable has two levels), you can use the paired *t*-test or non-parametric Wilcoxon test to see if the differences in scores are statistically significant. We discuss these tests in Chapter 18. If you have tested the same group of participants more than twice the parametric within-groups ANOVA or the non-parametric Friedman test is most appropriate. These analyses are covered in Chapter 19. If you find there is a statistically significant difference in ergophobia levels between the testing sessions, you will need to find out where these differences exist (the students' first year or second year, or did the change occur between the students' second year and third year, and so on). The post-hoc tests and planned comparisons you need to do this are covered in Chapter 20. If you want to construct a more sophisticated design you can examine the effect of two repeated measures variables on a dependent variable (this is known as a two-way within-groups ANOVA and is covered in Chapter 19) or one repeated-measures and one independent-groups design on a dependent variable (this is a mixed ANOVA design and is addressed in Chapter 21).

Getting Started

The critical stage of any research study is always the start. It is important to specify a hypothesis that is testable and actually addresses the question you are interested in (see Chapter 8 for more on hypotheses); your hypothesis must be informed by theory and previous research. At this early stage you also need to consider how you will analyse the data by deciding on the appropriate statistic; this will help you decide how to measure your variables, so you don't find yourself unable to address your hypothesis because you cannot perform the analysis you want with the data you have collected. Deciding on the appropriate statistical analysis also allows you to calculate the sample size you will need (see Chapter 11). If you do not recruit enough participants you are unlikely to discover a significant effect in your data even if one exists in the population, and your efforts will be a waste of time. When you are preparing your SPSS file, take time to label your data and assign values that are easy to read and will make sense when you re-visit them months later. It helps to keep a paper record of the labels and values you used so you can refer to them when you are running analyses. Remember to save your SPSS file regularly when you are entering your data. When the fateful day arrives and you begin to analyse your data, take a deep breath and relax. Give yourself plenty of time, take notes as you go along, save your appropriately named output files and allow yourself to make mistakes. SPSS will run statistics almost instantly so if you make a mistake (and you will) you can simply start again.

We advise you that the best time to consult a statistical advisor is when you are designing your study. They will be able to offer you advice on the type of data you should collect, the analyses you will have to conduct and the sample size you will require. Asking for help after the data has been collected may be too late!

Chapter 2

What Type of Data Are We Dealing With?

. . . .

In This Chapter

▶ Distinguishing between discrete and continuous variables

▶ Understanding nominal, ordinal, interval and ratio levels of measurement

▶ Knowing the difference between independent and dependent variables and covariates

. . . .

*W*hen you conduct a research study in psychology, you normally collect data on a number of variables. A *variable* is something you measure that can have a different value from person to person or across time, like age, self-esteem and weight. *Data* is the information that you gather about a variable. For example, if you gather information about the age of a group of people then the list of their ages is your research data. (Not everything that you can measure is a variable, though, as you can read about in the 'Constantly uninteresting' sidebar, later in this chapter.)

The data that you collect on all the variables of interest in a research study is often known as a *data set* – a collection of information about several variables. A data set often contains information on several different types of variables, and being able to distinguish between these variables is the essential first step in your analysis. No matter how complex your statistical analysis becomes, the first question you always need to address is: *What type of variables do I have?* Therefore, you can't be confident about conducting statistical analysis unless you understand how to distinguish between variables. This is a basic skill that you must know before attempting anything else in statistics. If you can get a handle on variables, statistics suddenly seems a lot less confusing.

You can classify a variable in psychological research by

> ✔ **Type:** Discrete or continuous
>
> ✔ **Level of measurement:** Nominal, ordinal, interval or ratio
>
> ✔ **Its role in the research study:** Independent, dependent or covariate

In this chapter, we discuss each of these ways of classifying a variable.

Constantly uninteresting

Everything that you can measure you can classify as either a constant or a variable; that is, its value is always the same (constant) or its value varies (variable). In psychological research, you're only interested in variables. Constants aren't interesting because you already know their value and you can do nothing with this. In psychology, research is generally concerned with how changes in one variable are associated with changes in another variable. Therefore, change (or difference) is essential for psychological research.

Understanding Discrete and Continuous Variables

In classifying a variable, you consider whether the variable measures discrete categories or a continuum of scores.

Discrete variables, sometimes called *categorical variables*, are variables that contain separate and distinct categories. For example, a person's gender is a discrete variable. Normally, gender is described as male or female in research studies. So, the variable 'gender' has two categories – male and female – so gender is a categorical (discrete) variable.

Imagine that we collect information about the age of a group of people (as part of a research study rather than general nosiness). We could simply ask people to record their age in years on a questionnaire. This is an example of a *continuous variable*. Age in years is a continuous variable because it's not separated into distinct categories – time proceeds continuously – it has no breaks and you can always place your age along a continuum. Therefore, someone might record her age as 21 years old; another person might record her age as 21.5 years old; another person might record her age as 21.56 years old and so on. The last two people in the example might appear a bit weird, but they've given a valid answer to the question. They've just used a different level of accuracy in placing themselves on the age continuum.

One trick to help you remember the difference between the two types of variables is this: generally, a continuous variable is a variable where fractions are meaningful and a discrete variable is a variable where fractions aren't meaningful, and which can take only specific values.

In the example, when you ask someone her age, she could give you any answer (theoretically, but in reality you won't find many people above 100 years old) in the form of a fraction if she wants – it would still be meaningful. If you ask someone their gender, they're likely to give you one of two possible answers – male or female.

Whether you record a variable as discrete or continuous depends on how you measure it. For example, you can't say that age is a continuous variable without knowing how age has been measured in the context of a research study. If you ask people to record their age and give them the following options: 'less than 25', '25 to 40' and 'older than 40' then you've created a discrete variable. In this case, the person can only choose one of the three possible answers and anything in between these answers (any fraction) doesn't make sense. Therefore, you need to examine how you measured a variable before classifying it as discrete or continuous.

Looking at Levels of Measurement

You can classify variables according to their measurement properties. When you record variables on a data sheet, you usually record the values on the variables as numbers, because this can facilitate statistical analysis. However, the numbers can have different measurement properties and this determines what types of analyses you can do with these numbers. The variable's *level of measurement* is a classification system that tells you what measurement properties the values of a variable have.

The measurement properties that the values in a variable can possess are

- Magnitude
- Equal intervals
- True absolute zero

And these three measurement properties enable you to classify the level of measurement of a variable into one of four types

- Nominal
- Ordinal
- Interval
- Ratio

We describe both the properties and the types in the sections that follow.

Measurement properties

The three measurement properties outlined in the following sections are hierarchical. In other words, you can't have equal intervals unless a variable also has magnitude, and you can't have a true absolute zero point unless a variable also has magnitude and equal intervals.

Magnitude

The property of *magnitude* means that you can order the values in a variable from highest to lowest. For example, take the example of age as measured using the following categories: 'less than 25', '25 to 40' and 'older than 40'. In your research study, imagine you give a score of 1 on the variable 'age' to people who report being less than 25; you give a score of 2 to anyone who reports being between 25 to 40; and you give a score of 3 to anyone who reports being older than 40. Therefore, your variable 'age' contains three values – 1, 2 or 3. These numbers have the property of magnitude in that you can say that those who obtained a value of 3 are older than those who obtained a value of 2 and they're older than those who obtained a value of 1. In this way, you can order the scores.

Equal intervals

The property of *equal intervals* means that a unit difference on the measurement scale is the same regardless of where that unit difference occurs on the scale. For example, take the variable temperature. The difference between 10 degrees Celsius and 11 degrees Celsius is 1 degree Celsius (one unit on the scale). Equally, the difference between 11 degrees Celsius and 12 degrees Celsius is also 1 degree Celsius. This one-unit difference is the same and means the same regardless of where on the scale it occurs.

This isn't true for the example of the age variable in the previous section. In this case, the difference between a value of 1 and a value of 2 is 1 (one unit) and the difference between the value of 2 and the value of 3 is also 1. However, these differences aren't equal and, in fact, don't really make sense. Effectively, we're asking: is the difference between 'less than 25' and '25 to 40' the same as the difference between '25 to 40' and 'older than 40'? The question doesn't make sense, which should tell you that this variable does *not* have the property of equal intervals.

True absolute zero point

The property of a *true absolute zero point* means that the zero point on the measurement scale is the point where nothing of the variable exists and, therefore, no scores less than zero exist. Take the example of weight measured in kilograms. At 0 kilograms, you consider the thing that you're measuring to have no weight, and there is no weight less than 0 kilograms.

But this isn't true for the example of temperature measured in Celsius (see the previous section). You can have temperatures below zero on this scale (and frequently do). For example, –12 degrees Celsius is a sensible value to report. An example of a temperature scale that does have a true absolute zero point is temperature measured in degrees Kelvin, because no temperature lower than zero degrees Kelvin exists (at least no temperature lower than this that scientists have been able to record). However, determining a true absolute zero point is rarely something you need to concern yourself with when doing psychological research, so don't worry too much about this measurement property.

Types of measurement level

In the following sections, we outline the four levels of measurement. You can always classify a variable into one of these four measurement levels.

Nominal

The *nominal* level of measurement means that a variable has none of the three measurement properties (see the earlier section 'Measurement properties'). You measure a variable at the nominal level when you're using the numbers in the variable only as labels.

For example, in your data set you might give a participant a score of 1 if he's male or a score of 2 if she's female. These numbers don't have any properties that you'd normally associate with numbers – they're simply shorthand labels. Because these numbers don't have any measurement properties, you can't do any arithmetic with them (add, subtract and so on). In other words, you couldn't add a score of 2 to a score of 1 and get a score of 3. This is equivalent to saying that you'd add a female to a male and get something that's not possible on your variable, because a score of 3 doesn't exist! You also can't order these scores, because the labels are completely arbitrary and it makes just as much sense to give someone a score of 2 if he's male and a score of 1 if she's female as it does to score 1 for male and 2 for female.

Ordinal

If you measure a variable at the *ordinal* level then the values on the variable have the measurement property of magnitude only (see the earlier section 'Magnitude'). You measure a variable at the ordinal level when the scores in the variable are ordered ranks.

For example, when measuring age using the categories 'less than 25', '25 to 40' and 'older than 40', you measure age at the ordinal level. Imagine that you give a score of 1 on the variable age to people who report being less than 25; you give a score of 2 to anyone who reports being between 25 to 40; and you give a score of 3 to anyone who reports being older than 40. These numbers (1, 2 and 3) don't tell you how much older (or younger) one person is compared to another, simply that one person is older (or younger) than another. The numbers here are ordered ranks and only tell you whether one score is greater or less than another score.

We're psychologists, not English teachers

People sometimes discuss whether you should use the word *data* in a plural or singular sense. The word *data* is the plural of *datum*, so it is correct to insist that it's used in a plural sense. Therefore, you should say something like 'these data have the property of magnitude' rather than 'this data has the property of magnitude'. However, our aim in this book is to ensure that you understand statistics, not to lecture you about the finer points of the English language. So, leave this type of debate to those who have time to engage in a bit of good old-fashioned pedantry.

In psychological research, you rarely want to distinguish between variables measured at the interval level and variables measured at the ratio level. Therefore, you often refer to variables measured at the interval/ratio level (see the next section). Sometimes you hear the measurement of variables at the interval/ratio level referred to as a *scale measurement*.

Interval/ratio

If you measure a variable at the *interval* level of measurement, it has the measurement properties of magnitude and equal intervals; if you measure a variable at the *ratio* level of measurement, it has the measurement properties of magnitude, equal intervals and a true absolute zero (see the earlier section 'Measurement properties'). Psychologists tend not to worry about identifying a true absolute zero point, and if the units on a variable are at equal intervals then the variable is at the interval/ratio level.

For example, consider the variable weight, measured in kilograms. Weight has the measurement property of equal intervals (and, by necessity, magnitude), and therefore is measured at the interval/ratio level.

Determining the Role of Variables

Research studies in psychology, which involve collecting *quantitative data* (that's any data that can be counted or rendered as numbers), usually require you to collect and store data on a data sheet about several variables. When it comes to conducting your statistical analyses on this data, you need to know what role each variable played in your research design. Generally speaking, you classify variables in psychological research designs as independent variables, dependent variables or covariates. (And if you got hung up on the phrase 'this data' in this paragraph, check out the 'We're psychologists, not English teachers' sidebar in this chapter.)

The way in which you measure a variable in a research study determines whether it's continuous or discrete (see the section 'Understanding Discrete and Continuous Variables') and whether it's measured at the nominal, ordinal or interval/ratio level (see the section 'Looking at Levels of Measurement'). However, it's the role of the variable in a research design that determines whether it's an independent variable, dependent variable or covariate, which we explain in the following sections. The role of the variable can change from one research study to another.

Independent variables

Independent variables are sometimes referred to as *predictor variables.* Strictly speaking, an *independent variable* is a variable that you manipulate so that you can study how the changes in the independent variable influence changes in other variables.

For example, imagine that you're conducting a research study to examine the effect of relaxation therapy in treating anxiety. You design a study where a group of people with anxiety receive a programme of relaxation therapy and another group of people with anxiety receive no additional treatment. In this simple research design the independent variable is the level of intervention, which has two categories (relaxation therapy versus no additional treatment).

In some cases, you refer to variables as independent variables even when you're not directly manipulating them. For example, you might design a research study to examine the effects of spending time in prison on a person's self-esteem. In this case you have two groups of participants – people who are in prison and people who aren't in prison and you wish to compare the self-esteem levels of these two groups. Here, whether or not you're in prison is the independent variable, but as the researcher you didn't control who went to prison and who didn't – this manipulation of the independent variable just occurs naturally. This type of independent variable is a *quasi-independent variable.*

Dependent variables

Dependent variables are sometimes referred to as *outcome variables* or *criterion variables.* A *dependent variable* is usually the variable that you expect to change when you manipulate the independent variable. In other words, the dependent variable is the variable that the independent variable affects. Therefore, the dependent variable is so called because its value depends on the value of the independent variable (at least in theory).

In the research design examining the effect of relaxation therapy on levels of anxiety (see the last section), the independent variable is the level of intervention and the dependent variable is the participants' level of anxiety. In this case, you hypothesise that the participants' level of anxiety will *depend* on whether or not they receive the relaxation therapy. In the second example mentioned in the previous section, the independent variable was whether or not a person is in prison, and the dependent variable is the person's level of self-esteem.

Covariates

A *covariate* is a broad term used for a variable in a research design that's neither an independent nor a dependent variable. In some designs you use a covariate to take account of other factors that might influence the relationship between the independent and dependent variable.

As an example, take the research design mentioned in the earlier section 'Independent variables', where the study aims to examine the effect of relaxation therapy on anxiety. In this example, you could probably think of lots of variables that aren't part of the intervention that might influence anxiety scores – for example whether the participants are taking any medication for their anxiety, the type of social support they receive at home, and so on. A good research design measures these variables so that you can account for their influence on anxiety scores in the analysis. Within this research design, these variables are *covariates*.

Covariates can also exist in research designs where no independent or dependent variables exist. For example, imagine you're designing a research study to examine the relationship between confidence and accuracy of eye witness testimony in court. Basically, you want to conduct a study to determine whether eye witnesses who are more confident about their testimony are also more accurate in their testimony. In this study you have two variables – confidence and accuracy. However, neither variable is being manipulated and you can't say that the values of one variable are dependent on the other. In fact, we believe that the relationship between the variables could work in either direction: that your confidence might depend on your accuracy or that your accuracy might depend on your confidence. In this case, you can't clearly identify an independent variable and a dependent variable. In this case, both variables are covariates, and are sometimes referred to as *correlates*.

Chapter 3

Inputting Data, Labelling and Coding in SPSS

In This Chapter

▶ Creating and defining variables in SPSS

▶ Inputting data to SPSS

▶ Manipulating variables in SPSS

▶ Saving output from SPSS

*W*hen you collect data as part of a research study, you need to store it in an accessible format, so that you can retrieve it when the data set is complete, to allow you to conduct your statistical analysis. The most convenient method of storing data is on a data file in a statistical software package. The advantages of doing this are as follows:

✔ You can make multiple copies of the data file and store these in separate locations, to guard against loss of information.

✔ You can keep a copy of the original data file in case you make any changes to the data that you wish to reverse.

✔ The data file stores the data in a way that makes it ready for statistical analysis.

✔ Statistical software packages have a variety of built-in statistical analyses routines that you can apply directly to your data.

This chapter addresses the basic information that you need to use the SPSS statistical software package. In this chapter, we discuss how to navigate your way around SPSS and how to manage data in SPSS. This knowledge brings you to the point where you're ready to begin your statistical analysis.

SPSS has three views. You can input information in the data view and the variable view, which are different views of your data file. SPSS generates the output view when you run a procedure or routine in SPSS. You can amend the information presented in the output view, but often you simply want to read and interpret the information presented in the output.

Variable View Window

The *variable view* window is often the first view that you use when creating a data file on SPSS. The variable view window allows you to label and define all the variables in your study and set up a data file with all the variable names inserted. By doing this, you make your data file ready to receive the data.

Before you begin to enter any information into the variable view window it looks like Figure 3-1. Along the top of the file you see a number of headings: name, type, width, decimals, label, values, missing, columns, align and measure. You input information about a variable under each of these headings, and we look at the meaning of each column heading in the sections that follow.

Imagine you've designed a research study to examine the levels of physical activity among people with a liver transplant. In your study, you want to know the following:

✔ How long the person has had his liver transplant (in months)

✔ How many minutes of moderate/vigorous exercise he takes every day

✔ Whether he finds exercise easy or difficult

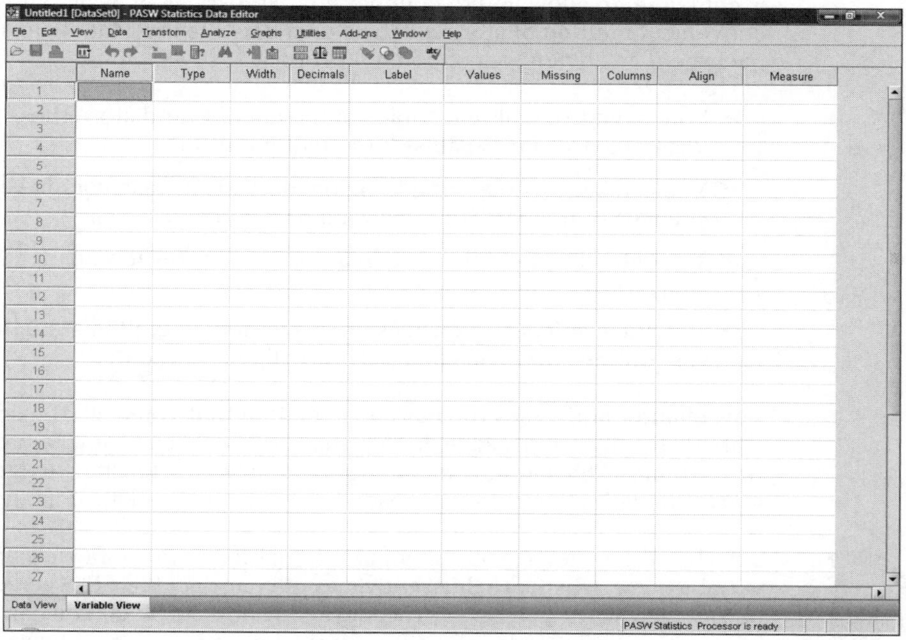

Figure 3-1: The variable view in SPSS.

Therefore, you have three variables in your study:

- ✔ Length of time since transplant
- ✔ Minutes of exercise
- ✔ Perception of exercise

Now we look at how you input these variables into SPSS.

Creating variable names

The first column in the variable view is headed Name. Completing this column is essential, because you tell SPSS what you want to call each of your variables. You need to specify the variables you've measured before you enter any data into SPSS. The name of the variable is a shorthand version of the variable name.

Here are a few points to keep in mind when entering variable names:

- ✔ The name can be up to 64 characters in length.
- ✔ Begin and end the variable name with letters rather than characters or punctuation marks.
- ✔ A variable name can't contain spaces, but you can separate words with, for example, an underscore (_).
- ✔ Each variable name must be unique.
- ✔ There are some combinations of letters that you can't use (for example EQ, ALL). You receive an error message if you try to use any characters that are not allowed.
- ✔ Keep variable names as short as possible.

In the example, your first variable is 'length of time since transplant'. You could shorten this to 'time' as a variable name. The second variable is 'minutes of exercise', which you could shorten to 'mins_exercise', and the third variable is 'perception of exercise', which could be 'perc_exercise'. You enter the variable names in separate rows, underneath each other in the variable view, as shown in Figure 3-2.

When you enter a variable name to SPSS, it automatically completes information under each of the other headings for this variable, for example how wide the column will be and the type of variable (see Figure 3-2). This information might not be the information you want to input for each variable, so you need to check these and modify as necessary.

When you begin to enter variable names to SPSS, save your data file intermittently, to ensure you don't lose any information. The first time you save your file, you need to name it.

Deciding on variable type

When you enter the variable name, SPSS automatically records the variable type as numeric. You can change the variable type by clicking on the right hand side of the box where the word 'numeric' is displayed (see Figure 3-3). This takes you to a window as shown in Figure 3-4. Here you can choose the type of variable. In most cases having a numeric variable is appropriate, but there are other options you may occasionally use, such as dates.

Even if your variable isn't numeric to begin with, often applying numeric values to it is best. Keep a record of what these numeric values mean, because some of the analyses in SPSS are only available to numeric variables (see the sections 'Using labels' and 'Using values').

	Name	Type	Width	Decimals	Label	Values	Missing	Columns	Align	Measure
1	time	Numeric	8	2		None	None	8	Right	Scale
2	mins_exercise	Numeric	8	2		None	None	8	Right	Scale
3	perc_exercise	Numeric	8	2		None	None	8	Right	Scale

Figure 3-2: Inserting variable names in SPSS.

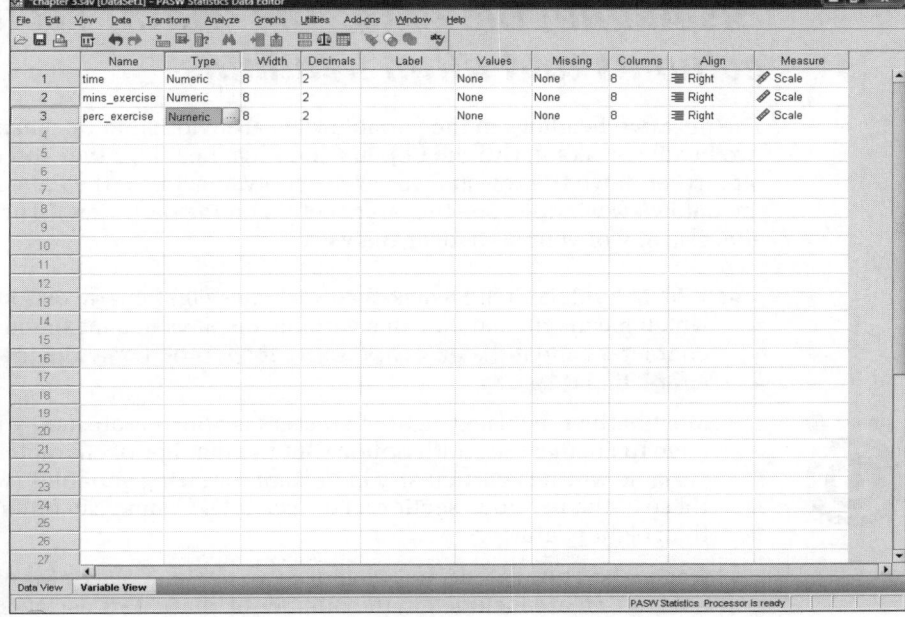

Figure 3-3:
Changing the variable type in the variable view window.

The other variable type that people use commonly in psychological research is the *string*. You can use a string variable when entering anonymous codes or pseudonyms for participants. Choosing this type of variable allows you to use letters rather than numbers when inputting data. However, we want to reiterate that applying this variable type limits the type of analyses you can do on SPSS.

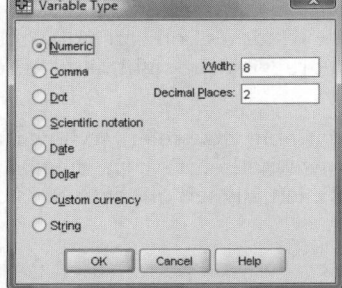

Figure 3-4:
Selecting the variable type.

Displaying the data: The width, decimals, columns and align headings

The next two headings in the variable view are Width and Decimals. These two headings, along with the Column and Align headings that you can find a bit further down the row in Figure 3-4, simply affect how the data displays in the data view window (see the later section on the data view). They have no effect on any of your statistical analyses.

✔ **Width:** By default SPSS makes all variables eight characters in width, which means the data for this variable displays in a maximum of eight characters and if the data inputted is longer then only the first eight characters display.

Most of the time using eight characters is appropriate, and you don't have to change the width option. But the number of characters for the variable width is particularly important for string variables (we explain these in the previous section). For example, a name can often be longer than eight characters.

✔ **Decimals:** The SPSS default includes two decimal places for each variable, which are included in the number of characters assigned to the width. If the data for a variable can only contain whole numbers (and not fractions) then reducing the number of decimal places to zero is useful, so that only whole numbers display. If you don't change this, then the output will contain decimal places which you will need to delete manually.

✔ **Columns:** The Column heading in the variable view window has a similar function as the width option. This controls the width of the column in which the variable is displayed in the data view window. By default it's eight characters in width, but you can increase this if you have a longer variable name.

In the data view and variable view windows you can make columns bigger or smaller by clicking and dragging the right-hand border of the column.

✔ **Align:** The Align heading in the variable view refers to how the data is displayed in the data view window: whether it's right aligned (which is the default for numeric variables), left aligned or centred.

Using labels

Under the Label heading you can type a longer name for the variable. You don't have to type any information in this column, so SPSS leaves it blank by default. However, you find it useful to use this column to type a longer name for your variables, in case you forget what the short variable name means. For example, you may forget whether time is measured in minutes, hours or weeks, or whether time refers to the amount of time spent exercising or the length of time since the transplant – include as much relevant detail as you feel is necessary here, which makes your analyses easier to interpret. You can type any characters under this heading, including spaces (see Figure 3-5).

If you type a longer variable label under the Label heading then this appears in any output that includes this variable (see the section on the output window, later in this chapter). If you leave the Label column blank then the output includes the variable name typed under the Name heading.

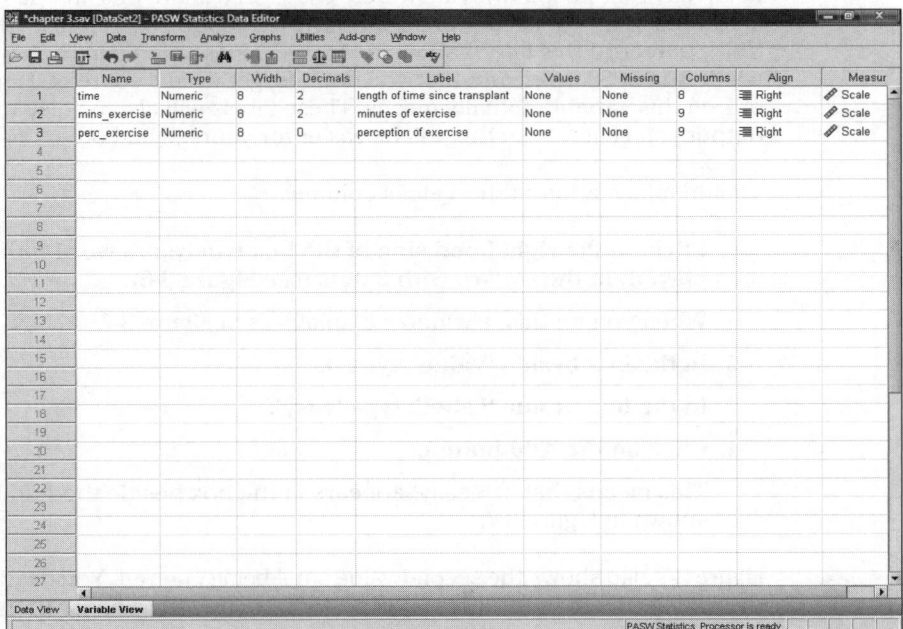

Figure 3-5: Variable labels in SPSS.

Using values

The column headed Values in the variable view window states 'none' by default. You don't have to change this. However, adding value labels to your data file can be very useful.

For some variables in psychological research, the numbers have an inherent meaning. In the example, you're asking participants about the minutes spent taking exercise. The answer to this question is a number and as long as you know what the number refers to (like the minutes of exercise) then you have all the information you need, as a score of 1 represents 1.

However, in other situations, you apply numbers to variables that aren't numerical to begin with. In the example, you're asking participants about their perceptions of exercise. The answer to this question is either 'easy' or 'difficult'. Clearly, these aren't numbers, but you want to record them as numbers to allow you to conduct statistical analysis on this variable in SPSS. So, you might say that people who answered 'easy' get a score of 0 and people who answered 'difficult' get a score of 1 on the perception of exercise variable. You can record this information under the Values column in the variable view window in SPSS, to ensure that you don't forget what a score of 0 and a score of 1 on this variable actually means. These labels will also be displayed in any output you generate so this will be easier for yourself and others to interpret.

To add information to the Values column:

1. **Click on the right-hand side of the box where the word *none* is displayed, in the square with 3 dots (see Figure 3-6).**

   When you do this, a window displays as in Figure 3-7.

2. **In the box beside 'Value', type 0.**

3. **In the box beside 'Label', type 'easy'.**

4. **Click on the Add button.**

   This means that '0 = easy' appears in the box beside the Add button, as shown in Figure 3-7.

Figure 3-7 also shows the second value label being entered. You need to press the Add button to make sure this is recorded in the box along with the other label. If you just type in the label but forget to press Add, SPSS doesn't save your label. You will be shown a warning if you do try to close without pressing Add.

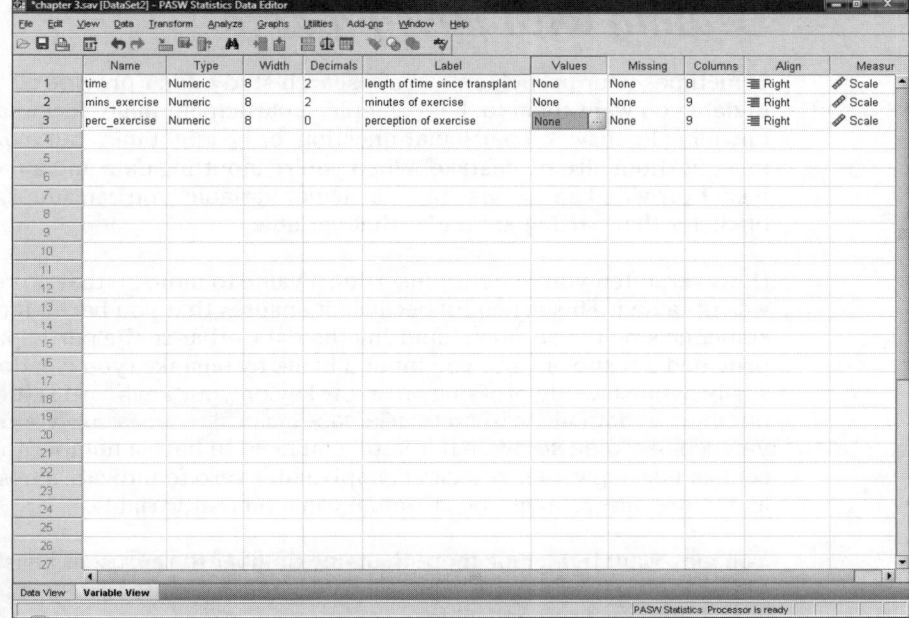

When you add value labels to your data file, you input only the numbers
when adding data (in the data view window in SPSS), but the labels display in
any output in SPSS.

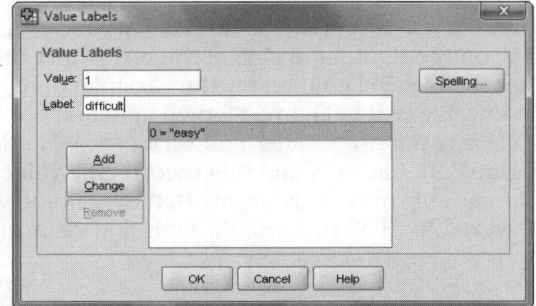

Dealing with missing data

Sometimes your participants in a research study don't provide all the pieces of data you want them to. For example, a participant might feel unable or unwilling to answer a particular question, or he might miss out a question in a questionnaire by mistake. When you're inputting data and a participant hasn't provided a response to a particular variable, you can simply leave a blank for that participant under that variable.

However, often you're better inserting a value to indicate that no response was obtained. This is helpful because it ensures that you haven't missed someone's response when inputting the data – that is, the participant has provided a response, but you input a blank by mistake (you can do this easily by mistakenly pressing an arrow key on your keyboard rather than a number). A data file with no blank spaces is best, to reassure yourself that you've missed no scores. Therefore, you need to have a number that represents a missing value. You can't simply enter zero to indicate a missing value, as a score of zero might be an actual value on that variable.

You may want to include more than one number to represent missing values, for example to distinguish between where there was no response and where a question was not applicable.

When choosing a number to represent a missing value, make it a number that's impossible to score on the variable and that's very different from any valid scores. For example, in the perceptions of exercise variable, the possible scores are 0 and 1. Therefore, you could assign a missing value with a score of 99.

To tell the computer not to treat a score of 99 on this variable as a score, but as a missing value, click on the right-hand side of the box where the word *none* is displayed under the Missing column for the variable 'perc_exercise' (see Figure 3-8). A window like that in Figure 3-9 then appears. Choose the radio button beside 'Discrete missing values' and then type 99 in the box below (as shown in Figure 3-9). Click OK and this records the value of 99 as a missing value for that variable only. This means that every time you enter the number 99 for this variable, SPSS realises it's a missing value and treats it appropriately.

For the other variables in the example, you need to think of alternative appropriate missing values. The variable 'length of time since transplant' is measured in months. Therefore, you need to choose a value that's well outside the possible range. Imagine that you're surveying people who've had their transplant for no more than five years (60 months). In this case, a missing value of 999 is appropriate.

The variable 'minutes of exercise' refers to the number of minutes of moderate/vigorous exercise taken every day. In this case a missing value of 999 is also appropriate because this is equivalent to over 16 hours of moderate/vigorous exercise every day, which is highly unlikely.

Assigning the level of measurement

The final column in the variable view window is headed Measure. For numeric variables, the default description is 'scale', which relates to any variables which are measured at the interval or ratio level. You can change this to 'nominal' or 'ordinal'. To change the description, click in the box where it states 'scale' and you then access a drop-down menu from which you can choose from the three descriptions (see Figure 3-10).

We discuss determining a variable's level of measurement in Chapter 2, and you must be able to do this before you embark on any type of statistical analysis. The 'scale' description on SPSS refers to variables that are measured at the interval or ratio level, as discussed in Chapter 2. However, defining the level of measurement on SPSS has no effect on your statistical analysis, so it doesn't matter whether you modify the level of measurement or not.

Figure 3-11 shows the variable view with all the information input for our example.

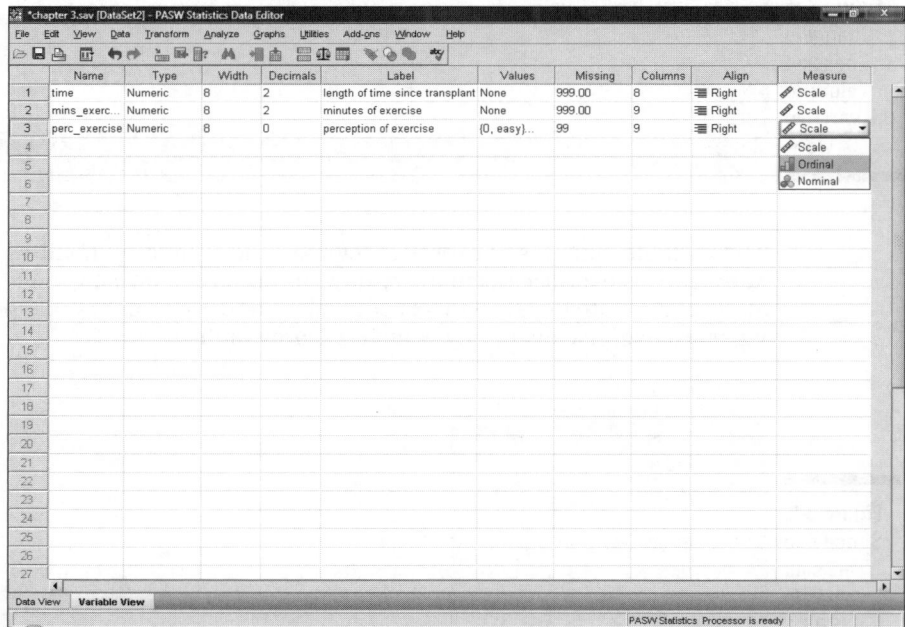

Figure 3-10: Choosing a variable's level of measurement.

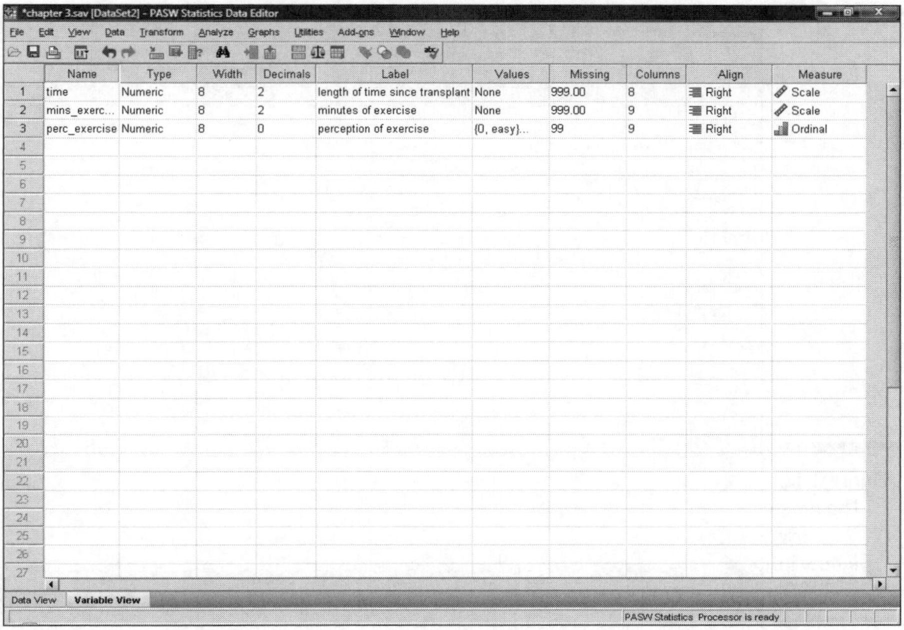

Figure 3-11:
A completed
variable
view.

Data View Window

The *data view window* in SPSS is where you enter your data that you collect from your research participants. The data view window is a data file that has all your variable names along the top. If you haven't already defined your variables in the variable view window (see the previous section on the variable view) then the top of each column in your data file reads 'var', indicating that it's waiting for a variable name. If you've defined your variables in the variable view then these labels automatically appear along the top of the data view (see Figure 3-12).

From the data view window you can add new variables, recode variables and sort variables. We discuss all these functions of the data view window in this section.

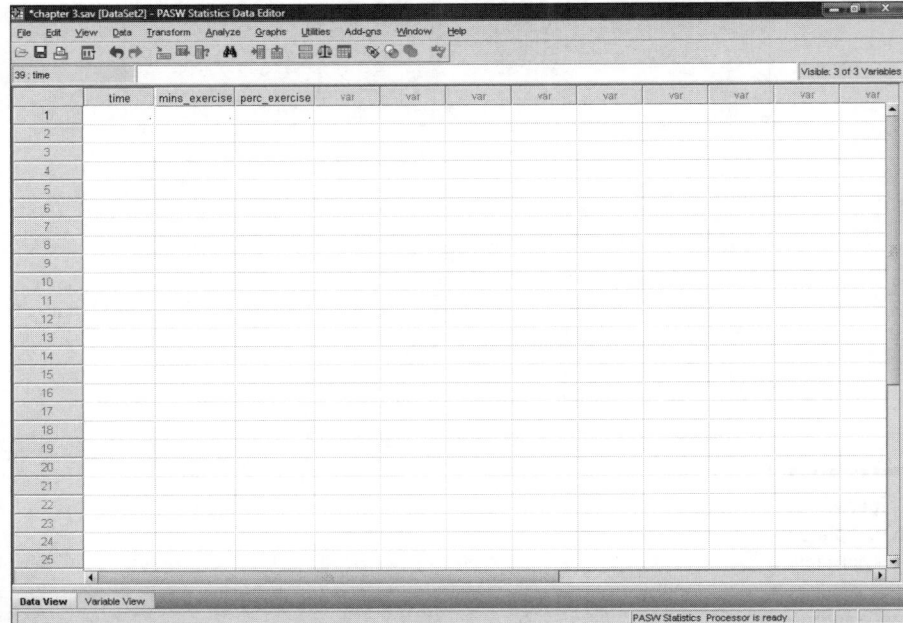

Figure 3-12:
The data
view
window in
SPSS.

Entering new data

The data view is organised so that you enter the data from each participant along a single row. For example, you enter the data from participant 1 in your study along row 1 in the data file (indicated by the number 1 on the left-hand side of the data file). It is common to record each participant's ID number as the first variable.

In this section we continue using the example we introduce in the earlier section 'Variable View Window' of a research study that examines the levels of physical activity among people with a liver transplant. You have three variables in your study: length of time since transplant (time), minutes of exercise (mins_exercise) and perception of exercise (perc_exercise; scored 0 for easy and 1 for hard). Say you've collected data on these variables from ten participants. The data set is provided in Table 3-1.

Table 3-1	Exercise Among People with a Liver Transplant		
Participant	*Time (Months)*	*Mins_exercise*	*Perc_exercise*
1	6	5	1
2	12	10	0
3	5	0	1

Participant	Time (Months)	Mins_exercise	Perc_exercise
4	18	15	0
5	10	10	0
6	9	5	0
7	6	5	1
8	20	20	1
9	20	10	1
10	12	15	1

The data in Table 3-1 is structured in the way that it should appear on the data view in SPSS, with all the scores for participant 1 entered along the first row; all the scores for participant 2 entered along the second row and so on. You can enter the data row-by-row (which we recommend) or column-by-column (where skipping a number is easier).

After entering a number, if you press the Tab key or the right arrow key, you move across the row, but if you press Enter you move down the column.

After you enter all the data in Table 3-1, the data file in SPSS looks like Figure 3-13.

Press this label button to display the value labels rather than numbers

Figure 3-13: The structure of data in SPSS.

REMEMBER

If you defined value labels in the variable view window (see the sections 'Using values' and 'Using labels', earlier in this chapter) then you can switch between these labels and the numbers you've input in the data view window by pressing the luggage label on the toolbar (see Figure 3-13).

Creating new variables

To add a new variable to your data file, you can return to the variable view window and add a variable onto the end of the list of variable names (see 'Variable View Window' in this chapter). You can also add a new variable in the data view window.

To add a variable in the data view window, you can just start to type the data in the next available column and SPSS will create a new variable for you. It will give it a name such as 'VAR0004' or similar. Obviously, you can think of a more suitable name than this, so you modify the name by going to the variable view window and then typing in a new name over this one.

Figure 3-14:
Inserting a
variable in
SPSS.

To insert a variable in between existing variables, find the variable that you want to be displayed to the right of your new variable and then right click on this column. You need to right click on this column when your mouse is pointing at the 'var' header at the top of the column. This allows you to choose the 'Insert Variable' option from the menu that appears (see Figure 3-14). For example, if you want to insert a new variable in between the 'time' and 'mins_exercise' variables, you point your mouse to the mins_exercise heading and then right click. When you choose 'Insert Variable', SPSS inserts the new variable to the left of the 'mins_exercise' variable.

Sorting cases

Often you want to sort cases in SPSS to identify, for example, the most extreme scores on a variable. *Sorting cases* means ordering a variable from the lowest to the highest score (ascending order) or the highest to the lowest score (descending order). You can order data on SPSS using the Sort Cases procedure (see Figure 3-15).

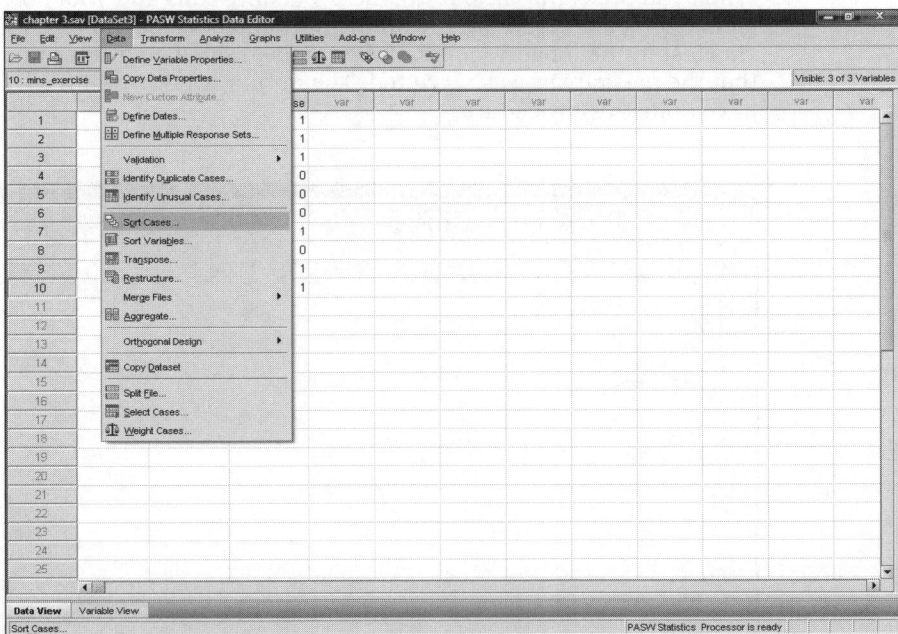

Figure 3-15: Finding the Sort Cases procedure.

When you select the Sort Cases procedure, another window appears asking you to select the variable that you want to sort and whether you want to sort the cases from the smallest to the largest value (ascending) or from the largest to the smallest value (descending). Choose the variable that you want to sort (time in this example) and move this to the box on the right headed 'Sort By' (see Figure 3-16) using the arrow in the middle.

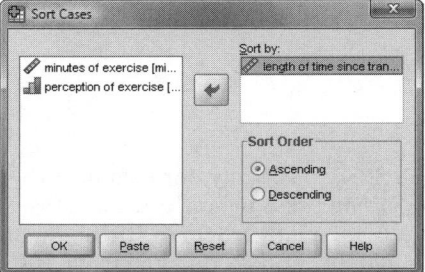

Figure 3-16:
Choosing a
variable
to sort
cases by.

When you press the OK button, the procedure runs and your sorted data file should look like Figure 3-17, with the participants listed in order from the shortest to the longest length of time since transplant, rather than by order that the participant was recruited. The output window will record that you have done this procedure.

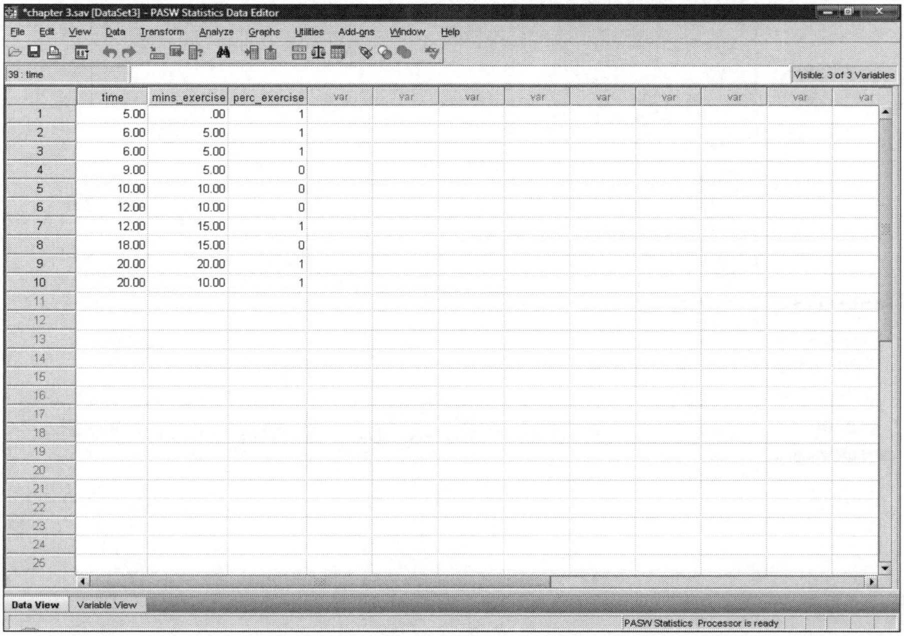

Figure 3-17:
Data sorted
by time.

Recoding variables

Recoding a variable means converting the data in a variable into new data as a new variable with a different meaning or measured on a different scale. For example, in the data set presented in Figure 3-13, the variable time is measured in months and ranges from 5 months to 20 months. Imagine that you want to conduct an analysis to examine the differences in amount of exercise taken between those who had their transplant less than 12 months ago and those who have had their transplant for 12 months or more. To enable this type of analysis, you need to have a variable in your data set that indicates which of these groups the participants belonged to (less than 12 months or 12 months and more). You already have information in your data set (under the variable 'time') that allows you to work this out, but SPSS can do this for you, by allowing you to recode the variable time into a new variable in your data set.

To recode a variable, choose the 'Recode into Different Variables' command from the 'Transform' menu (see Figure 3-18). It is important that you choose to recode in to different variables and not the same because this will overwrite the current variable. A window then appears and you can select the time variable from the left-hand side and move it across to the box on the right-hand side, using the arrow button (see Figure 3-19). In the section headed Output Variable you can then type the variable name of the new variable that you want to create ('time_categories' in this example) and press the Change button below this box. This moves the new variable name into the right-hand box (see Figure 3-20).

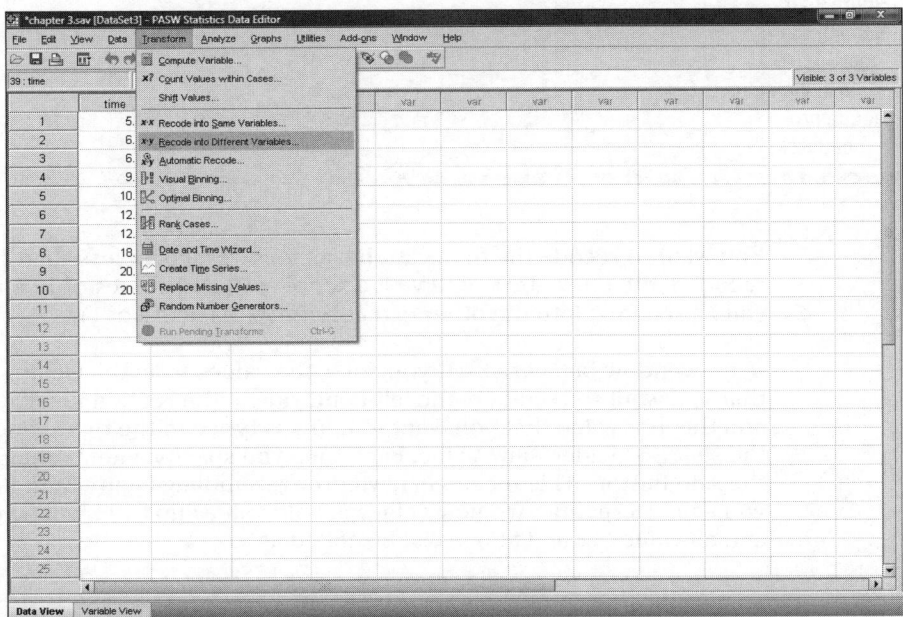

Figure 3-18: Choosing the recode command on SPSS.

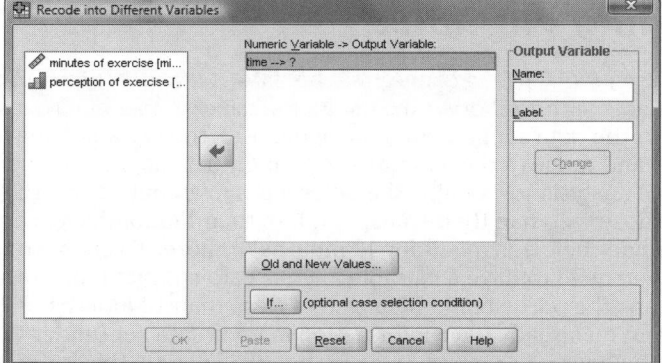

Figure 3-19:
Selecting a
variable to
recode.

To specify how you want the variable to be recoded, click on the Old and
New Values button, which takes you to the window in Figure 3-21.

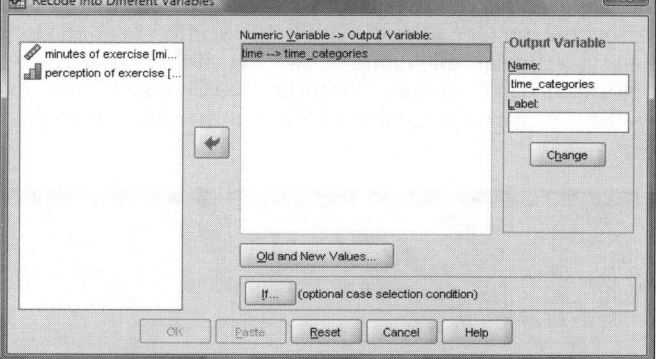

Figure 3-20:
Naming the
new vari-
able in the
recode pro-
cedure.

You want to recode the time variable as follows: scores less than 12 are
recoded into one category (give it a score of 0) and scores of 12 and more
will be recoded into the other category (give it a score of 1).

In the window in Figure 3-21, you enter the values from the existing variable
that you want to recode in the left-hand side in the section headed Old Value
and the new value that you want to apply is typed in the right-hand side in
the section headed New Value. Each time you specify a new value, click on
the Add button. This results in a window resembling Figure 3-22. In this case
you will be creating two new values; all old values up to 11 will be coded as 0
and all values 12 and above will be coded as 1.

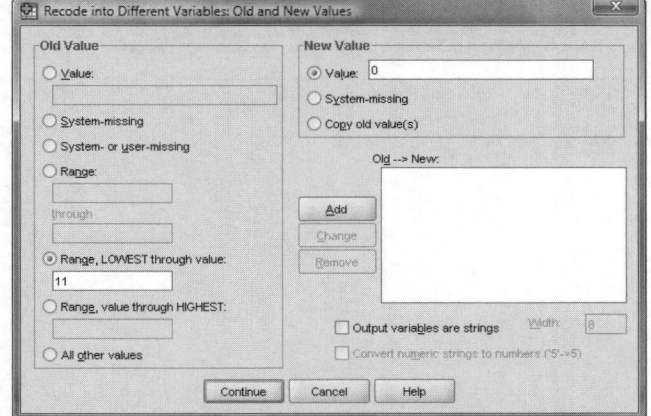

Figure 3-21:
Specifying
old and new
values in the
recode pro-
cedure.

Figure 3-22:
Specifying
all the val-
ues to be
recoded.

After you add all the values, click Continue and then click OK. SPSS creates
a new variable at the end of your data set to represent the new variable
(see Figure 3-23). At this point you might want to return to the variable view
window (see the earlier section on this view) to add value labels to this new
variable which would be 0 = less than 12 and 1 = 12 or above.

Enter your data into SPSS in its raw form where possible, before it has been
recoded. If you want you can then recode information on SPSS. However, if
you recode the data before entering it, you can't get SPSS to undo the recoding for you.

Figure 3-23:
The new variable created using the recode command.

Output Window

SPSS presents the results of any analyses you conduct in the *output window*. When you run an analysis or procedure for the first time in SPSS, an output window automatically opens. Thereafter when you conduct any analyses, the results are presented in the open output window.

When you run any procedures in SPSS which include opening an existing data-file, such as sorting cases or recoding cases (see the previous two sections) then SPSS presents any warnings that indicate these procedures haven't worked correctly in the output window. Therefore, you should check the output window after you run any procedures on SPSS. If the procedure has run correctly the output window will just show a description of what you have done.

Using the output window

Whenever we discuss statistical analyses throughout this book we present the results of these analyses as displayed by SPSS in the output window.

In most cases you can copy and paste the tables and charts displayed in the SPSS output window into a report document. However, you might want to make some changes to the output before copying and pasting it into a final report, to make it more in keeping with the style of your report. For example, you often want to modify charts in SPSS, because they're in colour in the output window and your final report document might not be presented in colour, or you might want to add a pattern to the chart to make it look more appealing. For output in the form of tables it is much easier to amend these once they have been copied and pasted into another program, rather than in SPSS.

To amend a chart in SPSS, double click on it. This takes you to an edit window. Figure 3-24 presents the edit window for a bar chart created for the perception of exercise variable in the example we introduced in the section 'Variable View Window' (see Chapter 6 for a discussion of bar charts). To amend the pattern of the bars, double click on one of the bars in the bar chart, which produces the window in Figure 3-25. Under the 'Fill & Border' tab, click on the drop-down menu beside the word 'Pattern' and choose a pattern to fill in the bars (see Figure 3-25). Then click on the Apply button, which changes the chart in the chart editor (see Figure 3-26). If you're happy with the look, click Close. The chart in the output window doesn't change until you close the chart editor.

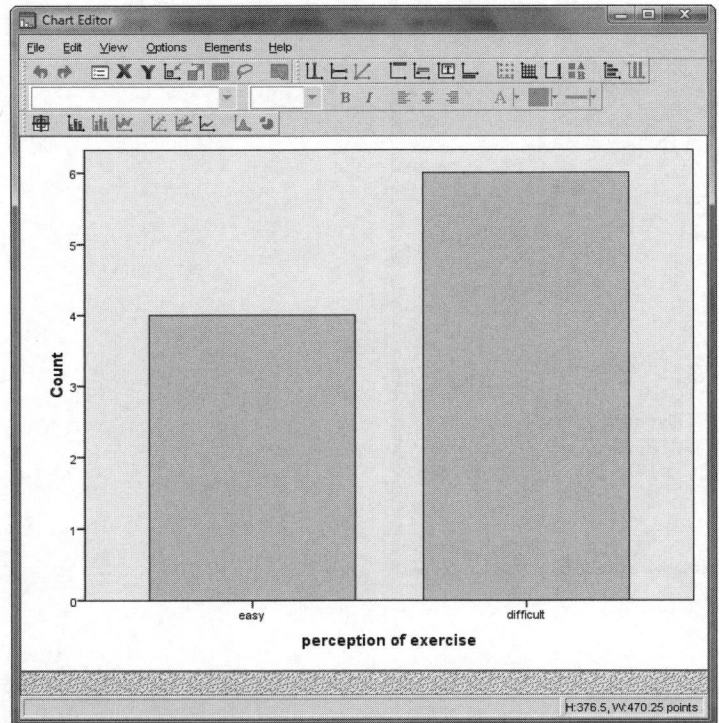

Figure 3-24:
The edit window in an SPSS output file.

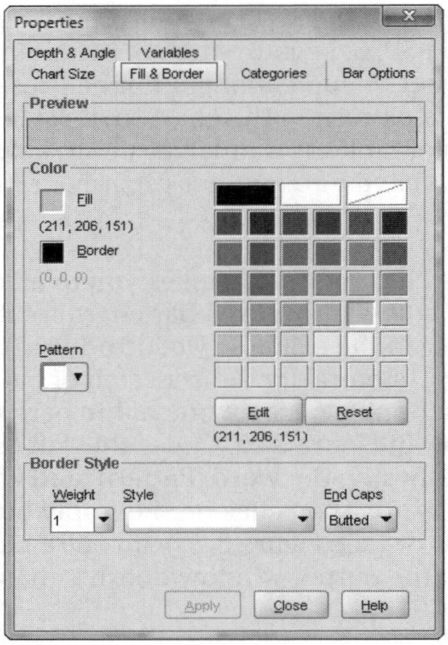

Figure 3-25:
Changing
the colour
or pattern of
a chart.

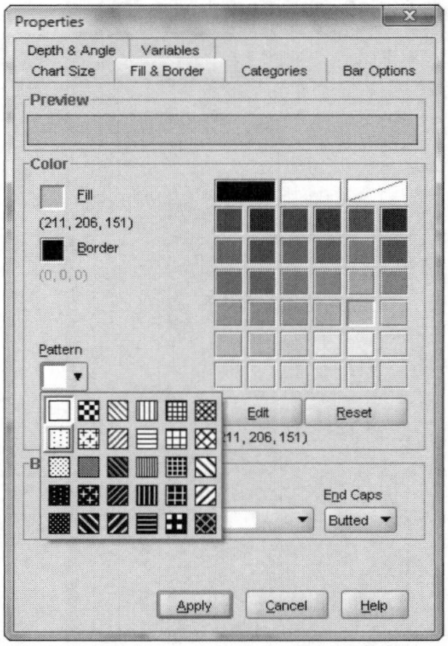

Figure 3-26:
Adding
a pattern
to a chart.

Saving your output

Save your output file as soon as you create some output from your first analysis and then ensure that you save the file intermittently from that point onwards. All output will be entered into the same output window, even if they are unrelated, so sometimes it may be appropriate to close one window and start a new one.

The first time you save your output file, you need to name it. You can give your output file the same name as your data file, because they have different suffixes. The output file has the suffix .spv, whereas the data file has the suffix .sav. Therefore, you can call your data file something like chapter3.sav and your output file chapter3.spv. In this way you see clearly which data file the output is based on.

Chapter 4

Measures of Central Tendency

. . . .

In This Chapter

▶ Understanding central tendency

▶ Calculating mode, median and mean

▶ Choosing between using mode, median and mean to summarise data

. . . .

*R*esearch is only useful if you communicate the information you collect during the research process (your data) to others. In other words, there is no point conducting a research study and gathering a large amount of data if you leave the data in your drawer, under a table or on a computer. Therefore, after you collect data as part of a research study, you need to produce a report which will (at the very least) tell people what this data looks like as well as being comprehensible, and giving people an idea of what the data shows.

One way of doing this is to print out a table with all your data from every participant in your research project. This might be okay if you have only a few participants in your project, but it isn't going to work very well when you have a larger group of participants, as is often the case in quantitative research studies in psychology. Imagine that you have amassed data from 50 participants in your research study – if you simply provide a list of the information gathered about every participant, you have a very large table that's very difficult for a reader to make sense of (not to mention making a considerable dent in the word count for your report!). Therefore, you need a way of summarising the data that you collect so that you can communicate it in a manageable way.

You need two pieces of information (as a minimum) to summarise the data you collect in your study: the *central tendency* of the data (a representative value from the data) and the *dispersion* of the data (how much the data deviates from this representative value). If you know the central tendency and dispersion of a set of data then you should have a fairly good idea about what the data look like. Therefore, when reporting the results of a research study, the central tendency and dispersion of the data are the first bits of information you report. In this chapter we examine central tendency only. Chapter 5 deals with measures of dispersion.

You communicate central tendency by using the mode, median or mean. In this chapter we look at a definition of each of these terms, the advantages and disadvantages of each and how you can generate the mode, median and mean using the SPSS statistical software package.

Defining Central Tendency

Central tendency describes a single number that aims to give you a sense of the most representative value in your data. In other words, if you were to choose one number that would best represent all the numbers on a variable in your data set, this would be it. In this way, central tendency is a summary of all the values on a variable in your data set (we explain variables in Chapter 2).

Central tendency always refers to a single variable. So, if you have several variables in your data set then you should generate a measure of central tendency for each variable. Central tendency summarises the values obtained by each participant on a single variable – it's a summary of the scores of a group of participants on a single variable. Therefore, if you have more than one group of participants in your research study, you might need to calculate a measure of central tendency for each group for a particular variable. For example, if looking at the example in Chapter 3 you may want to summarise anxiety scores for those who had received treatment separately from those who did not.

It's most important that when you calculate and report a measure of central tendency you're clear about who this measure of central tendency refers to and what variable it refers to. For example, imagine you've conducted a research study that includes male and female participants and one of the variables you measured was depression scores, using a questionnaire measure of depression. In this case you could calculate several measures of central tendency: a measure of central tendency for the depression scores of all participants, a measure of central tendency for the depression scores of females or a measure of central tendency for the depression scores of males. You just need to be clear about what you're reporting.

The label *central tendency* might cause you to believe that the central tendency value is a value at the centre of ordered values on a variable – that it's a value in the middle of all the values on that variable. However, this isn't always the case, as you see in the following sections when we examine the mode, median and mean separately. Some people therefore suggest that the term *central tendency* is an inappropriate umbrella term for the mean, median and mode. But no one's come up with a catchy alternative. If you can think of one, let us know – we need a better label for this concept!

The Mode

The mode is the simplest measure of central tendency to calculate, but can be the most problematic one to report. We look at the mode in detail in the following sections.

Determining the mode

The *mode* is the most frequently occurring score in a set of scores. Usually, you can ask a programme such as SPSS to calculate the mode for you. However, for the purposes of helping you to understand the mode (and because it's easy to calculate), we want to take you through the process of calculating the mode.

For example, take the research study we mention in the earlier section 'Defining Central Tendency' (part of which involves assessing depression scores among male and female participants) and imagine 20 people participate (10 males and 10 females). We present the scores on the depression questionnaire for all the participants, in the order they were obtained, in Table 4-1.

Table 4-1	Depression Scores for Males and Females	
Participant	*Gender*	*Depression Score*
A	Male	2
B	Male	10
C	Male	3
D	Female	12
E	Male	9
F	Female	15
G	Male	6
H	Female	10
I	Female	9
J	Male	11
K	Female	4
L	Male	5
M	Female	8
N	Male	7

(continued)

Table 4-1 *(continued)*

Participant	Gender	Depression Score
O	Male	8
P	Female	14
Q	Male	4
R	Female	12
S	Female	12
T	Female	14

Often one of the first things you do before generating any descriptive statistics, such as a measure of central tendency, is to order your data. *Ordering your data* means that you sort the cases in order from the lowest to the highest score on the variable in which you're interested. Ordering your data makes further calculations simpler. In a small data set like this, ordering the data is relatively easy. In a larger data set, SPSS can help you to order your data (see Chapter 3). Bear in mind, though, that when using a computer program to calculate central tendency there is no need to have the data in order.

Table 4-2 presents the data in Table 4-1 but now ordered on the basis of the variable 'depression score'. This means that the participants are now listed in order from the smallest to the largest depression score rather than by order that the participant was recruited.

Table 4-2   Ordered Depression Scores for Males and Females

Participant	Gender	Depression Score
A	Male	2
C	Male	3
K	Female	4
Q	Male	4
L	Male	5
G	Male	6
N	Male	7
M	Female	8
O	Male	8
E	Male	9
I	Female	9

Participant	Gender	Depression Score
B	Male	10
H	Female	10
J	Male	11
D	Female	12
R	Female	12
S	Female	12
P	Female	14
T	Female	14
F	Female	15

With the data ordered you can now more easily see how many times each score occurs in the data set. From Table 4-2 you can see that a depression score of 12 is obtained by three participants and the other scores in the data set are obtained by only one or two participants. This means that a score of 12 is the most frequently occurring score and so the mode is 12 for depression score within this data set.

To find the modal depression score for males and females separately, you need to separate the scores for males and females and then order each set of scores by the depression score variable. Again, this is reasonably straightforward to do with a small data set, but with a larger data set SPSS can help you to sort cases (see Chapter 3). Again, if you are using SPSS then it is unnecessary to sort the cases

If you separate males' and females' depression scores and then order the scores, you get a table of scores that looks like Table 4-3.

Table 4-3	Ordered Depression Scores for Males and Females Separately	
Participant	**Gender**	**Depression Score**
K	Female	4
M	Female	8
I	Female	9
H	Female	10
D	Female	12

(continued)

Table 4-3 *(continued)*		
Participant	**Gender**	**Depression Score**
R	Female	12
S	Female	12
P	Female	14
T	Female	14
F	Female	15
A	Male	2
C	Male	3
Q	Male	4
L	Male	5
G	Male	6
N	Male	7
O	Male	8
E	Male	9
B	Male	10
J	Male	11

Have a look at Table 4-3 and scan the females' scores. You can see that a score of 12 occurs three times and is the most frequently occurring score. Therefore, the modal depression score for females is 12. If you scan the depression scores for males, you can see that every male in the data set has a different score: every score occurs once. In this situation you can't calculate a modal depression score for males (which is obviously not very useful and is one of the disadvantages of the mode that we highlight in the next section).

Knowing the advantages and disadvantages of using the mode

As with any measure of central tendency, you need to consider several advantages and disadvantages before you decide which measure of central tendency to report for your data. Table 4-4 outlines the advantages and disadvantages of the mode.

Table 4-4	Advantages and Disadvantages of the Mode
Advantages	*Disadvantages*
You can calculate it easily, without the need for any mathematical formula.	Sometimes you can't calculate the mode (see example in the last section) and sometimes a variable might have more than one mode. For example, imagine that a score of 12 occurs 3 times and a score of 14 also occurs 3 times. There are two modes 12 and 14. When a variable has two modes it is known as having a *bimodal distribution*.
It is always an actual value on the variable rather than the possibility of a fraction between two possible scores. This isn't true of the mean and median.	It doesn't take account of all the data. Calculating the mode simply means that you look for the most frequently occurring score, so it doesn't matter what the other scores on the variable are and how close they are to the mode.

Obtaining the mode in SPSS

You can easily calculate the mode, as we demonstrate in the earlier section 'Determining the mode'. However, SPSS can calculate the mode for you, to avoid you needing to sort the data. To obtain the mode in SPSS:

1. **Go to the Frequencies command, as shown in Figure 4-1.**

2. **Move the variable containing your scores (depression scores in this example) into the window headed 'Variable(s)' (see Figure 4-2). When doing this you can enter as many variables as you want, so if you need to summarise more than one variable it is not necessary to run the procedure numerous times.**

3. **Click on the Statistics button and tick the box beside Mode in the section headed Central Tendency (see Figure 4-3).**

4. **Click Continue. If you don't want a frequency table you should also untick the 'Display frequency tables' box. A frequency table will show you how often each score on a variable occurs.**

5. **Click OK.**

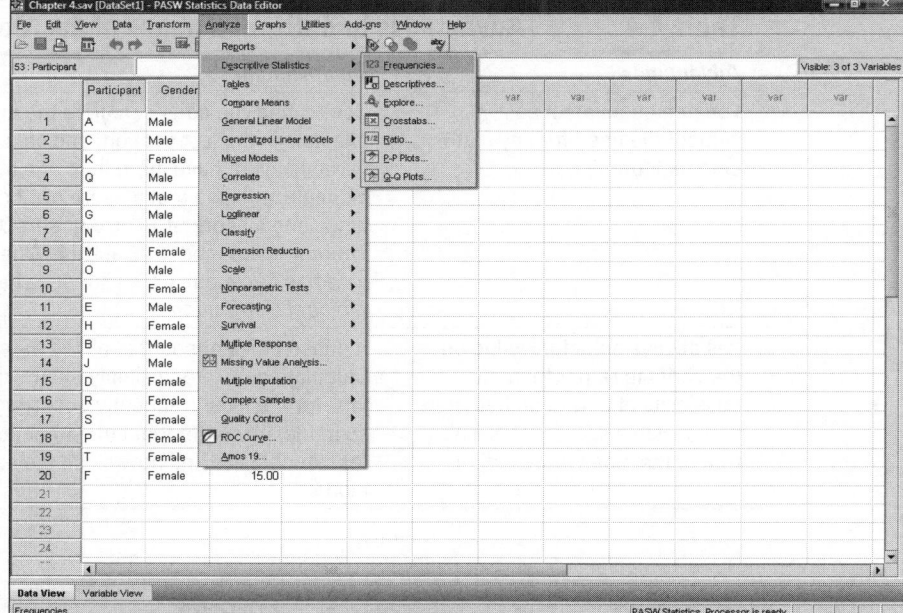

Figure 4-1:
Choosing the frequencies command to generate measures of central tendency.

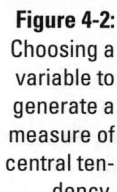
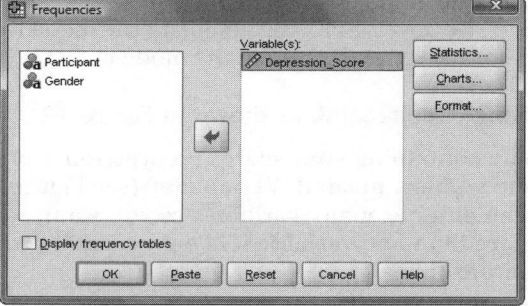

Figure 4-2:
Choosing a variable to generate a measure of central tendency.

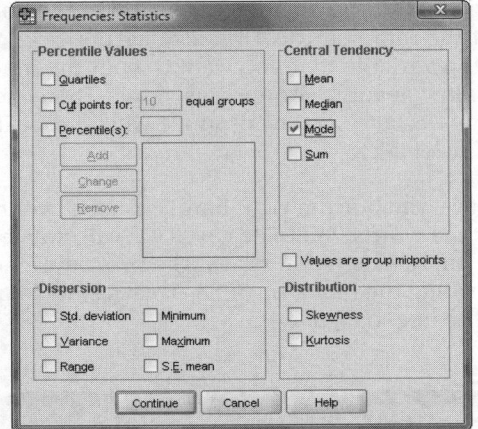

Figure 4-3:
Choosing
the mode.

When you've completed this procedure, the output window in SPSS displays a table like that in Figure 4-4.

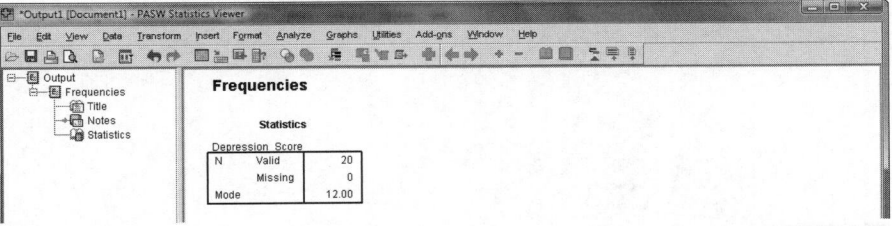

Figure 4-4:
The mode
as displayed
by SPSS.

The table in Figure 4-4 indicates that the mode for all 20 participants is 12. The number of participants is indicated by the letter N. If you want SPSS to generate the mode for males and females separately, then you need to split the file before running this procedure to obtain the mode. You can split the file using the 'Split File' command under the Data drop down menu (see

Figure 4-5). When you choose this command, it takes you to the Split File window, where you select the radio button 'Organize output by groups'. This then allows you to move the variable that you want to split the file by (in this case, gender) into the window headed 'Groups Based on'. Then click the OK button (see Figure 4-6). Any output you now produce will be repeated twice, once for males and once for females.

After you run this procedure, the bottom right-hand corner of your SPSS data sheet should display the words 'Split File On'. This will stay switched on until you manually turn it off. At this point, repeat the procedure outlined in Figures 4-1 to 4-3 for generating the mode on SPSS. This results in a table in your output window like the one in Figure 4-7.

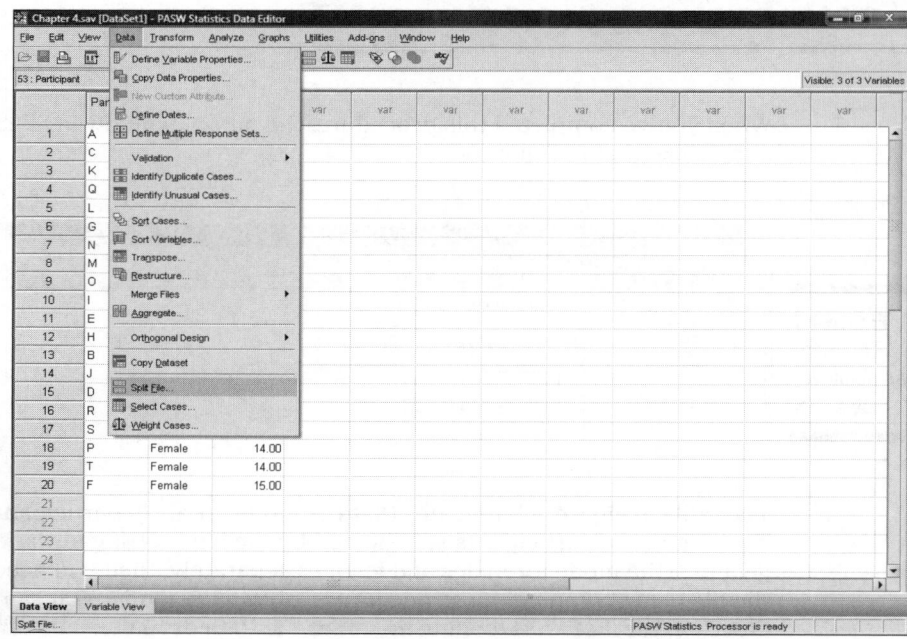

Figure 4-5:
Choosing the Split File command in SPSS.

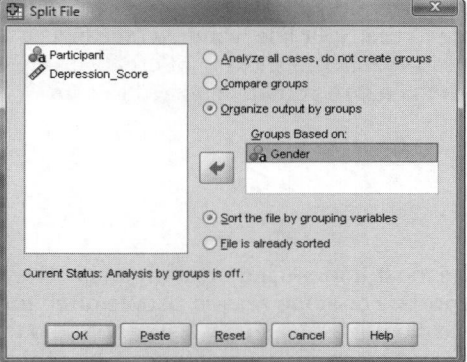

Figure 4-6:
Splitting a
file by gen-
der.

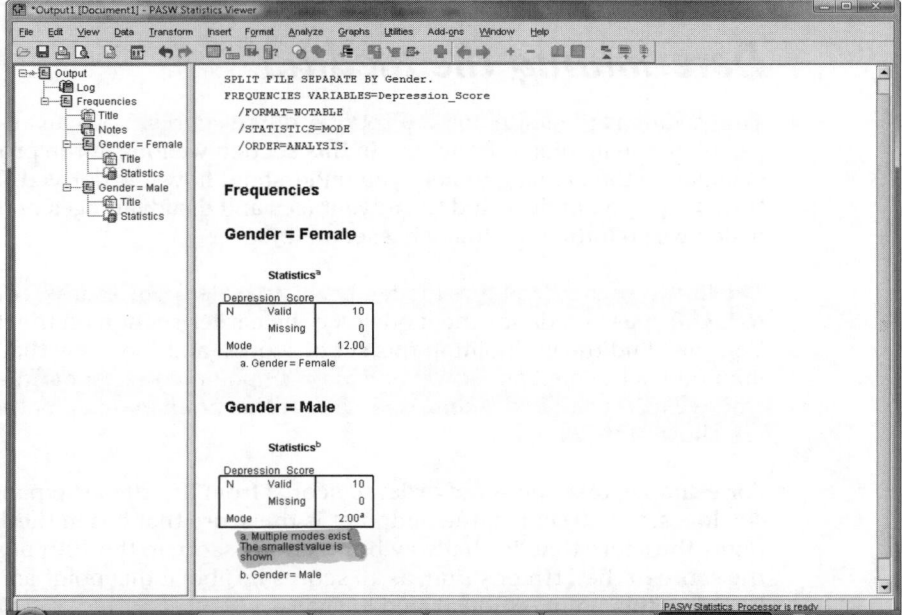

Figure 4-7:
The mode
as displayed
in SPSS for
split groups.

Note that in the output presented in Figure 4-7 SPSS generates a mode for
males but then indicates as a footnote to the table that multiple modes exist,
and that the smallest has been displayed. You won't know how many modes
exist until you look at the data.

If you do use the 'Split File' procedure, always remember to switch it off when you're finished by returning to the 'Split File' window (see Figure 4-6) and choosing the radio button 'Analyze all cases, do not create groups'. Check the bottom right of your screen to ensure you have turned this off.

The Median

The median is probably the most under-used measure of central tendency in psychological research reports. For some reason people often forget about the median – like Cinderella. So don't be an ugly sister but help the median to display its beauty when you can. (Okay, the analogy is a bit tenuous, but you get the picture!)

Determining the median

The *median* is the midpoint in a set of ordered scores. You can ask SPSS to calculate the median for you, but in this section we look at the process of calculating the median, to help you understand how it is derived. This, in turn, helps you understand the advantages and disadvantages of the median, which we go into in the following section.

The first step in calculating the median is to order your scores from lowest to highest, as you do for the mode (see the earlier section on the mode). You then find the midpoint in this set of scores, and the value that is at the midpoint is the median. The *midpoint* is the point in the set of ordered scores where exactly half of the scores are below this point and half of the scores are above this point.

For example, take the set of ordered scores from the 20 participants in Table 4-2. In a set of 20 scores, the midpoint is the score that lies in the 10.5th position – the score that lies halfway between the score in the 10th position and the score in the 11th position, as 10 scores lie above this point and 10 scores lie below this point, as illustrated in Figure 4-8.

In the data set, the score that lies at the 10.5th position is the score that lies halfway between a score of 9 (at position 10) and a score of 9 (at position 11). There isn't actually a score here, so you need to estimate what would be here. The only score that can lie between a score of 9 and a score of 9 in a set of ordered scores is another 9. Therefore, the median value for depression score for the 20 participants is 9.

Particpant	Gender	Depression Score	Position
A	Male	2	1
C	Male	3	2
K	Female	4	3
Q	Male	4	4
L	Male	5	5
G	Male	6	6
N	Male	7	7
M	Female	8	8
O	Male	8	9
I	Female	9	10 ← Score at the 10.5th position = median
E	Male	9	11
H	Female	10	12
B	Male	10	13
J	Male	11	14
D	Female	12	15
R	Female	12	16
S	Female	12	17
P	Female	14	18
T	Female	14	19
F	Female	15	20

Figure 4-8:
Finding the
median
in a set of
ordered
scores.

If Participant E (in position 11) had obtained a score of 10 rather than 9 then the median value would be the score that lies halfway between a score of 9 and a score of 10. Halfway between these scores is 9.5, so this would be the median value in that case.

A quick way to find which value is at the midpoint in a set of ordered scores is using the formula $(n+1)/2$, where n is the number of scores in the data set. So, with 20 scores, the formula becomes $(20+1)/2 = 21/2 = 10.5$. This is the position where you find the median, not the median value itself. You then need to find the score at the 10.5th position to find out what the median is.

If you want to find the median score for males' and females' depression scores separately, you need to order the scores separately for males and females (see Table 4-3).

Because there are 10 males and 10 females, the midpoint for males is at position 5.5 in their set of ordered scores, and the same is true for females. This means that for females, the median lies halfway between a score of 12 and a score of 12. Therefore, the median depression score for females is 12. For males, the median lies halfway between a score of 6 and a score of 7. Therefore the median depression score for males is 6.5 (see Figure 4-9).

Particpant	Gender	Depression Score	Position
K	Female	4	1
M	Female	8	2
I	Female	9	3
H	Female	10	4
D	Female	12	5
R	Female	12	6
S	Female	12	7
P	Female	14	8
T	Female	14	9
F	Female	15	10
A	Male	2	1
C	Male	3	2
Q	Male	4	3
L	Male	5	4
G	Male	6	5
N	Male	7	6
O	Male	8	7
E	Male	9	8
B	Male	10	9
J	Male	11	10

← Score at the 5.5th position = median

← Score at the 5.5th position = median

Figure 4-9: Finding the median for separate groups.

Knowing the advantages and disadvantages to using the median

Table 4-5 outlines the pros and cons of using the median.

Table 4-5	Advantages and Disadvantages of the Median
Advantages	**Disadvantages**
It is relatively easy to calculate, because you don't need a mathematical formula.	It may not be representative of the variable. For example, imagine you have a set of ordered scores from seven participants in a research study with the following values: 2, 2, 8, 9, 500, 500, 550. The median in this set of scores is the score that lies at position 4, which is a score of 9. Is a value of 9 truly representative of this set of scores?

Advantages	Disadvantages
It is always the central value in the variable and therefore is often a good representation of the other values in this variable. But it is not affected by extreme scores. For example, imagine that participant F in the data set in Figure 4-9 had a score of 1500 (if this was possible) rather than 15. In this case, the median depression score for females would still be 12, a good representation of the remainder of the scores.	It is not always an actual score in the variable. In the example in the last section, the median depression score for males was 6.5. However, only whole numbers are possible on the depression questionnaire, so a score of 6.5 could never occur.

Obtaining the median in SPSS

To obtain the median in SPSS, complete the steps from the earlier section 'Obtaining the mode in SPSS', but after you click the Statistics button, tick the box beside Median instead of Mode.

When you have completed this procedure, the output window in SPSS displays a table as shown in Figure 4-10.

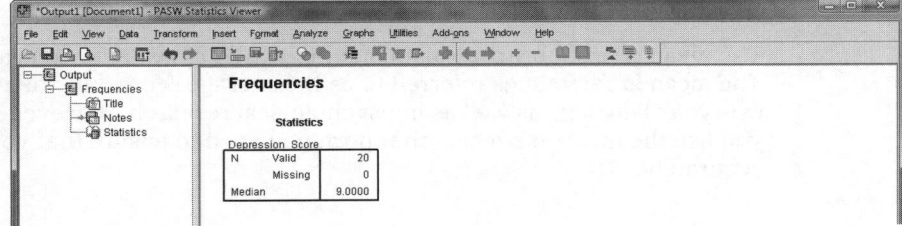

Figure 4-10: The median as displayed by SPSS.

The table in Figure 4-10 indicates that the median for all 20 participants is 9. If you want SPSS to generate the median for males and females separately then you need to split the file before running this procedure to obtain the median. Use the 'Split File' command as illustrated in 'Obtaining the mode in SPSS' (see Figures 4-5 and 4-6). Then repeat the procedure outlined in this section for generating the median on SPSS. This results in a table in your output window as shown in Figure 4-11.

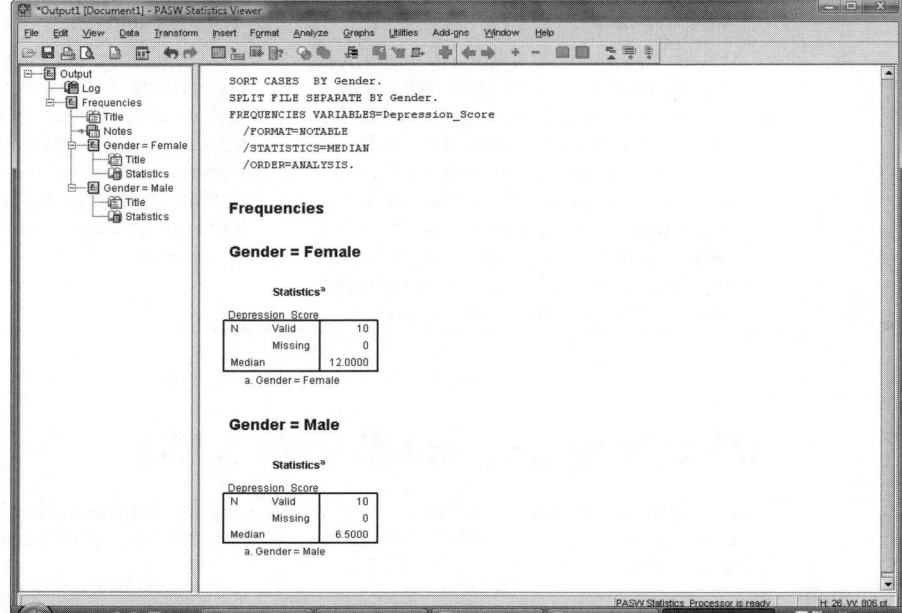

Figure 4-11:
The median as displayed in SPSS for separate groups.

The Mean

The mean is probably the most commonly used measure of central tendency. The mean is sometimes referred to as the average score and you use it in everyday language as well as in psychological research. However, when you use the mean in a research report, you need to ensure that you do so accurately.

Determining the mean

The *mean* is the arithmetical average of scores in a variable. You obtain the mean by adding together all the scores on a variable and then dividing by the number of scores. For example, if you add up all the participants' depression scores presented in Table 4-1, you get a total of 175. Twenty participants have contributed to this total score, so you get the mean score by dividing the total score (175) by the number of participants (20): 175/20 = 8.75. Therefore, the mean depression score for all participants is 8.75.

If you want to find the mean score for males' and females' depression scores separately, Table 4-3 separates the scores into those from male participants and those from females: you can add them up to find the total of 110 for female and 65 for male. You have 10 males and 10 females, so the mean depression score for females is: 110/10 = 11 and the mean depression score for males is: 65/10 = 6.5.

Knowing the advantages and disadvantages to using the mean

Table 4-6 takes you through what's good and bad about the mean.

Table 4-6	Advantages and Disadvantages of the Mean
Advantages	**Disadvantages**
It's widely understood and its calculation is straightforward.	It is affected by extreme scores. For example, imagine that participant F in Table 4-5 had a score of 1500 (if this was possible) rather than 15. In this case, the mean depression score for females would become 1595/10 = 159.5, not a good representation of the scores in the variable.
It takes account of all the data and can be determined with mathematical precision, even when only the sum of scores and the number of items are known.	It's not always an actual score in the data set. In the example the mean depression score for males was 6.5. However, only whole numbers are possible on the depression questionnaire, and a score of 6.50 could never occur.

Obtaining the mean in SPSS

To obtain the median in SPSS, complete the steps from the earlier section 'Obtaining the mode in SPSS', but after you click the Statistics button, tick the box beside Mean instead of Mode.

When you have completed this procedure, the output window in SPSS displays a table like that in Figure 4-12.

Figure 4-12 indicates that the mean for all 20 participants is 8.75. If you want SPSS to generate the mean for males and females separately then you need to split the file before running this procedure to obtain the mean. Use the 'Split File' command as illustrated in 'Obtaining the mode in SPSS' (Figures 4-5 and 4-6). Then repeat the procedure in this section for generating the mean on SPSS. This results in a table in your output window as in Figure 4-13.

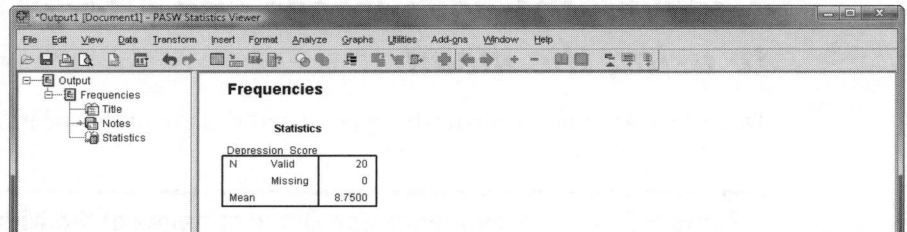

Figure 4-12: Displaying the mean in SPSS.

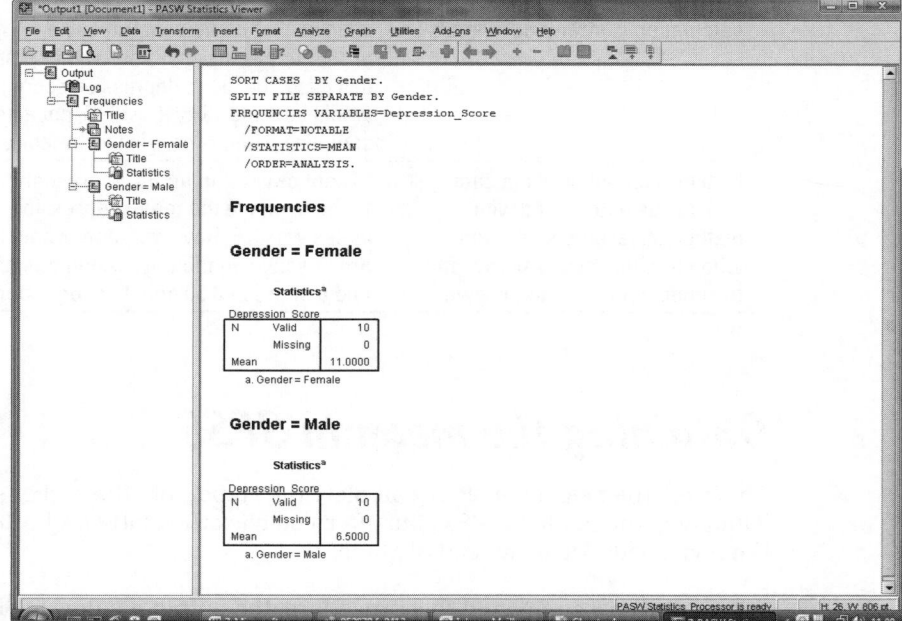

Figure 4-13: Displaying the mean in SPSS for separate groups.

Choosing between the Mode, Median and Mean

Of the three measures of central tendency – the mode, median and mean – which one should you report when you're describing a variable in a report of your research? When deciding on the most appropriate measure of central tendency to choose be guided by the advantages and disadvantages of each measure.

Weighing up the advantages and disadvantages of each measure leads you to the following conclusion: the most appropriate measure of central tendency for a variable depends on the *level of measurement* of the variable and the nature of the *distribution of scores* within that variable.

✓ **Level of measurement:** We examine the level of measurement of a variable in detail in Chapter 2. You need to distinguish between three levels of measurement (nominal, ordinal, and interval/ratio) when choosing a measure of central tendency.

✓ **Distribution of scores:** We explore the nature of the distribution of scores in Chapter 9. For the purposes of choosing a measure of central tendency, you need to know whether any extreme scores exist in your data set (often called *outliers*) or whether the distribution of scores is skewed.

 When you determine the level of measurement of your variable of interest and whether or not there is skewness and/or extreme scores in your data set then you can determine the most appropriate measure of central tendency, as follows:

✓ **Data measured at the nominal level:** Of the three measures of central tendency examined in this chapter, the mode is the only appropriate one as the scores cannot be ordered from smallest to largest in a meaningful way.

✓ **Data measured at the ordinal level:** The mode and the median are appropriate. The median is usually preferable, because it's more informative than the mode. The scores can be ordered from smallest to largest and this is meaningful, however they cannot be added up so the mean cannot be calculated.

✔ **Data measured at the interval/ratio level:** All three measures of central tendency are appropriate. The mean is usually preferable. However, the mean isn't appropriate when extreme scores and/or skewness exist in your data set. In this situation the median is usually best.

Chapter 5

Measures of Dispersion

. . . .

In This Chapter

▶ Understanding dispersion

▶ Calculating range, interquartile range and standard deviation

▶ Choosing between using range, interquartile range and standard deviation to summarise data

. . . .

You use measures of dispersion in conjunction with measures of central tendency to summarise the information you collect during the research process (your data). When you have a large amount of data, presenting data for each individual separately isn't feasible. This would mean providing a very large table, which could take up many pages in a report and would be unintelligible. Instead, you use summary statistics to provide an indication of what variables in a data set look like (we explain variables in Chapter 2).

As we explain in Chapter 4, you need two pieces of information (as a minimum) to summarise the data you collect in your study: the central tendency of the data, which we cover in Chapter 4, and the dispersion (or variability) of the data, which we examine in this chapter.

Dispersion of a variable basically means how spread out the data are. You communicate dispersion by using the range, interquartile range or standard deviation, and in this chapter we explain how to determine these, and the advantages and disadvantages of each.

Defining Dispersion

Dispersion describes a single number that aims to give you a sense of the spread or variability in a variable. In other words, a measure of dispersion is a number that's meant to give you a sense of how similar the scores in a variable are. The larger the dispersion score, the greater the variability and therefore the less similar the scores are. The data used in this chapter is the same as that used to explain central tendency in chapter 4: depression scores for males and females.

To interpret a measure of dispersion such as the standard deviation, you usually need to take account of the maximum and minimum possible scores on the measurement scale and the central tendency of the data (flick to Chapter 4 for details). A measure of dispersion is difficult to make sense of in isolation. For example, what does it mean when you state that a variable has a standard deviation of 10 – is this a large or small amount of dispersion? If the possible range of scores is only between 1 and 20 then a standard deviation of 10 is pretty large. However, if the possible range is between 1 and 100 then a standard deviation of 10 would be considered relatively small. If you only know what the central tendency of the variable is (for example, the mean of the variable) then you can use this information to answer this question. For example, a standard deviation of 10 would be considered large if the mean value was 1 but a standard deviation of 10 would be considered smaller if the mean value was 50. Therefore, you need to read the information in this chapter along with the information provided in Chapter 4.

If you have several variables in your data set then you need to generate a measure of dispersion for each variable. Additionally, if you have more than one group of participants in your research study, you might need to calculate a measure of dispersion for each group for a particular variable.

As we explain in Chapter 4 for measures of central tendency, you need to be clear about who the measure of dispersion refers to and what variable it refers to.

The Range

The range is the simplest measure of dispersion to calculate. The following sections look at the range in a detail.

Determining the range

The *range* is the difference between the highest score and the lowest score in a variable. These are the values that have been scored by participants and not necessarily the highest and lowest possible scores. Usually, you can ask a programme such as SPSS to calculate the range for you. But you also need to know how to do the calculation yourself.

Take the research study we introduce in Chapter 4 that involves assessing depression scores among 10 male and 10 female participants. The scores on the depression questionnaire for all the participants, in the order they were obtained, are presented in Table 4-1 (flick back to Chapter 4 to have a look).

Before generating any descriptive statistics, such as a measure of dispersion, order your data. Take a look at Table 4-2 in Chapter 4 to see the data set ordered by depression score.

With the data ordered you can now more easily see the lowest and highest values in the variable. From Table 4-2 you can see that a depression score of 2 is the lowest score obtained and a score of 15 is the highest score. The range is the difference between these two scores – the lowest score subtracted from the highest score (highest score – lowest score). The range for this set of scores is 15 – 2 = 13.

To find the range of depression scores for males and females separately, you need to separate the scores for males and females and then order each set of scores by the depression score variable. Table 4-3 in Chapter 4 shows you the ordered depression scores for males and females separately. If you scan the female scores in Table 4-3, you can see that the lowest score is 4 and the highest score is 15. Therefore, the range of depression scores for females is 11. If we scan the depression scores for males, we can see that the lowest score is 2 and the highest score is 11. Therefore, the range of depression scores for males is 9. This example shows the importance of looking at males and females separately as the range for both genders is smaller than when looking at all 20 participants together.

Knowing the advantages and disadvantages of using the range

You need to think about advantages and disadvantages before you decide which measure of dispersion to report for your data. Table 5-1 outlines the pros and cons of using the range.

Table 5-1	Advantages and Disadvantages of the Range
Advantages	**Disadvantages**
You can calculate it easily.	It doesn't take account of all the data. Calculating the range simply means that you look for the highest and lowest values. It really doesn't matter what the other scores in the variable are.
You can calculate it when you know the maximum and minimum value in the variable – you don't need to know every value in the variable.	It's affected by extreme scores and therefore might not be a good representation of the dispersion within a variable. For example, imagine that a participant F in the data set in Table 4-3 had a score of 1500 rather than 15.00 (if this was possible). This would mean that the range of depression scores for females would be 1496 rather than 11.

Obtaining the range in SPSS

SPSS can calculate the range for you. To obtain the range in SPSS:

1. **Go to the Frequencies command, as shown in Figure 5-1.**

2. **Move the variable containing your scores (depression scores in this example) into the window headed 'Variable(s)' (see Figure 5-2).**

3. **Click on the 'Statistics' button and tick the box beside 'Range' in the section headed 'Dispersion' (see Figure 5-3).**

4. **Click 'Continue'. If you don't want a frequency table you should also untick the 'Display frequency tables box'.**

5. **Click OK.**

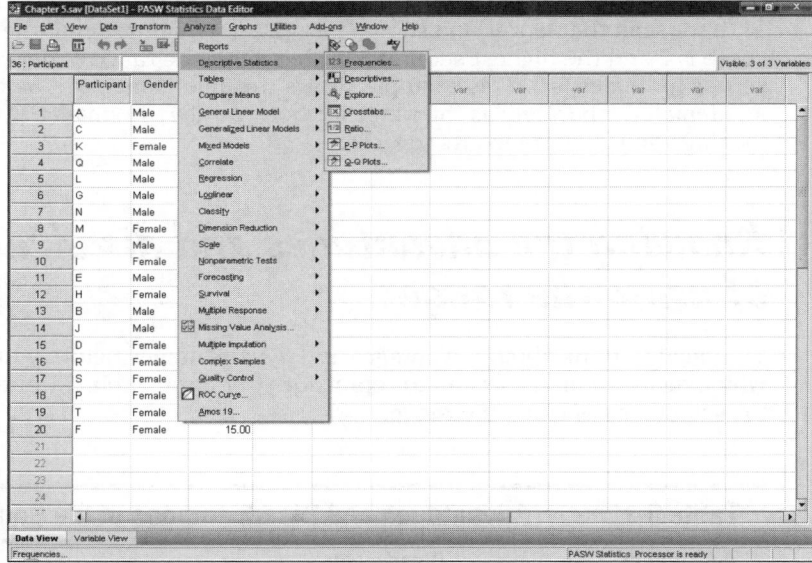

Figure 5-1:
Choosing the frequencies command to generate measures of dispersion.

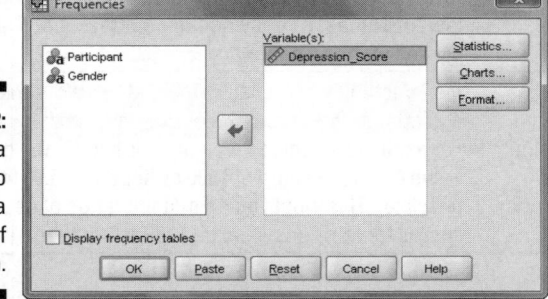

Figure 5-2:
Choosing a variable to generate a measure of dispersion.

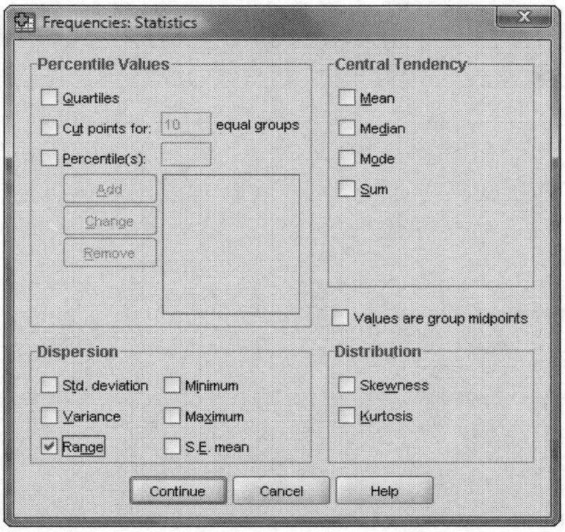

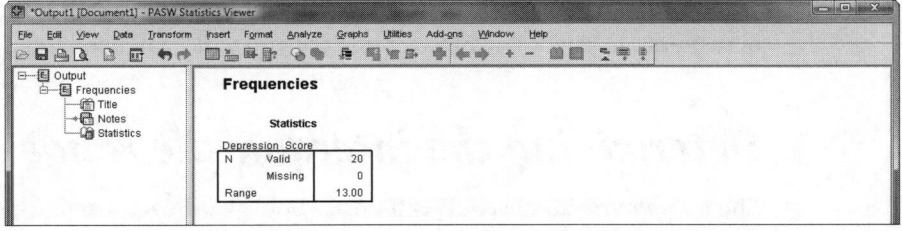

Figure 5-3:
Choosing
the range.

When you have completed this procedure, the output window in SPSS displays a table like that in Figure 5-4.

The table indicates that the range for all 20 participants is 13. If you want SPSS to generate the range for males and females separately, you need to split the file before running this procedure to obtain the mode. We explain how to do this in Chapter 4. This results in a table in your output window as shown in Figure 5-5.

Figure 5-4:
The range
as displayed
by SPSS.

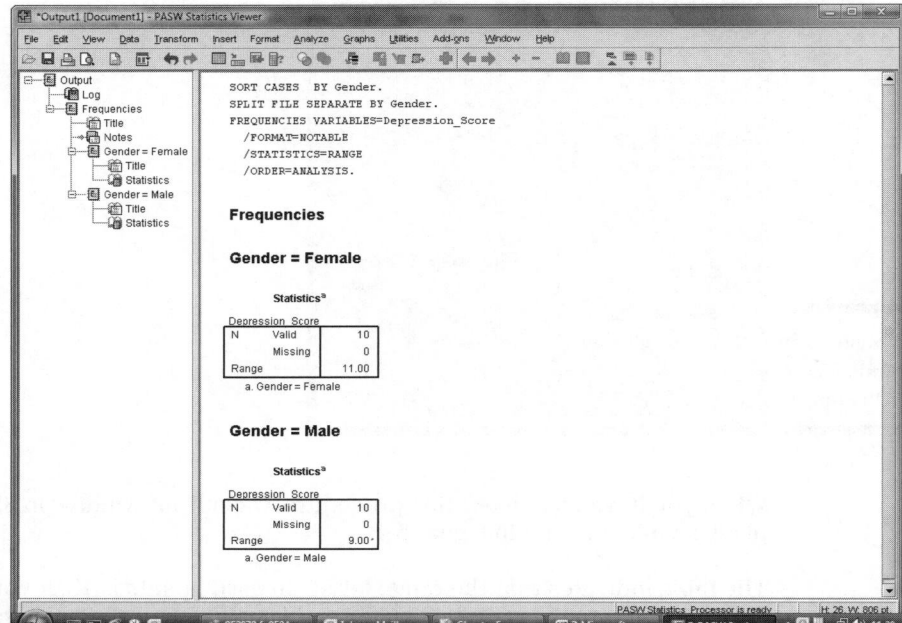

Figure 5-5:
The range as displayed in SPSS for split groups.

The Interquartile Range

The interquartile range is a useful but not very commonly employed measure of dispersion. The following sections tell you what you need to know.

Determining the interquartile range

The *interquartile range* is the difference between the upper quartile and the lower quartile in a set of ordered scores. Quartiles are formed by dividing a set of ordered scores into four equal-sized groups. It's easy to calculate when you find the upper and lower quartiles, so perhaps first we want to spend some time examining how you find these values.

The *upper* and *lower quartiles* bound the middle 50 per cent of the scores in the variable. That is, 50 per cent of all the scores in the variable lie within the upper and lower quartile. Therefore, the interquartile range tells you the range of the middle 50 per cent of scores in the variable.

The first step in finding the upper and lower quartiles (sometimes called the *75th* and *25th percentiles*, respectively) is to order your scores from lowest to highest. You then find the point in this set of scores below which 25 per cent (or one-quarter) of the scores lie. The value at this point is known as the *lower quartile* (25th percentile). You also need to find the point in this set of scores above which 25 per cent (or one-quarter) of the scores lie. The value at this point is known as the *upper quartile* (75th percentile).

A quick way to find the position of the upper and lower quartiles in a set of ordered scores is using the following formulae:

Position of the lower quartile = $(n + 1)/4$, where n is the number of scores in the data set.

Position of the upper quartile = $3(n + 1)/4$, where n is the number of scores in the data set.

So, with 20 scores, the formulae become:

Position of the lower quartile = $(20 + 1)/4 = 21/4 = 5.25$

Position of the upper quartile = $3(n + 1)/4 = 63/4 = 15.75$

These are the positions where the upper and lower quartiles can be found, not the upper and lower quartile values themselves. For example, take the set of ordered scores from the 20 participants in Table 4-2 (see Chapter 4). In a set of 20 scores, the lower quartile is the score that lies in the 5.25th position – the score that lies a quarter of the way between the score in the 5th position and the score in the 6th position. The upper quartile is the score that lies in the 15.75th position – the score that lies three-quarters of the way between the score in the 15th position and the score in the 16th position, as illustrated in Figure 5-6.

In the data set shown in Figure 5-6, the score that lies at the 5.25th position is the score that lies a quarter of the way between a score of 5 (at position 5) and a score of 6 (at position 6). There isn't actually a score here, so you need to estimate what would be here. The only score that can lie a quarter of the way between a score of 5 and a score of 6 in a set of ordered scores is a score of 5.25. This is the lower quartile. Note that in this case the position of the lower quartile and the value of the lower quartile is the same. This isn't always the case.

In the data set shown in Figure 5-6, the score that lies at the 15.75th position is the score that lies three-quarters of the way between a score of 12 (at position 15) and a score of 12 (at position 16). The only score that can lie in this position is another score of 12. This is the upper quartile.

Particpant	Gender	Depression Score	Position
A	Male	2	1
C	Male	3	2
K	Female	4	3
Q	Male	4	4
L	Male	5	5
G	Male	6	6
N	Male	7	7
M	Female	8	8
O	Male	8	9
I	Female	9	10
E	Male	9	11
H	Female	10	12
B	Male	10	13
J	Male	11	14
D	Female	12	15
R	Female	12	16
S	Female	12	17
P	Female	14	18
T	Female	14	19
F	Female	15	20

Score at the 5.25th position = lower quartile

Score at the 15.75th position = upper quartile

Figure 5-6: Finding the upper and lower quartiles in a set of ordered scores.

Now that you know that for the depression scores in this example the upper quartile is 12 and the lower quartile is 5.25, you can calculate the interquartile range by subtracting the lower quartile from the upper quartile (upper quartile – lower quartile). Therefore the interquartile range for depression scores is $12 - 5.25 = 6.75$.

If you want to find the interquartile range score for males' and females' depression scores separately, then you need to order the scores separately for males and females (see Table 4-3 in Chapter 4).

You have 10 males and 10 females, so the lower quartile for males is at position 2.75 in their set of ordered scores, and the same is true for females. The upper quartile for males is at position 8.25, and the same is true for females. This means that for females, the lower quartile lies three-quarters of the way between a score of 8 and a score of 9 and the upper quartile lies a quarter of the way between a score of 14 and a score of 14. Therefore, the lower quartile depression score for females is 8.75 and the upper quartile is 14, resulting in an interquartile range of $14 - 8.75 = 5.25$. For males, the lower quartile depression score lies three-quarters of the way between a score of 3 and a score of 4 and the upper quartile lies a quarter of the way between a score of 9 and a score of 10. Therefore the lower quartile depression score for males is 3.75 and the upper quartile is 9.25, resulting in an interquartile range of $9.25 - 3.75 = 5.50$ (see Figure 5-7).

Particpant	Gender	Depression Score	Position	
K	Female	4	1	
M	Female	8	2	Score at the 2.75th position = lower quartile
I	Female	9	3	
H	Female	10	4	
D	Female	12	5	
R	Female	12	6	
S	Female	12	7	
P	Female	14	8	Score at the 8.25th position = upper quartile
T	Female	14	9	
F	Female	15	10	
A	Male	2	1	
C	Male	3	2	Score at the 2.75th position = lower quartile
Q	Male	4	3	
L	Male	5	4	
G	Male	6	5	
N	Male	7	6	
O	Male	8	7	
E	Male	9	8	Score at the 8.25th position = upper quartile
B	Male	10	9	
J	Male	11	10	

Figure 5-7:
Finding the upper and lower quartiles for separate groups.

Knowing the advantages and disadvantages of using the interquartile range

Here are the main good and bad points of using the interquartile range.

Table 5-2	Advantages and Disadvantages of the Interquartile Range
Advantages	*Disadvantages*
It is reasonably straightforward to calculate.	The upper and lower quartiles aren't always actual scores in the variable. In the example, the lower quartile depression score for males was 3.75. However, only whole numbers are possible on the depression questionnaire, so a score of 3.75 could never occur.
It's not affected by extreme scores. For example, imagine that participant F in the data set in Figure 5-7 had a score of 1500 (if this was possible) rather than 15. In this case, the interquartile range for depression scores for females would still be 5.25, a good representation of the dispersion in the middle 50% of the scores.	

Obtaining the interquartile range in SPSS

The simplest procedure for obtaining the interquartile range in SPSS is to use the Frequencies command. Follow the process we outline in the earlier section 'Obtaining the range in SPSS', but after you click on Statistics, tick the box Quartiles in the section headed Percentile Values. After you complete this procedure, the output window in SPSS displays a table as shown in Figure 5-8.

The lower quartile is the value presented for the 25th percentile in Figure 5-8 and the upper quartile is the value presented for the 75th percentile in Figure 5-8. To find the interquartile range, you need to subtract these two values: 12 − 5.25 = 6.75.

If you want SPSS to generate the quartiles for males and females separately then you need to split the file before running this procedure to obtain the interquartile range (we explain how in Chapter 4). You get a table in your output window as shown in Figure 5-9.

The method doesn't actually generate the interquartile range in SPSS, but provides you with the quartiles to allow you to calculate the interquartile range. In all cases this is sufficient, because it only requires you to do a simple subtraction of two numbers.

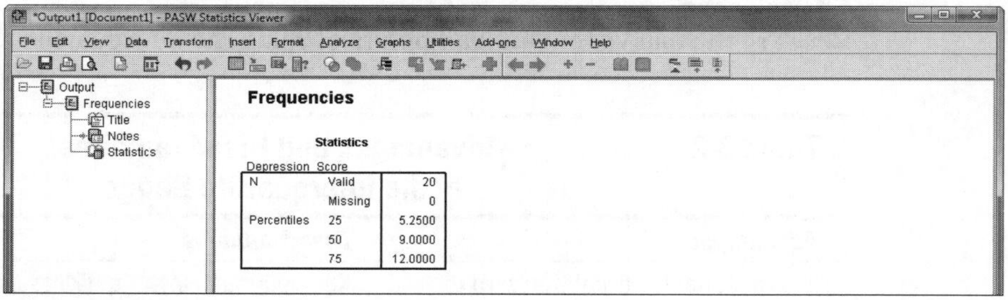

Figure 5-8:
The quartiles as displayed by SPSS.

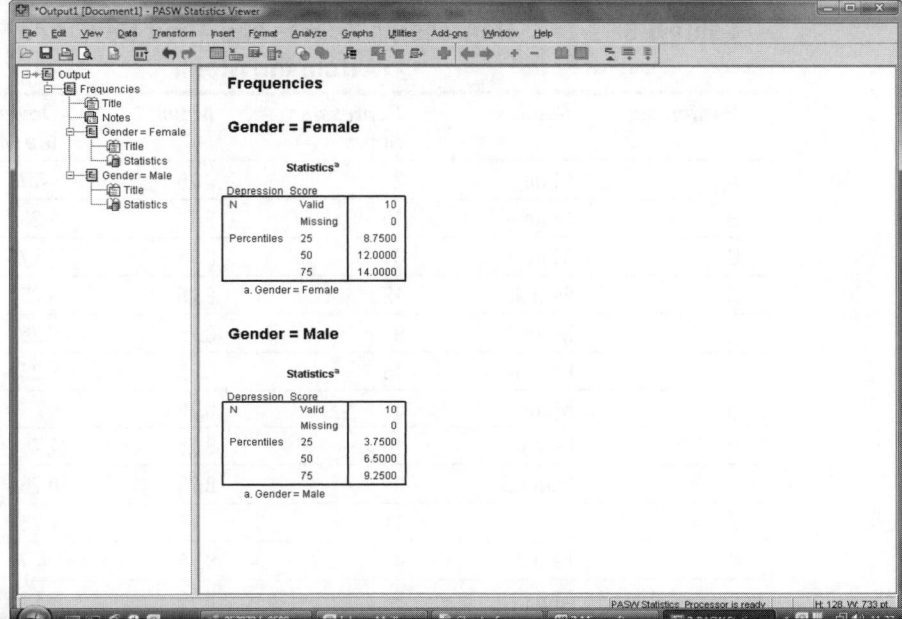

The Standard Deviation

The standard deviation is probably the most commonly used measure of dispersion. It is closely related to another measure of dispersion which is less commonly reported – the variance. Therefore it is important to know that the first steps of calculating the standard deviation also calculate the variance.

Defining the standard deviation

The *standard deviation* (often abbreviated to Std. Dev. or SD) is the average deviation of scores in your data set from their mean score for a particular variable. As we explain in Chapter 4, the *mean score* is the average of scores on a variable. The standard deviation indicates the extent to which the scores on a variable deviate from the mean score.

For example, Table 5-3 below presents the original scores presented in Table 4-1 in Chapter 4. The last row in the table is the mean depression score for all 20 participants (8.75). The last column in the table indicates the deviation of each score from the mean score. In other words, the deviation is the score you obtain if you subtract the mean score from each person's depression score (individual's depression score – mean depression score). For example, the depression score for Participant A is 2 and the mean depression score is 8.75. Therefore the deviation is 2 – 8.75 = –6.75.

Table 5-3		Depression Scores and Their Deviation from the Mean		
Participant	*Gender*	*Depression Score*	*Mean*	*Deviation from the Mean*
A	Male	2	8.75	−6.75
B	Male	10	8.75	1.25
C	Male	3	8.75	−5.75
D	Female	12	8.75	3.25
E	Male	9	8.75	0.25
F	Female	15	8.75	6.25
G	Male	6	8.75	−2.75
H	Female	10	8.75	1.25
I	Female	9	8.75	0.25
J	Male	11	8.75	2.25
K	Female	4	8.75	−4.75
L	Male	5	8.75	−3.75
M	Female	8	8.75	−0.75
N	Male	7	8.75	−1.75
O	Male	8	8.75	−0.75
P	Female	14	8.75	5.25
Q	Male	4	8.75	−4.75
R	Female	12	8.75	3.25
S	Female	12	8.75	3.25
T	Female	14	8.75	5.25
		Mean = 8.75		

Table 5-3 provides a list of deviation scores, but how can you summarise these deviation scores in a meaningful way? If you look at the depression scores in Table 5-3, you see that they're summarised by the mean score. The mean score is calculated by adding all the depression scores and dividing by the number of scores. Perhaps you could use the same principle to summarise the deviation scores? This seems like a good idea. So, in principle, you could add up all the deviation scores and divide by their number, giving you a mean deviation score. Let's see how that would work.

If you add up all the deviation scores you get a total of zero (0). This isn't helpful because you can't divide zero by the total number of scores (20). In fact, when you add up deviations from the mean, the answer is often zero or close to zero. This is because the mean tends to be a central point in your data set and, therefore, the deviations above the mean are similar to deviations below the mean. Because deviations below the mean are given a negative value, the negative scores and positive scores balance each other out and when you sum them you get zero or something similar.

To deal with this problem, you need to remove the negative values. One way of doing this (which is quite common in statistics) is to square the scores. *Squaring a score* means multiplying the score by itself. When you square a positive score, it remains positive; when you square a negative score, it becomes positive. So, by squaring the scores you have a handy method of making negative scores become positive. For example, the deviation score for Participant A is –6.75. If you square this value (multiply –6.75 by –6.75), you get 45.5625. Table 5-4 shows the squared deviations.

Table 5-4   Depression Scores and their Squared Deviations from the Mean

Participant	Gender	Depression Score	Deviation from the Mean	Squared Deviations from the Mean
A	Male	2	–6.75	45.5625
B	Male	10	1.25	1.5625
C	Male	3	–5.75	33.0625
D	Female	12	3.25	10.5625
E	Male	9	0.25	0.0625
F	Female	15	6.25	39.0625
G	Male	6	–2.75	7.5625
H	Female	10	1.25	1.5625
I	Female	9	0.25	0.0625
J	Male	11	2.25	5.0625
K	Female	4	–4.75	22.5625
L	Male	5	–3.75	14.0625
M	Female	8	–0.75	0.5625
N	Male	7	–1.75	3.0625
O	Male	8	–0.75	0.5625
P	Female	14	5.25	27.5625
Q	Male	4	–4.75	22.5625
R	Female	12	3.25	10.5625
S	Female	12	3.25	10.5625
T	Female	14	5.25	27.5625
		Mean = 8.75		Mean = 14.1875

You can now take the average of the squared deviations from the mean by adding these up and dividing by the number of scores. The total squared deviation from the mean is 283.75. The number of scores is 20. Therefore, the average of the squared deviations from the mean is 283.75/20 = 14.1875.

The average of the squared deviations from the mean is similar to the measure of dispersion known as the *variance*. The difference is that the average of the squared deviations from the mean is the sum of the squared deviations from the mean (283.75) divided by the total number of scores (20), whereas the variance is the sum of the squared deviations from the mean (283.75) divided by the total number of scores less one (19). Therefore the variance for the depression scores is 283.75/19 = 14.93.

The one that got away

When calculating the standard deviation you divided the sum of squared deviations by the number of scores less one ($n - 1$). Why is $n - 1$ used instead of n? If you're calculating the standard deviation of a population of scores rather than a sample (you don't want to use the standard deviation to make any extrapolations about your scores to a group of people bigger than your sample) then it's appropriate to divide the sum of the squared deviations by n rather than $n - 1$ (see Chapter 7 for a discussion of samples and populations).

However, when working with sample data, where you want to make extrapolations to a population then the deviations that you calculate should, in theory, be the deviations between the scores in your sample and the population mean. Yet often you don't know the population mean and so you use the sample mean in its place.

In most cases the data is closer to the sample mean than the population mean (the deviations are larger if you used the population mean) and therefore the standard deviation is smaller when based on the sample mean than when based on the population mean. To account for this, you divide the sum of squared deviations by a slightly smaller number ($n - 1$ rather than n), thereby making the standard deviation

slightly larger than if you had divided by n. It is appropriate to make this adjustment based on the sample size (n), because as the sample size increases, the sample mean becomes more like the population mean, and as the sample size increases, the difference between a standard deviation based on n and a standard deviation based on $n - 1$ becomes negligible.

Depending on the texts you read some will divide by n and others will use $n - 1$, so it is important to know the difference between the two. When using SPSS it will automatically divide by $n - 1$ as it will presume that you want to be able to apply your results to a wider population.

Formulas for the sample variance and sample standard deviation are usually presented as follows.

Variance: $\dfrac{\sum(x - \bar{x})^2}{n - 1}$

Standard deviation: $\sqrt{\dfrac{\sum(x - \bar{x})^2}{n - 1}}$

Where x is an individual's score in your data set; $\bar{x}$ is the sample mean and n is the total number of scores. The $\sum$ symbol means that you take the sum of the information that follows.

But remember that you set out to find the standard deviation of the depression scores. The standard deviation is the square root of the variance. Remember also that you squared all the deviation scores to remove negative values. Therefore, you need to reverse this process to return to the original units. The reverse of squaring a number is to take its square root. So, if you take the square root of the variance then you can express dispersion in terms of the original units of the variable. This is known as the standard deviation. The standard deviation for depression scores is the square root of 14.93, which is 3.86. This means that, on average, the depression scores deviate by about 3.86 points from the mean.

Knowing the advantages and disadvantages of using the standard deviation

Keep the following pros and cons in mind when using the standard deviation.

Table 5-5	Advantages and Disadvantages of the Standard Deviation
Advantages	*Disadvantages*
It is widely understood and its calculation is straightforward.	It is affected by extreme scores. For example, imagine that participant F in the data set in Table 5-5 had a score of 1500 (if this was possible) rather than 15. In this case, the standard deviation for depression scores would become 333.55 rather than 14.93.
It takes account of all the data and can be determined with mathematical precision.	
It can be determined when only the sum of scores and the number of items are known.	

Obtaining the standard deviation in SPSS

Use the procedure we explain in the earlier section 'Obtaining the range in SPSS' to obtain the standard deviation in SPSS, but after you click on Statistics, tick the box beside 'Std. deviation' in the section headed 'Dispersion'. After you complete this procedure, the output window in SPSS displays a table as shown in Figure 5-10.

Chapter 4 shows you how to split the file so you can generate the standard deviation for males and females separately. When you do so you see a table like that in Figure 5-11.

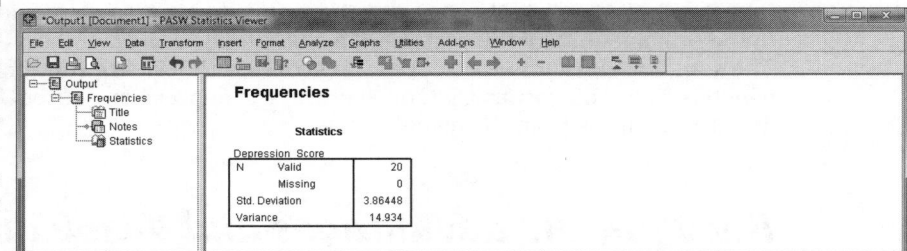

Figure 5-10: The standard deviation and variance as displayed by SPSS.

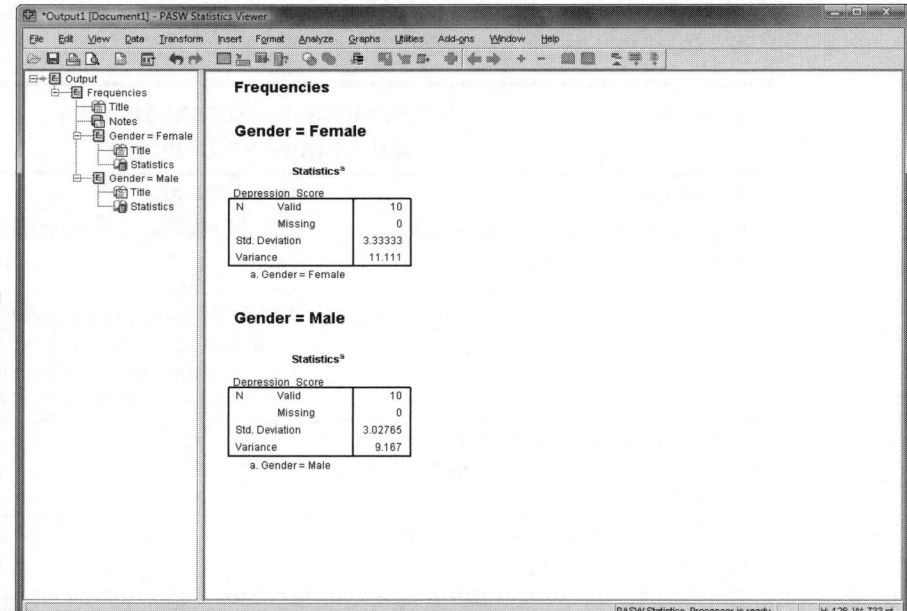

Figure 5-11: The standard deviation (and variance) as displayed in SPSS for separate groups.

Choosing between the Range, Interquartile Range and Standard Deviation

Take a look at Chapter 4, where we explain what you need to keep in mind when choosing your measures of central tendency – the same advice applies here.

You determine the most appropriate measure of dispersion as follows (for details of these three levels of measurement, flick to Chapter 2):

- **Data measured at the nominal level:** As all of the three measures of dispersion examined in this chapter require data to be ranked or summed, none of them are appropriate for data measured at the nominal level.

- **Data measured at the ordinal level:** The range and interquartile range are appropriate. The interquartile range is usually preferred, as it is more informative than the range.

- **Data measured at the interval/ratio level:** All three measures of dispersion we have examined are appropriate. The standard deviation is usually preferred. However, the standard deviation (or variance) isn't appropriate when there are extreme scores and/or skewness in your data set. In this situation the interquartile range is usually preferred.

Chapter 6

Generating Graphs and Charts

. . . .

In This Chapter

▶ Generating a histogram to display data

▶ Making a bar chart

▶ Using a pie chart

▶ Creating a box and whisker plot

. . . .

*B*efore you embark on any statistical analyses of your data, you need to have a sense of the shape of the distribution of scores on any variables that you want to include in your analyses (Chapter 2 explains variables). The shape of the distribution of scores influences your choice of simple descriptive statistics such as measures of central tendency (see Chapter 4) and dispersion (see Chapter 5) as well as your choice of inferential statistical tests (see Parts III–V). Therefore, you need to become comfortable with examining data on a graph and making decisions about the shape of that data.

In this chapter we look at several commonly used approaches to displaying data – the histogram, bar chart, pie chart, and box and whisker plot. We discuss when it is appropriate to use each of these types of charts and how to generate them on the SPSS statistical software package. For a further discussion of how these charts help you to say something about the shape of a distribution, check out Chapter 9.

Whatever type of graph or chart you use to display your data, make sure you label the axes and include a title for the graph or chart.

The Histogram

People often use histograms to display data from a continuous variable in a chart when conducting basic statistical analysis. Your ability to understand a histogram is crucial in determining your ability to choose appropriate statistics for your data.

Understanding the histogram

A *histogram* is a method of displaying scores on a variable in pictorial form. You usually use a histogram to indicate how often each score occurs in a variable – in other words, to display the frequency of each score. Histograms have two axes – the horizontal axis (or *x* axis) and the vertical axis (or *y* axis). Normally, you display the full range of scores on a variable from your dataset on the horizontal axis and the frequency with which each score occurs on the vertical axis.

For example, imagine you're conducting a study to examine the extent to which students pay attention to anti-drink-driving advertising messages. You conduct the study by asking students to watch the messages on a television screen and then rate their level of interest on a sliding scale between 0 and 100, where 0 means no interest and 100 means extremely interested. You conduct the study with 25 participants. Table 6-1 shows their responses.

Table 6-1	Students' Level of Interest in Anti-Drink-Driving Messages
Participant	**Interest Score**
A	50
B	45
C	55
D	43
E	50
F	46
G	56
H	55
I	50
J	72
K	49
L	30
M	81
N	20
O	51
P	65
Q	60

Participant	Interest Score
R	35
S	40
T	35
U	56
V	61
W	32
X	70
Y	70

Displaying the scores from each participant, as shown in Table 6-1, isn't very informative. All the information you need to make sense of the data is there, but it is not presented in a way that's easy to interpret. This is where a chart such as a histogram becomes useful.

To convert the information in Table 6-1 into a histogram, you draw a horizontal axis and add the range of scores to this axis. This can be the range of possible scores (0 to 100 in this case) or the range of actual scores (20 to 81 in this case). Take a look at Figure 6-1 to see the histogram.

Presenting the range of possible scores on the axis is useful to provide the reader with a sense of where the scores actually obtained lie in relation to the scores that could be obtained. But if you present the range of actual scores, and these don't begin at zero then indicate this by a double slash through the beginning of the horizontal axis - this tells the reader that there are possible scores lower than that indicated on the chart (see Figure 6-1).

One of the things you notice about the histograms in Figure 6-1 is that the scores on the horizontal axis are in line with the beginning of each bar (or column) on the chart. Therefore, the bars represent a range of scores (in this case) rather than just a single score. As the bars are all the same width, then the range of scores represented by each bar must be the same. In the example in Figure 6-1, each bar represents a range of 10 points on the variable. For example, the first bar on the histogram represents the scores that range from 20 up to but not including 30. You see from Table 6-1 that only one score lies in this range (a score of 20 obtained by Participant N). Therefore, this bar's height is level with a frequency of 1 on the vertical axis. You often have to use bars that represent a range of scores with continuous data, because you will often have cases such as this where each individual score only has a frequency of 1 or 2. When that happens, having each bar represent an individual score would not give any useful information.

All charts should have a title to indicate what the chart contains. For example: "A histogram of the frequency of interest scores"

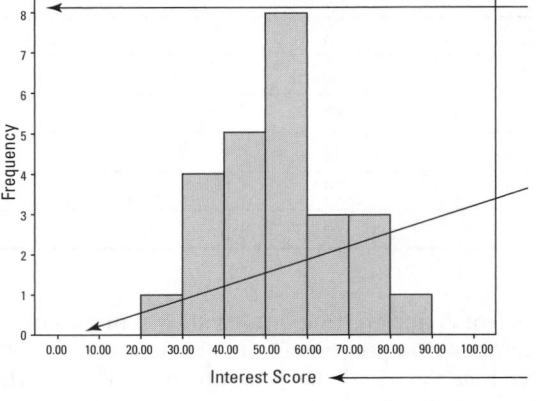

The vertical axis on a histogram usually refers to the frequency of scores and should be labelled accordingly

There are blank spaces here because no one has obtained these scores

The horizontal axis on a histogram usually refers to the range of scores on the variable of interest and should be labelled accordingly

Figure 6-1:
Histograms showing the possible range of scores (top chart) and the actual range of scores (bottom chart).

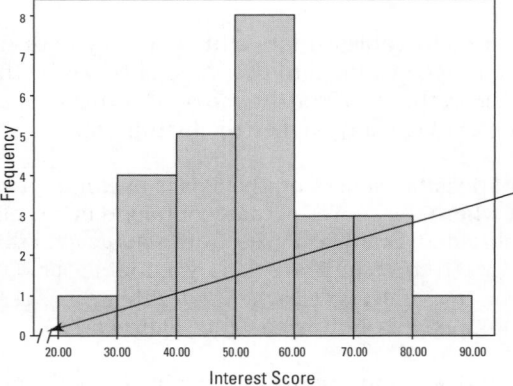

A double slash here indicates that there are possible scores lower than that recorded, but no-one obtained these scores

The bars on a histogram touch each other: there is no space between the bars unless there are scores on the variable that no one obtained. (Contrast this with the bars on a bar chart – see the following section.) This means that the variable on the horizontal axis is being treated as a continuous variable, and the horizontal axis on a histogram is meant to portray one continuous range of scores. Therefore, displaying a discrete (or categorical) variable on a histogram is never appropriate (as we explain in Chapter 2, discrete variables contain separate and distinct categories, and continuous variables contain a continuous range of scores).

Sometimes a bar on a histogram represents only a single score (usually when the range of scores is small) rather than a range of scores. In this case, the score on the horizontal axis is in the middle of the bar it refers to (see Figure 6-2).

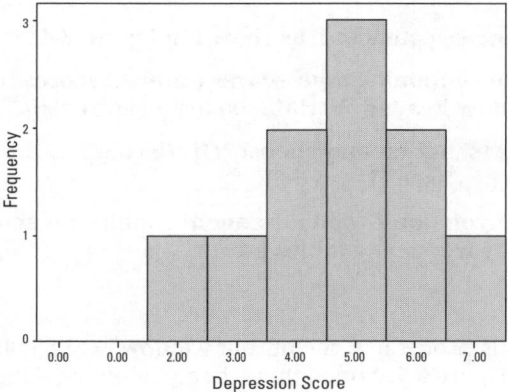

Figure 6-2:
Histogram
with bars
represent-
ing single
scores
rather than
a range of
scores.

When you look at a chart, the scales used on the axes of the chart can affect your perception of the shape of the data, as it can if you choose to display only the range of scores obtained and not the whole possible range. Therefore, in addition to simply looking at the shape of the data on a chart, pay attention to the scale of the axes. For example, take a look at Figure 6-3. It displays the same information as that displayed in the top histogram in Figure 6-1, but with the scale of the vertical axis amended. A quick glance at these histograms might lead you to believe that they display different information and this might influence your interpretations. Therefore, always check the scale used on the axes.

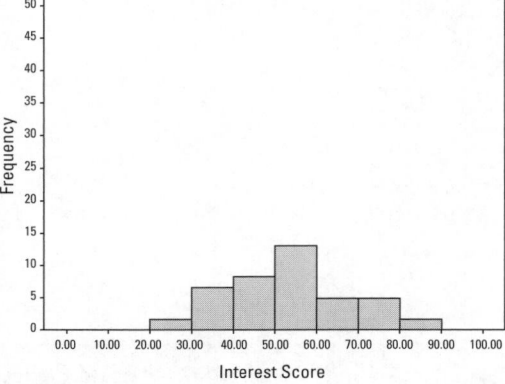

Figure 6-3:
Histogram
with
amended
vertical axis.

Obtaining a histogram in SPSS

You can generate a histogram in SPSS in a number of ways. The simplest method is as follows:

1. **Go to the Frequencies command, as shown in Figure 6-4.**

2. **Move the variable containing your scores (interest scores in this example) into the window headed 'Variable(s)' (see Figure 6-5).**

3. **Click on the 'Charts' button and choose 'Histograms' in the section headed 'Chart Types' (see Figure 6-6).**

4. **Click Continue. If you don't want a frequency table you should also untick the 'Display frequency tables box'.**

5. **Click OK.**

When you complete this procedure, the output window in SPSS displays a histogram like that in Figure 6-7. Notice that when you obtain a histogram in SPSS it (by default) provides you with the mean, standard deviation and sample size (N) for the variable on the histogram. We discuss the mean in Chapter 4 and the standard deviation in Chapter 5.

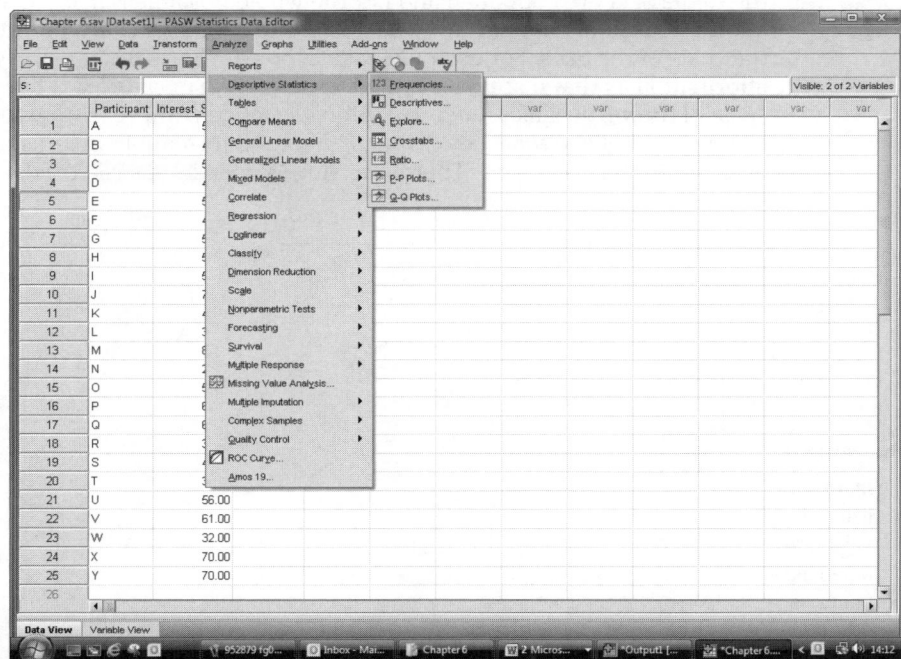

Figure 6-4: Choosing the frequencies command to generate charts.

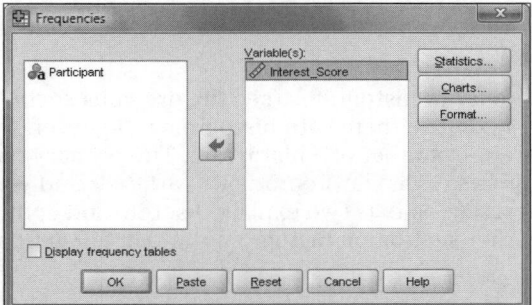

Figure 6-5:
Choosing a
variable to
generate a
chart.

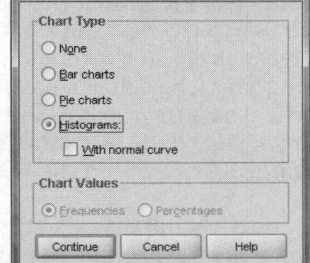

Figure 6-6:
Choosing
the
histogram.

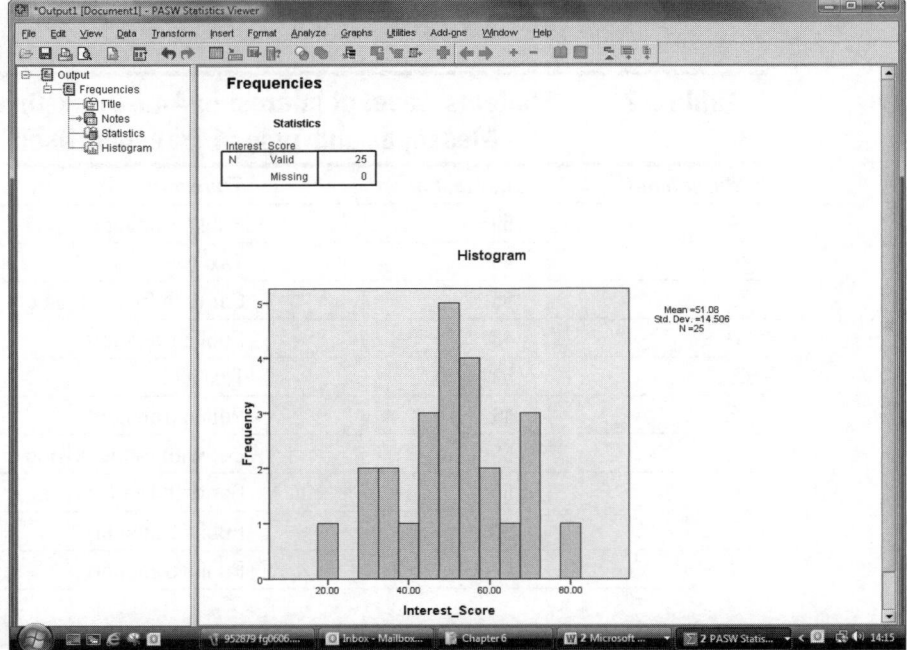

Figure 6-7:
A histogram
as displayed
by SPSS.

The Bar Chart

Bar charts are very similar to histograms (see the previous section) and therefore people often confuse them with histograms. However, the purpose of a bar chart is different from that of a histogram. The primary difference is that you use histograms to display continuous variables and you use bar charts to display discrete variables (we explain discrete and continuous variables briefly in the earlier section on histograms, and in full in Chapter 2).

Understanding the bar chart

A *bar chart* is a method of displaying a variable in pictorial form. You usually use a bar chart to indicate how often each category occurs in a variable, such as how many males and how many females are in a sample. As with the histogram (see the earlier section on histograms), bar charts have two axes – the horizontal axis (or *x* axis) and the vertical axis (or *y* axis) - and you normally show each category on a variable from your dataset on the horizontal axis and the frequency with which each category occurs on the vertical axis.

Continuing the student anti-drink-driving study we introduce in the earlier histogram section, imagine that in addition you ask the students to report the type of transport they normally take when they've consumed alcohol (they can choose between 'public transport', 'taxi', or 'car with friend driving'. Table 6-2 shows their responses.

Table 6-2	Students' Level of Interest in Anti-Drink-Driving Messages and Type of Transport Used	
Participant	**Interest Score**	**Transport**
A	50	Public transport
B	45	Taxi
C	55	Car with friend driving
D	43	Public transport
E	50	Taxi
F	46	Public transport
G	56	Car with friend driving
H	55	Car with friend driving
I	50	Public transport
J	72	Public transport

Participant	Interest Score	Transport
K	49	Car with friend driving
L	30	Public transport
M	81	Taxi
N	20	Public transport
O	51	Taxi
P	65	Public transport
Q	60	Car with friend driving
R	35	Public transport
S	40	Car with friend driving
T	35	Public transport
U	56	Car with friend driving
V	61	Public transport
W	32	Car with friend driving
X	70	Taxi
Y	70	Public transport

A bar chart is helpful in displaying the information about the type of transport used, as presented in Table 6-2. To convert the information in Table 6-2 into a bar chart, you draw a horizontal axis and add the three 'Transport' categories to this axis. You then indicate the frequency with which each category occurs by drawing a bar up to the appropriate frequency level on the vertical axis (see Figure 6-8).

Figure 6-8: Bar chart displaying the frequency of transport categories

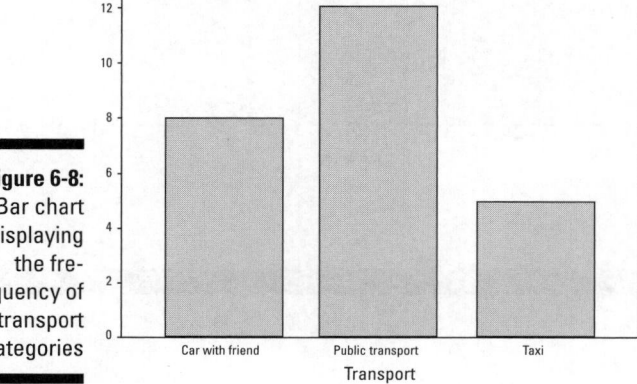

REMEMBER

The bars on a bar chart don't touch each other; there is always a space between the bars. (Contrast this with the bars on a histogram; see the previous section.) This means that the variable on the horizontal axis is being treated as a categorical variable – the visual representation is that the categories are separate and discrete. Therefore, it is not appropriate to display a continuous variable on a bar chart.

Obtaining a bar chart in SPSS

To generate a bar chart in SPSS, follow the same procedure we outline in the earlier section 'Obtaining a histogram in SPSS', but in the Charts box select 'Bar charts' in the section headed 'Chart Type'. SPSS displays a bar chart in the output window like that in Figure 6-9. When you generate a bar chart in SPSS, you have the option of displaying the vertical axis as a frequency score or as a percentage score (you can obtain the percentage score by choosing 'percentages' under the 'Chart Values' section in Figure 6-6).

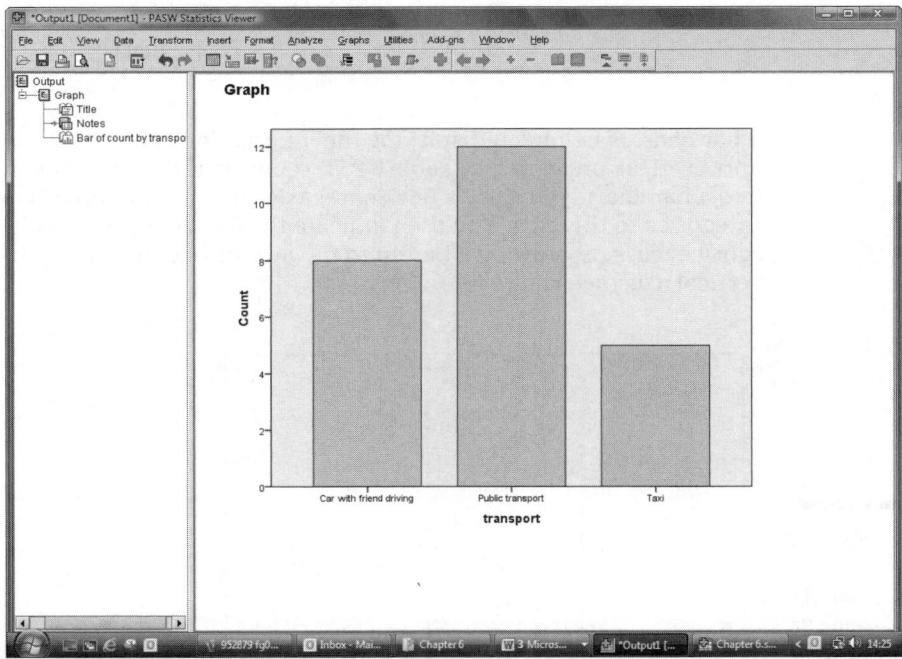

Figure 6-9:
A bar chart as displayed by SPSS.

The Pie Chart

Pie charts display similar information to bar charts (see the previous section) but are often favoured because they look nice! The other advantage of a pie chart is that they're a useful way of indicating, visually, the proportion of cases in each category on a variable. You mostly use pie charts to display discrete variables (we explain discrete and continuous variables briefly in the earlier section on histograms, and in full in Chapter 2). You can use a pie chart to display a continuous variable, but only when the range of the variable is small, otherwise you have a pie chart which is difficult to make sense of.

Understanding the pie chart

Pie charts are employed to indicate the relative frequency of each score or category within a variable – in other words, to display the percentage or proportion of cases within each category. Pie charts are called pie charts because they're round (like a pie) and each score or category is represented by a segment on the chart (a slice of the pie). The higher the relative frequency of a category, the bigger the slice of pie attributed to that category.

Take another look at the example we introduce in 'The Histogram' section and at Table 6-2. A simple pie chart is helpful in displaying the information about the type of transport used, as presented in Table 6-2. To convert the information in Table 6-2 into a pie chart, you first need to work out the relative frequency of each transport category. You do this by calculating the frequency of each category and then dividing each frequency by the total frequency. For example, Table 6-3 shows that 12 people out of the 25 participants reported taking public transport. Therefore, the relative frequency for public transport is 12/25 = 0.48. You can also convert a relative frequency into a percentage by multiplying the relative frequency by 100. Therefore, a relative frequency of 0.48 becomes 0.48 × 100 = 48 per cent.

Table 6-3	Converting Frequencies into Relative Frequencies		
Transport Categories	*Frequency*	*Relative Frequency*	*Percentage*
Public transport	12	0.48	48
Taxi	5	0.20	20
Car with friend driving	8	0.32	32
Total	**25**	**1.00**	**100**

Slicing up the pie

For those of you who want to know the mechanics of converting relative frequencies to a pie chart, this is how it works. The entire pie chart is a circle and we know that a circle turns through 360 degrees. Therefore, your 25 cases (100 per cent) is equivalent to 360 degrees and you need to work out how much of this 360 degrees should be attributed to each category in the variable. The answer is to multiply the relative frequency of a category by 360. For example, in Table 6-3, the relative frequency for 'public transport' is 0.48. If you multiply 0.48 by 360, you get 172.8. This tells you that the segment (or slice of pie) that is attributed to 'public transport' should have an angle of 172.8 degrees, as shown in the figure. The relative frequency for 'taxi' is 0.2, therefore, the angle for that slice of pie should be 0.2 x 360 = 72 degrees; the relative frequency for 'car with friend driving' is 0.32, so the angle for this slice of pie should be 0.32 x 360 = 115.20 degrees. To accurately represent this by hand you would need a compass and a protractor, so it is much easier to use a computer to do it. See Figure 6-10 for an illustration.

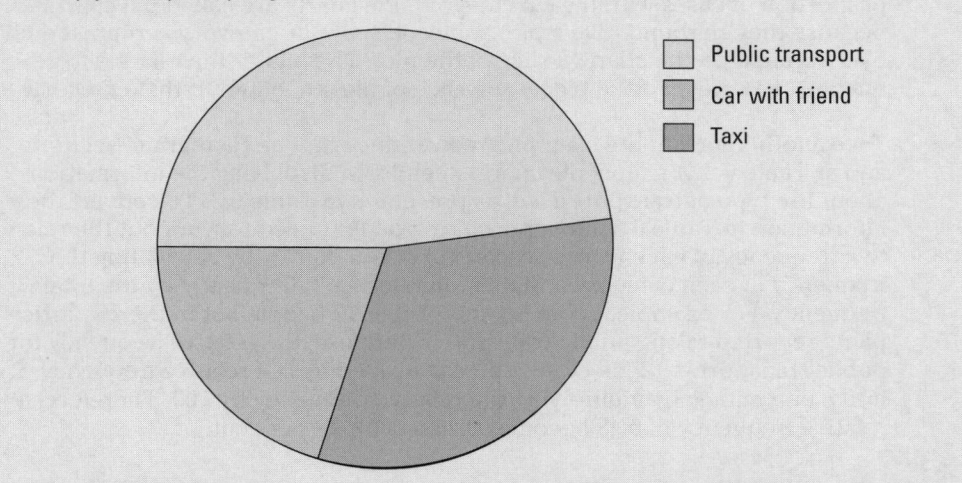

☐ Public transport
▨ Car with friend
▨ Taxi

After you calculate the relative frequency (or percentage) for each category, you need to transform this information into a pie chart. This can be a bit fiddly and is best done with the help of an appropriate computer software package, like SPSS (see the following section).

Obtaining a pie chart in SPSS

To make a pie chart in SPSS, follow the same procedure we outline in the earlier section 'Obtaining a histogram in SPSS', but in the Charts box select 'Pie charts' in the section headed 'Chart Type'. The result is a pie chart like that in Figure 6-10.

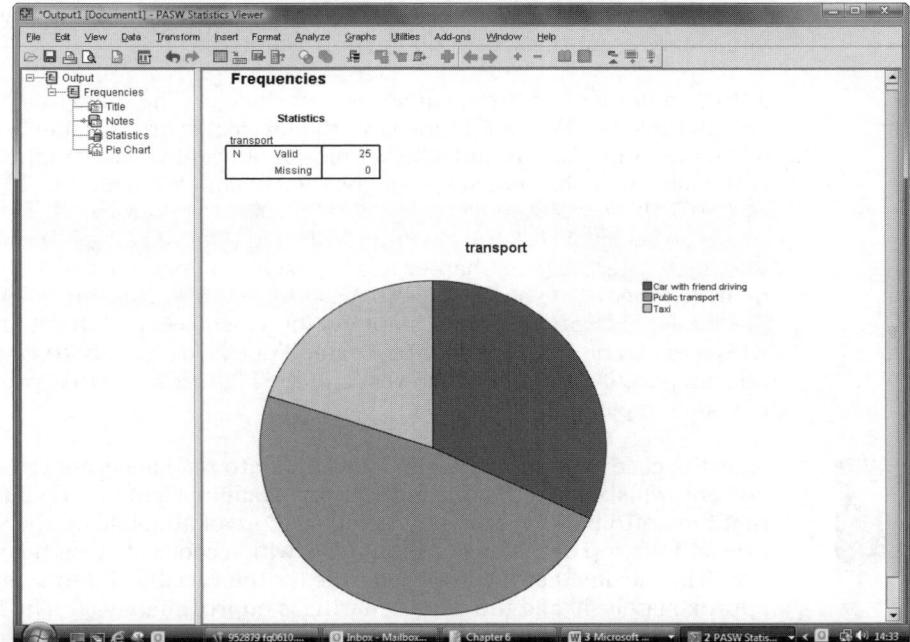

Figure 6-10:
A pie chart
as displayed
by SPSS.

The Box and Whisker Plot

Box and whisker plots (sometimes called boxplots) are a very useful way of displaying data on a chart that provides you with a considerable amount of information. Unfortunately, box and whisker plots are not used as commonly as they could be in the analysis of psychological research data. This is probably because the box and whisker plot uses the median, and psychological researchers tend to avoid the median and prefer to use the mean (see Chapter 4), sometimes even when it is not appropriate to do so. We have yet to work out exactly why this is the case.

Understanding the box and whisker plot

A *box and whisker plot* is a method of displaying data on a variable in pictorial form and of providing information about the central tendency (see Chapter 4) and dispersion (see Chapter 5) of that variable. You can use a box and whisker plot to display any type of numerical data: variables that are measured at the ordinal, interval or ratio level (see Chapter 2 for a discussion of these levels of measurement). Usually, the vertical axis on a box and whisker plot refers to the range of scores on the variable, although sometimes you may present the scores on the horizontal axis.

Take another look at the example we introduce in 'The Histogram' section and at Table 6-2. Figure 6-11 displays the interest score variable from Table 6-2 in the form of a box and whisker plot. A box and whisker plot contains two main elements – not surprisingly, the box and the whiskers! The box in a box and whisker plot represents the interquartile range, that is, the bottom of the box is level with the lower quartile and the top of the box is level with the upper quartile (see Chapter 5 for a discussion of quartiles and the interquartile range). The box also contains a thicker line. This line is level with the median for this variable (see Chapter 4 for a discussion of the median). The whiskers in a box and whisker plot extend outwards from both ends of the box and stretch as far as the lowest and the highest score that you obtained in your sample on this variable.

As is the case with many charts, it is difficult to read accurate values from a box and whisker plot. For example, if you examine Figure 6-11, you can see that the bottom of the box is level with a score of about 40 on the vertical axis and the top of the box is about level with a score of 60 on the vertical axis. This means that the lower quartile for the variable 'interest score' is approximately 40 and the upper quartile is approximately 60. The *interquartile range* is the difference between the upper and lower quartile, so the interquartile range in this example is approximately 20. The line inside the box is about level with a value of 50, suggesting that the median interest score is approximately 50. In Figure 6-11, the bottom whisker extends downwards and ends about a score of 20, indicating that the minimum obtained value on the variable is approximately 20. The top whisker extends upwards and ends at about a score of 80, indicating that the maximum obtained value on the variable is approximately 80 (although an examination of Table 6-2 indicates that it is 81).

The box and whisker plot also indicates *extreme scores* or *outliers*, which are scores that are much higher or much lower than all the other scores in the data set. None are indicated in Figure 6-11. Outliers can be classified as mild or extreme and they're indicated on a box and whisker plot using different symbols. Normally, a circle is used to indicate a mild outlier and an asterisk is used to indicate an extreme outlier. For example, if participant M in our data set had obtained an interest score of 90 rather than 81, this would be considered a mild outlier and the box and whisker plot would look like Figure 6-12. In this case, you can see that the upper whisker extends to the maximum obtained score on the variable, not including the outlier. The outlier is considered separately and highlighted using a circle.

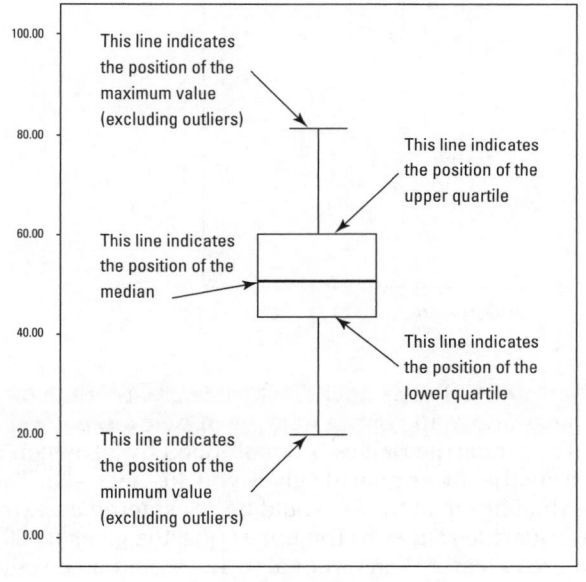

Figure 6-11:
A box and whisker plot of interest scores.

A *mild outlier* is defined as any score which is greater than or equal to 1.5 interquartile ranges above the upper quartile or below the lower quartile. For example, from Figure 6-12, you can estimate that the upper quartile is approximately 60 and the lower quartile is approximately 40. Therefore, the interquartile range is 60 – 40 = 20. Consequently, 1.5 interquartile ranges is 1.5 multiplied by 20 which is 30. Subtracting this from the lower quartile gives you 40 – 30 = 10. Therefore, any scores lower than or equal to 10 would be considered a mild outlier. Adding 1.5 interquartile ranges to the upper quartile gives us 60 + 30 = 90. Therefore, any scores greater than or equal to 90 would be considered a mild outlier.

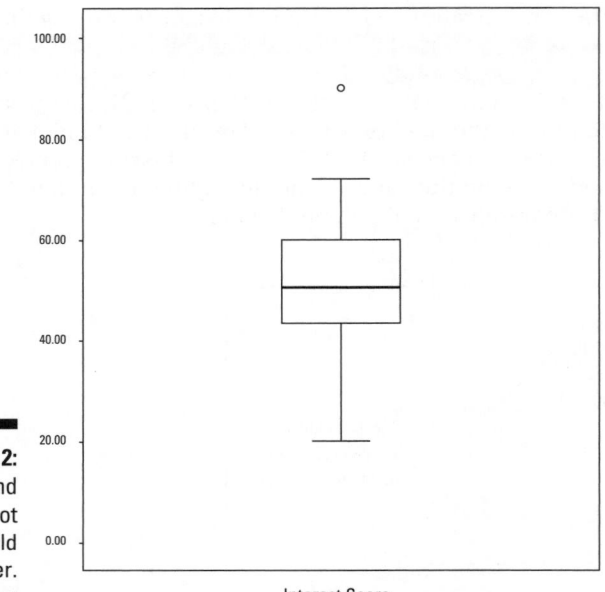

Interest Score

An *extreme outlier* is defined as any score which is greater than or equal to 3 interquartile ranges above the upper quartile or below the lower quartile. In this example, 3 interquartile ranges is 3 multiplied by 20, which is 60. Subtracting this from the lower quartile gives you 40 – 60 = –20. Therefore, any scores lower than or equal to –20 would be considered an extreme outlier. Adding 3 interquartile ranges to the upper quartile gives us 60 + 60 = 120. Therefore, any scores greater than or equal to 120 would be considered an extreme outlier.

To illustrate an extreme outlier on a box and whisker plot, imagine participant M in our data set had obtained an interest score of 120 rather than 81. This would be considered an extreme outlier and the box and whisker plot would look like Figure 6-13. In this case, you can see that the upper whisker extends to the maximum obtained score on the variable, not including the outlier. The outlier is considered separately and highlighted using an asterisk.

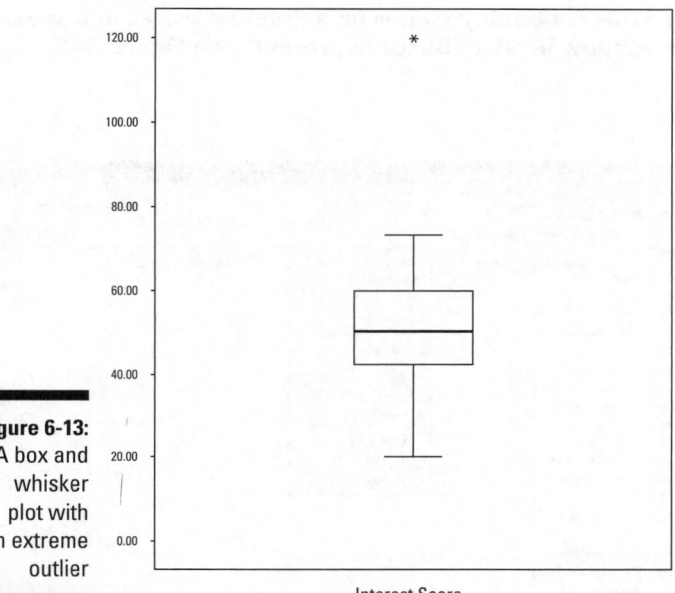

Figure 6-13:
A box and
whisker
plot with
an extreme
outlier

Interest Score

When outliers are present in a box and whisker plot, the whiskers extend to the maximum and minimum values on the variable after the outlier has been ignored. The outliers will then be displayed separately from the whiskers.

Obtaining a box and whisker plot in SPSS

Here's the simplest method of generating a box and whisker plot in SPSS:

1. **Go to the Boxplot command, under the Graphs menu as shown in Figure 6-14.**

2. **Define the type of boxplot you want. For the type of boxplot discussed in this chapter, choose the simple boxplot and the 'Summaries of separate variables'.**

3. **Click Define (see Figure 6-15).**

4. **Move the variable containing your scores (interest scores in this example) into the window headed 'Boxes Represent' (see Figure 6-16).**

5. **Click OK.**

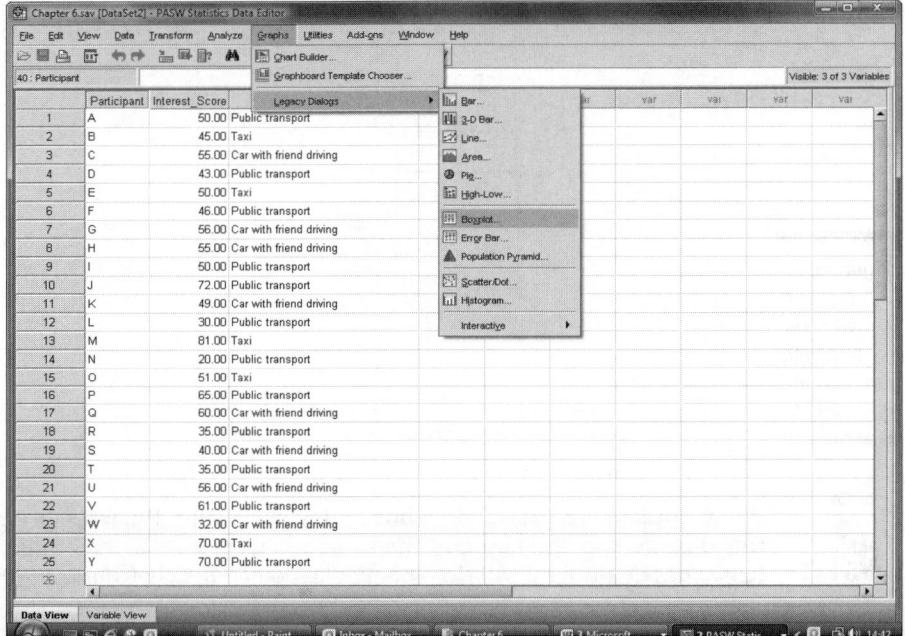

Figure 6-14:
Obtaining
a box and
whisker plot
in SPSS.

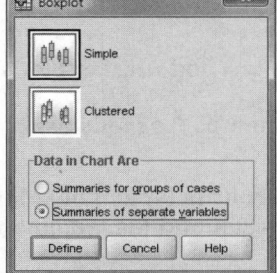

Figure 6-15:
Define the
type of box-
plot.

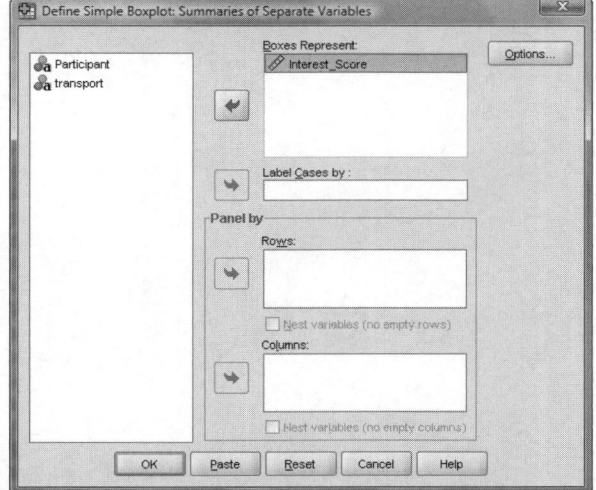

Figure 6-16:
Choose the
variable
for which
you want to
construct a
boxplot.

When you have completed this procedure, the output window in SPSS displays a box and whisker (see Figure 6-17).

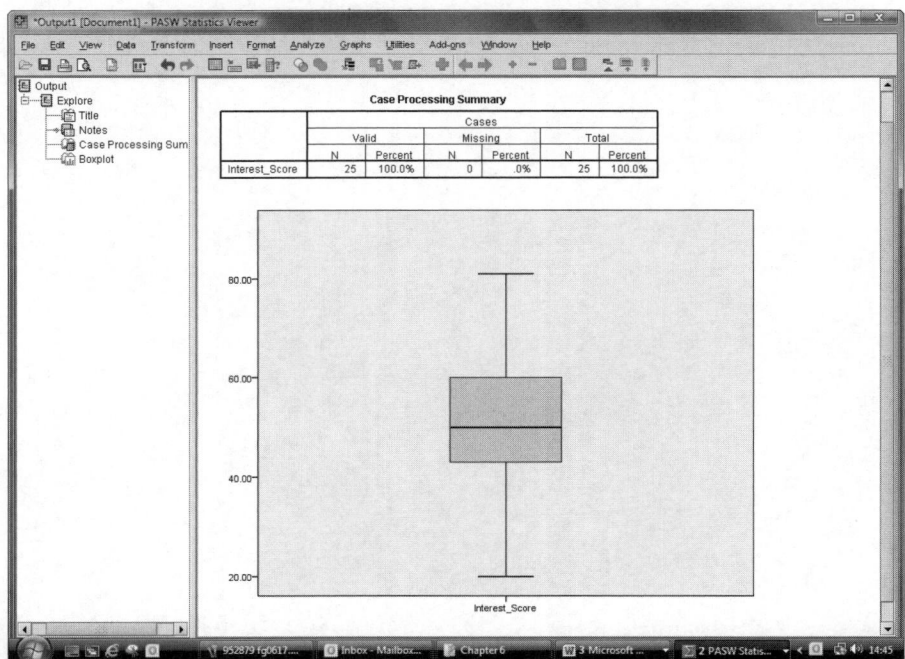

Figure 6-17:
A box and
whisker plot
as displayed
by SPSS.

Part II
Statistical Significance

"You & your 95% confidence & certainties."

In this part . . .

This part concentrates on some of the concepts which are most important for understanding and interpreting statistics. If you don't know the difference between null and alternative hypotheses, are unsure why you have to report the *p*-value and an effect size, or have never really been confident of what statistical inference actually means, then you're in the right place. Here we'll show you the inside track on probability and inference, set you straight on testing your hypotheses, and delve into distribution.

Chapter 7

Understanding Probability and Inference

Inferential statistics are the statistical techniques you use to make inferences about a larger group (the population) based on the results from a smaller group (the sample). These statistical techniques allow you to make powerful statements about psychological phenomena and, therefore, researchers widely use them. However, in the words of Peter Parker's (Spiderman's) Uncle Ben, 'with great power comes great responsibility'. In other words, it is important to know how to use these statistical techniques correctly and how to report them correctly, otherwise you make impressive statements about your research findings that may be inappropriate.

This chapter examines the difference between descriptive statistics and inferential statistics; explores the foundation of inferential statistics, probability; and discusses the definition of the terms *sample* and *population* as used in statistical terminology.

Examining Statistical Inference

The statistical analyses you conduct can be broadly grouped into two types: descriptive statistics and inferential statistics. In this section we explain both, and show the types of situations when inferential statistics are used and why they're a useful tool in psychological research.

Looking at the population and the sample

Inferential statistics are statistics that allow you to make inferences about a population. In other words, they are statistical techniques that allow you to infer something about a population based on the results from your sample. So, before you can develop an understanding of inferential statistics, you need to be able to discriminate between a population and a sample.

Population

A *population* refers to a (usually large) group that you wish to draw conclusions about in your research. Often, in psychological research, this means a group of people but sometimes psychological research is conducted with animals (for example, exploring the welfare of animals). Therefore, you usually refer to a population of cases.

Don't assume that the term *population* when used in relation to statistical analysis means the same thing as when you use the term population in a geographical sense. In the latter case, a population is defined by some geographical boundary, for example the population of a country means everyone who lives in that country; the population of a county means everyone who lives in that county, and so on. In statistics, a population means everyone in a group that is defined by the researcher. The researcher might use geographical boundaries to define the population but in psychological research you're more likely to use different criteria for defining your population; for example the population of adult males with depression, or the population of breast cancer survivors in the UK. Consequently, a population is defined within the context of each research study.

Given that populations are defined by the researcher, it is important to do this clearly when writing a research report, otherwise the readers of your report don't know what your population of interest looks like.

Sample

Usually when you conduct a psychological research study, you can't include everyone in the population in your study. The populations of interest are often large and no single research study has the resources to collect data from every case in the population. In these situations an appropriate strategy is to include a selection of cases from the population of interest in your study, in the hope that the information you collect from this selection of cases is a good representation of the information you would have obtained if you had included everyone in the population in your study. This selection of cases from the population is known as your study *sample*.

The way you select a sample for your study from the population is your *sampling strategy*. Your sample is more likely to be a good representation of the population if the sampling strategy isn't biased. Your sampling strategy is less likely to be biased if the cases are selected from the population at random. For example, random sampling means that everyone in the population has an equal chance of being selected for your sample. Basically, simple random sampling means that everyone in the population is listed and then cases are selected from this list at random (like drawing names out of a hat) until you reach the number you need for your sample. In this way, you have no influence over who is selected for the sample, it is a matter of chance, and so you can't bias the sample. Any good research methods book provides more detail on sampling strategies.

The number you need for a sample is based on a sample size calculation, which we discuss in Chapter 11.

Knowing the limitations of descriptive statistics

Part I of this book deals with *descriptive statistics*, which are the statistics you use to describe the data you've collected from your sample. You describe this data in terms of central tendency (see Chapter 4) and dispersion (see Chapter 5). Statistical analysis using descriptive statistics is very important because it allows you to make sense of your data and summarise its key features.

But if you want to make conclusions about a population then descriptive statistics don't allow you to do this, unless you include everyone from the population in your research study. Sometimes this is possible, when you're interested in a small and easily accessible population. In this situation, descriptive statistics are sufficient because there isn't a larger group that you want to make inferences about. But in most cases in psychological research your sample is a sub-group of the population and you need to use inferential statistics to make inferences about the population based on your sample.

For example, imagine you conduct a research study to examine how quickly 6 month old babies recognise their mothers' faces. You conduct this study by presenting a picture of women's faces (one of which is the baby's mother) to each baby and then observing the baby's reaction. You also time how long it takes before the baby makes a move towards the picture of their mother. Your population in this example is 6 month old babies and you have a sample of 100 babies.

It's all Greek to me

Often, when you read statistics books, you see formulas for calculating different statistics. These formulas use different symbols to indicate that they refer to either a sample or a population. When referring to a population, statistical notation usually uses Greek letters. For example, the letter 'mu' (μ) refers to the mean in a population and the letter 'sigma' (σ) refers to the standard deviation in a population. When referring to a sample, the mean is denoted by 'x-bar' ($\bar{x}$) and the standard deviation is denoted by the letter 's'.

When conducting your statistical analyses for this study, you could calculate the average length of time it takes the 100 babies in your sample to make a move towards their mother's picture (see the section on the mean in Chapter 4 for a discussion about how to do this). However, this only tells you about the 100 babies in your sample, not about *all* the babies in your population. Nevertheless, on the basis that your sampling strategy was appropriate, the average reaction time for the babies in our sample is probably a good estimate of the average reaction time for all babies in the population. Inferential statistics tell you about the accuracy of this estimate for all the babies in your population. In other words, inferential statistics allow you to say something about the average reaction time of all babies in the population, based on the descriptive statistics in your sample.

Aiming to be 95 per cent confident

When you use inferential statistics to say something about a population based on a sample, you can never be completely (100 per cent) certain about your conclusions. Remember, you haven't collected data from everyone in the population, so you can't make conclusions about the population with 100 per cent certainty. The inferences you make about the population, based on a sample, represent your best guess about the population.

However, your best guess should be a very good guess because:

✔ Your guess is based on real data that you collected from your sample.

✔ The sample was selected from the population in an unbiased way, meaning that the sample should be a fair representation of the population.

In addition, you need to be at least 95 per cent sure that your conclusions about the population are accurate. In psychology, as in many other disciplines, being 95 per cent certain about your conclusions is the minimum level of certainty that is acceptable to readers of your research. In other words, it is not acceptable for you to state your conclusions and simply to say that this is your best guess. A reader wants to know how certain you are about your estimates and isn't convinced unless you can state that you are at least 95 per cent certain.

Take the example of taking your car to a mechanic to fix a problem. When the mechanic gives you an estimate of how much the work will cost (for example, £100), it's an estimate, not the actual price you pay (it's probably impossible for the mechanic to give you a completely accurate price until he begins to take the car apart to find out exactly what's wrong). However, you want to know how certain the mechanic is about this estimate. If he tells you that he's only 50 per cent sure then you might understandably be concerned that the estimate will bear little resemblance to the final price you pay and you might go to another mechanic. If he tells you that he's 95 per cent sure (or more) then you expect the final price to be very similar to the estimate. The same principle applies in statistics: you want to be quite confident (at least 95 per cent confident) that the information you provide is accurate.

But why is 95 per cent an acceptable level of confidence rather than, say, 94 per cent or 96 per cent? It might surprise you to know that there is no particular reason why 95 per cent is considered the minimum acceptable level of confidence. No-one has calculated it using any mathematical formula. It has been chosen because it is a high number. It could just as easily be 96 per cent or 94 per cent, but 95 per cent seems like a more memorable number. In any case, it has become convention now and there is no good reason for not choosing 95 per cent as the minimum acceptable level of confidence, so we don't think it will change anytime soon.

Making Sense of Probability

All inferential statistics (see the earlier section 'Examining Statistical Inference') are based on the concept of probability. You use inferential statistics to make inferences about a population based on the results from a sample. As described in the previous section in this chapter, it's not possible to be completely certain about the inferences made about a population based on a sample, but you can indicate your level of certainty about these inferences. In other words, you can indicate the probability of your conclusions being accurate. Given that the conclusions from inferential statistical analyses are based on probability, you need to understand the concept of probability before using these statistics.

Defining probability

Probability is the likelihood (or chance) of something occurring. For example, if you're asked 'how likely is it that it will rain today?', then you are being asked for your probability estimate that it will rain today. Most people answer this question with a vague probability statement such as 'it's very likely that it will rain today'. But in statistical terms, probability statements are exact numerical values, usually expressed in the form of a percentage value. For example, a statistical answer to the question (that a meteorologist might give) is 'there is an 85 per cent chance that it will rain today'.

When expressed as a percentage, probability ranges from 0 per cent to 100 per cent. A probability of 0 per cent means that the event definitely will not happen; a probability of 100 per cent means that the event definitely will happen. Sometimes, you may express probability as a proportion, ranging from 0 to 1, where a probability of 0 again means that the event definitely will not happen and a probability of 1 means that the event definitely will happen. In inferential statistics, you can never be completely certain about the inferences you make, therefore your conclusions never have a probability of 0 or 1 (or never have a probability of 0 per cent or 100 per cent). Conclusions based on inferential statistical analysis always have a probability somewhere between these two extremes.

When estimating the probability of an event occurring, that event can be anything you want. Therefore, you need to clearly define the event that you're making a probability statement about. In shorthand, you use the notation *P[event]* to indicate the probability of an event, where the event is defined within the square brackets. For example, *P[will rain today]* denotes the probability that it will rain today and *P[will rain today] = 0.85* indicates that the probability that it will rain today is 0.85, or 85 per cent.

The probability that an event will not happen is 1 minus the probability that the event will happen. In notation: P[event A does not occur] = 1 – P[event A occurs]. Therefore, if you know the probability that something will happen, you can work out the probability that it will not happen, and vice-versa. For example, if the probability that it will rain today is 0.85, then the probability that it will not rain today must be 0.15, or 15 per cent.

Considering mutually exclusive and independent events

When calculating the probability of more than one event occurring, whether the events are mutually exclusive and/or independent affects your calculations.

Mutually exclusive events

Events are *mutually exclusive* if the occurrence of one event means that the other cannot occur – both events cannot occur at the same time. For example, it can't rain and stay dry at the same time, so when it is raining, no possibility exists of it staying dry at the same time, and vice versa.

In statistical analysis, you should aim to have mutually exclusive events. In other words the values that an individual obtains on a variable should be mutually exclusive. For example, an individual in your study should be able to obtain only one score or value on any variable at any one point in time. If you're recording the age of people in your study then they will have only one value for the variable 'age' at any one point in time. If a person records his age as 36 years old then he can't record another, different value for his age at the same point in time. If the design of your research study permits participants to do this then it's probably a flawed design and the data you collect will be incredibly difficult, if not impossible, to analyse statistically.

Independent events

Events are *independent* if the occurrence of one event has no influence on the occurrence of the other event. For example, imagine you have a container with 20 balls in it, numbered from 1 to 20. You select a ball from this container at random and then put it back in the container. You then select another ball from the container. The number of the ball you selected the first time has no influence on the number of the ball you selected the second time. Therefore, these events are independent. Now imagine that you select the first ball from the container and do not put it back before selecting the second ball. Then these events are not independent, because the ball that you selected the first time cannot be selected the second time (because it's no longer in the container). Consequently, the result of the first event affects the result of the second event.

In statistics, it is important to determine whether your data is independent or not, because you use different statistical techniques for independent and non-independent data. For example, if you administer a self-esteem questionnaire to all participants within your study then the information you obtain from each person could be considered independent data: the data provided by one participant doesn't influence the data provided by another participant (assuming the questionnaires are completed confidentially). However, if you ask participants to complete the self-esteem questionnaire at several different points in time then the data obtained about each individual across the time points isn't independent, because a person's self-esteem at one point in time is likely to influence their self-esteem at a later point in time.

Whether or not events are independent also determines how you calculate the probability of events. For example, take the case where you have a container with 20 balls, numbered 1 to 20. What is the probability of selecting the number 5 ball on the first draw and then replacing it and selecting the number 6 ball on the second draw? As the first ball is replaced, these events are independent. The rules of probability tell you that the probability of one event occurring and then another event occurring is the probability of the first event occurring multiplied by the probability of the second event occurring, if the events are independent. In notation form:

P[selecting number 5 and then number 6 with replacement]

= P[selecting number 5] × P[selecting number 6]

Because there are 20 balls in the container, the probability of selecting any one of the balls is 1 out of 20 or 0.05, so:

P[selecting number 5] = 0.05 and P[selecting number 6] = 0.05. Therefore:

P[selecting number 5 and then number 6 with replacement]

= 0.05 × 0.05 = 0.0025

You can change this scenario to make the events non-independent, by asking what is the probability of selecting number 5 followed by number 6 without replacing the first ball. When events aren't independent then the probability of one event occurring and then another event occurring is the probability of the first event occurring multiplied by the probability of the second event occurring taking account of the effect of the first event. In notation form for the example:

P[selecting number 5 and then number 6 without replacement] = P[selecting number 5] × P[selecting number 6 after taking account of the first selection]

In this case the probability of selecting number 5 remains at 0.05. However, the probability of selecting number 6 is now altered because there is 1 ball fewer in the container. For the second draw there are only 19 balls in the container, so the probability of selecting number 6 is 1 out of 19, which is approximately 0.0526. So:

P[selecting number 5 and then number 6 without replacement] = 0.05 × 0.0526 = 0.0026

In this case we can see that the probability has not changed much, but is very slightly higher, as you are slightly more likely to select a 6 the second time as there is one ball fewer in the container.

Understanding conditional probability

Probability refers to the likelihood of an event occurring. *Conditional probability* refers to the likelihood of an event occurring under certain conditions. For example, take the example of a research study that examines babies' reaction times to their mothers, that is, how long it takes a 6 month old baby to react to a picture of their mother's face. In this study you sample 100 babies and record the reaction time as fast (less than 5 seconds) or slow (5 seconds or more). You also record the babies' gender (there are 50 males and 50 females). We summarise the results in Table 7-1.

Table 7-1	Reaction Time and Gender of 100 Babies	
	Fast Reaction	*Slow Reaction*
Male	20	30
Female	40	10

On the basis of this data, you can ask 'What is the probability that a baby selected at random will have reacted slowly to their mother's face?' This is a simple *probability* calculation. There are 40 babies who reacted slowly (30 males and 10 females) and there are 100 babies in total. Therefore, the probability is 40/100, or 0.4.

On the basis of the data in Table 7-1, you can also ask 'What is the probability that a male baby selected at random will have reacted slowly to their mother's face?' This is a *conditional probability*, because you are being asked the probability of the baby reacting slowly, given that (on the condition that) the baby is male. There are 50 male babies in the sample and 30 of these babies reacted slowly. Therefore, the probability is 30/50 or 0.6.

In notation form a conditional probability is indicated by P[A|B]. This means 'the probability of A given B'. In our example above, the conditional probability question could be denoted as: P[slow reaction | baby is male].

You need to know whether a probability statement that you're interpreting is a conditional or an unconditional probability, because this affects your understanding of its meaning. In statistics, the probability statements that result from conducting inferential statistical analyses are conditional probability statements. They are probabilities calculated under the condition that the null hypothesis is true (see Chapter 8 for a discussion of the null hypothesis and probability statements based on inferential statistics).

Knowing about odds

Odds are similar to probability in that they try to convey the likelihood of an event occurring. However, odds are calculated differently from probability. Probability determines the chance of an event occurring by calculating the fraction of the specified event divided by the total number of possible events. For example, say you have 20 balls in a container, numbered 1 to 20, and you select a ball from the container. There are 20 balls, so the probability of selecting a ball with the number 6 is 1 out of 20 or 0.05.

Odds are calculated as the probability that the event will occur divided by the probability that the event will not occur. Therefore, the odds of selecting ball number 6 from the container of 20 balls is 1/20 divided by 19/20, which is equivalent to 1/19 or 0.053. That is, there is one chance of getting a 6 divided by 19 chances of not getting a 6.

Whereas probability ranges from 0 to 1, odds range from 0 to infinity. Odds of zero are equivalent to a probability of zero, indicating that the event will definitely not happen. Odds of 1 are equivalent to a probability of 0.5. This indicates that there is a 50 per cent probability of an event happening or the odds are that the event is as likely to happen as not.

However, whereas probability is bounded by 1, indicating that an event definitely will happen, odds don't have an upper boundary. For example, imagine that you have 20 balls in a container and 19 of the balls are coloured yellow. What is the probability that a ball selected from the container will be yellow? In probability terms, the answer is 19/20 which is 0.95. In odds terms, the answer is 19/1, which is 19. But imagine that all balls in the container are yellow. Then the probability is 20/20, which is 1, but the odds are 20/0, which is an indefinable number (remember you cannot divide by zero). However, this outcome is in reality a certainty, or a sure thing in terms of odds.

Most people are more comfortable with probabilities than with odds, which is probably why odds are quoted when you bet on events, rather than probabilities (because odds are a bit more difficult to understand and the bookmakers don't want you to get a good understanding of what they're doing!).

In inferential statistics, you mostly work with conditional probabilities, and are less concerned with odds.

Chapter 8

Testing Hypotheses

In This Chapter

▶ Discriminating between the null and alternative hypotheses

▶ Testing hypotheses

▶ Understanding the role of Type I and Type II errors in hypothesis testing

▶ Applying one-tailed and two-tailed hypotheses

*I*n Chapter 7 we introduce you to inferential statistical analysis. Conducting inferential statistical analysis is a way of testing your hypothesis about the population based on the data obtained from your sample (see the section on samples and populations in Chapter 7). In other words, you develop a hypothesis about the population and then conduct statistical analysis (on your sample data) to determine whether your hypothesis seems reasonable or not.

Research is really about generating and testing hypotheses. No single research study provides conclusive answers to a question. However, by conducting a series of research studies that generate, test, refine and retest hypotheses, you can begin to assemble a body of information that allows you to provide meaningful and evidence-based answers to your research question. So, view any research study you conduct as part of an ongoing process, rather than an isolated event.

In this chapter we discuss the different types of hypotheses you use in statistical analysis, how to test a hypothesis and what sort of conclusions you can draw based on the results of your hypothesis test.

Understanding Null and Alternative Hypotheses

In all inferential statistical analyses you need to define the null and alternative hypotheses. Defining these hypotheses clarifies what you're actually testing when you conduct your statistical analysis. Normally, in research reports you only state the alternative hypothesis, but you should define the null hypothesis for yourself.

Testing the null hypothesis

The *null hypothesis* is the hypothesis that you test when you conduct an inferential statistical test. The null hypothesis states that there is no difference/relationship/association between the variables being tested. For example:

- ✔ If you're conducting a study to determine whether there is a difference between males and females on a measure of altruism then your null hypothesis is: 'There is no difference between males and females on the measure of altruism'.

- ✔ If you're conducting a study to examine the relationship between test anxiety and self-efficacy among students then your null hypothesis is: 'There is no relationship between test anxiety and self-efficacy among students'.

Usually, the null hypothesis isn't the outcome that you expect to find (which is stated within your alternative hypothesis; see the next section). Nevertheless, the null hypothesis is always the hypothesis that you test when you conduct an inferential statistical test. You are testing to see whether or not you can be confident in saying that the null hypothesis is not supported.

Defining the alternative hypothesis

The *alternative hypothesis* is so called because it is the alternative to the null hypothesis. The null hypothesis is what is tested, but probably not what you expect the outcome of the test to be. The alternative hypothesis is a statement of what you expect the outcome of the test to be. This is an expectation based on your knowledge about the topic before any data was collected. For example:

- ✔ If you're conducting a study to determine whether there is a difference between males and females on a measure of altruism then your alternative hypothesis might be: 'There is a difference between males and females on the measure of altruism'.

- ✔ If you're conducting a study to examine the relationship between test anxiety and self-efficacy among students then your alternative hypothesis might be: 'There is a relationship between test anxiety and self-efficacy among students'.

An alternative hypothesis can be one-tailed or two-tailed (refer to the section 'Looking at One- and Two-Tailed Hypotheses', later in this chapter).

Deciding whether to accept or reject the null hypothesis

The null hypothesis is always the hypothesis that you test. The principle is that you presume the null hypothesis to be true and only reject it in situations where the statistical analysis is convincing that it's not true (see the 'Reasonable doubt' sidebar in this chapter). This means that in situations where your statistical analysis isn't convincing that the null hypothesis should be rejected then the default position is to retain the null hypothesis. Where the statistical analysis supports the alternative hypothesis, the null hypothesis is rejected.

You either reject or do not reject (retain) a null hypothesis. That is, either you have information that convinces you to reject your null hypothesis or you don't. Technically, a null hypothesis isn't accepted, because you don't conduct your statistical analysis with the aim of accepting the null hypothesis. You conduct your statistical analysis with the aim of rejecting the null hypothesis and you either meet this aim or not.

Given the nature of the null hypothesis (look at the examples in the section 'Testing the null hypothesis'), which is always a bit bland, then no groundbreaking or controversial conclusions will ever be reached by failing to reject the null hypothesis. This is a safeguard built into your statistical analysis. It means that the default position is to reach an uncontroversial conclusion when you conduct your statistical analysis. Only in extreme situations do you move to a position of suggesting that the alternative hypothesis is supported.

So how extreme, or how convincing, should the statistical analysis be before you can reject the null hypothesis? In statistics, the minimum level of certainty required is 95 per cent (see a discussion of this in Chapter 7). This means you need to be more than 95 per cent sure that your analysis doesn't support the null hypothesis before you reject the null hypothesis. An alternative, and more common way, of stating this is that there needs to be less than a 5 per cent chance that you would have found the results from your statistical analysis if the null hypothesis was true. As we explain in Chapter 7, this is a conditional probability statement.

Therefore, every time you conduct an inferential statistical test, you're asking the question: 'How likely is it that I would have found this test result if the null hypothesis is true?' If the answer is that the likelihood is less than 5 per cent then you reject the null hypothesis. If the answer is that the likelihood is 5 per cent, or more, then you fail to reject the null hypothesis.

Calculating the *p* value

If you know the *p* (significance) value associated with an inferential statistical test, you can decide whether or not to reject the null hypothesis. You might be wondering how the *p* value is calculated. Basically, the *p* value is obtained from a (hypothetical) distribution of scores, where the probability of obtaining any particular score is known.

For example, imagine the scores on variable *x* range from 1 to 20 and they are known to have a uniform distribution among the population. A uniform distribution is shown in the figure in this sidebar – it means every score occurs with the same frequency.

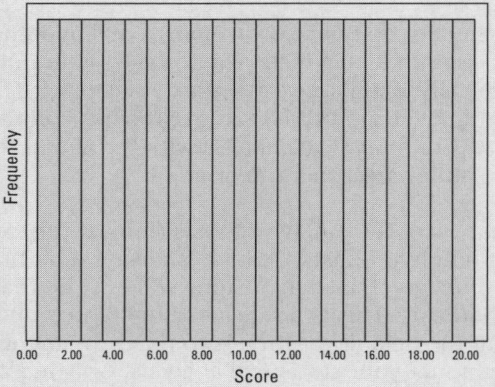

Because there are 20 scores, and each score occurs with the same frequency, then the probability of randomly selecting any specified score is 1/20, or 5 per cent (see Chapter 7 for a discussion on probability). Consequently, the probability of randomly selecting a score of 19 or less is 19/20, or 95 per cent; the probability of selecting a score between 2 and 19 (inclusive) is 18/20, or 90 per cent; the probability of selecting a score of 9 is 5 per cent; and so on. These probability values are conditional probability values, that is, they are true on the condition that the distribution of scores looks like that in the figure,

including being centred on a score of 10.5. On this assumption, the conditional probability of obtaining a particular score or range of scores can be calculated, and presented as a *p* value.

Unfortunately, most variables do not take this shape and so calculating the probability of a particular score occurring isn't as straightforward as this, although the principle is the same. In fact, most variables in psychology take the shape of a normal distribution and we examine how to calculate a *p* value based on a normal distribution in Chapter 10.

In SPSS (and other statistics software packages), every time you conduct an inferential statistical test, the computer calculates this likelihood value for you. It will be presented as either a *p value*, a *significance value* or a *sig. value* and will be expressed as a number between 0 and 1 rather than as a percentage (if you want to determine the *p* value yourself, take a look at the nearby sidebar 'Calculating the *p* value'). For example, if the likelihood is 4 per cent that you would have found your test result if the null hypothesis is true then this will be presented as 0.04. By interpreting this value, you can conclude whether or not to reject the null hypothesis. In this case there is a 4 per cent probability of obtaining these results assuming the null hypothesis is true; this makes the null hypothesis seem unlikely, so you can reject your null hypothesis.

When testing a null hypothesis, you can't conclude that you can *prove* or *disprove* the null (or alternative) hypothesis. Inferential statistics are based on probability and allow you to assess your certainty in rejecting the null hypothesis. You can never be completely certain about your conclusions about the null or alternative hypothesis, so you can never prove or disprove anything. You can state your conclusions with a high degree of certainty, but this isn't conclusive proof. When you're writing up your research, say that the results support (or fail to support) your hypothesis.

Taking On Board Statistical Inference Errors

The conclusion about whether or not to reject the null hypothesis (see the previous section) that you make from an inferential statistical test is based on probability. Therefore, you don't know whether your conclusion is absolutely correct and you need to accept that there is some chance that your conclusion isn't correct. There are two types of errors that can be made when you form a conclusion on the basis of an inferential statistical test: Type I and Type II. Table 8-1 provides a summary.

Table 8-1	Drawing Conclusions from Inferential Statistical Tests	
Conclusion	*Null Hypothesis Is True in Reality*	*Null Hypothesis Is False in Reality*
Reject Null Hypothesis	Type I error	Correct conclusion
Fail to reject Null Hypothesis	Correct conclusion	Type II error

It's important to note that these errors aren't a result of something you did wrong when conducting your statistical analysis. They're errors that are an inevitable part of conducting statistical analysis. They aren't your fault!

Knowing about the Type 1 error

A *Type I error* occurs when you decide to reject the null hypothesis (because the p value for the test is less than 0.05), but the null hypothesis is true in reality. In other words your conclusion based on your sample is incorrect; you have concluded that there was a statistically significant effect where one doesn't exist.

You decide to reject the null hypothesis because the p value associated with your statistical test indicates that results from your sample would be found less than 5 per cent of the time if the null hypothesis was true. There are two possible reasons for this:

- ✔ The null hypothesis is not true.
- ✔ The null hypothesis is true and your sample is unusual.

If the null hypothesis isn't true then you have made the correct conclusion. If your sample is unusual and the null hypothesis is true, then you have made a Type I error. But here's the problem – you won't know whether your null hypothesis is actually true or not! (If you did, you wouldn't need to conduct the statistical test.) So, you won't know when you have made a Type I error. The solution to this problem is to stop searching for certainty when none exists. You just have to work with the knowledge that every time you conduct a statistical test, there is a chance that you'll make a Type I error. Helpfully, you can work out what this chance is.

The chances of making a Type I error when you conduct a statistical test is equivalent to the p value obtained from the test, because this is the probability of finding your test result when the null hypothesis is true. Traditionally, it is not acceptable to reject a null hypothesis unless the p value from a test is less than 0.05 (5 per cent). Therefore, the maximum acceptable chance of making a Type I error is 0.05 (5 per cent).

Considering the Type 11 error

A *Type II error* occurs when you fail to reject the null hypothesis (because the p value for the test is 0.05 or more), but the null hypothesis is false in reality. In this case you have concluded that there was no statistically significant effect when in fact one does exist but you failed to find it!

You fail to reject the null hypothesis because the *p* value associated with your statistical test indicates that results from your sample would be found at least 5 per cent of the time if the null hypothesis was true. There are two possible reasons for this:

✔ The null hypothesis is true.

✔ The null hypothesis is not true but your sample did not allow you to detect this.

If the null hypothesis is true, then you have made the correct conclusion. If the null hypothesis is not true, then you have made a Type II error. But, why might your sample not allow you to detect a false null hypothesis? There are many reasons for this. For example, if your null hypothesis is wrong, but only slightly wrong, then this will be difficult to detect and you need a large sample size to help you find this small difference (see Chapter 11 for a discussion of sample size and rejecting the null hypothesis).

You won't know whether your null hypothesis is actually true or not, so, as with the Type I error, you won't know when you have made a Type II error. Again, you just have to work with the knowledge that every time you conduct a statistical test, there is a chance that you will make a Type II error and we can work out what this chance is.

The chances of making a Type II error when you conduct a statistical test is related to the power of the test (see Chapter 11). Traditionally, the maximum acceptable chance of making a Type II error is 0.20 (20 per cent).

Be more comfortable with making a Type II error than with making a Type I error, because Type I errors have more serious ramifications (see the 'Reasonable doubt' sidebar in this chapter).

Getting it right sometimes

You notice in Table 8-1 that although there is a chance of making a Type I error and a chance of making a Type II error every time you conduct a statistical test, there is also a chance that the conclusion you draw will be correct. In fact, if the maximum acceptable probability of making a Type I error is 5 per cent then the chances of correctly concluding that the null hypothesis is true must be at least 95 per cent. Additionally, if the maximum acceptable probability of making a Type II error is 20 per cent then the chances of correctly concluding that the null hypothesis is false must be at least 80 per cent. This should reassure you that when you use statistical tests appropriately, the chances are high that the conclusions you make are correct.

Reasonable doubt

Many people have drawn a comparison between the process of testing the null hypothesis in statistics and testing someone's innocence in a court.

In statistics you have two possible realities – either the null hypothesis is true or it isn't but you don't know which is correct. A court also works on the principle that there are two realities – either the defendant is innocent or not but the court doesn't know which is correct. Therefore, in both situations, you gather and weigh up the evidence and decide, on the basis of probability, what conclusion you will draw from this evidence. In statistics, like courts, there is always a chance that your conclusions will be incorrect (because they are based on probability). In statistics, you call your mistakes Type I and Type II errors (see Table 8-1). In a court you call these mistakes sending an innocent person to jail or setting a guilty person free. The big difference between statistics and law is that the impact of errors in court judgments are much more serious than statistical errors!

However, the principle in both systems is the same – that the evidence should be convincing (beyond a reasonable doubt) before you reject the status quo (the null hypothesis in statistics and a person's innocence in law). The court works on the standard that a person is innocent until evidence suggests otherwise. This assumes that it would be a worse mistake to send an innocent person to jail than for a guilty person to remain free. Statistics works on the standard that a null hypothesis should be considered to be true until evidence suggests otherwise, which assumes that it would be a worse mistake to reject a true null hypothesis (make a Type I error) than to fail to reject a false null hypothesis (make a Type II error). So, decision making in statistics is designed to ensure that the probability of making a Type I error is considerably smaller than the probability of making a Type II error.

Looking at One- and Two-Tailed Hypotheses

When you conduct a statistical test, you test a null hypothesis (see the earlier section 'Understanding Null and Alternative Hypotheses'). This is usually not what you believe the outcome of the test will be. Your expectation for the outcome of the test is presented in the alternative hypothesis. You can express an alternative hypothesis either as a one-tailed hypothesis or a two-tailed hypothesis.

Using a one-tailed hypothesis

The *one-tailed hypothesis* is so called because it allows for a difference/relationship to occur in a specified direction only. In other words, it allows you to state the specific nature of the alternative hypothesis. For example:

- ✔ If you're conducting a study to determine whether there is a difference between males and females on a measure of altruism then your one-tailed alternative hypothesis might be: 'Females will score higher than males on the measure of altruism'.

- ✔ If you're conducting a study to examine the relationship between test anxiety and self-efficacy among students then your one-tailed alternative hypothesis might be: 'There is a negative relationship between test anxiety and self-efficacy among students'.

You present a one-tailed alternative hypothesis when you have a good rationale for expecting the result to be in the specified direction. You base this rationale on evidence from theoretical discussions and/or previous research in the area.

When possible use a one-tailed alternative hypothesis, because this makes your statistical test more powerful (see Chapter 11).

You can use a one-tailed hypothesis only when you are examining the relationship/association between two variables or when you are investigating the difference between two groups. When you have more than two variables or more than two groups in your hypothesis then you can't formulate a single one-tailed alternative hypothesis. In those situations you need to use a two-tailed alternative hypothesis.

Applying a two-tailed hypothesis

The *two-tailed hypothesis* is so called because it allows for a difference/relationship to occur in any direction. In other words, it allows you to state an alternative hypothesis without specifying the direction of the difference/relationship. For example:

- ✔ If you're conducting a study to determine whether there is a difference between males and females on a measure of altruism then your two-tailed alternative hypothesis is: 'There is a difference between males and females on the measure of altruism'.

- ✔ If you're conducting a study to examine the relationship between test anxiety and self-efficacy among students then your two-tailed alternative hypothesis is: 'There is a relationship between test anxiety and self-efficacy among students'.

When you have more than two variables or more than two groups in your hypothesis then you must use a two-tailed alternative hypothesis (i.e. you can't use a one-tailed hypothesis). For example, if another variable (exam performance) was added to the second hypothesis above, then it would become: 'There is a relationship between test anxiety, self-efficacy and exam performance among students' and this could not be converted into a one-tailed hypothesis.

Confidence Intervals

This chapter has dealt with testing a null hypothesis as a way of making inferences about a population based on a sample. An alternative, but related, approach to making inferences about a population based on a sample is to generate *confidence intervals*.

Confidence intervals can be generated for many different statistics but often you will want to generate a confidence interval around a mean.

Confidence intervals also differ in terms of the amount of confidence you want to have about the interval produced. As a minimum, you would expect to see 95 per cent confidence in inferential statistics (see Chapter 7). So, you will commonly encounter 95 per cent confidence intervals, although sometimes you will see confidence intervals with a higher level of confidence, for example 99 per cent.

Defining a 95 per cent confidence interval

A 95 per cent confidence interval around a sample mean is a range of values. It is the range of values above and below the sample mean within which you are 95 per cent certain that the true population mean lies. In other words, you are telling the reader of your report that within the range of values presented you will find the population mean, with 95 per cent probability.

There is a clear parallel here with the hypothesis testing approach to inferential statistics discussed in the other sections of this chapter. The principle of hypothesis testing is that when your sample mean is so extreme that it is likely to be found less than 5 per cent of the time, then your hypothesis about the population mean is likely to be false and we should reject our hypothesis about this mean.

As with hypothesis testing, when you use a 95 per cent level of probability it means that there is a 5 per cent chance that the conclusions you make about the population mean are wrong. However, if you want to be more certain, for example 99 per cent, about your estimate then the confidence intervals calculated will be wider (all else remaining constant). So, in a sense, you are trading confidence for accuracy.

For example, let's imagine you have conducted a research study to examine the scores obtained by 10 male and 10 female psychology students on a statistics exam. You calculate the 95 per cent confidence interval around the mean score for all 20 students to be: 59.07 to 68.63. (Don't worry about how the confidence interval is calculated for now – information about that is presented in the next section). This means that you are 95 per cent confident that the mean score on the statistics exam for all psychology students lies somewhere within the range of values: 59.07 to 68.63.

If you wanted to be more confident about your estimate of the population mean, then you could generate a 99 per cent confidence interval. For the same data the 99 per cent confidence interval is: 57.31 to 70.39. Compare this with the 95 per cent confidence interval.

Calculating a 95 per cent confidence interval

Let's look in more detail at how a confidence interval is calculated, using the scores of psychology students on a statistics exam as an example. The results for the 20 students who sat the statistics exam are presented in Table 8-2.

Table 8-2	Statistics exam scores
Gender	*Statistics exam score*
Male	45
Male	55
Male	62
Male	75
Male	80
Male	62

(continued)

Table 8-2 *(continued)*

Gender	Statistics exam score
Male	65
Male	62
Male	65
Male	58
Female	52
Female	58
Female	65
Female	75
Female	90
Female	65
Female	68
Female	58
Female	62
Female	55

As you want to calculate a confidence interval around the mean, the first thing you need to do is to calculate the mean (see Chapter 4). The mean score for the 20 students is 63.85.

The relationship of a confidence interval to the mean score depends on the hypothesised shape of the population distribution. In psychology, we often believe that the distributions of scores we are interested in are normal in shape. Even when they are not, and we have a sufficiently large sample size, we can assume they are normal in shape (see Chapter 9), so a confidence interval based on the normal distribution is most common.

Using the standard error in the calculation of a confidence interval

A 95 per cent confidence interval based on the normal distribution will be centred on the mean. That is, the maximum value in the confidence interval will be the same distance from the mean as the minimum value in the confidence interval. This distance is sometimes known as the *critical distance*. The critical distance is based on the standard deviation (see Chapter 5). More accurately, it is based on the standard deviation (SD) of the sampling distribution, which is the standard deviation divided by the square root of the sample size (see Chapter 9 for a discussion of the sampling distribution). This is known as the *standard error* (SE) of the mean.

For the data in Table 8-2, the standard deviation is 10.22 and the sample size is 20. The square root of 20 is 4.47. Therefore, the standard error for the data in Table 8-1 is 10.22/4.47 = 2.29.

Using probability in the calculation of a confidence interval

The level of confidence you desire from your confidence interval will determine the exact size of the critical distance. For example, if you want a 95 per cent confidence interval, then the critical distance will be approximately twice the standard error.

We say 'approximately twice' the standard error, because the exact number depends on the number of people in your sample. For example, for a sample of 20 people (as in Table 8-2), the number you multiply the standard error by is 2.093. For a sample of 10 people, the number you multiply the standard error by is 2.262. This number is obtained from a distribution of scores known as t scores (see Chapter 9). There is usually no need for you to find this number, because when you ask a computer to calculate a confidence interval, it will work out this number for you.

So, for our sample of 20 students, the critical distance for a 95 per cent confidence interval is: $2.093 \times$ SE, which is: $2.093 \times 2.29 = 4.79$. You need to add this critical distance to the mean score to get the upper value for the confidence interval and subtract it from the mean score to get the lower value for the confidence interval. So, the 95 per cent confidence interval for the sample of 20 students will range from $63.85 - 4.79$ to $63.85 + 4.79$, which is 59.06 to 68.64. This is very similar to the 95 per cent confidence interval presented earlier for this data (which was calculated using a computer). The small differences are due to differences in rounding or use of more or fewer decimal places.

Obtaining a 95 per cent confidence interval in SPSS

If you input the data in Table 8-2 to SPSS, you can obtain a confidence interval as follows. Go to the Analyze menu, choose Descriptive Statistics and then choose Explore (see Figure 8-1).

Move the variable containing the data that you want a confidence interval for (in this case 'stats_exam') from the box on the left to the box on the right headed 'Dependent List'. In this example, if you moved the variable 'gender' into the box headed 'Factor List', SPSS would generate separate confidence intervals for males and females. Under the heading 'Display', choose 'Statistics'. Then press the Statistics button on the top right of this window (see Figure 8-2).

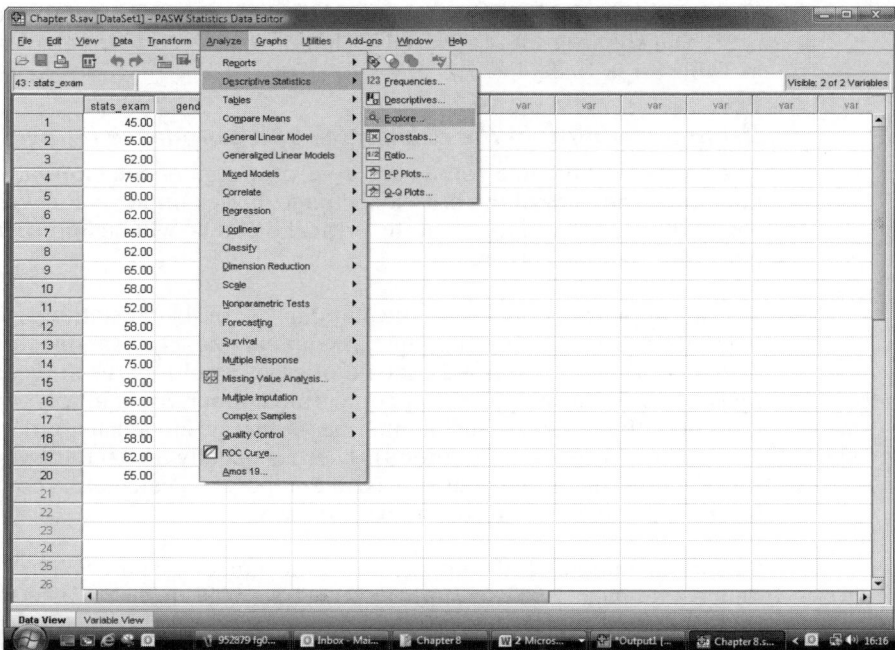

Figure 8-1:
Choosing
the Explore
procedure
in SPSS.

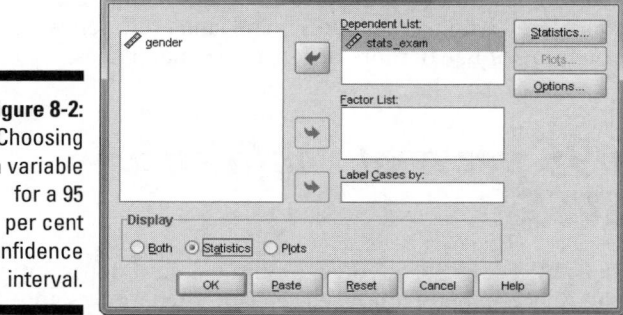

Figure 8-2:
Choosing
a variable
for a 95
per cent
confidence
interval.

This will open a new window. In this window tick the box next to 'Descriptives' and ensure that the confidence interval being requested is set at 95 per cent (see Figure 8-3).

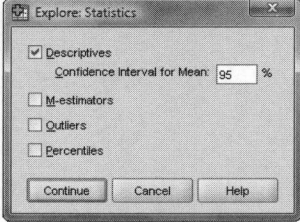

Figure 8-3:
Obtaining a
95 per cent
confidence
interval in
SPSS.

This will generate a box with more information than you need (see Figure 8-4). Within the table, the second and third numbers shown in the column headed 'Statistic' are the lower and then upper values of the 95 per cent confidence interval for the mean.

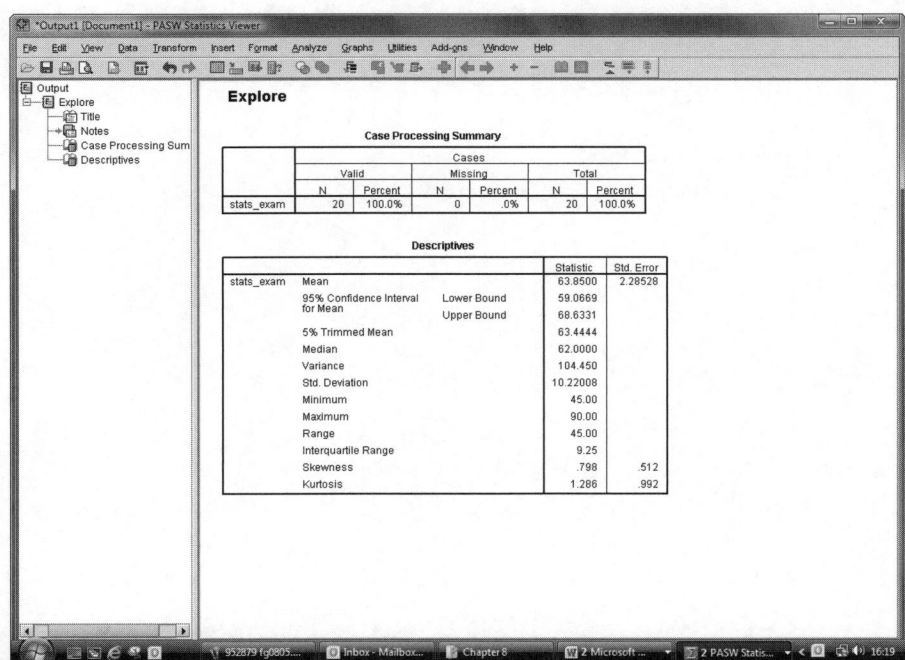

Figure 8-4:
95 per cent
confidence
interval as
displayed by
SPSS.

Chapter 9

What's Normal about the Normal Distribution?

*W*hen you collect scores on a variable and display these scores on a table or chart, the result is a *data distribution*. Data distributions are most often displayed on a chart such as a histogram or a bar chart, because this gives you information about the shape of the data distribution (see Chapter 6).

The shape of the distribution is interesting in itself, and you should be able to describe the shape of the distribution of data in your sample. However, the shape of a data distribution is also important in the calculation of probability statements about the null hypothesis when conducting statistical tests (see Chapter 8).

You might be surprised to know that variables are often distributed with similar shapes – the distribution of some variables looks the same as others. As a result, you can use several distributions of known shapes in statistics (for example the normal distribution, the binomial distribution, the uniform distribution and so on). Therefore, when assessing the shape of a data distribution, the first question you ask yourself is: 'Does this distribution look like any of the known distributions?' There is a good chance that it will and then you can simply describe the distribution by referring to its name: you can state that the distribution is, for example, normal in shape, or exponential in shape. This is a useful shortcut to describing the characteristics of a distribution.

In psychology, many of the variables that you deal with have a distribution that looks very like the normal distribution. Consequently, we focus on the normal distribution in this chapter. This is appropriate because the normal distribution is one of the few distributions you need to know about, but it is also important to realise that the normal distribution is only one of several standard distributions used in statistics (for a list of other distributions, see *Statistical Distributions*, Fourth Edition, by Forbes, Evans, Hastings and Peacock, published in 2011 by Wiley).

Understanding the Normal Distribution

The normal distribution is the name given to a distribution of data when it follows a particular shape (see Figure 9-1). In other words, if you have a set of scores on a variable and you plot these scores on a chart and the shape of the chart is similar to that in Figure 9-1, then you have a normal distribution. The normal distribution is also referred to as the Gaussian distribution (after Gauss, the German mathematician who's often credited with defining the distribution). It is only normal in the sense that the term *normal* derives from the Latin word for perpendicular (*normalis*), which was used in the original description of the distribution.

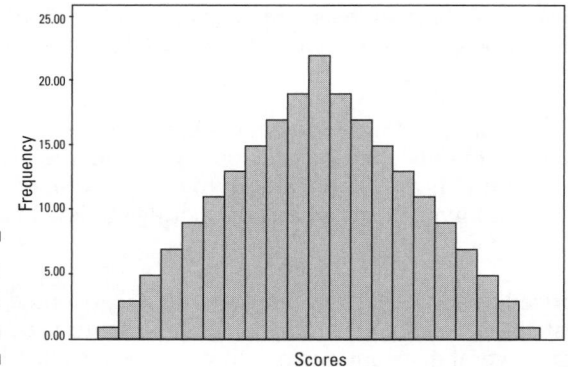

Figure 9-1:
The normal
distribution.

Defining the normal distribution

For a distribution to be considered normal in shape, the following characteristics must be present:

✔ The distribution is symmetrical about the midpoint (see the section on skewness later in this chapter).

✔ The mean, mode and median are the same (see Chapter 4).

✔ The variable in the distribution is continuous (see Chapter 2).

✔ The distribution looks like a bell, in that the greatest frequency of scores is around the midpoint of the distribution and then the frequency of scores tails off as the scores move away from the midpoint (see Figure 9-1 to get a sense of this shape).

Often you're content to describe a variable as approximately normal in shape in that it doesn't need to meet these characteristics exactly, but approximates them.

Determining whether a distribution is approximately normal

In a real life setting you don't usually find a distribution that's perfectly normal in shape, but lots of variables have a distribution that's approximately normal. However, this begs the question: 'How do you know when your distribution is close enough to a normal distribution to be considered approximately normal?' You can answer this question in two ways:

✔ Inspect a histogram of the distribution of scores and determine whether the distribution is approximately normal, based on your own judgement.

✔ Use a statistic to tell you whether your distribution deviates significantly from a normal distribution.

Most statisticians prefer the first of these two options, but most novices in statistics are very uncomfortable with this option and choose the second option.

There are a couple of ways of using statistics to tell you whether your distribution deviates significantly from the normal distribution. The first method is to examine the skewness statistic (see the section 'Determining Skewness' in this chapter). The second method is to use the Kolmogorov–Smirnov test.

As an example, imagine you conduct a research study during which you ask people who smoke to estimate the age they'll live to. We present the data from ten participants in Table 9-1.

Table 9-1	Longevity as Estimated by People Who Smoke
Participant	*Estimated Age at Death*
A	78
B	67
C	75
D	81
E	64
F	88
G	76
H	83
I	69
J	70

To obtain the Kolmogorov–Smirnov statistic in SPSS for this data:

1. **Go to the Analyze menu in SPSS and choose Nonparametric tests.**
2. **Choose the 1-sample K-S test (see Figure 9-2).**

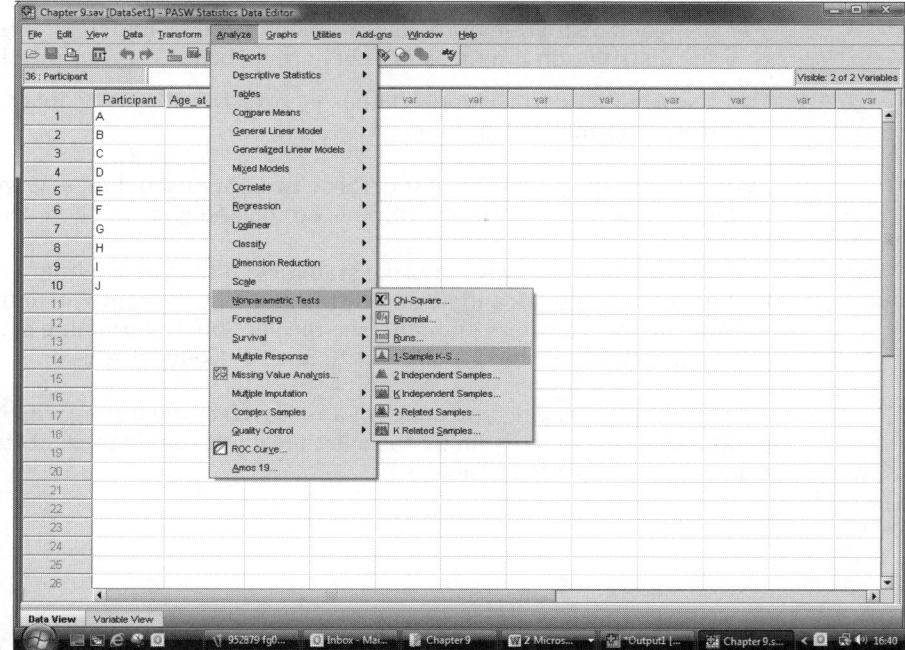

Figure 9-2: Choosing the Kolmogorov-Smirnov test in SPSS.

3. **Select the variable that contains the data you want to compare against the normal distribution (in this example the variable is called 'age at death') and move this variable across to the box headed 'Test Variable List' (see Figure 9-3). Ensure that there is a tick beside the word 'Normal' in the Test Distribution List.**

4. **Click OK.**

The output that you obtain looks like Figure 9-4. The Kolmogorov–Smirnov test statistic is 0.468.

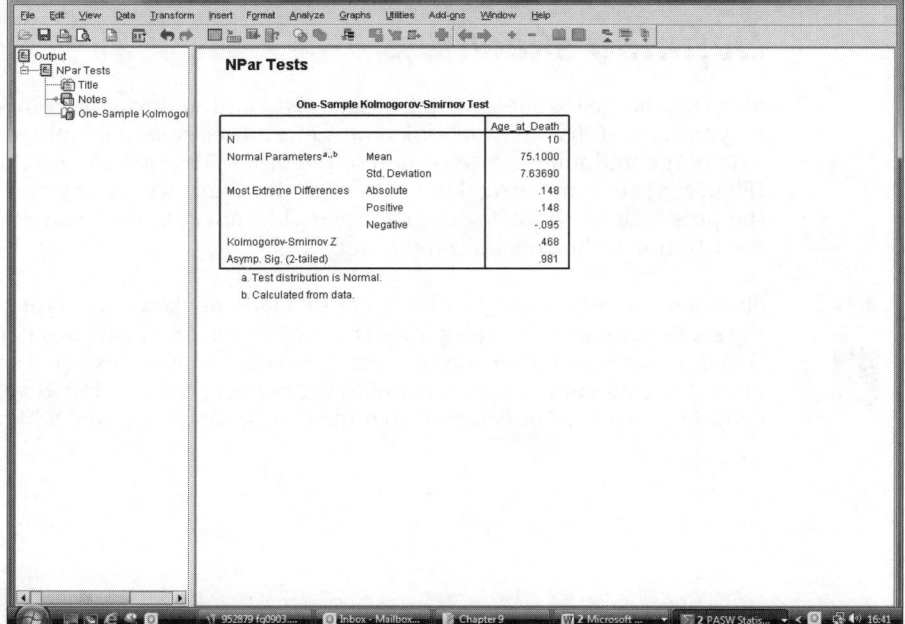

Figure 9-3:
Choosing a variable for the Kolmogorov-Smirnov test.

Figure 9-4:
The Kolmogorov-Smirnov test, as displayed by SPSS.

The Kolmogorov-Smirnov test tests the null hypothesis that your distribution is the same as the normal distribution (see Chapter 8 for a discussion of null hypothesis testing). Therefore, if the significance value (p value) associated with the test is less than 0.05, you reject the null hypothesis and conclude that your distribution isn't similar to the normal distribution. In this example, the significance value is 0.981 and so you can conclude that this distribution isn't significantly different from the normal distribution; that is, it is approximately normal.

Using a statistical method of determining normality can be problematic when you have a large sample size. With large sample sizes, even very small deviations from normality register as significant deviations from a normal distribution. Therefore, when you have a large sample size, we don't advise that you use a statistic to determine approximate normality (see section 'Considering the sampling distribution', later in this chapter).

Determining Skewness

The amount of skewness in a data distribution is important in determining the appropriate measures of central tendency (see Chapter 4) and dispersion (see Chapter 5). It is also important in determining whether a distribution follows a standard shape, such as the normal distribution (see the earlier section 'Understanding the Normal Distribution') and, therefore, the inferences that can be made about this distribution.

Defining skewness

Skewness is the extent to which a data distribution deviates from symmetry. A symmetrical distribution looks the same either side of its midpoint – one side of the midpoint is a reflection of the other. The normal distribution (Figure 9-1) is symmetrical but other distributions are also symmetrical, so the presence of symmetry is a necessary but not sufficient condition for a distribution to be considered normal.

Skewness can be caused by outliers or by inherent skewness in the data (see the section on box and whisker plots in Chapter 6 for a discussion of outliers). When outliers exist in the distribution it means that a few extreme scores have been detected but the remainder of the data might be distributed symmetrically. Inherent skewness means that the distribution is skewed without outliers

Figure 9-5a illustrates skewness due to outliers. You can see that most of the scores in the distribution are bunched together on the left hand side of the chart but there are two scores on the right hand side of the chart that are separate from the rest. These scores are outliers because they are unusually high scores in relation to all the other scores in the distribution.

Figure 9-5b illustrates inherent skewness. Here all the scores in the distribution are bunched together (there are no outliers) but the scores are not symmetrical and tail off to the right side of the chart.

Figure 9-5:
Skewness
due to
outliers (a)
and inherent
skewness (b).

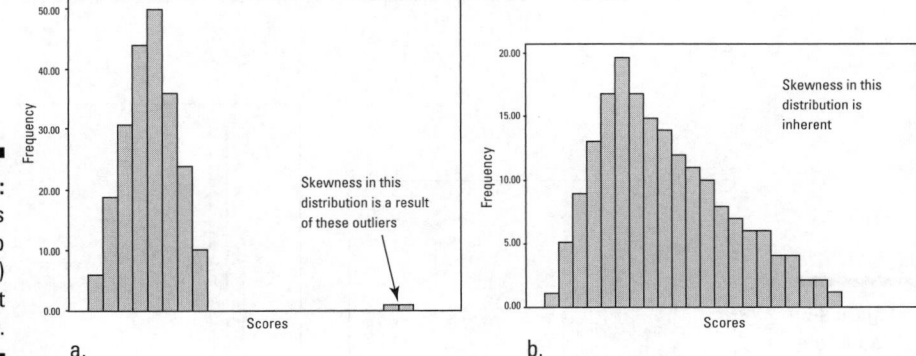

Assessing skewness graphically

Skewness can be assessed by plotting the data distribution on a histogram or a box and whisker plot (see Chapter 6 for a discussion of histograms and box and whisker plots). Real data is unlikely to be perfectly symmetrical when plotted on a chart, so determining skewness from a histogram or box and whisker plot requires you to use your judgement to determine the amount of skewness that exists. Figure 9-6 displays data distributions with a moderate and severe degree of skewness, using a histogram. Figures 9-6a and 9-6b display moderate and severe skewness with a left tail, which is commonly referred to as negative skew. Figures 9-6c and 9-6d display moderate and severe skewness with a right tail, which is commonly referred to as positive skew.

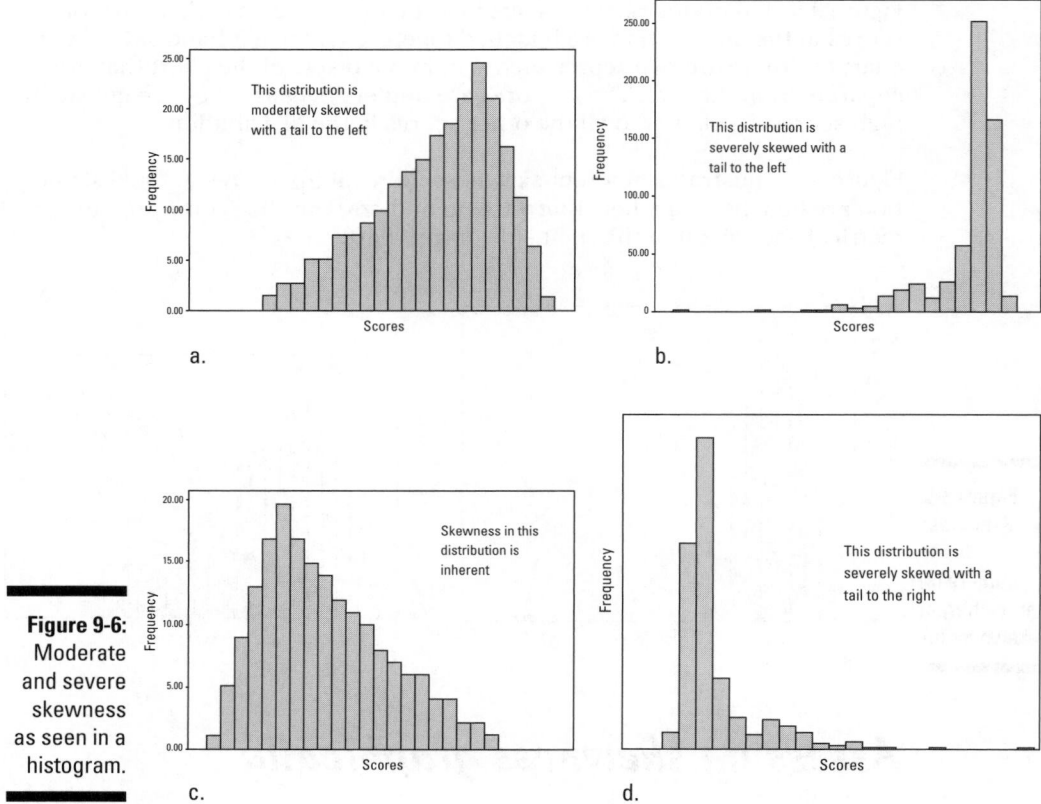

Figure 9-6:
Moderate
and severe
skewness
as seen in a
histogram.

Figure 9-7 displays data distributions with a moderate and severe degree of skewness, using a box and whisker plot. In Figure 9-7a the slightly longer whisker at the bottom indicates moderate skew with a left tail, and in Figure 9-7b the longer whisker at the bottom and the presence of outliers indicates severe skew with a left tail. In Figure 9-7c the slightly longer whisker at the top indicates moderate skew with a right tail, and in Figure 9-7d the longer whisker at the top and the presence of outliers indicates severe skew with a right tail.

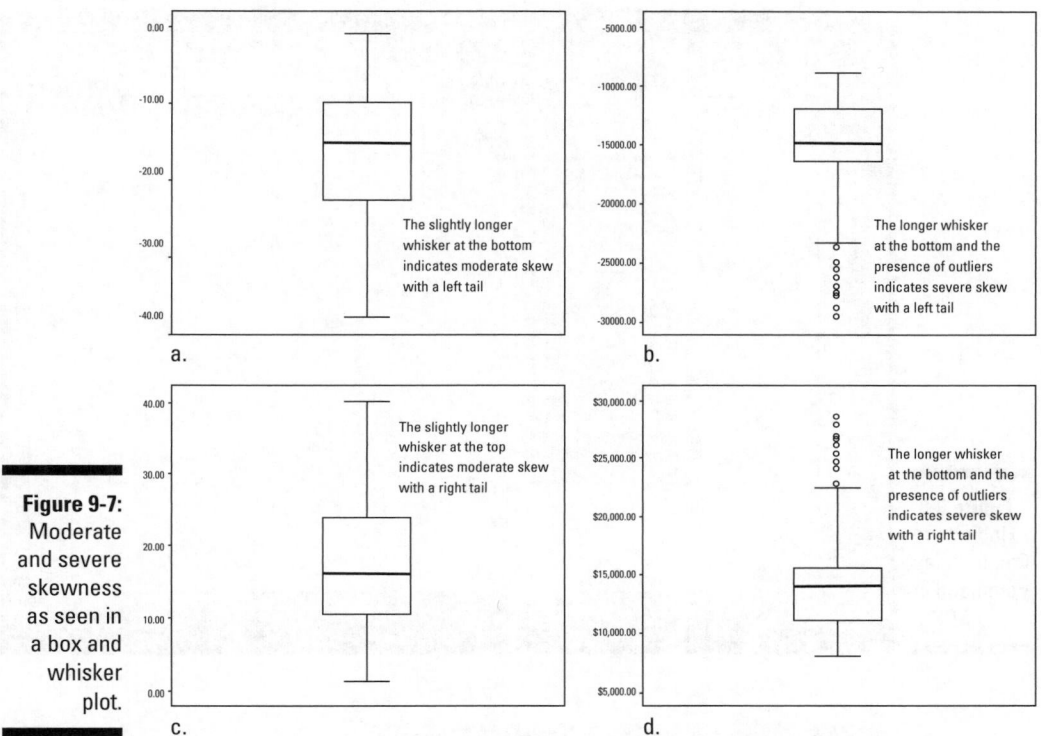

a.

b.

c.

d.

Figure 9-7:
Moderate
and severe
skewness
as seen in
a box and
whisker
plot.

Obtaining the skewness statistic in SPSS

Sometimes when you examine a histogram or box and whisker plot, the skewness in the distribution is obvious, but sometimes it is more subtle and not easy to detect on a graph. In this case, the skewness statistic can be useful.

Table 9-1, earlier in the chapter, presents the results for a research study during which you ask people who smoke to estimate the age they will live to. You obtain the skewness statistic in SPSS as follows:

1. **Go to the Frequencies command, as shown in Figure 9-8.**

2. **Move the variable containing your scores ('age at death' in this example) into the window headed 'Variable(s)' (see Figure 9-9).**

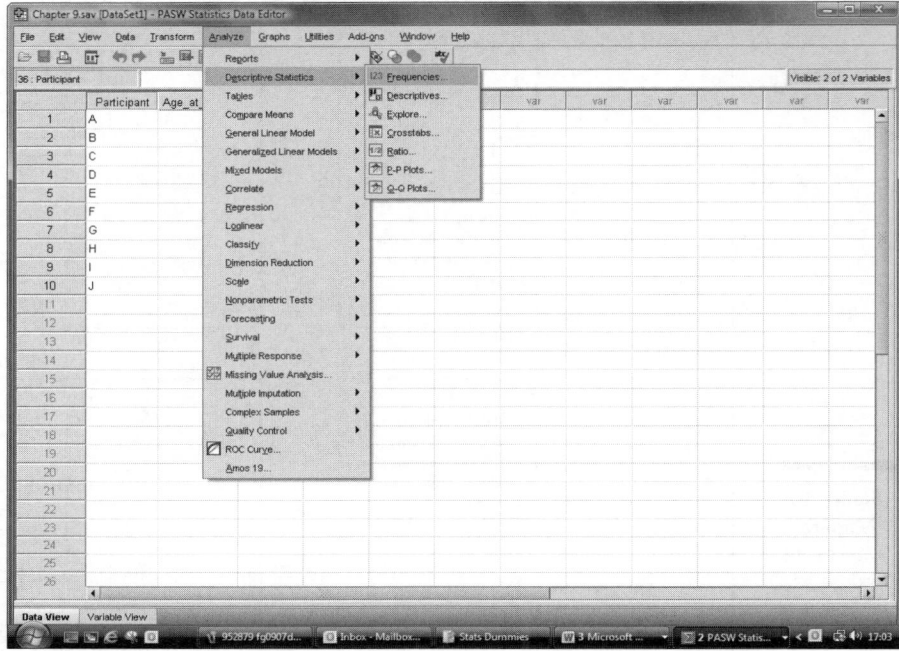

Figure 9-8:
Finding the
Frequencies
command in
SPSS.

Figure 9-9:
Choosing
a variable
for which
to calcu-
late the
skewness
statistic.

3. Click on the 'Statistics' button and tick the box beside 'Skewness' in the section headed 'Distribution' (see Figure 9-10).

4. Click Continue. If you don't want a frequency table you should also untick the 'Display frequency tables box'.

5. Click OK.

SPSS then provides output that looks like Figure 9-11. Figure 9-11 tells you that the skewness statistic is 0.191. To interpret this output, you need to know that a perfectly symmetrical distribution has a skewness statistic of zero. The further away from zero that the skewness statistic is, the more skewness exists in the distribution. A skewness statistic with a positive value indicates that there is positive skewness in the distribution (the distribution is skewed with a right tail). A skewness statistic with a negative value indicates that there is negative skewness in the distribution (the distribution is skewed with a left tail).

In this case, a skewness statistic of 0.191 indicates some positive skewness in the distribution. But is the skewness represented by a value of 0.191 something to be concerned about? The answer to this question is determined by comparing the skewness statistic with its standard error. The general guideline is that if the skewness statistic is more than twice its standard error then the distribution is considered to differ significantly from a symmetrical distribution.

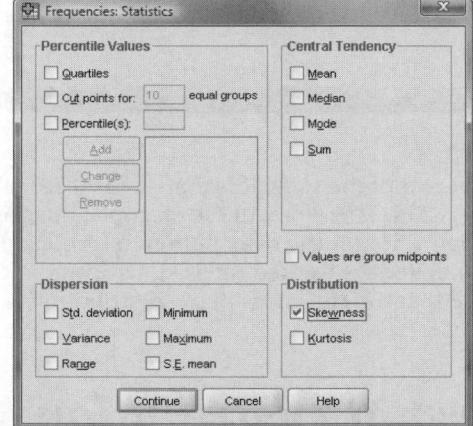

Figure 9-10:
Obtaining the skewness statistic in SPSS.

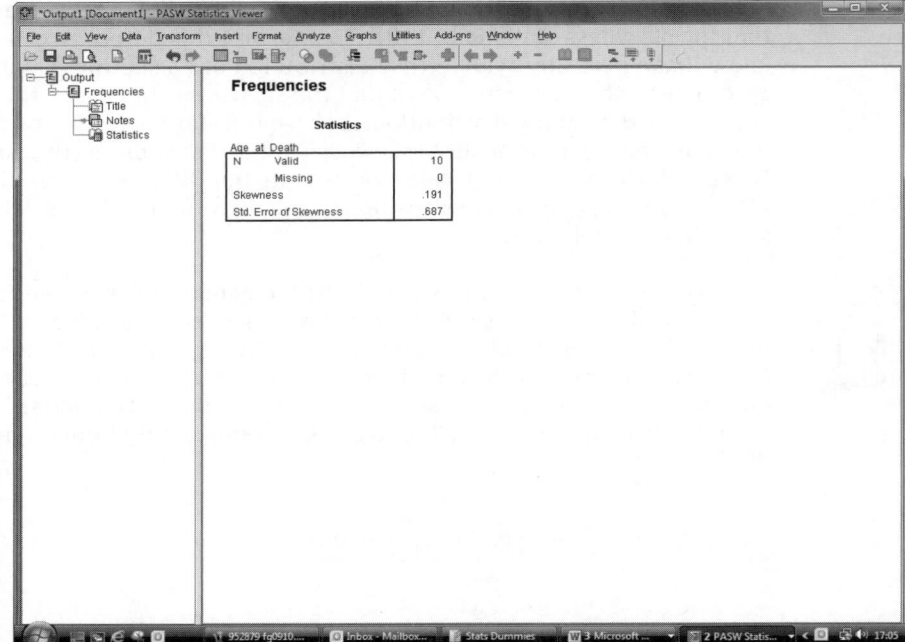

Figure 9-11:
The
skewness
statistic as
displayed by
SPSS.

In Figure 9-11, the standard error of the skewness statistic is 0.687. Twice the standard error is $0.687 \times 2 = 1.374$. Therefore, in the example, the skewness statistic needs to be greater than 1.374 for the distribution to be considered significantly different from symmetry. As the skewness statistic in the example is 0.191 then you can conclude that the skewness in the distribution is very mild.

Looking at the Normal Distribution and Inferential Statistics

The normal distribution is an important distribution in statistics because its properties allow you to make the probability statements that are the outcome of inferential statistical tests (see Chapter 8). This section aims to outline the key features of the normal distribution and how you use it in inferential statistics.

Making inferences about individual scores

The normal distribution follows a particular shape and its properties are known (see the section 'Understanding the Normal Distribution' in this chapter). Because of this, you can calculate the probability of obtaining a score or range of scores within the normal distribution. We provide an example of calculating the probability of scores in a different type of distribution (the uniform distribution) in Chapter 8. The same principle applies here.

Calculating the probability of a range of scores occurring under the normal distribution is mathematically quite complex (well, more complex than we want to present), so we won't go into the details here. Suffice to say that clever mathematicians went to the trouble of doing this for you, so you don't have to. The mathematicians say that the probability of obtaining a score within a particular range of scores in the normal distribution is as presented in Figure 9-12. The scores in Figure 9-12 are presented in terms of the mean score and standard deviations (see Chapter 4 for a discussion of the mean and Chapter 5 for a discussion of the standard deviation). This allows the information in Figure 9-12 to be applied to any variable, regardless of the original units of measurement, as long as it follows a normal distribution.

Figure 9-12 shows that the probability of obtaining a score between the mean score and 1 standard deviation is 0.3413, or 34.13 per cent. The probability of obtaining a score between the mean score and 2 standard deviations is 0.3413 + 0.1359 = 0.4772, or 47.72 per cent. Notice that 0.9544 or 95.44 per cent of the distribution lies between a standard deviation of –2 and a standard deviation of 2, and 0.9974 or 99.74 per cent of the distribution lies between a standard deviation of –3 and a standard deviation of 3.

Figure 9-12: The probability under a normal distribution.

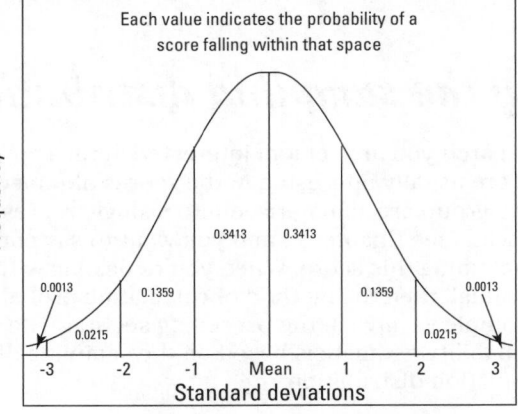

This information allows a computer package, such as SPSS, to calculate the *p* value (significance value) associated with a statistical test. You don't need to do this, because SPSS does it for you, but an example is useful to aid understanding.

Imagine you give a (randomly selected) person an IQ test and he obtains a score of 115. You assume that IQ scores are normally distributed in the population with a mean score of 100 and a standard deviation of 15. What is the probability that the individual you tested would have obtained an IQ score of at least 115?

To use the information in Figure 9-12 to calculate the answer, you first need to convert your score of interest (115) into standard deviations. If you know that the mean score in the distribution is 100 and the standard deviation is 15 then a score of 115 represents 1 standard deviation above the mean. So, you can rephrase the original question to become: 'What is the probability that the individual you tested would have obtained an IQ score of at least 1 standard deviation above the mean?'

So, you want to know the probability of a score in the normal distribution lying at 1 standard deviation or above. The probability of obtaining a score above the mean in a normal distribution is 0.5, or 50 per cent (remember you're only interested in scores above the mean). Figure 9-12 tells you that the probability of obtaining a score between the mean and 1 standard deviation is 0.3413, or 34.13 per cent. Therefore, the probability of obtaining a score of at least 1 standard deviation is 0.5 – 0.3413 = 0.1587, or 15.87 per cent.

The answer is that the probability that someone will obtain a score of at least 115 is 15.87 per cent, if your assumptions are correct (if the distribution is normal, with a mean of 100 and a standard deviation of 15). This is a conditional probability statement (see the section on conditional probability in Chapter 7).

Considering the sampling distribution

In psychological research you are seldom interested in the scores obtained by individuals. You are usually interested in the scores obtained by groups. Scores obtained by a group are summarised into a single representative score such as the mean (see Chapter 4) and you want to say something about the probability of obtaining this score. When you're dealing with a group, rather than an individual, then the method of calculating probability differs slightly from the example we give in the preceding section. The main difference is that the probability estimate is based on the sampling distribution rather than the population distribution.

There are three types of distributions referred to in statistics:

✔ A *sample distribution* is the distribution of scores on a variable obtained from individuals in a sample (see Chapter 7 for a discussion of the differences between samples and populations).

✔ A *population distribution* is the distribution of scores on a variable obtained from all individuals in a population (because usually you can't access everyone in a population, this distribution is hypothetical).

✔ A *sampling distribution* is the distribution of a statistic calculated from repeated samples. For example, the sampling distribution of the mean is the distribution that you'd obtain if you repeatedly took an infinite number of random samples (of a specified size) from a population, calculated the mean score on a variable for each sample and then plotted the means.

So, when you want to say something about the probability of the score of an individual, you need to compare the individual's score with all the possible individual scores, which is the population distribution. When you want to say something about the mean score of a group of people, you need to compare the mean score you obtained with all the possible mean scores (from samples of the same size), which is the sampling distribution of the mean.

The sampling distribution has three important properties (these are known as the *Central Limit Theorem*):

✔ The larger the sample size, the more the sampling distribution will approximate a normal distribution. Sampling distributions are normal if the population distribution is normal or if the sample size is large. In other words, you can assume that a sampling distribution is normal in shape as long as your sample size is large (*large* in this case means about 50 or more, although some statisticians suggest that a sample size of 30 or more should be considered large).

✔ The mean of the sampling distribution is equal to the mean of the population distribution.

✔ The standard deviation of the sampling distribution is equal to the standard deviation of the population distribution divided by the square root of the sample size. This value is known as the *standard error* (of the mean).

Making inferences about group scores

In the section 'Making inferences about individual scores' we look at an example of calculating the probability of an individual obtaining a particular range of scores on an IQ test. Let's look at that example again, but this time with a group rather than an individual.

For example, imagine you're conducting a research study during which you give a (randomly selected) sample of four people an IQ test and they obtain a mean score of 115, i.e. the mean score for the sample is 115. You assume that IQ scores in the population are normally distributed with a mean score of 100 and a standard deviation of 15. What is the probability that the group you tested would have obtained a mean IQ score of at least 115?

To use the information in Figure 9-12 to calculate the answer, we first need to convert your score of interest (115) into standard deviations. If you know that the mean score in the population distribution is 100 then the mean score of the sampling distribution is also 100 (see previous section). If you know that the standard deviation in the population is 15 then the standard deviation of the sampling distribution must be 15 divided by the square root of the sample size which is 4 (see the previous section). The square root of 4 is 2, so the standard deviation for this sampling distribution is 15 / 2 = 7.5.

A mean score of 115 is 15 points above the mean, or 2 standard deviations (standard errors) above the mean of the sampling distribution. So, you can rephrase our original question to become: 'What is the probability that the group you tested would have obtained a mean IQ score of at least 2 standard deviations above the mean?'

The probability of obtaining a score above the mean in a normal distribution is 0.5, or 50 per cent. Figure 9-12 tells you that the probability of obtaining a score between the mean and 2 standard deviations is 0.4772, or 47.72 per cent. Therefore, the probability of obtaining a score of at least 2 standard deviations is 0.5 − 0.4772 = 0.0228, or 2.28 per cent.

The answer is that the probability that a group of 4 people will obtain a mean IQ score of at least 115 is 2.28 per cent, if your assumptions are correct (if the population distribution is normal, with a mean of 100 and a standard deviation of 15). If your sample size was large (at least 30) then you would be comfortable with the assumption of normality (see the previous section).

If you're convinced that the assumption of normality is warranted then you would have found a very unusual group in this example. This might indicate to you that the assumption about the mean score in the population isn't correct. This is the basis of hypothesis testing (see Chapter 8).

Chapter 10

Standardised Scores

In This Chapter

▶ Understand standardised scores

▶ Calculating Z scores

▶ Using Z scores in inferential statistics

*O*ften in statistics you need to convert the scores you obtain on a particular variable (sometimes referred to as the *raw data*) to standardised scores. *Standardised scores* are scores placed in context. For example, if you're told that you were awarded a mark of 50 in your statistics test, you're unlikely to be satisfied with this information. You will at least want to know what the maximum possible score was (for example, did you get 50 out of 50, or 50 out of 100), so that you could put your mark in context. In statistics, as you might expect, the context is a little more complex, but don't worry, in this chapter we explain all you need to know about standardising scores.

Knowing the Basics of Standardised Scores

In statistics you need two important pieces of information, as a minimum, to make sense of the distribution of data on a variable (Chapter 2 explains variables): a measure of central tendency, such as the mean (see Chapter 4), and a measure of dispersion, such as the standard deviation (see Chapter 5). When making sense of scores, you place the scores in the context of the data distribution from which they came; so you place them in the context of the mean and standard deviation. This is what happens when you standardise a score.

Defining standardised scores

A *standardised score* tells you how a score compares to the mean score on the variable. For example, as we explain in the introduction, you're unlikely to be satisfied with being told that you were awarded a mark of 50 in your statistics test; you will at least want to know the maximum possible mark. In fact, you probably want to know more information than that. Most people also want to know how their mark compares to the marks obtained by everyone else who took the test. In other words, you probably want to know how your mark compares to the mean score for your class. So, if you're told that your mark is 50 out of 100 and that the mean mark for the class is 60, are you happy with this amount of information?

Most people probably would be happy with this information and would interpret this as having scored 10 marks below the mean. But, as someone who's knowledgeable about statistics (yes, you), you shouldn't be content with this information because you know that a vital piece of information is missing: information about the dispersion of scores: the standard deviation (see Chapter 5). If you have the standard deviation then you can determine whether 10 marks below the mean is a lot (in relation to the scores obtained by the rest of the class) or not.

For example, if the mean score for the class is 60 and the standard deviation is 2 then this indicates that the marks obtained by the class didn't differ much from the mean and that most people obtained a score close to 60. Therefore, your score (a score of 50) seems quite low in comparison. However, if the mean score for the class is 60 and the standard deviation is 10 then this indicates that the marks obtained by the class were quite spread out across the range of scores. Therefore, your score (a score of 50) seems quite close to the mean score in comparison.

In summary, a standardised score tells you how far your score is from the mean, in terms of standard deviations.

Calculating standardised scores

Several different types of standardised scores exist but the most commonly used one is the *Z score*.

You convert a raw score on a variable to a Z score by subtracting the mean from the raw score and dividing by the standard deviation. Expressed as a formula, this looks like:

Z = (raw score − mean) / standard deviation

Take as an example the situation where you obtained a score of 50 on your statistics test (see the previous section). You need to place the score in the context of the mean score for the class, which was 60. If the standard deviation is 2, then your score of 50 is converted to a Z score as follows:

Z = (50 − 60) / 2 = −10 / 2 = −5

In this situation a score of 50 converts to a Z score of −5. In other words, a score of 50 is 5 standard deviations below the mean.

If you change the standard deviation to 10 then a score of 50 converts to a Z score as follows:

Z = (50 − 60) / 10 = −10 / 10 = −1

In this situation a score of 50 converts to a Z score of −1. In other words, a score of 50 is 1 standard deviation below the mean.

If you convert all the scores on a variable into Z scores then the standardised variable has a mean of 0 and a standard deviation of 1. SPSS can standardise all the scores on a variable for you as follows.

Say you have input all the test scores for your sample into SPSS under the variable heading test_score. If you want to standardise the scores on this variable into Z scores, do the following:

1. **Choose the Analyze menu, then choose Descriptive Statistics and then choose Descriptives, as shown in Figure 10-1.**

2. **In the window that appears, move the variable that you wish to standardise (in this case test score) from the box on the left to the box on the right.**

3. **Tick the box at the bottom left of the window, where it states 'Save standardised values as variables' (see Figure 10-2).**

4. **Click OK.**

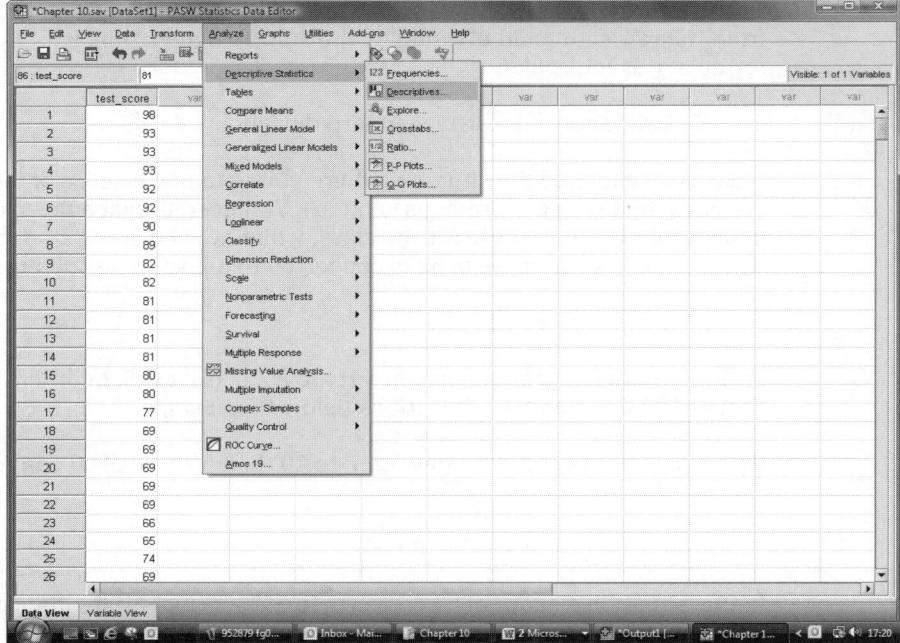

Figure 10-1:
Choosing
the
Descriptives
option in
SPSS.

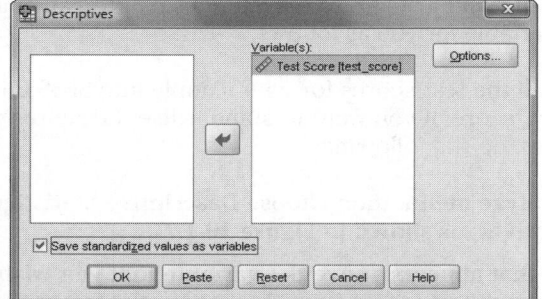

Figure 10-2:
Standardising
variables
in SPSS.

This procedure creates a new variable in your data sheet, which has the same name as the original variable, but with a Z in front. So, in this case, the new variable is called 'Ztest_score' (see Figure 10-3).

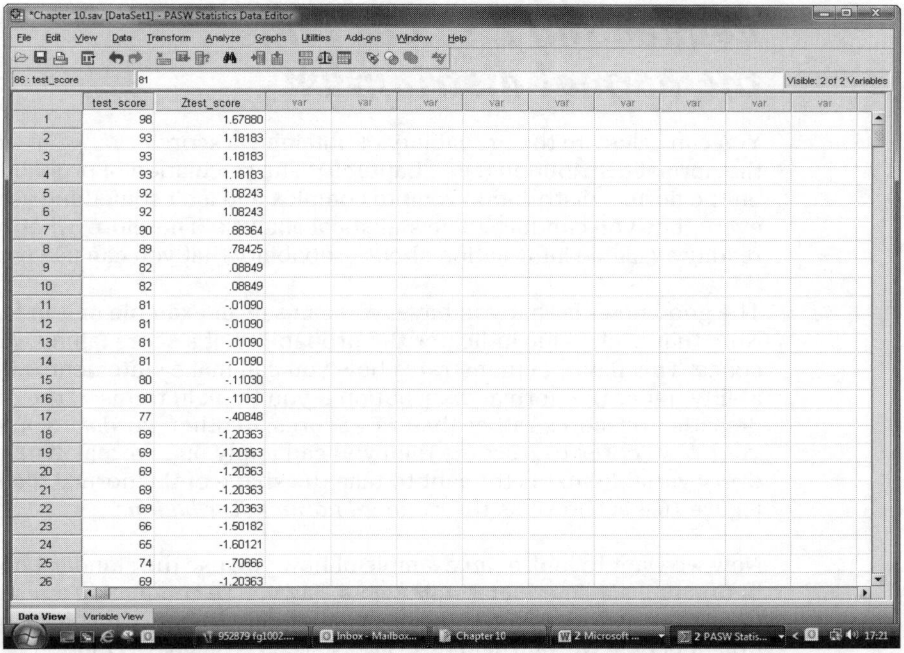

Figure 10-3: A standardised variable in SPSS.

Using Z Scores in Statistical Analyses

You can use Z scores in statistics to describe a score in the context of other scores on a variable. For example, in the previous section we explain how you use Z scores to provide a sense of how a score on a test compares with the scores obtained by everyone else who took the test. However, you can also use Z scores to help you make inferences about sample scores based on probability statements (see Chapters 7 and 8 for a discussion of probability and inferential statistics). You make inferences by calculating the probability of obtaining your sample result (for example, the sample mean), assuming that your variable takes on a particular shape, such as the normal distribution (see Chapter 9).

Connecting Z scores and the normal distribution

You can calculate the probability of obtaining a score or range of scores within the normal distribution (see Chapter 9). The calculation of probability based on the normal distribution is quite complex and isn't something you want to do every time you conduct some statistical analysis. Therefore, what you want is readily available information about probability that you can use repeatedly.

The good news is that you have: you can see an example of it in Figure 10-4. Note that each value indicates the probability of a score falling within that space. This figure demonstrates how you can make statements about probability under the normal distribution if you think in terms of the standard deviation of scores rather than raw scores. In other words, if you convert your raw scores to Z scores then you can apply one normal distribution to every variable that is thought to take the shape of the normal distribution. Figure 10-4 is known as the *standard normal distribution*.

Now we want to look at an example of how you use the standard normal distribution to make inferential statements. Say you're conducting a research study to test the hypothesis that the mean score on a memory test for a population of people with Alzheimer's Disease is 50. You give a (randomly selected) sample of 25 people with Alzheimer's Disease the memory test and they obtain a mean score of 52, so the mean score for the sample is 52. You assume that the memory test scores in the population are normally distributed with a standard deviation of 10. Is your hypothesis (that the population mean score is 50) likely to be true? In other words, what is the likelihood of your sample obtaining a mean score of at least 52, on the basis that the population mean is 50?

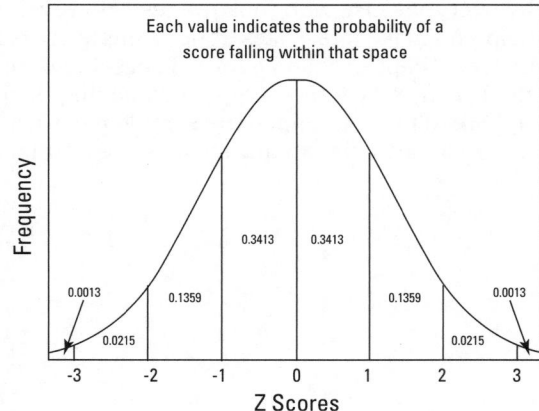

Figure 10-4:
The standard normal distribution.

To use the information in Figure 10-4 to calculate the answer, you first need to convert your score of interest (52) into a Z score.

When you're converting a group score to a Z score, the standard deviation that you use is the group standard deviation divided by the square root of the sample size. This is known as the *standard deviation of the sampling distribution* or the *standard error of the mean* (see the section on the sampling distribution in Chapter 9).

If you know that the standard deviation in the population is 10 then the standard deviation of the sampling distribution must be 10 divided by the square root of 25 (the square root of 25 is 5), which is 10 / 5 = 2.

The Z score that corresponds with a raw score of 52 in this example is:

$$Z = (52 - 50) / 2 = 2 / 2 = 1$$

So, you can rephrase our original question to become: 'What is the likelihood of your sample obtaining a Z score of 1 or more?'

Look at Figure 10-4 and locate the point that represents a Z score of 1. If you add up the probability values to the right of this point, you get: 0.1359 + 0.0215 + 0.0013 = 0.1587. Therefore, the probability of obtaining a Z score of at least 1 is 0.1587, or 15.87 per cent.

The answer is that the probability that a group of 25 people will obtain a mean memory test score of at least 52 is 15.87 per cent, if your assumptions are correct (if the population distribution is normal, with a mean of 50 and a standard deviation of 10). In other words, it is not unlikely that a sample of 25 people will obtain a mean score of 52 if the population mean is 50. This is the basis of hypothesis testing in inferential statistics (see Chapter 8).

Of course, sometimes the Z score you're interested in isn't a whole number and then Figure 10-4 doesn't provide you with the information you need to calculate probability. So use a computer, then you don't have to refer to a very large and detailed graph or table to find the probability value information.

Using Z scores in inferential statistics

The purpose of inferential statistics is to make statements about the population based on the results from your sample; for example, to test a hypothesis about the population mean based on the sample statistics (see Chapter 8). Yet the example in the previous section assumes that you know the standard deviation of scores in the population. If this was true then you wouldn't need to generate an hypothesis about the population mean: you could simply work it out.

In inferential statistics you don't have information about the population mean and standard deviation; that's why you need to make inferences. The whole point of inferential statistics is to hypothesise about the population mean and then determine the likelihood of your hypothesis being correct. To do this you need to use standardised scores, but how can you calculate standardised scores without the population standard deviation?

The solution is to use the best information you have. So if you don't have the population standard deviation (and in reality you won't) then use the sample standard deviation. Unfortunately, the probability values that we present in Figure 10-4 aren't true when you use the sample standard deviation to calculate Z scores. In fact, the probability values presented in Figure 10-4 change every time your sample size changes, because, as we explain in Chapter 5, the sample size partly determines the sample standard deviation.

In situations where you have used the sample standard deviation to calculate a standardised score, the standardised score you use is the *t score*. The *t* score is similar to the Z score but it is based on the sample standard deviation. Consequently, there is no single *t* score distribution, but there is a different *t* score distribution for every sample size. In statistical terms we define *t* score distributions by their *degrees of freedom (df)*.

Degrees of freedom are the number of values in a data distribution that are free to vary, given the expected result. For example, if you have five scores in a data distribution and you know that the sum of these scores is 10, then four of these scores can take any value but the fifth score will need to be fixed to make the sum of the scores equal 10. Therefore, in this case you have 4 degrees of freedom.

Degrees of freedom for a t distribution are defined by the sample size minus 1. We present the probability underlying a *t* score distribution with a $df = 24$ and a *t* score distribution for a $df = 25$ in Figures 10-5 (a) and (b) respectively. You can see that with a change of only 1 df, the probability values change only slightly, but they do change, and they are different from the probability values presented in Figure 10-4 for the Z score distribution.

So, when you're reporting the results of a statistical test based on a t score distribution, you need to report the *t* score, the probability value and the df.

Given the possible number of different *t* score distributions, using a computer is the only efficient means of generating inferential statistical analyses.

Figure 10-5:
Probability
under two
t score
distributions.

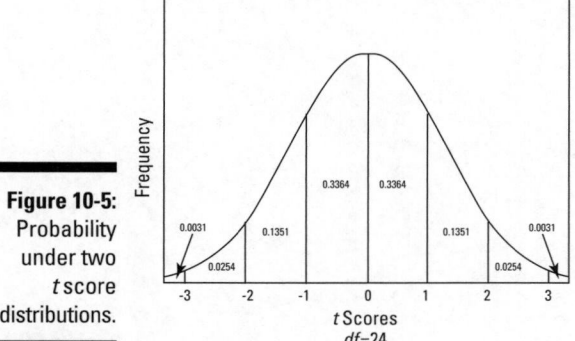

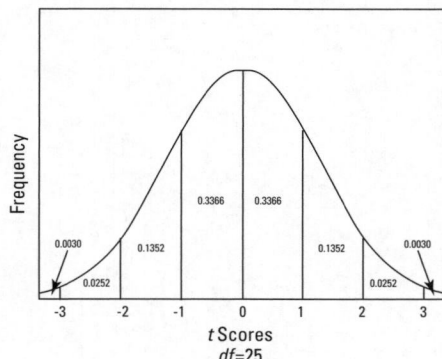

Chapter 11

Effect Sizes and Power

• •

In This Chapter

▶ Knowing the difference between effect size and statistical significance

▶ Obtaining effect sizes

▶ Getting a grip on statistical power

▶ Calculating sample size based on statistical power

• •

Statistical power refers to the probability that you will find a statistically significant result when it is appropriate. Statistical power depends, to a large extent, on the effect size. However, effect sizes are important in their own right and you should be able to make sense of effect sizes and use them on a regular basis when conducting statistical analyses.

In this chapter, we discuss the importance of effect sizes and how they are calculated. We also examine the relationship between effect sizes and statistical power and the implications this relationship has for estimating the number of participants you require in a research study.

Distinguishing between Effect Size and Statistical Significance

Several chapters help you to understand the concept of statistical significance. Given the amount of space devoted to the topic, you might get the impression that statistical significance is the only important outcome of statistical analyses, but that's not true. Psychologists talk about statistical significance a lot, but they also mention effect size.

The effect in an effect size is the relationship/association/difference that you have set out to investigate in your research study. When writing a research report, the American Psychological Association indicates that you should report the effect size associated with your statistical analysis in addition to reporting information about statistical significance. So you clearly indicate the effect size in your research question/hypothesis.

The effect size is standardised so that effect sizes can be compared, regardless of the units of the variables that are being investigated (if you need more info on variables, head to Chapter 2).

Statistical significance provides information that allows you to make inferences about the population based on your sample (see Chapters 8 and 9). Basically, a significance test asks whether the hypothesis we have about the effect in the population is likely to be true or not. Surely it would be useful to know not only whether your hypothesis is likely to be true, but also how close your results are to your hypothesis. This is the value of the effect size.

An alternative approach to stating effect sizes is to state the confidence interval for your statistic (see Chapter 8).

Exploring Effect Size for Correlations

Correlation coefficients (which we describe in full in Chapter 12) are the statistics that you generate when you want to analyse the relationship between two variables. For example, say you conduct a research study, with 20 participants, with the following research question: 'What is the relationship between the amount of time spent reading this book and a statistics exam mark?'. This research question lends itself to analysis using a *correlation coefficient*, which tells you the size of the relationship between two variables on a standardised scale (see Chapter 12). Therefore, the correlation coefficient is an effect size.

To find out how to obtain a correlation coefficient in SPSS, go to Chapter 12.

The correlation coefficient is reported on a scale between 0 and 1, with plus and minus signs indicating the direction of the relationship. Zero indicates no relationship and the further the coefficient is from 0 (the closer to +1 or −1), the stronger the relationship – so, the larger the effect.

Think of a correlation coefficient of 0.1 up to 0.3 indicating a small effect, a correlation coefficient of 0.3 to 0.5 indicating a medium effect, and a correlation coefficient of above 0.5 indicating a large effect.

Imagine you obtain a correlation coefficient of 0.135 in the example. This is a small effect, suggesting that only a small relationship exists between the amount of time spent reading this book and statistics exam score. I know you're wondering how that can be true, given that this book is so informative! (Perhaps it's not the amount of time you spend reading a book but the extent to which you understand it that's important.)

Considering Effect Size When Comparing Differences Between Two Sets of Scores

When comparing differences between two sets of scores, these sets of scores can be scores from independent groups or scores from repeated measurements. For example, imagine you're conducting a research study to address the following research question: 'Are males better drivers than females?' This study would result in two sets of scores from independent groups (males and females). We discuss analyses to compare differences between two independent groups in Chapter 15.

As another example, imagine you're conducting a study to address the following research question: 'Is your mood more positive when you eat chocolate?' In this study you assess the mood (via questionnaire) of 20 people before they eat anything that day. The following day, you assess the mood of the same 20 people after they've eaten chocolate. In this case you have two sets of scores on the same variable (mood) from the same people, which is known as _repeated measurement_. We discuss analyses to compare differences between two repeated measurements in Chapter 17.

The effect sizes for both types of designs are similar.

Obtaining an effect size for comparing differences between two sets of scores

In these situations the easiest effect size to calculate is obtained by finding the difference between the mean score for each set of scores and dividing by the standard deviation (we discuss the mean in Chapter 4 and standard deviation in Chapter 5). In notation form this is:

$$(\text{mean}_1 - \text{mean}_2) / SD$$

The order that you put the mean scores into this formula determines whether you get a positive or negative effect size, but the size of the effect remains the same.

Calculating this effect size is straightforward, except for the choice of standard deviation. There are two sets of scores here (either two groups or two repeated measurements). There will, therefore, be two means and you use both of these in calculating the effect size. You also have two standard deviations (one for each set of scores), but you need only one standard deviation to calculate the effect size, so which one should you use? The answer partly depends on whether you're examining differences between two groups or differences between two repeated measurements.

Effect size for the difference between two groups

In this case, the standard deviation that you use to calculate the effect size should be the average of the standard deviation for each group. So, you add the standard deviation for one group to the standard deviation of the other and then divide by two. The answer is the standard deviation that you use to calculate the effect size.

For example, say you conduct a study to address the research question: 'Are males better drivers than females?'. In this study 10 males and 10 females take a driving test and the driving examiner awards each person a score out of 100. Table 11-1 presents the mean and standard deviation for the results of each group in the study.

Table 11-1	Driving Test Scores for Males and Females	
	Males	*Females*
Mean	62.20	65.50
Standard deviation	9.02	11.54

To find the effect size in this case:

1. **Subtract the mean scores (65.50 − 62.20), which equals 3.30.**

2. **Divide the result of Step 1 by the average of the two standard deviations in Table 11-1.**

   The average of the two standard deviations is (9.02 + 11.54) / 2 = 10.28. Therefore, the effect size is: 3.30 / 10.28 = 0.32.

You could subtract the mean score for females from the mean score for males, rather than the other way round as in the example. In this case you get a negative effect size value, but the size of the effect is the same. The negative sign simply tells you the direction of the effect. Therefore, you're best presenting the effect size as a positive value and just describing the direction of the effect, as in the example in the later section 'Interpreting an effect size for differences between two sets of scores'.

Effect size for the difference between two repeated measurements

In this case, you have two choices for the standard deviation in the effect size formula:

- ✔ Use the standard deviation obtained at the first measurement point. The principle here is that the standard deviation is more appropriate because it represents the scores as they were originally, for example more similar to a population that has not undergone an experimental condition.

- ✔ Use the standard deviation of the difference scores. So, calculate the difference between the two repeated measurements for each person in the dataset, so that you have a set of difference scores, and then work out the standard deviation of this set of difference scores.

Say you conduct a study to address the research question: 'Is your mood more positive when you eat chocolate?'. In this study you assess the mood (via questionnaire) of 20 people before they eat anything that day. The following day, you assess the mood of the same 20 people after they've eaten chocolate. Each participant rates mood out of a total possible score of 100, with higher scores representing more positive mood. Table 11-2 presents the mean and standard deviation for the results at each time point in the study. It also presents the mean and standard deviation for the difference scores. You obtain difference scores by subtracting the score obtained by a person at one point in time from the score obtained by the same person at the other point in time, resulting in a single set of difference scores. You can then calculate the mean and standard deviation of this set of difference scores.

Table 11-2   Positive Mood Scores With and Without Chocolate

	Without Chocolate	With Chocolate	Difference Scores
Mean	65.05	63.85	1.20
Standard deviation	13.83	10.22	8.38

To find the effect size in this case:

1. **Subtract the mean scores (65.05 – 63.85), which equals 1.20.**

   Notice that this is the same value you get if you work out the difference scores for all participants and take the mean of these (see Table 11-2).

2. **Divide the mean difference by a standard deviation.**

   As outlined, you have two options for this standard deviation.

   • **Use the standard deviation from the first time point (the 'without chocolate' situation in this case).**

      This standard deviation in Table 11-2 is 13.83. Therefore, using this option, the effect size is 1.20 / 13.83 = 0.09.

   • **Use the standard deviation of the difference scores.**

      This standard deviation in Table 11-2 is 8.38. Therefore, using this option, the effect size is 1.20 / 8.38 = 0.14.

If you use the first option, then the effect size you calculate is commonly referred to as *Cohen's d*. If you use the second option, the effect size you calculate is commonly referred to as the *standardised response mean*. These labels are used as a shorthand way of telling the reader how you calculated your effect size.

The note in the previous section about subtracting the other way around also applies here.

Interpreting an effect size for differences between two sets of scores

Cohen's *d* or the standardised response mean (see the previous section) tell you the size of the difference between the two sets of scores, expressed in terms of their standard deviation. In other words, if the effect size is 0.5 (using Cohen's *d*), this tells you that the difference between group 1 and group 2 was approximately 0.5 standard deviations. A standard deviation is a measure of how much you expect the scores to vary on average, so expressing a difference in terms of standard deviations provides some context for the size of the difference.

Consider an effect size small when it has a value of 0.2 up to 0.5, medium when it has a value of 0.5 to 0.8 and large when it has a value of greater than 0.8.

This means that the effect size for the difference in driving ability between males and females, which was 0.32 in the example, tells you that females scored higher than males on a test of driving ability, but the difference between males and females is small.

In the repeated measurements example in the previous section, which examines the effect of chocolate on mood, the effect size was 0.09 (or 0.14 if calculated differently). In this case, the effect size tells you that the participants reported more negative mood after eating chocolate, compared with not eating chocolate, but the difference between the two conditions is very small.

Looking at Effect Size When Comparing Differences between More Than Two Sets of Scores

When comparing differences between three or more sets of scores, these sets of scores can be scores from independent groups or scores from repeated measurements. For example, imagine you're conducting a research study to address the following research question: 'Are left-handed people, right-handed people or ambidextrous people better drivers?' This study results in three sets of scores from independent groups (lefties, righties and ambidextrous people). We discuss analyses to compare differences between more than two independent groups in Chapter 16.

As another example, imagine you're conducting a study to address the following research question: 'Is your mood more positive when you eat chocolate or fruit?'. In this study you assess the mood (via questionnaire) of 20 people before they eat anything that day. The following day, you assess the mood of the same 20 people after they've eaten chocolate and the following day you assess the mood of 20 people after they've eaten a piece of fruit. In this case you have three sets of scores on the same variable (mood) from the same people, which is known as *repeated measurement*. See Chapter 19 for more on analyses to compare differences between more than two repeated measurements.

The effect size for both types of designs is the same.

Obtaining an effect size for comparing differences between more than two sets of scores

A statistical test commonly used to examine differences between more than two sets of scores is the analysis of variance test (ANOVA). There are different ANOVA tests for different research designs and you can read about these in detail in chapters 16, 19 and 21. The information you obtain from an ANOVA allows you to calculate an effect size known as eta-squared (the symbol is: η^2). We don't provide the details of how you calculate eta-squared because letting the computer do this for you is easier.

The method of obtaining eta-squared in SPSS is slightly different depending on whether you have an independent groups design or a repeated measurements design.

Effect size for the difference between more than two groups

Imagine you're conducting a research study to address the research question 'Are left-handed people, right-handed people, or ambidextrous people better drivers?'. You collect data on driving test scores from seven lefties, seven righties and six ambidextrous people.

You obtain partial eta-squared for independent groups via the analysis of variance (ANOVA) procedure in SPSS (for an explanation of partial eta-squared, head to 'Interpreting an effect size for differences between more than two sets of scores', later in the chapter):

Go to the Analyze menu, choose 'Compare Means' and then choose 'Means' (see Figure 11-1).

1. **In the window that opens move the variable that represents the groups (in this case 'handedness') into the box headed 'Independent List'.**

2. **Move the variable with the scores of interest (in this case 'driving_test') into the box headed 'Dependent List' (see Figure 11-2).**

3. **Click on the Options button.**

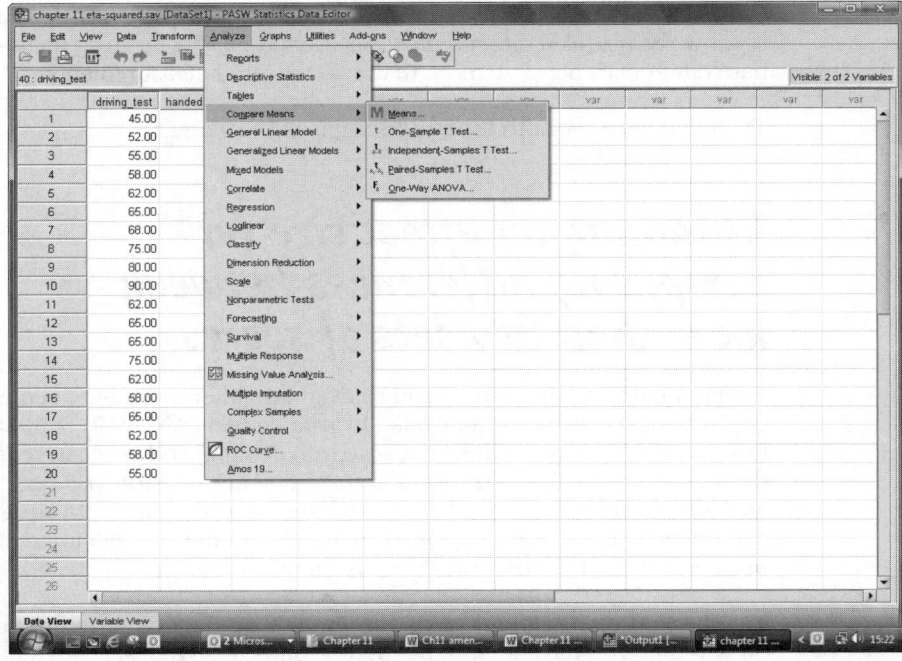

Figure 11-1: Comparing means for independent groups in SPSS.

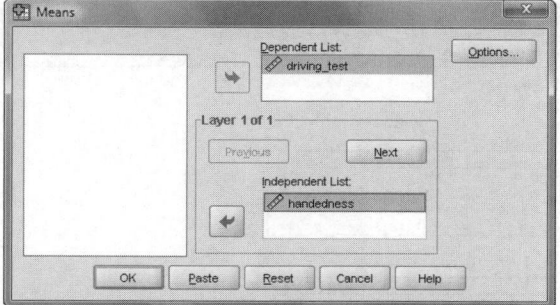

Figure 11-2:
Choosing
the
variables
for the
calculation
of eta-
squared.

4. **In the window that opens choose a number of statistics to be presented by moving them from the box on the left to the box on the right. By default, the mean, standard deviation and number of cases are in the box on the right and you needn't add anything further in this case. However, make sure that you tick the box beside 'Anova table and eta' in the list headed 'Statistics for First Layer' (see Figure 11-3).**

5. **Click Continue and then OK.**

The resulting output looks like Figure 11-4. The output also contains an ANOVA table, which isn't of interest to you when determining effect size (see Chapter 16 for a discussion of ANOVA).

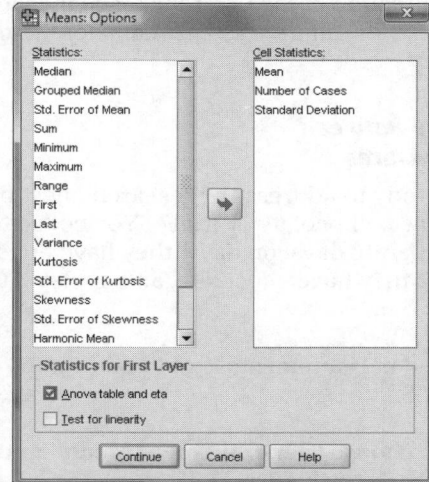

Figure 11-3:
Selecting
the effect
size in SPSS
for more
than two
independent
groups.

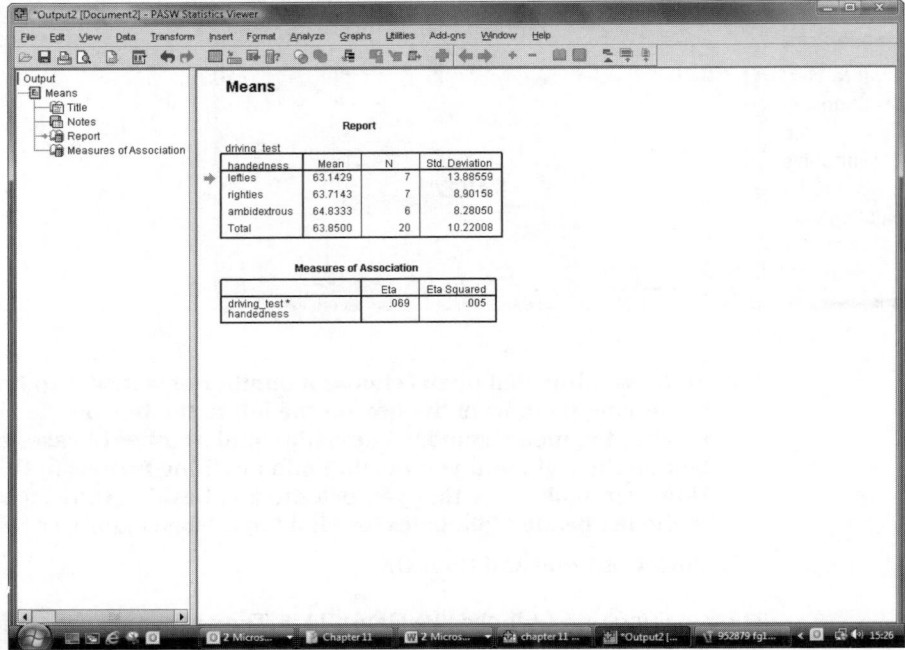

Figure 11-4:
Eta-squared
for indepen-
dent groups
as displayed
by SPSS.

The eta-squared value in Figure 11-4 is 0.005 and the mean scores in the figure help you interpret the direction of the difference (see the later section below 'Interpreting an effect size for differences between more than two sets of scores').

Effect size for the difference between more than two repeated measures

Imagine you're conducting a study to address the research question 'Is your mood more positive when you eat chocolate or fruit?'. You collect data about the mood of 20 people on 3 separate days: on day 1 they have no food before reporting their mood; on day 2 they have chocolate; and on day 3 they have a piece of fruit.

Partial eta-squared for repeated measurements is obtained via the General Linear Model procedure in SPSS.

1. **Go to the Analyze menu, choose 'General Linear Model' and then choose 'Repeated Measures' (see Figure 11-5).**

2. **In the window that opens you see that 'factor1' appears in the box headed 'Within-Subject Factor Name'. Under this is a box headed 'Number of Levels'. In this box you type in the number of repeated measurements in the analysis: In the example there are three repeated measurements (see Figure 11-6).**

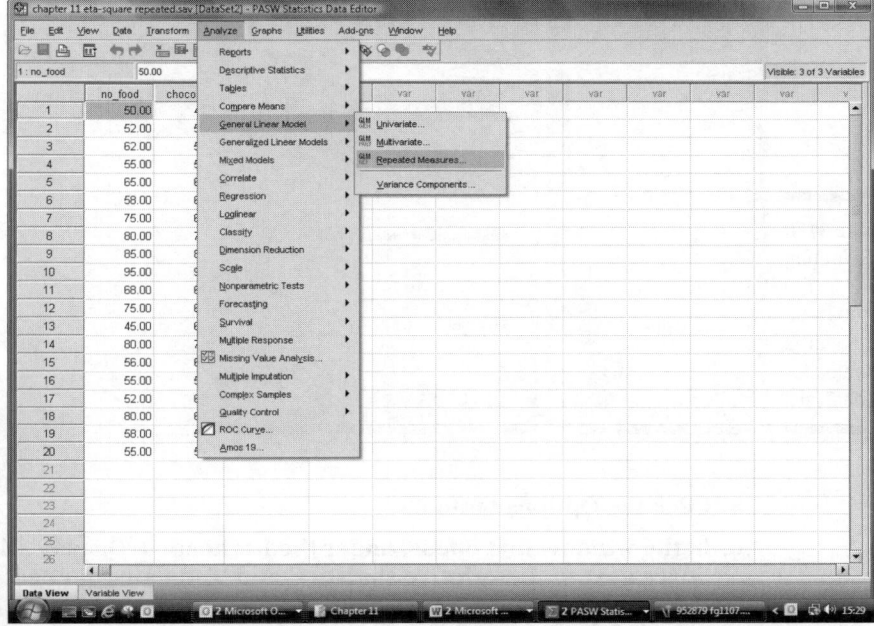

Figure 11-5: Selecting a repeated measures analysis in SPSS.

Figure 11-6: Defining the number of repeated measurements to be analysed.

3. Click 'Define'.

4. In the window that opens move the variables that represent the scores at each of the three time points (in this case 'no-food', 'chocolate', and 'fruit') into the box headed 'Within-Subjects Variables' (see Figure 11-7). Make sure that the variables are listed in the order they occurred, so in the example the no food condition was first, the chocolate condition was second and the fruit condition was third, so that is the order the variables should appear.

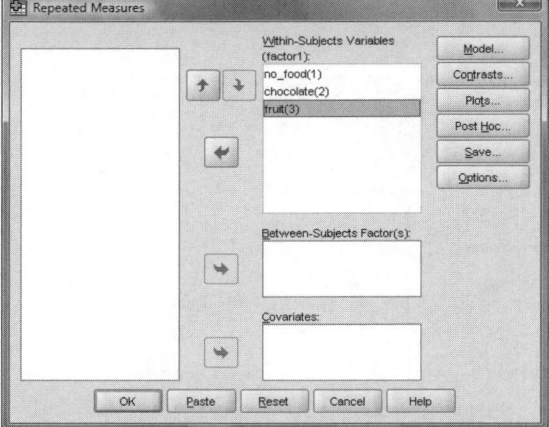

Figure 11-7:
Selecting
the
repeated
measures
variables for
analysis.

5. **Click the Options button.**

6. **In the window that opens, under the list headed 'Display', tick the boxes next to 'Descriptive statistics' and 'Estimates of effect size' (see Figure 11-8).**

7. **Click Continue and then OK.**

The resulting output contains a considerable amount of information that you don't need for interpretation of the effect size. Figure 11-9 shows the important information for interpreting the effect size (see Chapter 19 for a discussion of the other information, including the ANOVA table).

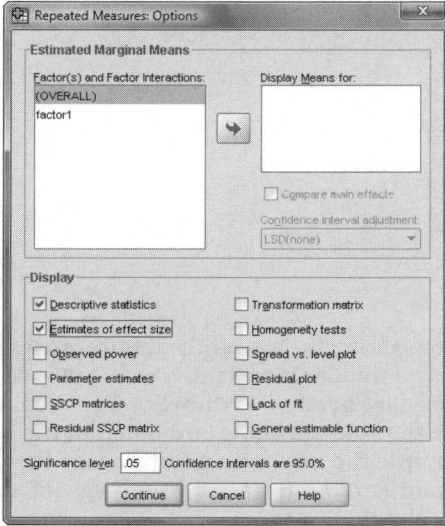

Figure 11-8:
Selecting
the effect
size in SPSS
for more
than two
repeated
measure-
ments.

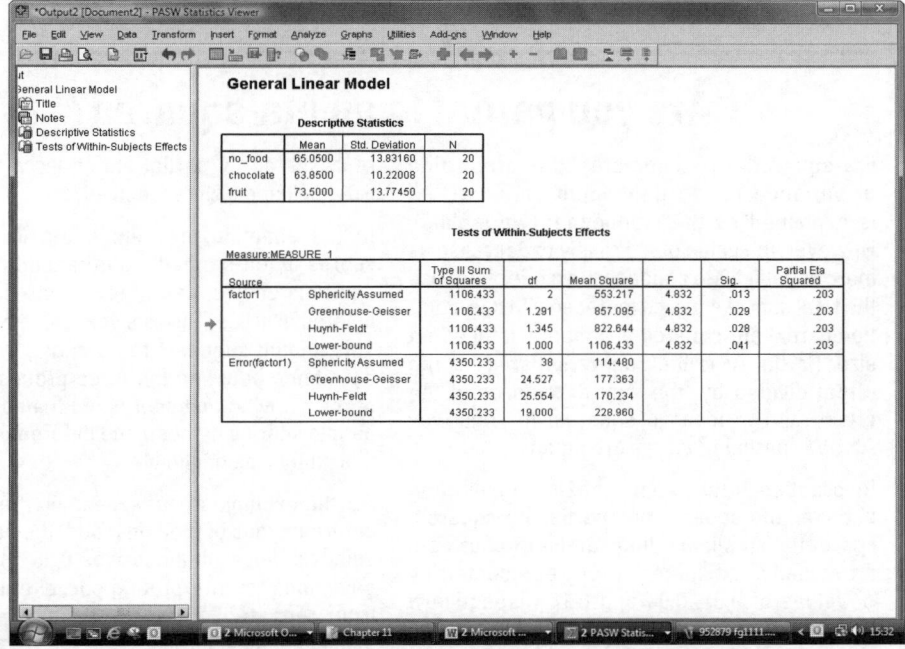

Figure 11-9:
Eta-squared
for repeated
measure-
ments as
displayed by
SPSS.

The eta-squared value in Figure 11-9 is 0.203. Notice that it's referred to as partial eta-squared, and that the mean scores in the figure help you interpret the direction of the difference – two aspects we cover in the following section.

Interpreting an effect size for differences between more than two sets of scores

Strictly speaking, eta-squared is produced by SPSS when you have a research design that can be analysed using a one-way between groups ANOVA (see chapter 16) or a one-way within-groups ANOVA (see chapter 19). When you have a research design that needs to be analysed using a two-way between-groups ANOVA (see chapter 16) or a two-way within-groups ANOVA (see chapter 19) or a mixed ANOVA (see chapter 21), then the effect size you obtain is more correctly known as *partial eta-squared* (see the nearby sidebar 'Are you partial to an eta-squared?' for an explanation of the difference between eta-squared and partial eta-squared).

Are you partial to an eta-squared?

Eta-squared (η^2) estimates the proportion of variance in the dependent variable that is explained by the independent variable(s). However, the value of η^2 is likely to decrease as more variables are added to the model, because the total sum of squares increases. In this situation partial eta-squared is a more useful effect size. Partial η^2 is the sum of squares for the effect divided by (the sum of squares of the effect + the error sum of squares). In a one-way ANOVA, partial η^2 and η^2 are equal.

In practice, few people make a distinction between eta-squared and partial eta-squared. For both, small, medium and large effects are usually considered to be represented by η^2 values of 0.01, 0.06 and 0.14 respectively. However, when using repeated measurements, these values might overestimate the effect and more appropriate guidelines are based on the guidelines for effect sizes of correlation coefficients (see the section 'Exploring Effect Size for Correlations', earlier in this chapter). Therefore, for repeated measures designs, small, medium and large effects could be considered to be

represented by partial eta-squared values of 0.01, 0.09 and 0.25 respectively.

In the example, examining the driving test scores of left-handed, right-handed and ambidextrous people, partial eta-squared was calculated as 0.005. This is a very small effect size. This finding suggests that although there is a difference between the three groups in terms of their driving test scores (with ambidextrous people scoring highest), the difference found in this study was negligible.

For the example about examining the effect of different types of food on mood, the partial eta-squared value obtained was 0.203. Using the guidelines for interpreting partial eta-squared from repeated measures designs, this is a medium, almost large, effect. The mean scores in Figure 11-12 tell you that there was little difference in mood scores when people had no food and when they ate chocolate, but when they ate fruit, the mood score was reported as much more positive. This difference is likely responsible for the big effect size.

Understanding Statistical Power

As we explain in Chapter 8, you use inferential statistical tests to help you make conclusions about hypotheses: to determine whether you can reject a hypothesis (the null hypothesis; see Chapter 8) or not. The conclusion (about whether or not to reject the null hypothesis) that you make from an inferential statistical test is based on probability. Therefore, you don't know whether your conclusion is absolutely correct and you need to accept that there is some chance that your conclusion will not be correct. In Table 8-1 in Chapter 8 we show you the two types of errors (Type I and Type II) and two correct decisions that can be made when you form a conclusion on the basis of an inferential statistical test.

One of these correct conclusions occurs when you reject a null hypothesis that is false in reality (see Table 8-1). The probability of making this correct conclusion is known as *statistical power*. In other words, statistical power is the likelihood that you'll find a statistically significant result which is correct. Generally, if a null hypothesis is false you want to be quite confident that your analysis will reject it, so it is important that your statistical analysis has high power.

Also, by increasing statistical power, you decrease the probability of making a Type II error (because power is equal to 1 minus the probability of making a Type II error).

These are two good reasons for ensuring that the power in your statistical analysis is maximised. By convention, it is preferable to have statistical power of at least 90 per cent, although a minimum of 80 per cent is considered acceptable. In other words, it is preferable to have a 90 per cent chance of rejecting the null hypothesis when it is false, but you settle for an 80 per cent chance, as an absolute minimum.

Seeing which factors influence power

A number of factors determine the level of statistical power in your analysis. These factors interact with one another, but in basic terms the following is true:

- ✔ The larger the effect size, the higher power you have in your analysis.

- ✔ The more liberal your cut-off point (known as *alpha*) for determining statistical significance, the more power in your analysis. By convention, the maximum alpha value acceptable is 5 per cent (this is the 0.05 cut-off point that you use to conclude whether a statistical test is significant or not). If you choose a more conservative alpha value (for example 0.01 rather than 0.05) then the power decreases.

- ✔ As the standard deviations of the variables included in your analysis decrease, the power of that analysis increases.

- ✔ Power is greater when you use a one-tailed hypothesis test rather than a two-tailed hypothesis test (see Chapter 8).

- ✔ As your sample size increases, power increases.

In practice, the only thing that you have much control over in terms of increasing power is the sample size. You can't arbitrarily set the effect size, because the effect size is what you find it to be in your analysis. You can't increase the alpha value beyond 0.05 because this would be unacceptable to an informed reader of your research report. And you can't arbitrarily change the standard deviations of the variables in your analysis, because these are what you find them to be. So, you rely on ensuring that your sample size is sufficient to ensure that the power in your analysis is at the required level. In fact, psychologists use the concept of power to work out the sample size required for a research study before they begin collecting data. In this way, they ensure that the amount of data collected gives them the power they need in their analysis.

Considering power and sample size

Constraints on resources usually mean that you aim for the minimum sample size necessary for a research project. So, when calculating sample size, researchers often base the calculation on an alpha (cut-off) value of 0.05 (or 5 per cent) and statistical power of 0.8 (or 80 per cent). To calculate sample size you also need to know the likely statistical analysis that you'll be conducting and the effect size for this analysis.

Calculating an effect size is relatively easy when you have data (as you can see in the preceding sections in this chapter), but when you want an effect size to calculate sample size, you're estimating the likely effect size before you collect any data! In other words, you're estimating the outcome of your analysis so that you can work out how many people you need to recruit for your research project in order for you to conduct your analysis! If it seems a bit back-to-front, that's because it is.

Here are some solutions:

- Use data from a pilot study to calculate an effect size.

- Use data reported in similar previously published studies to calculate effect size.

- Estimate an effect size based on the minimum effect size you consider to be important. The idea is that you ensure that you have a sufficient sample size to detect any important effects but not any effects smaller than this. For example, if you use questionnaire scores then you want to know the minimum change on the questionnaire score that would be considered meaningful. People with experience in using this questionnaire might be able to help with this decision.

- If you can't estimate a specific effect size, estimate whether you expect the effect to be small, medium or large. You can then convert this into an effect size value using the guidelines presented in the different sections in this chapter, depending on the analysis you intend to use.

Calculating sample size

For correlation analysis, use the following formulae:

> Sample size required to attain 80 per cent power, with alpha = 0.05, using a one-tailed test = $1 + (2.5 / r)^2$

> Sample size required to attain 80 per cent power, with alpha = 0.05, using a two-tailed test = $1 + (2.8 / r)^2$

> where r = the expected effect size (correlation coefficient)

For independent *t*-tests use the following formulae:

> Sample size required per group to attain 80 per cent power, with alpha = 0.05, using a one-tailed test = $2*(2.5 / ES)^2$

Sample size required per group to attain 80 per cent power, with alpha = 0.05, using a two-tailed test = $2*(2.8 / ES)^2$

where ES = the expected effect size expressed as Cohen's *d*.

For paired t-tests, use the following formulae:

> Sample size required per group to attain 80 per cent power, with alpha = 0.05, using a one-tailed test = $(2.5 / ES)^2$

> Sample size required per group to attain 80 per cent power, with alpha = 0.05, using a two-tailed test = $(2.8 / ES)^2$

where ES = the expected effect size expressed as Cohen's *d*.

When you have all this information, you can calculate some sample sizes by hand. For more complex designs you need a sample size calculator. You can download sample size calculators from the internet. A particularly useful calculator is G*Power (www.psycho.uni-duesseldorf.de/abteilungen/aap/gpower3/). If you prefer to do the calculations yourself, take a look at the nearby sidebar 'Calculating sample size'.

Part III
Relationships between Variables

"I never got the chance to ask him about the meaning of life — I just said I'm a psychology student."

In this part . . .

*H*ere's where we deal with inferential statistics, the ones that examine relationships or associations between variables, including correlations, regression and tests for categorical data. We explain each technique clearly – what it is used for and when you should use it, and follow up with instructions on how to perform the necessary analysis in SPSS. We also show you how to interpret the subsequent output and write up the results in both the correct statistical format and plain English.

Chapter 12

Correlations

*O*ften in psychology you want to examine the relationship between two variables. One way to do this is to visually examine a plot of the two variables (we explain variables in Chapter 2) to see how change in one variable is related, or not, to change in another. Alternatively, you can obtain a *correlation coefficient*, which is a number that offers a standardised way to express the magnitude and direction of a relationship. You can get several different types of correlation coefficients using the SPSS statistical software package. This chapter outlines when to use each technique, how to run the analysis using SPSS and how to interpret and report the subsequent results.

Using Scatterplots to Assess Relationships

One of the quickest and most accessible methods of looking at the relationship between two variables is to draw a *scatterplot*; a simple graph with one variable on the *x*-axis and the other on the *y*-axis (it doesn't matter which way round they are). The number of data points you have is equal to the number of cases or participants you have (if they each have unique scores) or less than your sample size (if some participants have exactly the same scores on both variables).

Scatterplots are most useful if the variables have a reasonably wide range of scores and you have a large sample size, otherwise you may find seeing relationships hard.

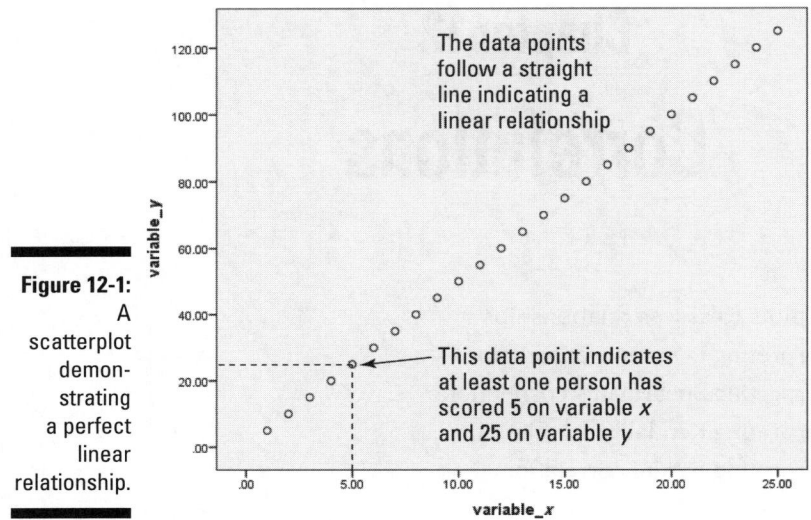

Figure 12-1:
A
scatterplot
demon-
strating
a perfect
linear
relationship.

Inspecting a scatterplot

Visually inspecting any scatterplot can inform you about the relationship between two variables. These relationships can take many shapes, but the only one you're interested in for now is the straight line, or *linear relationship*. If you look at Figure 12-1 you see a clear linear relationship running from the bottom left corner to the top right corner of the plot, or uphill; as one variable increases in magnitude, the second variable also increases in magnitude. This is known as a *positive relationship* and it represents a very strong relationship because the linear relationship is very clear.

Now look at Figure 12-2. You see a positive linear relationship, but it's not perfect as in Figure 12-1. An increase in one variable tends to be related to an increase in the second variable. For example, students who have high marks in their first year tend to have higher marks in the final year, but this relationship isn't perfect. This is more like the relationships you observe when conducting your analysis: it is very unlikely you will ever find two variables that have a perfect relationship.

You can also have a negative relationship between two variables where an increase in one variable is related to a decrease in the second variable. For example, Figure 12-3 illustrates the relationship between participants' health scores and number of sick days. The data points run from the top left corner of the plot towards the bottom right corner, or downhill, representing a strong negative relationship. Higher health scores relate to lower numbers of sick days.

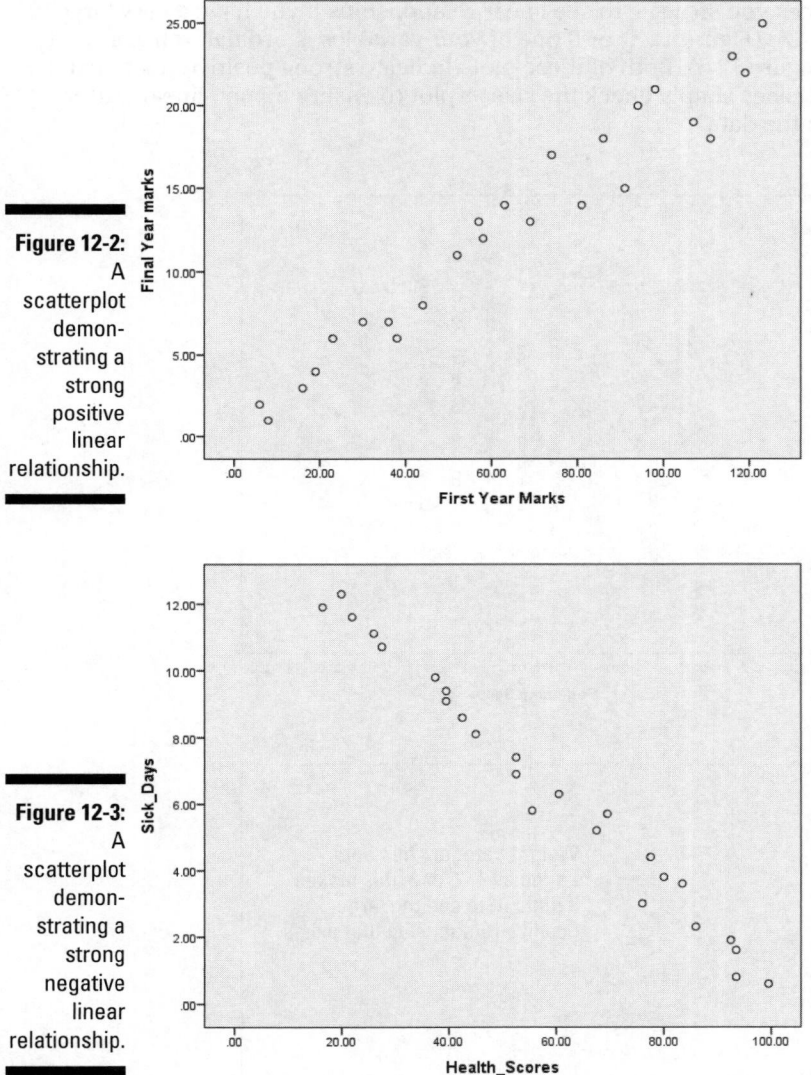

Figure 12-2:
A scatterplot demonstrating a strong positive linear relationship.

Figure 12-3:
A scatterplot demonstrating a strong negative linear relationship.

Of course the relationship between your variables doesn't have to be linear. Perhaps after an initial linear trend the relationship plateaus; it could form a wave shape or perhaps form two separate trends suggesting two separate sub-populations. All these non-linear relationships are interesting, but you can't interpret them the same way as with a linear (straight-line) relationship and their treatment, you'll be glad to know, is beyond the scope of this book.

Sometimes you struggle to see linear relationships if you have a very large sample size (Figure 12-4) or if one of your variables is ordinal or has a small range (Figure 12-5). Both of these plots indicate strong positive relationships. In these cases simply check the scatterplot to ensure no non-linear pattern exists in the data.

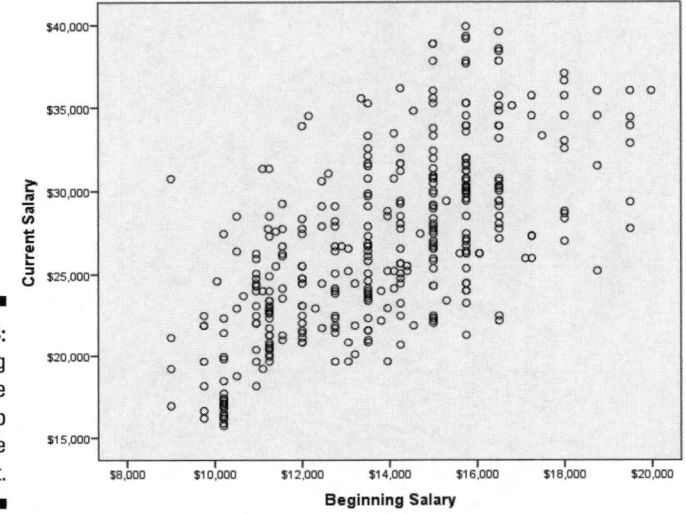

Figure 12-4:
A strong positive relationship in a large data set.

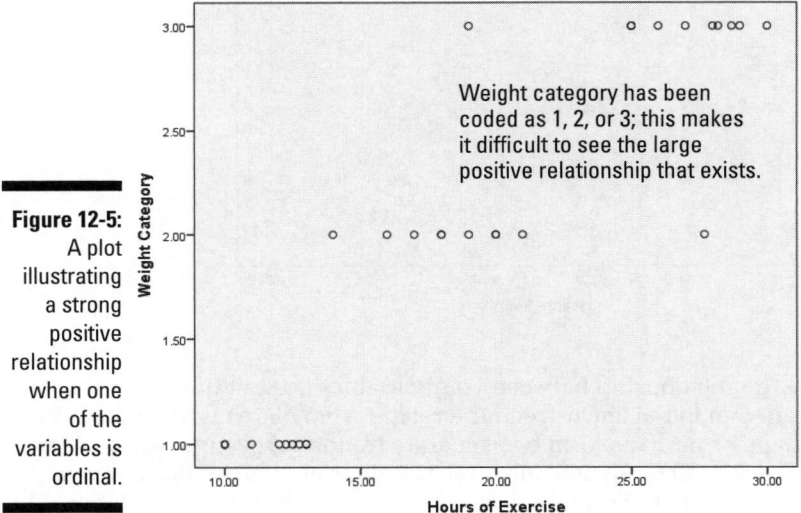

Weight category has been coded as 1, 2, or 3; this makes it difficult to see the large positive relationship that exists.

Figure 12-5:
A plot illustrating a strong positive relationship when one of the variables is ordinal.

Drawing a scatterplot in SPSS

You can draw graphs in many ways in SPSS; the following steps illustrate the most straightforward way.

1. **Along the top toolbar select Graphs and Legacy Dialogs from the drop-down menu. A choice of graphs appears; select the Scatter/Dot option (see Figure 12-6).**

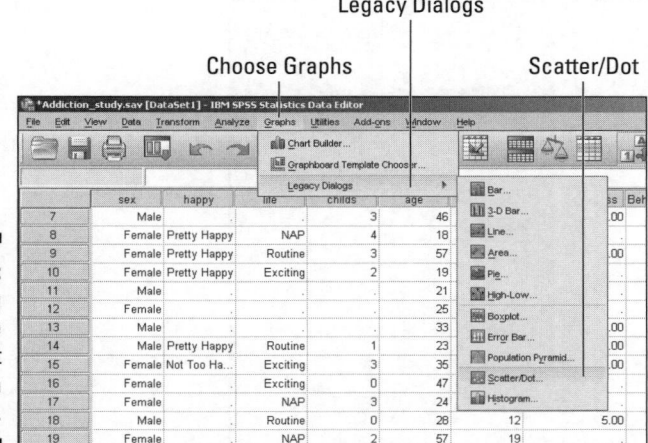

Figure 12-6: Choosing the scatterplot option in SPSS.

2. **SPSS asks you what type of scatter plot you require. The default option is the Simple Scatter and this is the option you want, so simply select Define (Figure 12-7).**

Choose Simple Scatter

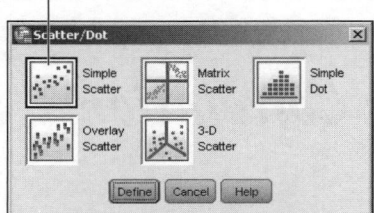

Figure 12-7: Choosing the simple scatterplot option in SPSS.

3. **A new Simple Scatterplot window appears allowing you to select the two variables you want to plot. Move one of the variables into the *y*-axis box and the other variable into the *x*-axis box. See Figure 12-8.**

The decision to place a variable into the *x* or *y* axes is completely arbitrary; it really doesn't matter which way round they go. To move the variables into the box simply click on the variable of interest then click on arrow button next to the relevant axis box or alternatively you can drag and drop the variable name into the axis box.

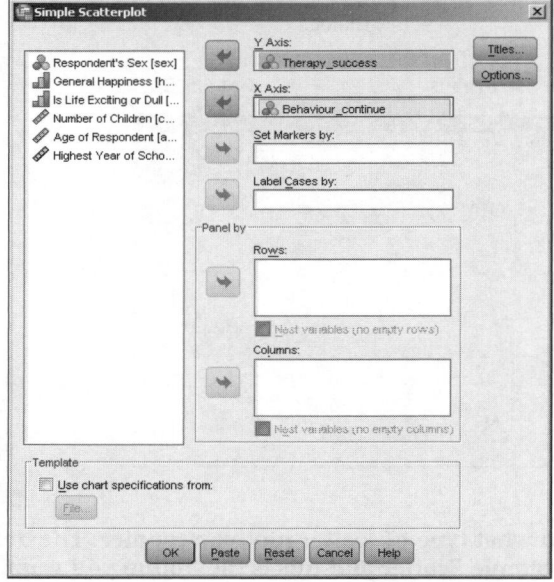

Figure 12-8:
Specifying
the
variables
for a scatter
plot.

4. **Click on the OK button at the bottom of the Simple Scatterplot window, and now you can examine the Scatter Plot in the Output window.**

Understanding the Correlation Coefficient

Looking at scatterplots is all very well, but wouldn't it be nice if there was a more objective way of assessing linear relationship? *Correlation coefficients* are a numerical way of expressing a linear relationship or a standardised way to report how the variables co-vary.

The correlation coefficient is reported on a scale between 0 and 1, with + and – signs indicating the direction of the relationship. Correlations can tell you two pieces of information: the strength and the direction of the relationship. The further the coefficient is from 0 (the closer to +1 or –1), the stronger the relationship, that is, the larger the effect. Zero indicates no relationship. As a guideline a correlation coefficient of 0.1 indicates a small effect, a correlation coefficient of 0.3 indicates a medium effect, and a correlation coefficient of 0.5 indicates a large effect.

A negative correlation coefficient (the number has a minus sign in front) indicates a negative relationship where an increase in one variable is related to a decrease in the second variable (see Figure 12-3). A positive number (with no sign in front) signifies that the relationship is positive where an increase in one variable is related to an increase the second variable (see Figure 12-2).

Several different types of correlation coefficients exist (for example, Pearsons, Spearman's or Kendall's) but you can interpret them all in a similar way, as we outline here.

Correlations do not imply causality! Correlations only indicate the strength and direction of a relationship between two variables. Irrespective of the magnitude or strength of the correlation, never imply that one variable causes a change in other variable. For example, over the past 60 years the Western world has seen substantial increases in both obesity and the number of hamsters kept as pets; therefore you could obtain a large correlation between obesity and the number of pet hamsters. This doesn't mean hamsters cause obesity! The reverse is also true; simply because a small correlation exists between two variables doesn't mean no causal relationship exists. For example, the correlation between the amount of sex people have and the number of babies they produce is typically very small, despite the fact that this is (normally) a causal relationship!

Examining Shared Variance

When thinking about correlations you can think about the degree to which two variables overlap. Think of this relationship as two overlapping circles; the larger the degree of overlap, the larger the correlation or the degree to which the two variables co-vary. You can quite easily determine the amount of overlap or shared variance by squaring the correlation co-efficient. If you have a large correlation of 0.5 this indicates a shared variance of 25 per cent $(0.5 \times 0.5 = 0.25)$ and a small correlation of 0.1 indicates a shared variance of 1 per cent $(0.1 \times 0.1 = 0.01)$. A perfect correlation of 1 results in the two circles being perfectly aligned and overlapping 100 per cent.

Consider an example where class test scores is correlated with the number of revision hours undertaken by group of students and results in a large correlation coefficient of 0.82. You can work out that the amount of shared variance in this relationship is 67 per cent. That means two thirds of the variance in class test scores can be explained by variances in revision hours. Of course that leaves you with 33 per cent variance that is unexplained in this relationship and could be to do with other variables (for example, quality of revision, IQ, whether they have read this book and so on).

When comparing relationships you find it's often best to compare the shared variance rather than the correlation coefficients. A large correlation of 0.5 looks to be 5 times stronger than a correlation of 0.1, but actually if you look at the shared variance you can see there is 25 times more variance explained!

Using Pearson's Correlation

Like any correlation co-efficient, you use the Pearson's correlation to assess the relationship between two variables. It's the most common correlation co-efficient you see reported and is the one you want to use as long as your data meets the assumptions.

Knowing when to use Pearson's correlation

Pearson's correlation is what is called a *parametric statistic*, which means it makes assumptions about the distributions of your data and the population from which your sample is drawn. These types of statistics can lead to powerful and accurate estimates but only if the assumptions are met. Before conducting a Pearson's correlation you must ensure your data meets the following three assumptions:

- ✔ Your variables must be measured at the ratio or interval level (see Chapter 2).

- ✔ Data for both variables approximate a normal distribution (see the sidebar 'Checking normality'). This can be done by checking each variable graphically, or by assessing the skewness statistics as explained in Chapter 9.

- ✔ There are no substantial extreme scores or outliers (see Chapter 6 and Figure 12-9).

If your data doesn't meet each of these assumptions, use a non-parametric statistic (such as Spearman's or Kendall's correlations; see the later sections on these).

When conducting a correlation, always check that the relationship between your variables is approximately linear (which you can check using the scatterplot; see the earlier section 'Using Scatterplots to Assess Relationships'). If the relationship between the two variables isn't approximately linear SPSS will still provide you with a correlation co-efficient, but it's not appropriate to interpret or report it; these correlations are only appropriate for assessing linear relationships.

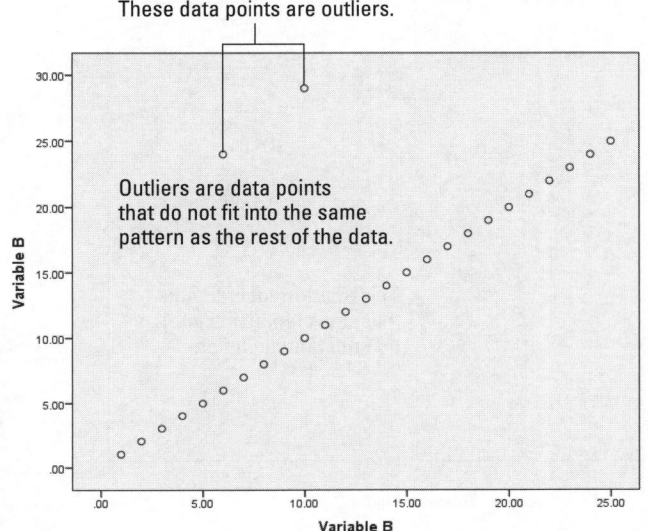

These data points are outliers.

Outliers are data points that do not fit into the same pattern as the rest of the data.

Figure 12-9: Always check your scatterplot for outliers!

Performing Pearson's correlation in SPSS

Our tutorial students didn't seem to believe us when we told them that the amount of time spent revising would be related to their exam marks. Therefore, we tried to establish this empirically by asking each of them how many hours they had spent revising in the past week and their most recent class test scores. We wanted to test the hypothesis that a significant relationship existed between class test scores and the number of hours spent revising.

The first step you always carry out before asking SPSS to provide you with a correlation coefficient is to visually check the relationship between the two variables. The way to do this is to draw a scatter plot of the two variables of interest, as in Figure 12-10. We explain how to obtain a scatterplot in SPSS earlier in this chapter. Assessing the scatterplot allows you to check whether the relationship between the variables is approximately linear and whether there are any major outliers.

Checking normality

Although most books (including this one) tell you to check the distribution of the sample by using histograms and skewness statistics, this isn't always necessary. The assumption of normality refers to the sampling distribution and we know that the sampling distribution will be normal when sample sizes are large (approximately 30 or more). So, checking the normality of your sample data is only necessary with small samples. In other situations (regression and analysis of variance covered in this book), the normality assumption also applies to the residual scores. We explain what residuals are and how to test this assumption in Chapter 13.

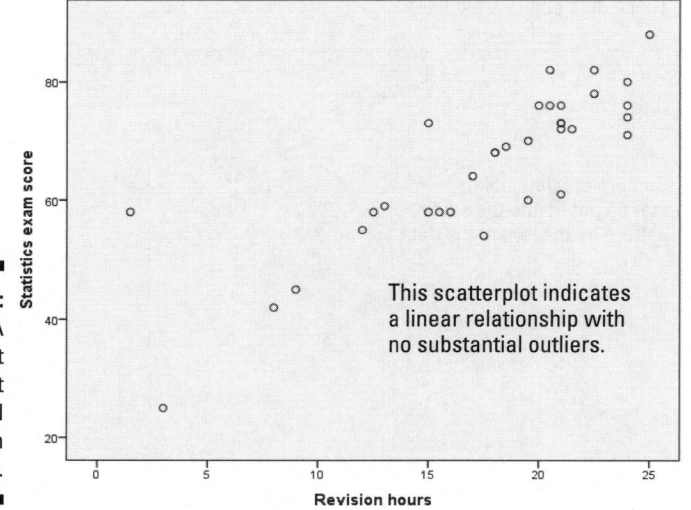

Figure 12-10:
A
scatterplot
of class test
scores and
revision
hours.

This scatterplot indicates
a linear relationship with
no substantial outliers.

Now you can get SPSS to calculate the correlation coefficient.

1. **Along the top toolbar select Analyze then choose Correlate from the drop-down menu. You get three choices but the one you should select is Bivariate, because you want to assess how two (bi-) measures vary.**

Select Analyze, Correlate and Bivariate

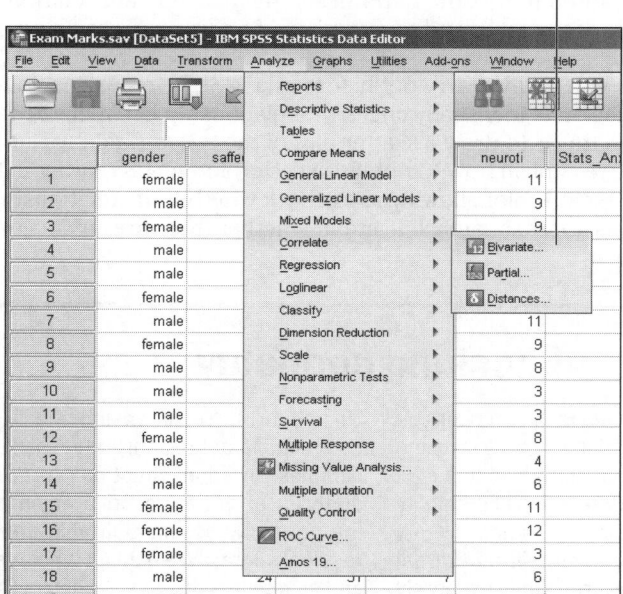

Figure 12-11:
Obtaining
a bivariate
correlation
in SPSS.

2. **A new Bivariate Correlations window appears allowing you to select the two (or more) variables you wish to correlate. Simply move both of the variables into the right hand variables box.**

3. **SPSS offers you a choice of correlation coefficients (Pearson's, Kendall's and Spearman's). Pearson's coefficient is the default option so you do not need to change this.**

4. **Specify if you are testing a one-tailed or a two-tailed hypothesis (remember one-tailed hypotheses specify direction whereas two-tailed hypotheses don't – see Chapter 8). Because the aim in this example is simply to see whether a relationship exists between the number of hours spent revising and class test scores, you can leave the default two-tailed option selected.**

5. **Leave the 'flag significant correlation' box checked so SPSS draws attention to significant correlation coefficients with a small asterisk. This can be useful when you are checking more than one correlation at a time.**

6. **Click OK.**

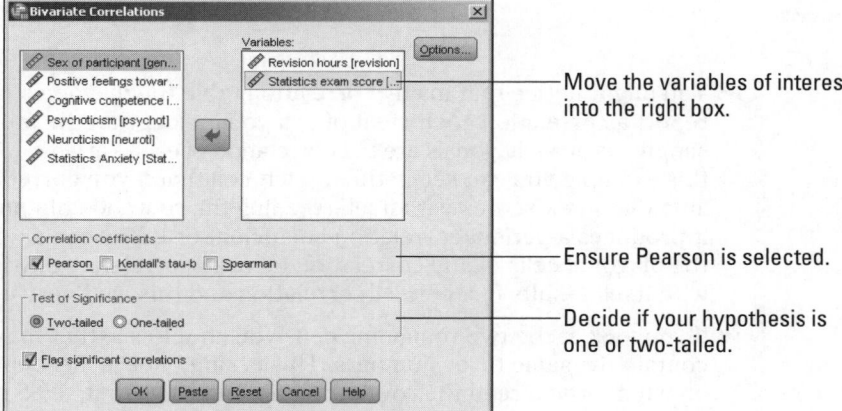

Figure 12-12:
Specifying
a Pearson's
correlation.

Move the variables of interest into the right box.

Ensure Pearson is selected.

Decide if your hypothesis is one or two-tailed.

Interpreting the output

The correlation table is produced in the output window (see Figure 12-13). Here's a breakdown of how you interpret what you see:

Correlations

		Class test scores	No. of revision hours
Class test scores	Pearson Correlation	1	.820**
	Sig. (2-tailed)		.001
	N	12	12
No. of revision hours	Pearson Correlation	.820**	1
	Sig. (2-tailed)	.001	
	N	12	12

**. Correlation is significant at the 0.01 level (2-tailed)

The correlation coefficient
Statistical significance
No. of cases or participants

Figure 12-13:
The Pearson's correlation table as produced by SPSS.

✔ You might notice that in any correlation table the diagonals always report a correlation coefficient of 1. If you look at that the table that's simply because diagonals are the correlation of each variable with itself. In this example you can see in the top left cell that if you correlate the variable Class test scores with itself (reading the row and column headings) it produces a perfect correlation coefficient of 1! You can always ignore the diagonal cells in any correlation table as correlating any variable with itself results in a perfect correlation and this isn't very interesting.

✔ If you look at the two remaining cells you should see that they each contain the same three numbers. This is simply because, depending on whether you read the row or column headings first, SPSS presents the class test scores correlated with the number of revision hours or the number of revision hours correlated with class test scores – this is exactly the same thing! It therefore doesn't matter which one of these cells you report.

✔ *Pearson's correlation* indicates the strength and the direction of the relationship between the two variables and always ranges somewhere between +1 and –1. In this example the correlation coefficient is 0.82; this tells you that it is a positive relationship (it is a positive number) and also that the relationship is quite strong because this number is approaching the maximum value of 1.

✔ *Sig*, the second value in the table, is the statistical significance. The value of .001 means that that there is a 0.001 probability (or .1 per cent) that you would have obtained this size of relationship with this sample size (assuming the null hypothesis is true); in other words, you're very unlikely to have obtained this result by chance. As you usually regard any value less than 0.05 as statistically significant, you can report that this relationship is indeed statistically significant.

✔ The third figure, labelled *N*, is simply the number of observed cases used to calculate the statistic; in this case you had 12 cases or 12 participants.

Writing up the results

The *American Psychological Association Publication Manual (2010)* suggests that you should report the correlation coefficient (denoted by the symbol *r*) value rounded to two decimal places, with the degrees of freedom in parentheses, followed by the significance level (denoted by *p*). The degree of freedom for a bi-variate correlation coefficient is always $n - 2$, which is the sample size minus 2; in the current example it is 10 (12 – 2 = 10). Taking the example reported in Figure 12-13, you would report the result as follows:

r (10) = .82, p = .001

When you're reporting your result, always report it in the statistical or numerical format and also in words. You need to describe the magnitude of the relationship, the direction of the relationship and whether it is statistically significant or not:

There was a strong, positive, statistically significant relationship between class test scores and the number of revision hours; r (10) = 0.82, p = 0.001.

We also recommend adding an extra sentence to describe what this result means in practical terms:

More time spent revising was related to higher class test scores.

It's not black magic . . .

It is important to realise that there is nothing supernatural or Machiavellian in calculating statistics. These days we use software packages like SPSS to circumvent the tedious number crunching required to arrive at our chosen statistic but you can (if you feel particularly masochistic) calculate by hand any of the statistics covered in this book. For example, if you wish to calculate Pearson's correlation coefficient for two variables you simply require the sample size as well as the raw scores, means and standard deviations for each variable. The formula can be presented in several ways but it normally looks something like:

$$r = \frac{\left[\sum\left(a_i - \bar{x}_a\right)\sum\left(b_i - \bar{x}_b\right)\right]}{\left[\left(N-1\right)\left(SD_a - SD_b\right)\right]}$$

Which can be expressed in words as:

Pearson's correlation coefficient = [The total sum of (each score on variable A minus the mean for variable A) multiplied by the total sum of (each score on variable B minus the mean for variable B)] divided by [(sample size minus 1) multiplied by (standard deviation for variable A – standard deviation for variable B)]

You will notice that there aren't pages of equations and proofs for each statistic in this book; that is because we believe there is no benefit in calculating statistics by hand, as it is more time consuming and you are more prone to errors compared to using a software package like SPSS.

Using Spearman's Correlation

Spearman's correlation co-efficient is the most commonly used non-parametric correlation. This means it's subject to less stringent assumptions than the parametric Pearson's correlation (see the previous section).

Knowing when to use Spearman's correlation

If you have ordinal level variables (flip to Chapter 2 for an explanation of levels of measurement) that you want to correlate, you use Spearman's correlation. Alternatively, if the interval or ratio level variables you want to correlate don't approximate a normal distribution or contain substantial outliers, Spearman's correlation is the most appropriate analysis to run.

So how does Spearman's correlation manage to avoid the assumptions we tell you to check when performing a Pearson's correlation (in the section 'Knowing when to use Pearson's correlation')? When calculating Spearman's correlation SPSS doesn't use the actual values of the data you enter; instead it ranks all the scores (that is, the lowest score becomes 1, the second lowest score becomes two and so on). This method of ranking means Spearman's correlation is less prone to influence of outliers or strange distributions.

So you may ask, why bother with Pearson's correlation at all? Non-parametric tests tend be less powerful (*power* is the ability to detect a significant effect if one exists; see Chapter 11) than their parametric counterparts, so you should use Pearson's correlation unless your data dictates that doing so isn't appropriate. However, you still need to check that the relationship between your variables is approximately linear (which you can check using the scatterplot; see the section 'Using Scatterplots to Assess Relationships', earlier in this chapter).

Performing Spearman's correlation in SPSS

One of our postgraduate students was quite rightly worried about the amount of time her friends wasted watching *The X Factor,* so she decided to design a brief intervention therapy for her friends to show them the error of their ways. At the end of the therapy session each participant was required to rate how successful they felt the therapy was and also how likely they were to continue the appalling behaviour of watching the programme. As these rating scales are ordinal level variables, she has correctly decided to use Spearman's correlation. Her hypothesis was that higher therapy success scores would be related to a reduced intention to continue the behaviour.

Before conducting the correlation coefficient you always inspect the scatterplot (see Figure 12-14). Correlations are only appropriate to assess a linear or straight-line relationship. It looks like there is negative linear relationship running from the top left corner of the plot towards the bottom right corner; a high score on one variable tends to be related to a low score on the other variable. One of the data points doesn't seem to follow this trend. The point in the top right corner is an outlier; it looks like this person has reported she felt that therapy was successful but still intends to continue the behaviour.

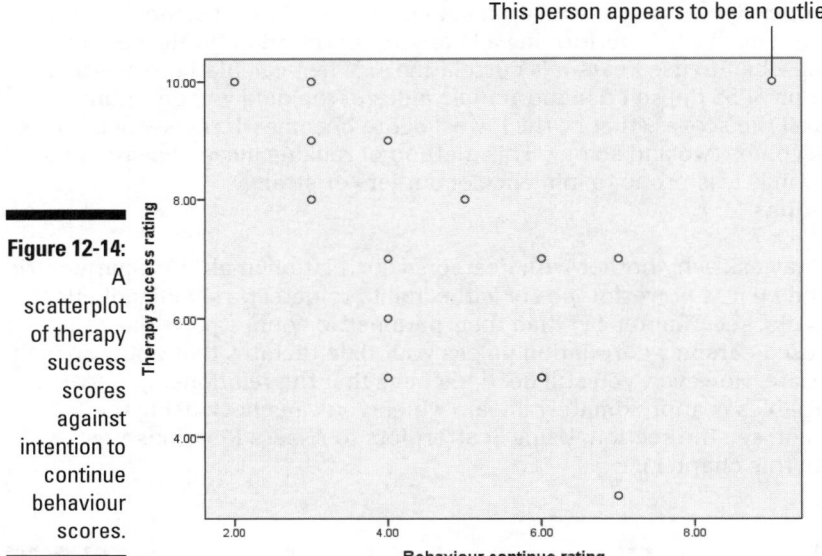

Figure 12-14:
A
scatterplot
of therapy
success
scores
against
intention to
continue
behaviour
scores.

Now you can get SPSS to calculate the correlation coefficient.

1. **Along the top toolbar select Analyze then choose Correlate and Bivariate (see Figure 12-11).**

2. **A new Bivariate Correlations window appears allowing you to select the two (or more) variables you wish to correlate. Simply move both of the variables into the right hand variables box.**

3. **SPSS offers you a choice of correlation coefficients (Pearson's, Kendall's and Spearman's). Select 'Spearman's' as the correlation coefficient and de-select the Pearson's option (see Figure 12-12). If you do not de-select the default Pearson's option SPSS will produce two separate correlation tables; Pearson's and Spearman's.**

4. **Specify if you are testing a one-tailed or a two-tailed hypothesis (remember one-tailed hypotheses signify direction whereas two-tailed hypotheses don't – see Chapter 8). Select the one-tailed hypothesis as in this example you predicted direction (see Figure 12-12).**

5. **Leave the 'flag significant correlation' box checked so SPSS draws attention to significant correlation coefficients with a small asterisk. This can be useful when you are checking more than one correlation at time.**

6. **Click OK.**

Interpreting the output

Your correlation table appears in the output window (see Figure 12-15). Each of the cells contains three numbers which we will address now.

- ✔ **Correlation**: Spearman's correlation coefficient indicates the strength and the direction of the relationship between the two variables and will always range somewhere between +1 and –1. In this example the correlation coefficient is –0.45; this tells you that it is a negative relationship (it is a negative number) and also that the relationship is of moderate strength.

- ✔ **Sig**: This is the statistical significance. As the value of .046 is less than .05 we can report this relationship as statistically significant.

- ✔ **N**: The third figure (N) is simply the number of observed cases used to calculate the statistic; in this case we had 15 cases or 15 participants.

Correlations

			Therapy success	Behaviour continue
Spearman's rho	Therapy success	Correlation Coefficient	1.000	–.450*
		Sig. (1-tailed)	.	.046
		N	15	15
	Behaviour continue	Correlation Coefficient	–.450*	1.000
		Sig. (1-tailed)	.046	.
		N	15	15

*. Correlation is significant at the 0.05 level (1-tailed).

The correlation coefficient ⎯
Statistical significance ⎯
No. of cases or participants ⎯

Figure 12-15:
The Spearman's correlation table as produced by SPSS.

Writing up the results

The APA Manual suggests that you should report the correlation coefficient (denoted by the symbol ρ or sometimes just by r) value rounded to 2 decimal places, with the degrees of freedom in parentheses, followed by the significance level (denoted by p). The degrees of freedom for a bi-variate correlation coefficient is always $n - 2$ which is the sample size minus 2; in the current example it is $15 - 2 = 13$. Taking the example reported in Figure 12-20, we would report the result as follows:

$\rho(13) = -.045, p = .046$

When you are reporting your result you should always report it in the statistical or numerical format and also in words. You need to describe the magnitude of the relationship, the direction of the relationship and whether it is statistically significant or not:

There was a moderate, negative, statistically significant relationship between therapy success scores and the intention of continue the behaviour scores; $\rho(13) = -.045, p = .046$.

It is also helpful to add an extra sentence to describe what this result means in practical terms:

> Higher therapy success scores were related to lower intentions to continue the behaviour.

You can find the ρ symbol (pronounced rho) in the symbol option under the Greek and Coptic subset in Microsoft Word.

Using Kendall's Correlation

Kendall's correlation (or *Kendall's tau-b rank correlation co-efficient* if you want to be formal) is a non-parametric statistic just like Spearman's correlation. It therefore is subject to less stringent assumptions than the parametric Pearson's correlation.

When calculating Kendall's correlation SPSS doesn't use the actual values of the data you have entered; instead it ranks all the scores, which means it is less prone to influence of outliers or strange distributions. Spearman's correlation is the most commonly used non-parametric correlation (because it was originally easier to calculate by hand), but Kendall's coefficient is most appropriate if you have *tied ranks* (data points with the same scores) in your data sets. This often happens if your variables have a narrow range; for example, if you're using Likert scales with a small number of responses or if the sample you're testing tends to give the same answers. Consider an example where people are asked to estimate their weight and height as high, medium or low; if two people answer medium on the same question then this is a tied rank.

Performing Kendall's correlation in SPSS

The Impact of Events Scale is a short questionnaire that attempts to measure aspects of post-traumatic stress disorder (PTSD). Participants choose one of five responses for each of the items. Two of the items are 'I tried not to talk about it' and 'I tried not to think about it'. In this example, you investigate whether any relationship exists between responses to these two items in a sample of 100 participants who suffered a recent traumatic experience. The hypothesis is that there would be a significant relationship between responses on the two items.

First, you visually check the relationship between the two variables. Figure 12-16 demonstrates the difficulty of trying to assess a linear relationship when your variables have a narrow range! There does not appear to be a liner relationship as far as you can see, but likewise there does not appear to any other shape of relationship that would suggest that a correlation would be inappropriate. The one (and perhaps only) interesting thing you notice is that there are only 12 data points despite the fact that there were 100 people in the sample. This should reassure you Kendall's coefficient was the correct correlation to use because lots of people had the same scores (tied ranks).

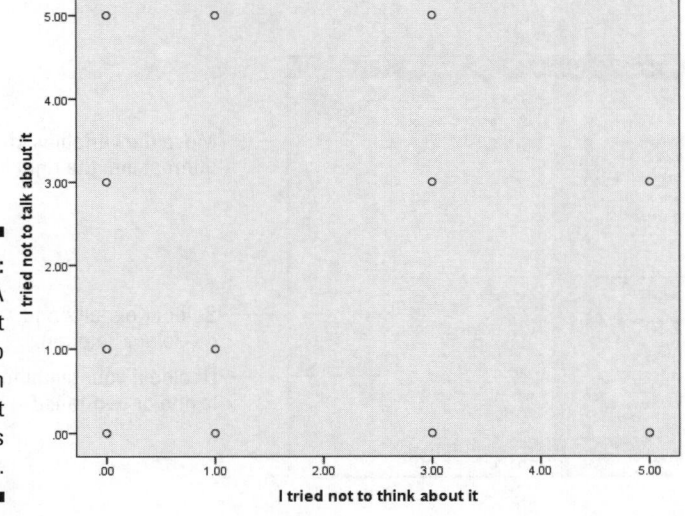

Figure 12-16: A scatterplot of the two items from the Impact of Events Scale.

Now you can get SPSS to calculate the correlation coefficient (see Figure 12-17). Follow the steps we provide in the earlier section 'Performing Pearson's correlation in SPSS', but in Step 3 choose Kendall's as the correlation coefficient (see Figure 12-18).

Select Analyze, Correlate and Bivariate

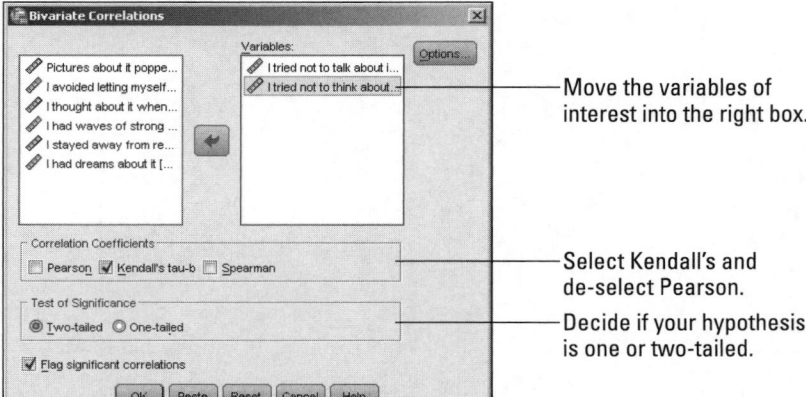

Figure 12-17:
Obtaining
a bivariate
correlation
in SPSS

Move the variables of
interest into the right box.

Select Kendall's and
de-select Pearson.

Figure 12-18:
Specifying
Kendall's
correlation

Decide if your hypothesis
is one or two-tailed.

Interpreting the output

Your correlation table appears in the output window (see Figure 12-19). Each
of the cells contains three numbers which we will address now.

✔ **Correlation:** Kendall's correlation coefficient indicates the strength and the direction of the relationship between the two variables and will always range somewhere between +1 and −1. In this example the correlation coefficient is .042; this tells you that it is a positive relationship (it is a positive number) and also that the relationship is very weak as this number is approaching zero.

✔ **Sig:** This is the statistical significance. As this value is greater than .05 we can report this relationship is not statistically significant.

✔ **N:** The third figure, simply the number of observed cases used to calculate the statistic; in this case we had 100 cases or 100 participants.

Correlations

			I tried not to talk about it	I tried not to think about it
Kendall's tau_b	I tried not to think about it	Correlation Coefficient Sig. (2-tailed) N	1.000 . 100	.042 .648 100
	I tried not to think about it	Correlation Coefficient Sig. (2-tailed) N	.042 ← .648 ← 100 ←	1.000 . 100

Correlation coefficent ————
Statistical significance ————
No. of cases or participants ————

Figure 12-19: The Kendall's correlation table as produced by SPSS.

Writing up the results

The APA manual suggests that you should report the correlation coefficient (denoted by the symbol τ or sometimes just by r) value rounded to 2 decimal places, with the degrees of freedom in parentheses, followed by the significance level (denoted by p). The degrees of freedom for a bi-variate correlation coefficient is always $n − 2$, which is the sample size minus 2; in the current example it is $100 − 2 = 98$. Taking the example reported in Figure 12-18, we would report the result as follows:

$$\tau (98) = .04, p = .65$$

When you are reporting your result you should always report it in the statistical or numerical format and also in words. You need to describe the magnitude of the relationship, the direction of the relationship and whether it is statistically significant or not:

> There was a very weak, positive, non-significant relationship between the responses of the two items; τ (98) = .04, p = 0.65

You can find the τ symbol (pronounced tau) in the symbol option under the Greek and Coptic subset in Microsoft Word.

Using Partial Correlation

Pearson's, Kendall's and Spearman's correlations are all very useful when looking at the relationship between two variables. In statistics, as in life, relationships are often more complex. More than one variable is likely to be related to exam scores, distress or whether someone watches *The X Factor* (see the examples in the previous sections). *Partial correlation* is a useful technique that allows you to test the relationship between two variables while controlling for (or *partialling out*) the influence of other variables on the relationship. The type of partial correlation that is calculated in SPSS is based on Pearson's correlation (see the previous section) and therefore has the same assumptions.

Performing partial correlation in SPSS

In a small country called Statsville a government official has noticed that there appears to be a very strong, positive, statistically significant correlation between ice-cream sales and the number of drownings over a 12-month period $r(10)$ = .96, $p<.001$); higher monthly ice-cream sales were related to an increase in the deaths due to drowning. The local media has picked up on the finding and are asking whether ice-cream causes drowning or whether people at funerals tend to buy a lot of ice-cream. However, you have an alternative suggestion; perhaps a third variable is influencing the relationship. Where it is warm people tend to buy more ice-cream in an effort to cool down. Similarly, where it is warm more people tend to go swimming and therefore more people get into difficulties and may unfortunately drown. You suggest that temperature may be influencing the relationship. To test this hypothesis you conduct a partial correlation.

Along the top toolbar select Analyze, choose Correlate from the drop-down menu and then select the Partial option (see Figure 12-20).

Select Analyze, Correlate and Partial

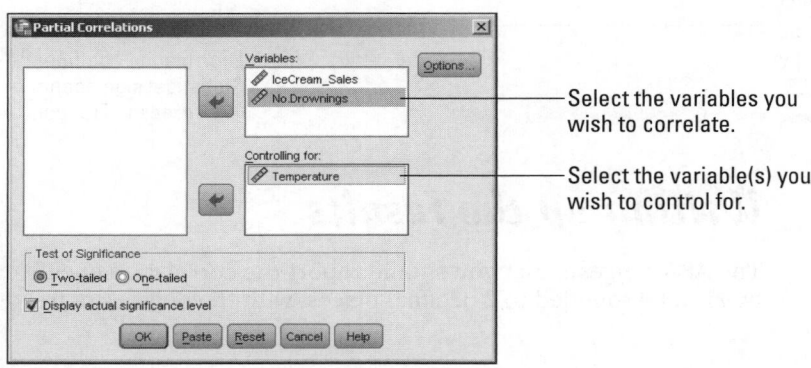

Figure 12-20:
Obtaining a
partial
correlation
in SPSS

A new Partial Correlations window will now appear allowing you to select the
two (or more) variables you wish to correlate (see Figure 12-21). Simply move
both of the variables into the right hand variables box. Then select the variable
or variables (you can control for more than one variable) you wish to control
for. In this example we wish to correlate ice-cream sales and drownings while
controlling for the influence of temperature. Below this again you can specify
if you are testing a one-tailed or a two-tailed hypothesis. A final option asks
if you wish to display the actual significance level; you should always report
the statistical significance so leave this box checked. Finally click OK.

Figure 12-21:
Specifying a
partial
correlation

Interpreting the output

The partial correlation table SPSS produces (see Figure 12-22) is very similar to any other form of correlation table. The diagonal cells are always one and then the information we want to interpret is duplicated. You should notice that the table does state that is controlling for temperature. The three values of interest are:

- **Correlation:** The first figure is partial correlation coefficient and can be interpreted in the same way as any other correlation coefficient. In this example the partial correlation coefficient 0.30 indicates a positive, medium relationship between ice-cream sales and the number of drownings when temperature is controlled for.

- **Significance (2-tailed):** The statistical significance indicates that this relationship is not statistically significant.

- **Df:** This stands for degrees of freedom; the degrees of freedom for a partial correlation is always the number of cases minus 3.

Correlations

Control Vaiables			Ice Cream sales	Drownings
Temperature	IceCream sales	Correlation	1.000	.296
		Significance (2-tailed)	.	.377
		df	0	9
	Drownings	Correlation	.296	1.000
		Significance (2-tailed)	.377	.
		df	9	0

Partial correlation coefficent
Statistical significance
Degrees of Freedom

Figure 12-22: The partial correlation table as produced by SPSS.

Writing up the results

The APA suggests that you should report the correlation coefficient (denoted by *r*) value rounded to 2 decimal places, with the degrees of freedom in parentheses, followed by the significance level (denoted by *p*). Taking the example reported in Figure 12-27, we would report the result as follows:

r (9) = .30, *p* = .38

To describe the relationship in words you must state the magnitude and direction of the relationship, whether it is statistically significant or not and, importantly, what variables were controlled for:

> There was a positive, medium relationship between ice-cream sales and the number of drownings when temperature is controlled for; *r* (9) = .30, *p* = .38

When you are writing up the results it is often useful to compare the partial correlation to the original Pearson's correlation to draw the reader's attention to the change in the relationship when a variable is controlled for. For example:

> There was a very strong, positive, statistically significant correlation between ice-cream sales and the number of drownings over a 12-month period (*r* (10) = .96, *p*<0.001) but when the temperature was controlled for this strength of this relationship decreased and it was no longer statistically significant; it therefore appears if the relationship between ice-cream sales and drownings is influenced by temperature.

Chapter 13

Linear Regression

*R*egression allows you to see whether one or more variables can predict an outcome variable (for the lowdown on variables, head to Chapter 2). Regression can determine the amount of variance in one variable that is explained by other variables.

Consider an example where you hypothesise that the number of hours spent revising predict exam scores. A regression can tell you, for example, that 68.5 per cent of the variance in exam scores can be predicted by revision hours. Furthermore, it can tell you which variables are important predictors and which aren't. If you have a good model you can even make predictions. For example, if you have range of variables (revision hours, gender, attitude and so on) that you think might predict exam score then you conduct a regression. This tells you which variables are important predictors and how much of exam score they can influence, and you can even estimate what exam score someone should obtain by only using your predictor variables.

In this chapter, we limit our discussion to linear regression. This means we're only interested in linear relationships or straight line relationships between interval or ratio level variables. In this case the variables are directly proportional to one another. It is worth noting that there are other types of regression which deal with non-linear relationships and discrete outcome variables, but we will not be addressing these models as they more complicated and not as commonly used as linear regression. This chapter first outlines simple regression and then addresses multiple regression. Finally, we show you how to check the important assumptions of regression in SPSS.

Getting to Grips with the Basics of Regression

As we explain in Chapter 12, correlations tell you the extent to which two variables co-vary by indicating the strength and the direction of the relationship. Regression takes the idea of looking at relationships between variables a little further. Regression can tell you how one variable affects or influences another variable. Correlations simply indicate the extent to which two variables are related or co-vary. For example, you can use a correlation to investigate the hypothesis that there is relationship between revision hours and exam mark. But by using regression you can test the hypothesis that revision hours predict exam marks. This is a subtle but important difference.

Regression also allows you to estimate or make predictions (assuming you have a good regression model). For example, if you knew how long someone spent revising you could estimate what exam score they should achieve.

Because statisticians like to make your life as complicated as possible, we have specific names for the types of variables used in regression. The variable that you hypothesise is having an effect or predicting an outcome is called the *independent variable* or *predictor*. The variable that is being affected is known as the *dependent variable* or *criterion*. So in the example outlined in the paragraph above, the time revising is the predictor variable and the exam score is the dependent variable or criterion.

When you run any regression model you're inferring a direction in the relationship between the variables. For example, revision hours influences exam mark. No matter how good your regression model turns out, this does not mean revision hours is causing a change in exam scores. As with correlations (see Chapter 12) you can't prove causality. If you enter the variables the other way round you get exactly the same result, which suggests that exams marks influence revision hours. This doesn't make sense, because people revise first and subsequently take an exam. You must use common sense when building any regression model and use the terminology that one variable predicts or is associated with another.

Adding a regression line

The first step of looking at any relationship between two variables is to draw a scatterplot (see Chapter 12). You should be able to tell that there is a linear positive relationship between the two variables in Figure 13-1; as revision hours increased exam scores also tended to increase. This reflects a strong, positive correlation. In Chapter 12, when we talk about drawing a scatterplot for assessing a correlational relationship, we say it doesn't matter which variables are associated with which axes. However, it does matter when you add a regression line. The convention is that the predictor variable should be on the *x*-axis and the dependent variable or the criterion should be on the *y*-axis.

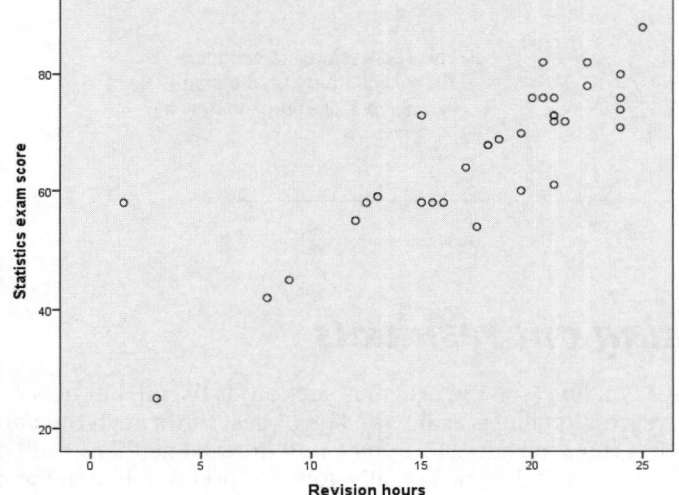

Figure 13-1:
A scatterplot of revision hours and exam score.

When you conduct a regression you can draw exactly the same scatterplot as for a correlation coefficient, except this time you can ask SPSS to impose a line of best fit. This is known as the *regression line.* This represents the linear relationship between the two variables and also allows you to make predictions. For example, to estimate what exam score someone should obtain if they revise for 10 hours, trace vertically up from 10 hours on the *x*-axis until your reach the regression line then trace horizontally across to the *y*-axis. We estimate from the plot that someone who revised for 10 hours should score around 50 in his exam (see figure 13-2).

If you want to fit a regression line, double click your scatterplot in the output file, choose Elements along the top toolbar and then choose the Fit Line at Total option. When the new properties window opens you're offered a range of lines you fit to your plot. Select the Linear option and then press Apply to finish.

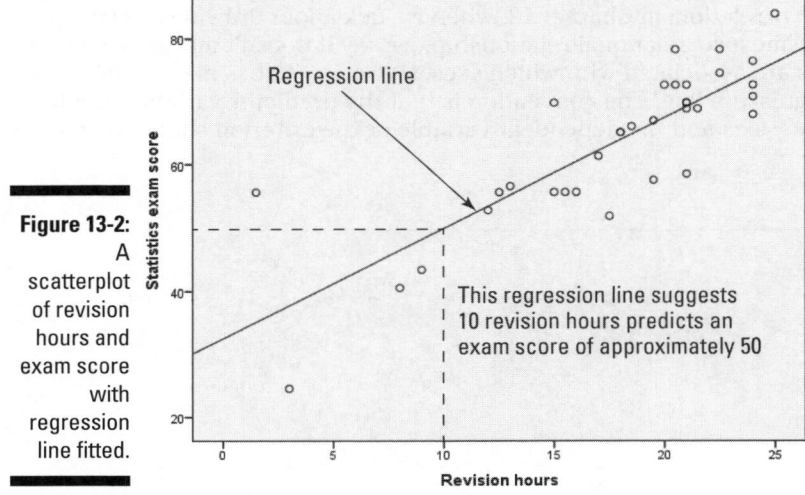

Working out residuals

The regression line (see the previous section) is useful, but how are you sure that this regression line is really the line of best fit through the data points? If you took a ruler to Figure 13-1 you could draw a line that would fit the data points pretty well. If the line is really good for predicting then the differences between the actual and predicted figures will be small (and vice versa). These differences between the actual scores and predicted scores are called *residuals*.

If you look at the first two scores on Figure 13-3, you can see data points with large residuals. If you look at the first data point A you can use the axis to see that this person revised for 1.5 hours and obtained an exam score of 58 (Figure 13-3). If you were to predict what score a person should obtain after revising for 1.5 hours by using the regression line (trace vertically up from 1.5 hours on the x-axis until your reach the regression line then trace horizontally across to the y-axis), you have a predicted score of approximately 36. The difference between the actual score of 58 and the predicted score of 36 results in a residual of 22 (58 – 36).

If you look at figure 13-3 you can see data point B, which represents a student who reported they undertook 3 hours of study and obtained an exam score of 25. If we use the regression to predict an exam score for someone who undertook 3 hours of study we would predict a mark of 39. The residual would be –14 (25 – 39). Residuals can be positive or negative.

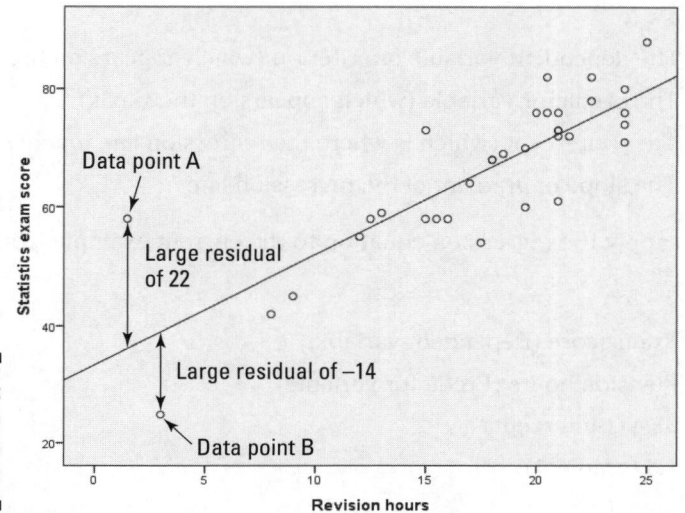

Figure 13-3:
An
illustration
of residuals.

The *linear regression line* is therefore the straight line that passes through the data points that results in the smallest residuals.

There are several ways of fitting a line to a scatterplot to try to minimise the residuals. In SPSS, the particular type of method used for fitting a regression line is known as the *least sum of squares regression* or *least squares regression*. This method fits a straight line to the scatterplot with the aim of minimising the value obtained if you add up all the squared residuals. (If you added up the residuals without squaring them, you would get a figure of zero, due to the fact that you have positive and negative residuals. Squaring any number always results in a positive number.) In practice SPSS calculates the regression line and residuals for you.

The better the points cluster around the regression line, the better the regression model will be. If the points fail to cluster tightly around the regression line it means the relationship is weaker and your predictions may not be as accurate.

Using the regression equation

A benefit of the regression line (see the earlier section 'Adding a regression line') is that as a straight line it can be denoted by a very simple equation (don't panic – it really is quite straightforward).

$y = a + bx$

y = The dependent variable or criterion (which appears on the y-axis)

x = The predictor variable (which appears on the x-axis)

a = The y-intercept (which is where the regression line touches the y-axis)

b = The slope or gradient of the regression line

So if you apply the regression equation to the current example, you get:

$y = a + bx$

y = Exam score (Dependent variable)

x = Revision hours (Predictor variable)

a = 33.4 (y-intercept)

b = 1.8 (gradient)

Don't worry too much about obtaining the values for the Y-intercept and gradient from the plot; SPSS will present you with these figures when you actually run your regression.

This allows you to complete the regression equation for this example:

$y = a + bx$

Exam score = 33.4 + (1.8 × Revision hours)

When you're writing out your regression equation always use the names of your variables for both y and x and then use numbers for a and b.

The importance of this regression equation is that it allows predictions. For example, if you want to estimate what score someone would obtain on his statistic exam if he studied for 10 hours, you can simply use the regression equation.

Exam score = 33.4 + (1.8 × Revision hours)

Exam score = 33.4 + (1.8 × 10)

Exam score = 33.4 + (18)

Exam score = 51.4

Using the scatterplot in Figure 13-2, we predicted that a person who revised for 10 hours would obtain an exam score of around 50. Using the regression equation provides a similar but more accurate answer. However, remember that this prediction might not be a very good prediction if the regression line has large residuals (see 'Working out residuals' above).

Using Simple Regression

You use simple regression when there are two variables of interest and you think one variable predicts or influences the other variable (unlike correlation when you simply hypothesise the variables are co-vary). In simple regression you have one predictor variable and one dependent variable (or criterion). It is important you have a clear idea, based on theory, which variable predicts the other before you start your analysis.

Performing simple regression in SPSS

In this section we show you how to perform a regression in SPSS by continuing to use the hypothesis that revision hours predict exam marks.

1. **Select Analyze along the top toolbar and Regression from the drop-down menu.** SPSS offers a list of various different types of regressions but the only one you're interested in is Linear (see Figure 13-4).

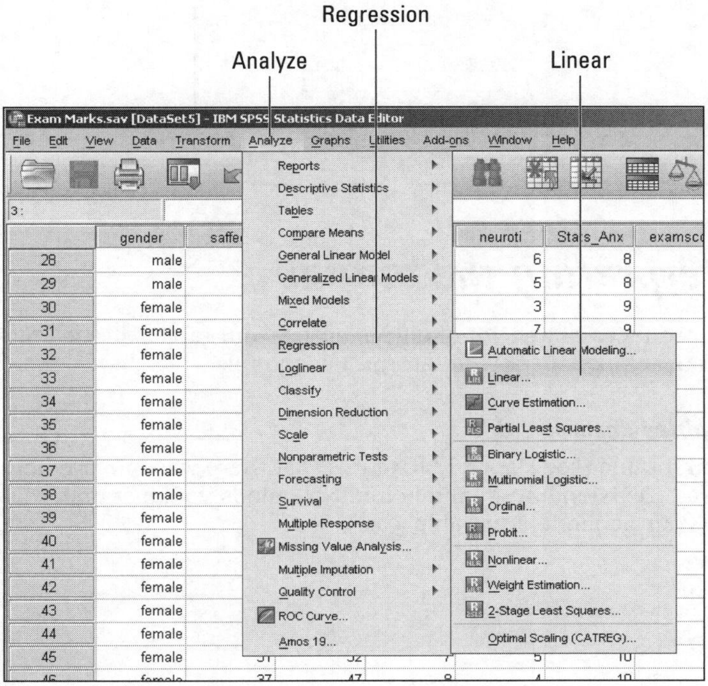

Figure 13-4: Obtaining a linear regression in SPSS.

2. **A new Linear Regression window opens.** Move your dependent variable into the Dependent box (either by using the arrow or simply by clicking and dragging) and then move the predictor variable over to the Independent(s) box (see Figure 13-5).

   In this case you move the statistics exam score into the dependent box (this is the variable you're trying to predict or explain) and revision hours goes in the Independent(s) box (this is the predictor which you think may influence exam score).

3. **Click OK.**

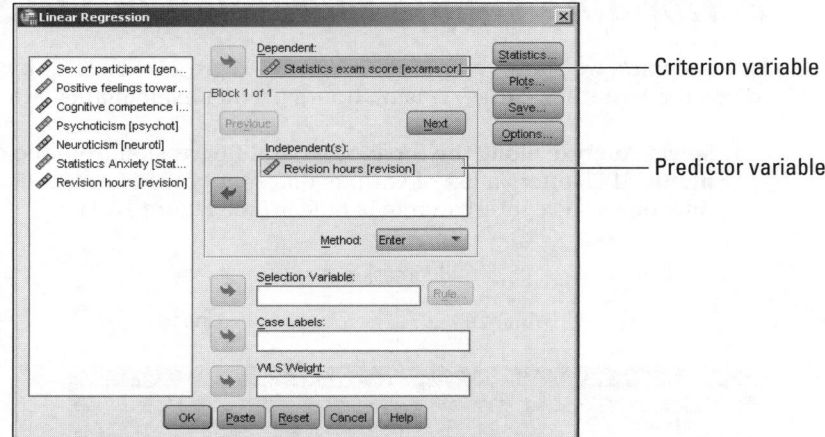

Figure 13-5:
Specifying a simple linear regression.

Interpreting the output

SPSS produces quite a lot of output across four tables. In the following sections we explain how to interpret each table.

Variables entered table

The first table (see Figure 13-6) states that there was one predictor variable entered (revision hours) and helpfully reminds you, just under the table, what your dependent variable was.

Variables Entered/Removed[b]

Model	Variable Entered	Variables Removed	Method
1	Revision hours	.	Enter

Figure 13-6:
Variables
entered
table.

a. All requested variables entered.
b. Dependent Variable: Statistics exam score

Model summary table

The second table (Figure 13-7) contains information about the relationship between the predictor variable and the criterion.

- ✔ *R:* This is simply the correlation coefficient between your two variables. If you carry out a Pearson's correlation (see Chapter 12) between revision hours and exam scores you would get exactly the same figure. This tells you that there is a large, positive relationship between revision hours and exam scores ($r = .83$).

- ✔ *R Square:* This figure is the correlation coefficient squared and therefore represents the amount of shared variance. It is the amount of variance in the dependent variable that can be accounted for by the predictor. R^2 ranges between 0 and 1. It makes most sense to report this figure as a percentage (simply multiply by 100). In this example 69 per cent of the variance in exam scores can be explained by variances in revision hours. This seems quite a substantial amount. We obviously don't know what accounts for the other 31 per cent variance in exam scores (it could be quality of revision, previous experience, IQ, whether they have this book and so on).

- ✔ **Adjusted R^2:** This figure is R^2 adjusted for the number of predictor variables in your model. It normally is a little bit less than R^2 to give you a more realistic and generalisable estimate. This is probably the most important figure in the table and the one we advise you to report it. The adjusted R^2 indicated that 68.5 per cent of the variance in exam scores can be explained by variances in revision hours.

- ✔ **Std. Error of the Estimate:** The standard error is an estimate of how accurate the estimate is likely to be. You can ignore this information at this stage.

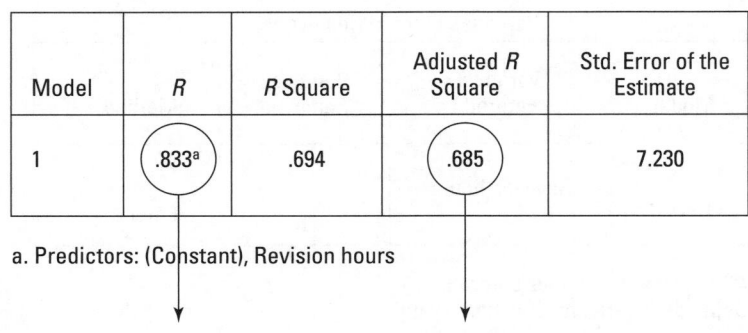

Model	R	R Square	Adjusted R Square	Std. Error of the Estimate
1	.833[a]	.694	.685	7.230

a. Predictors: (Constant), Revision hours

Figure 13-7:
Model summary table.

This is the correlation between the predictor and criterion variable

68.5% of the variance in the criterion variable (exam score) can be explained by the predictor variable (revision hours).

ANOVA table

The ANOVA table in Figure 13-8 (see Chapter 16 for a discussion of ANOVA) tests the null hypothesis that the predictor doesn't explain any variance in the dependent variable (more than simply using the mean; to recap on the mean in Chapter 4). If the ANOVA result is statistically significant, the result is unlikely to have occurred by chance (assuming the null hypothesis is true). If the ANOVA table indicates that the regression model isn't statistically significant, you can't be confident your results didn't occur by chance; therefore you simply state the regression model isn't statistically significant and you don't interpret the remainder of the output.

In this example the ANOVA table suggests that the model is significant, because the sig value is less than 0.05 (it explains a big chunk of the variance in the dependent variable) and is therefore unlikely to have occurred by chance.

Model	Sum of Squares	df	Mean Square	F	Sig.
1 Regression	3799.296	1	3799.296	72.678	.000[a]
Residual	1672.822	32	52.276		
Total	5472.118	33			

a. Predictors: (Constant), Revision hours
b. Dependent Variable: Statistics exam score

Figure 13-8:
ANOVA table.

If sig. is less than 0.05 it indicates we have a statistically significant model

Coefficients table

The final table (see Figure 13-9) contains quite a lot of interesting information.

Coefficients[a]

Model	Unstandardized Coefficients		Standardized Coefficients	t	Sig.
	B	Std. Error	Beta		
1 (Constant)	33.446	4.041		8.276	.000
Revision hours	1.852	.217	.833	8.525	.000

a. Dependent Variable: Statistics exam score

Figure 13-9:
Coefficients
table.

This gives the value of *a* in the regression equation

This gives the value of *b* in the regression equation

This tells you whether the variable is a significant predictor or not

✔ **Unstandardized Coefficients B:** In simple regression the coefficients table displays two figures under the column headed 'Unstandardized Coefficients' and the column headed 'B', which are the values of *a* and *b* in the regression equation. The value that represents the constant is the *y*-intercept or *a*; in this example it's 33.4. The value related to the predictor variable (revision hours) is the gradient of the regression or *b*; in this example it is 1.8. By checking these two figures you can complete the regression equation (see the earlier section 'Using the regression equation').

$y = a + bx$

y = Exam score (Dependent variable)

x = Revision hours (Predictor variable)

a = 33.4 (*y*-intercept)

b = 1.8 (gradient)

Exam score = $33.4 + (1.8 \times \text{Revision hours})$

The value of *b* or the regression line gradient also tells you the predicted increase in the dependent variable if the predictor variable increases by 1 unit; in this example the regression line gradient indicates that if revision hours increase by 1 unit (1 hour), exam score should increase by 1.8 marks.

✔ **Unstandardized Coefficients Std. Error:** The standard errors for the values of a and b. These values enable SPSS to work out the t-value and statistical significance for the predictor variable (see the final bullet point). Because SPSS automatically calculates t-values and statistical significance you don't need to worry about the standard errors.

✔ **Standardized Coefficients Beta:** The unstandardized coefficient B in the first column, which has been standardised. We cover standardisation in Chapter 10 if you want more detail. This figure allows you to predict the increase of the dependent variable in standard deviations if the predictor variable increases by one standard deviation. This is very useful when interpreting multiple regression, but not particularly interesting when dealing with simple regression.

✔ **t and Sig:** This is the t-value and associated significance level (see Chapter 15 for t-tests). In simple regression, SPSS presents two sets of values; one for the constant (or y-intercept) and one for the predictor value. You're usually not interested whether the constant (y-intercept) is statistically significant; therefore, you focus your attention on the predictor value. These values test the null hypotheses that the regression gradient is zero or, to phrase it differently, these values test whether the predictor variable is a significant predictor of the dependent variable. A significant result indicates that the predictor variable is a significant predictor (and this relationship is unlikely to have occurred by chance, assuming the null hypothesis is true). In this example you can conclude that revision hours is a statistically significant predictor of exam score ($t = 8.52$, $p < .001$).

Writing up the results

When writing up the results of a simple regression, include the ANOVA result, the adjusted R^2 value, the t-value and associated significance values for the predictor variable and the regression equation. If you were to write up the results of the current example it would look like this:

Simple linear regression was carried out to determine influence of revision hours on exam scores. This was a statistically significant model ($F(1,32)$ = 72.68, $p < .001$). The adjusted R^2 indicated that 68.5% of the variance in exam scores can be explained by the variance in revision hours. Revision hours was shown to be a statistically significant predictor of exam score ($t = 8.52$, $p < .001$). The regression model suggested that each increased revision hour was related to a 1.8 mark improvement in exam score. The regression equation for this model was: Exam score = 33.4 + (1.8 × Revision hours).

Working with Multiple Variables: Multiple Regression

In multiple regression you have more than one predictor variable and one dependent variable (see Figure 13-10). You could have many predictor variables but you can only ever have one dependent variable.

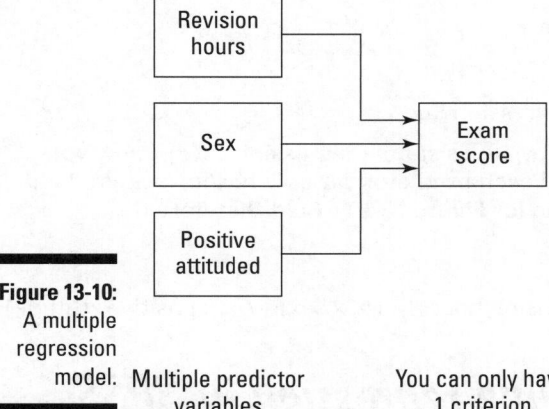

Figure 13-10: A multiple regression model.

Multiple predictor variables

You can only have 1 criterion

Importantly, multiple regression informs you about the relationship between each predictor and the criterion, after controlling for the effect of all other predictors in the model. This means that the regression attempts to calculate the unique variance between a predictor and the criterion while eliminating the variance from the other predictor variables in the model. For example, it assesses the relationship between statistics exam score and revision hours after controlling for the influences of positive attitudes and gender in the model.

In simple regression you have one predictor variable so the regression equation (see 'Using the regression equation', earlier in the chapter) is:

$y = a + bx$

y = The dependent variable or criterion

x = The predictor variable

a = The y-intercept

b = The slope or gradient of the regression line

If there is more than one predictor variable it means we have to expand the regression equation slightly. In multiple regression you have more than one predictor so you will have more than one x (predictor variable) and more than one b (gradient of each regression line). If there were 3 predictor variables in your analysis you would have 3 xs and 3 bs, as each predictor variable has its own b value. The regression equation would then look like this:

$y = a + b_1x_1 + b_2x_2 + b_3x_3$

y = The dependent variable or criterion

x = The predictor variable

a = The y-intercept

b = The gradient of the regression line

The regression has the same format as simple regression except now you have 3 predictor variables and each predictor variable has its own gradient (or b). The regression equation for Figure 13-10 would therefore be:

$y = a + b_1x_1 + b_2x_2 + b_3x_3$

Exam score = $a + (b_1 \times \text{Revision hours}) + (b_2 \times \text{sex}) + (b_3 \times \text{positive attitude})$

Performing multiple regression in SPSS

You perform a multiple regression in SPSS in the same way as you perform a simple regression. We will test the example that revision hours, sex of the student and positive attitudes all predict exam mark (see Figure 13-10). Select Analyze along the top toolbar and Regression from the drop down menu then choose the Linear option.

A new Linear Regression window will open (see Figure 13-11). Simply move your dependent variable into the Dependent box and then move all the predictor variables over to the Independent(s) box. In this case we have moved the statistics exam score into the dependent box (this is the variable we are trying to predict or explain) and revision hours, sex and positive attitudes are placed in the independent(s) box. Click OK.

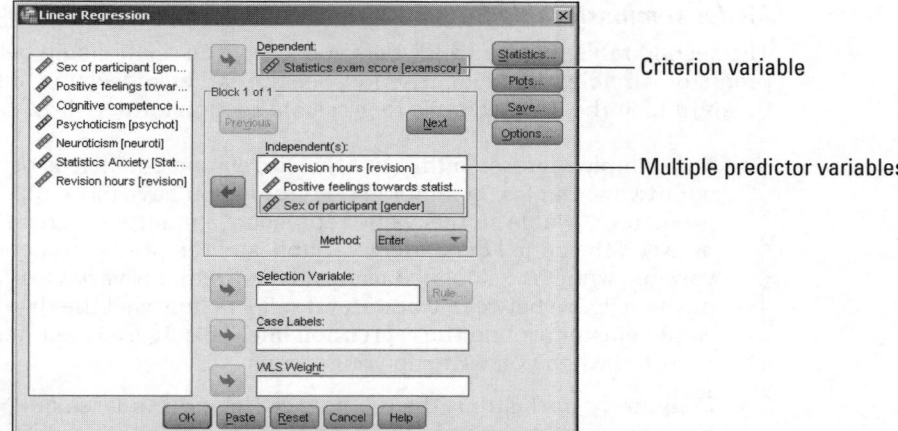

Figure 13-11:
Specifying
a multiple
regression

Interpreting the output

The same four tables that are produced in simple regression are produced in multiple regression.

Variables entered table

The first table (Figure 13-12) table reminds you what predictor variables were entered.

Model	Variables Entered	Variables Removed	Method
1	Sex of participant, Revision hours, Positive Attitude towards stats		Enter

Figure 13-12:
Variables
entered
table

a. All requested variables entered.
b. Dependent Variable: Statistics exam score

Model summary table

The second table (Figure 13-13) tells you about the relationship between the predictor variables and your criterion. See the earlier subsection 'Interpreting the output' in the 'Using Simple Regression' section for details of each.

- ✔ **R:** In simple regression this was the correlation coefficient between your two variables. In multiple regression you have more than one predictor variable so this value represents a multiple correlation between the actual dependent variable and the predicted dependent variable which is calculated using all the predictor variables. It's a positive figure between 0 and 1 and reflects how well the data points would cluster around the regression line. This figure is not normally reported when you write up your results.

- ✔ **R Square:** This figure is the multiple correlation squared and represents the amount of variance in the dependent variable that can be accounted for by the all predictors. In this example 73.8 per cent of the variance in exam scores can be explained by variances in sex, revision hours and positive attitudes.

- ✔ **Adjusted R^2:** This figure is R^2 adjusted for the number of predictor variables in your model. The adjusted R^2 indicates that 71.2 per cent of the variance in exam scores can be explained by variances in sex, revision hours and positive attitudes.

- ✔ **Std. Error of the Estimate:** An estimate of how accurate the estimate is likely to be; just ignore this.

Model	R	R Square	Adjusted R Square	Std. Error of the Estimate
1	.859[a]	.738	.712	6.910

a. Predictors: (Constant), Sex of participant, Revision hours, positive Attitude towards stats

Figure 13-13: Model summary table.

71% of the variance in exam score (criterion) can be explained by your predictor variables

ANOVA table

See the earlier subsection 'Interpreting the output' in the 'Using Simple Regression' section for details of the ANOVA table. In this example the ANOVA table (see Figure 13-14) suggests that the model is a significant fit to the data and is therefore unlikely to have occurred by chance.

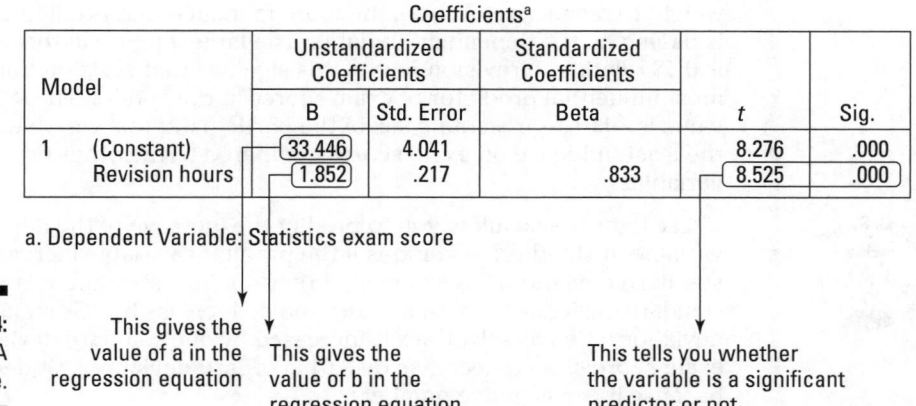

Coefficients^a

Model		Unstandardized Coefficients		Standardized Coefficients	t	Sig.
		B	Std. Error	Beta		
1	(Constant)	33.446	4.041		8.276	.000
	Revision hours	1.852	.217	.833	8.525	.000

a. Dependent Variable: Statistics exam score

Figure 13-14:
ANOVA
table.

This gives the value of a in the regression equation

This gives the value of b in the regression equation

This tells you whether the variable is a significant predictor or not

Coefficients table

See the earlier subsection 'Interpreting the output' in the 'Using Simple Regression' section for details of the coefficients table. Here we provide details relevant to the multiple regression example.

✔ **Unstandardized Coefficients B:** This column provides the values for a and b used in the regression equation. The value that represents the constant is the a or the y-intercept; in this example it is 24.63. Each predictor value has its own related b value or gradient. The b value for revision hours is 1.30, the b value for positive attitude is 0.55 and the b value for sex is –0.45. Now you can complete the regression equation (see the earlier section 'Using the regression equation'):

$$y = a + b_1 x_1 + b_2 x_2 + b_3 x_3$$

Exam score = a + (b_1 × Revision hours) + (b_2 × sex) + (b_3 × positive attitude)

Exam score = 24.63 + (1.30 × Revision hours) + (–0.45 × sex) + (0.55 × positive attitude)

✔ **Unstandardized Coefficients Std. Error:** You don't need to worry about the standard errors.

✔ **Standardized Coefficients Beta:** These figures are simply the unstandardized coefficient B values in the first column which have been standardised. Standardisation is covered in chapter 10 if you want more detail. Each of the variables is measured on different units. It is therefore hard to compare 1.3 hours in time with half a sex score with 0.4 on an attitude scale! One of the benefits of standardisation is that all the variables are converted to the same units (measured in standard deviations; see Chapter 5). That means you can make direct comparisons between the predictor variables. The greater the value of the standardised beta weight (irrespective of sign), the more influence that predictor variable is having on the dependent variable. The largest figure in this column is 0.58 relating to revision hours; this signifies that revision hours is the most influential predictor of exam scores in this model. The smallest value is –0.01 representing sex of the participant; this variable is having the least influence on exam scores compared to the other two predictor variables.

These figures also allow you to predict the increase of the dependent variable in standard deviations if the predictor variable increases by one standard deviation. For example, if revision hours are increased by one standard deviation then exam score should increase by 0.58 standard deviations. Conversely, if sex is increased by one standard deviation then exam score should decrease by 0.01 standard deviations (it decreases because it is a negative number).

✔ **t & Sig:** This is the t-value and associated significance level for each predictor variables. These values test the null hypotheses that each regression gradient is zero or, to put it another way, tests whether each of the predictor variables is a significant predictor of the dependent variable. A significant result indicates that the particular variable is a significant predictor of the criterion. In this example you can conclude that revision hours ($t = 84.04$, $p < .001$) and positive attitude ($t = 2.24$, $p = .033$) are statistically significant predictors of exam score. The sex of the participant is not a significant predictor of exam score ($t = -.12$, $p = .905$). We are not interested in the constant (y-intercept).

Model	Unstandardized Coefficients		Standardized Coefficients		
	B	Std. Error	Beta	t	Sig.
1 (Constant)	24.628	6.812		3.615	.001
Revision hours	1.301	.322	.585	4.037	.000
Positive hours	.548	.245	.325	2.242	.033
Positive Attitude	−.445	3.686	−.011	−.121	.905
Sex of participant					

a. Dependent Variable: Statistics exam score

Figure 13-15: Coefficients table.

Unstandardised coefficients give you the values of $a + b$ in your regression equation

Standardised coefficients allow you to compare the relative strength of predictors

t-scored and associated significance value allows you to assess which variables are significant predictors and which are not.

Writing up the results

When writing up the results of a multiple regression include the ANOVA result, the adjusted R^2 value, the *t*-value and associated significance values for the predictor variable and explain to the reader the relevant contribution made by the variables. As well a written summary of your finding it is useful to provide a summary table of the main results. Here's how you write up the current example with a paragraph and a summary of the results (see Table 13-1).

> Multiple linear regression was carried out to determine the effect of revision hours, positive attitudes and sex of the participant on exam scores. This was a statistically significant model (F (3,30) = 28.20, $p<.001$) indicating these results were unlikely to have arisen by chance (assuming the null hypothesis to be true). The adjusted R^2 indicated that 71.2 per cent of the variance in exam scores can be explained by variances in the three predictor variables. The analysis suggested that revision hours (β = .58) was the most influential predictor and sex of the participant (β = −.01) was the least influential predictor in the model. Revision hours (t = 4.04, $p < .001$) and positive attitudes (t = 2.24, p = .03) were shown to be statistically significant predictors of exam score. Sex of the participant was shown not to be a statistically significant predictor of exam score (t = −.12, p = .91).

Table 13-1	Regression Model with Exam Score as the Criterion Variable			
	Unstandardised Coefficients	**Standardised Coefficients**	**t**	**Sig.**
Constant	2.63			
Revision hours	1.30	0.58	4.04	<.001
Positive attitude	0.55	0.32	2.24	.033
Sex of participant	−0.44	−0.01	−0.121	.905

Adjusted R^2= 71.2 per cent; F (3,30)= 28.20; p<.001

Checking Assumptions of Regression

It is important to ensure your data is suitable for regression analysis. SPSS will produce the output irrespective of whether or not your data is suitable which means you could produce and interpret results which are not accurate or appropriate. You must therefore check the assumptions of regression before you report the results; the assumptions addressed in this section are:

- ✔ Normally distributed residuals
- ✔ Linearity
- ✔ Outliers
- ✔ Multicollinearity
- ✔ Type of data

Normally distributed residuals

The residuals in a regression should be approximately normally distributed with a mean around zero. If the residuals were highly skewed this may suggest that the regression line doesn't really fit the data. The easiest way to check this assumption is simply to look at a histogram of the residuals and judge whether it approximates a normal distribution. Open the regression window as before (Select Analyze, Regression, then Linear) then select the Plots option button. This will open a second Plots window. Select the Histogram option and then continue. Finally select OK on the regression window to produce the histogram in the output file (see Figure 13-16).

Your task is to decide whether the histogram approximates a normal distribution. It is unlikely that any histogram demonstrates a perfect normal distribution. We would say Figure 13-17 is acceptable and doesn't violate this assumption. For more information on assessing the normal distribution, refer to Chapter 9.

Select plots

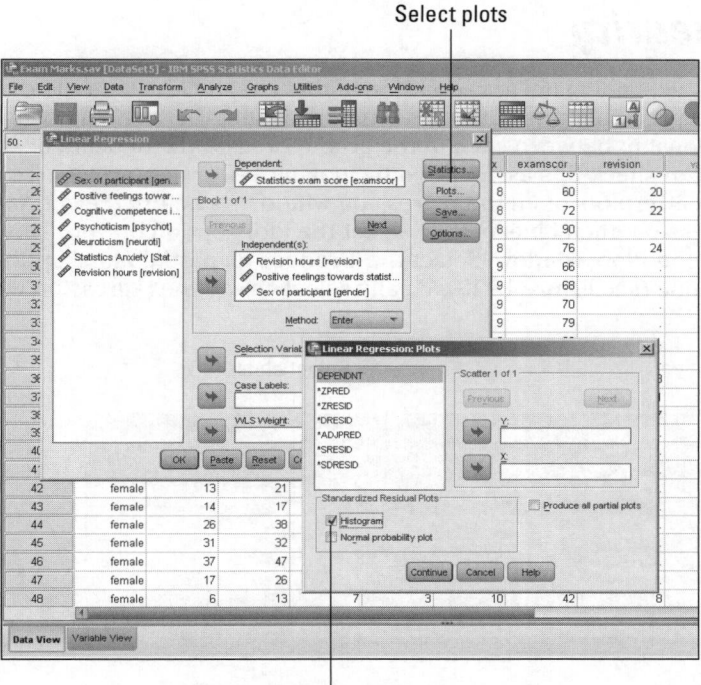

Check Histograms

Figure 13-16:
Obtaining a
histogram
of the
residuals

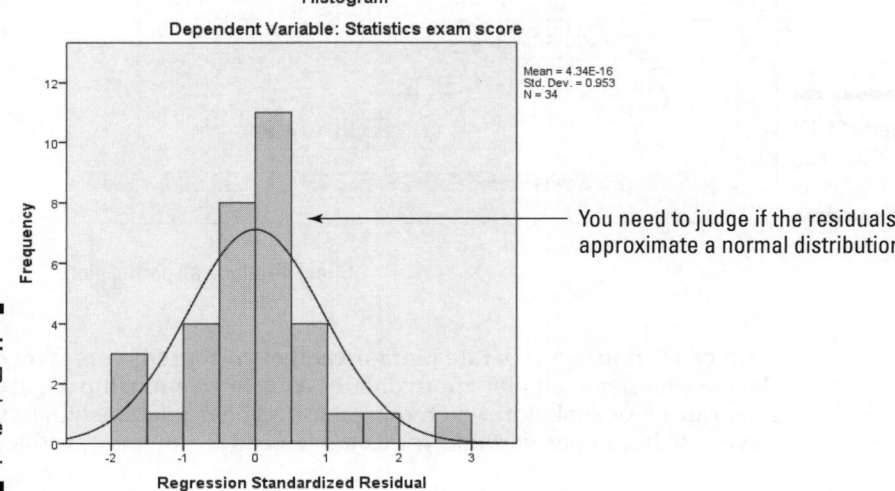

You need to judge if the residuals
approximate a normal distribution

Figure 13-17:
Interpreting
the histo-
gram of the
residuals.

Linearity

We're explaining linear regression in this chapter, so it should come as no surprise that one of the assumptions is that there should be a linear relationship between each of the predictors and the dependent variable. You can check this assumption by looking at the scatterplots. To obtain the scatterplots open the regression window as before (Select Analyze, Regression, then Linear) then select the Plots option button. This will open a second Plots window. Select the 'Produce all partial plots' option and then continue (see Figure 13-18). Finally select OK on the regression window.

Select plots

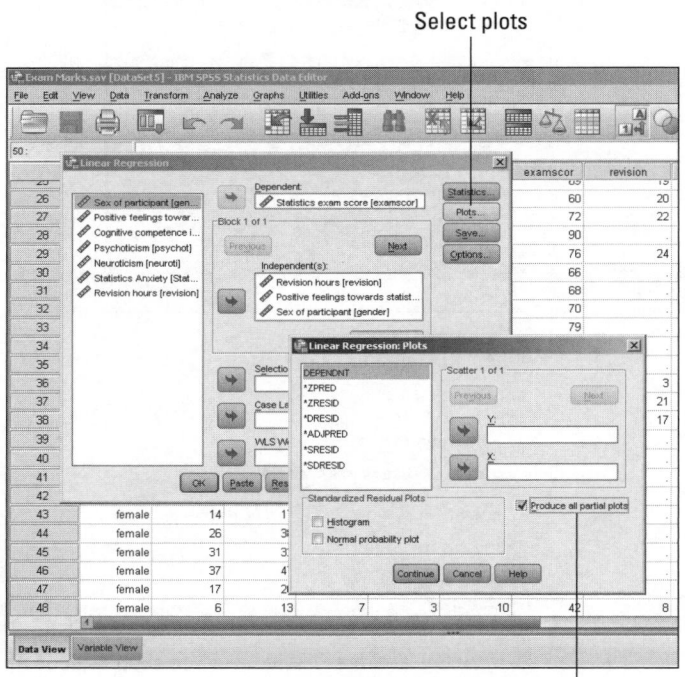

Figure 13-18:
Obtaining
partial plots

Check Produce all partial plots

SPSS can produce a separate plot for each of your predictors. You should decide whether each plot approximates a linear relationship. Figure 13-19 illustrates a typical plot, which represents a linear relationship. But if you have a dichotomous variable, for example gender, you may produce a plot similar to Figure 13-20; although this doesn't look like a linear relationship it is simply because your two predictor variable only had two possible scores and is acceptable. For more information on assessing linear relationships, go to Chapter 12.

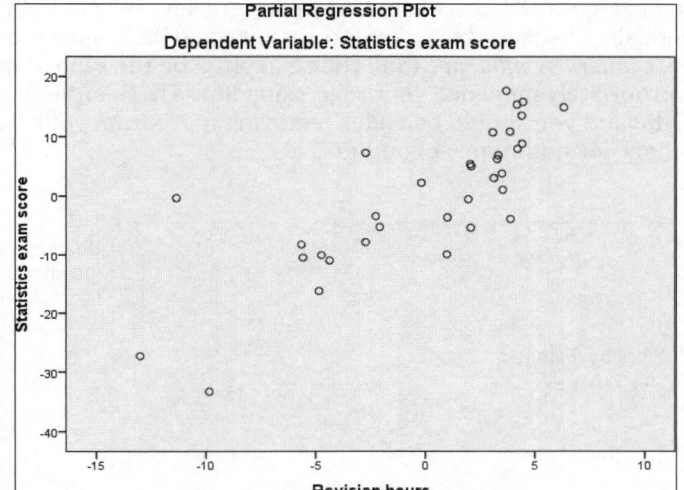

Figure 13-19: Interpreting the partial plots 1.

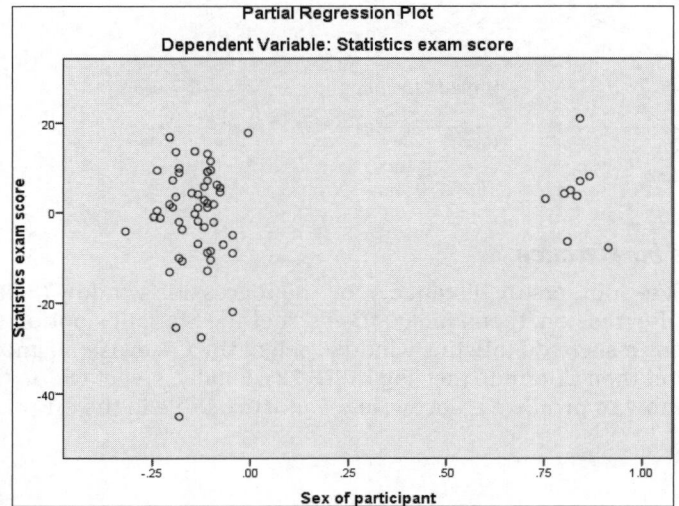

Figure 13-20: Interpreting the partial plots 2.

Outliers

Outliers (extreme scores; see Chapter 6) can have a major influence on your regression analysis and any conclusions you draw from it. The two main types of outliers are outliers by distance and outliers by influence, as illustrated in Figure 13-21. *Outliers by distance* are simply data points with large residuals. Check these outliers to ensure the data has been entered correctly. *Outliers by influence* (and they can often be the same data points) can inappropriately influence your regression line. These outliers are more problematic and you should consider removing these from your data set. Always check for both types of outliers.

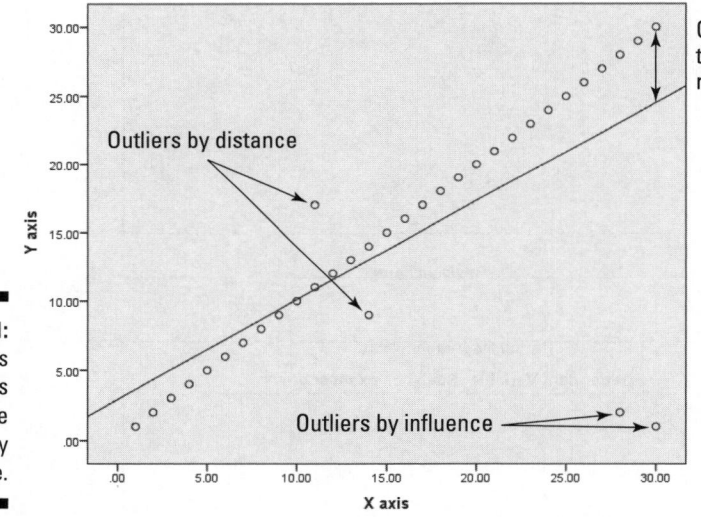

Figure 13-21: Examples of outliers by distance and by influence.

Outliers by distance

To check for outliers by distance open the regression window (Select Analyze, Regression, then Linear) then select the Statistics option button. This opens a second Statistics window. Select the Casewise diagnostics option and then Continue (see Figure 13-22). Finally, select OK on the regression window to produce a Casewise diagnostics table in the output file.

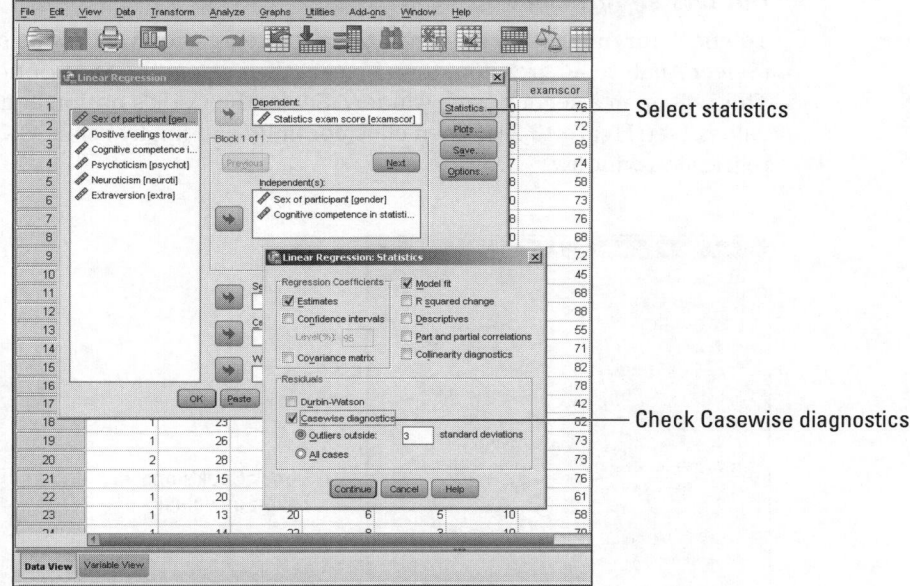

Figure 13-22:
Obtaining
the case-
wise
diagnostics
table.

Check Casewise diagnostics

The Casewise Diagnostics table displays any data points that are outliers by distance as in Figure 13-23. In this example participant 29 has been flagged as an outlier. They have a large standardised residual of 3.76. The actual statistics exam score the person achieved was 58 but according to the regression model their predicted exam score was 38.9.

Case Number	Std. Residual	Statistics exam score	Predicted Value	Residual
29	3.760	58	38.93	19.071

Figure 13-23:
Casewise
diagnostics
table

This table will display
any participants with
large residuals; in case
there was only one

Outliers by influence

To check for outliers by influence open the regression window as before (Select Analyze, Regression, then Linear) then select the Save option button. This will open a second Save window. Select the Cook's option and Leverage values (see Figure 13-24). Then click continue and finally select OK on the regression window.

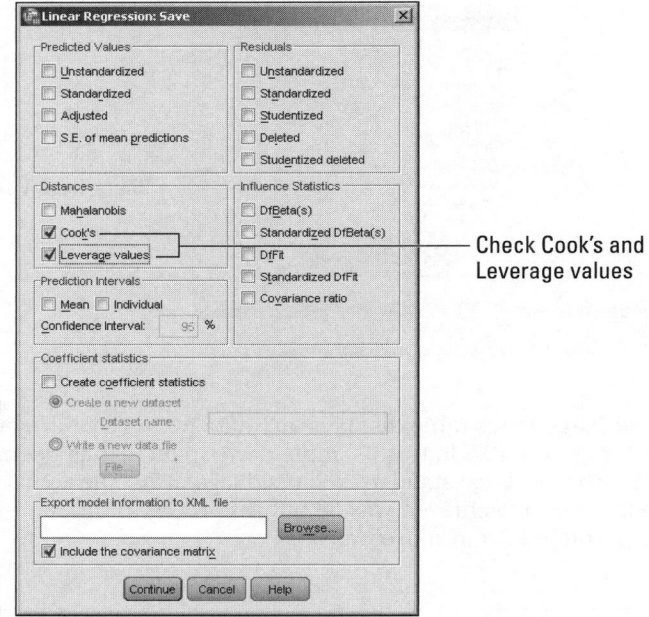

Figure 13-24: Obtaining Cook's distances and leverage values

Check Cook's and Leverage values

In the output window you see a new residual statistics table summarising descriptive statistics for various measures of residuals (Figure 13-25). To assess whether there are any outliers by influence you should check the figures for Cook's Distance and Centred Leverage Value.

Roughly speaking, a Cook's distance over 1 indicates an outlier by influence. If you check the maximum and minimum figures of Cook's distance for the data set you can see they range from 0 to 1.15. This tells you at least one data point is an outlier by influence, but you don't know what particular data points these are.

	Minimum	Maximum	Mean	Std. Deviation	N
Predicted Value	34.85	81.36	66.24	11.064	34
Std. Predicted Value	−2.837	1.367	.000	1.000	34
Standard Error of Predicted Value	1.331	3.864	2.222	.839	34
Adjusted Predicted Value	30.84	81.54	66.28	11.352	34
Residual	−12.275	19.071	.000	6.589	34
Std. Residual	−1.776	3.760	.000	.953	34
Stud. Residual	−2.143	3.293	−.003	1.058	34
Deleted Residual	−17.858	27.160	−.048	8.195	34
Stud. Deleted Residual	−2.289	4.052	.012	1.149	34
Mahal. Distance	.254	9.347	2.912	3.092	34
Cook's Distance	.000	1.150	.070	.216	34
Centered Leverage Value	.008	.283	.088	.094	34

a. Dependent Variable: Statistics exam score

Figure 13-25:
Residuals
statistics
table.

Check whether any Cook's
distance value exceeds 1.00

Check whether any leverage
value exceeds 3 times
its mean

A Centred Leverage Value greater than 3 times its mean may also be an outlier by influence. In this example the mean leverage value was 0.088 so any value over 0.264 (which is 3×0.088) is of concern. If you check the maximum and minimum figures of the leverage values for the data set you can see they range from 0.008 to 0.283. Because the maximum exceeds 0.264 this tells you at least one data point is an outlier by influence, but you don't know what particular data points these are.

Here's the clever bit. If you now look at your data file (not the output window) SPSS has created two new columns of Cook's distances and leverage values for each case or participant. You can now check to see which of these values exceed the cut-off values. You should check both Cook's distance and the Centered Leverage Values. In this example participant 29 is an outlier by influence (see Figure 13-26).

Check the new columns to see if any
figures exceed the cut-off values

	extra	examscor	COO_1	LEV_1
18	10	82	.02161	.04863
19	9	73	.00051	.04863
20	6	73	.00011	.09502
21	3	76	.00726	.01037
22	10	61	.00199	.00301
23	10	58	.00457	.01037
24	10	70	.00067	.00543
25	9	64	.04108	.09722
26	6	80	.00866	.01085
27	5	76	.00606	.00759
28	5	75	.00001	.09921
29	4	75	1.14587	.26518
30	5	73	.00093	.02326
31	10	72	.00415	.15610
32	10	66	.00008	.00301
33	10	72	.00047	.01849
34	10	69	.00047	.00759
35	9	79	.00714	.01085
36	9	25	.14308	.01085
37	10	58	.07826	.12858
38	10	56	.00716	.01037
39	9	66	.00052	.00797
40	4	78	.01044	.01037

Figure 13-26:
Checking
Cook's dis-
tance and
the leverage
value in
your data
file.

Multicollinearity

In most regression models the predictor variables will be correlated to some
degree. This is fine and it makes sense that similar predictor variables
should be correlated. However, predictor variables correlating very highly
suggests the variables are measuring similar things and you can't confidently
ascertain the unique influence of each predictor. If a predictor variable demonstrates *multicollinearity* (very high correlations with other predictors in
your model) it is best to remove it from your analysis.

To check for muliticollinearity open the regression window (Select Analyze,
Regression, then Linear) then select the Statistics option button. This opens
a second Statistics window. Select the Collinearity diagnostics option and
then Continue (see Figure 13-27). Finally select OK on the regression window.

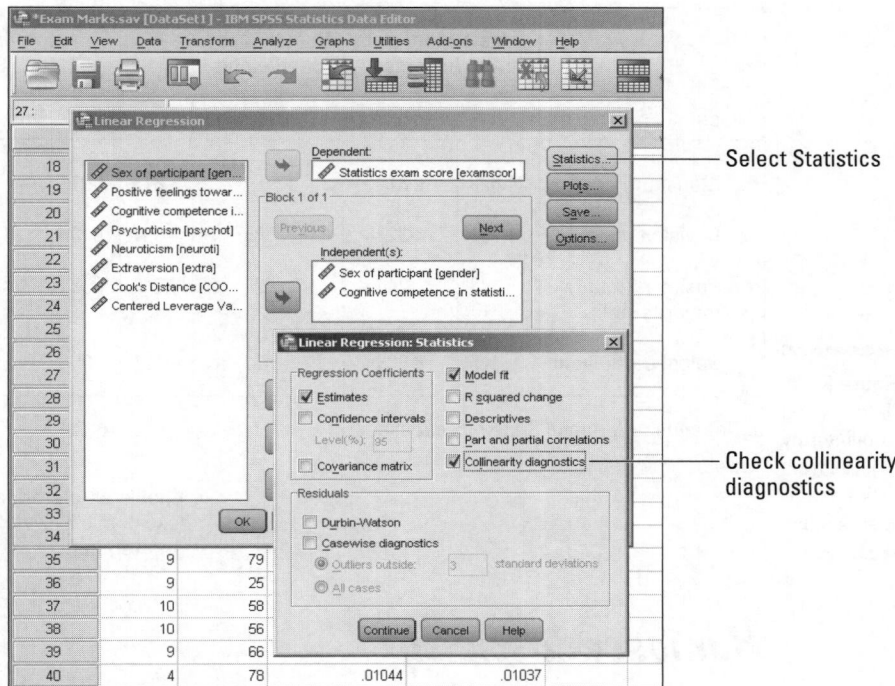

Select Statistics

Check collinearity diagnostics

Figure 13-27:
Obtaining
collinearity
figures

If you check your coefficients table in the output file you should notice there are two new columns at the end of the table (Figure 13-28). These columns display tolerance and VIF (Variance Inflation Factor) figures for each variable. These are measures of multicollinearity. It doesn't matter which one you check because they both do the same thing (in fact they are simply inverted versions of the each other: Tolerance = 1/VIF and VIF = 1/Tolerance). Using the tolerance values, a figure of 1 indicates that the predictor variable isn't correlated to the others and therefore has no multicollinearity. Lower tolerance values indicates a higher degree of multicollinearity; values below 0.2 indicate problematic multicollinearity. Higher VIF values indicates a higher degree of multicollinearity; values above 5 indicate problematic multicollinearity.

Model	Unstandardized Coefficients		Standardized Coefficients	t	Sig.	Collinearity Statistics	
	B	Std. Error	Beta			Tolerance	VIF
(Constant)	24.628	6.812		3.615	.001		
Revision hours	1.301	.322	.585	4.037	.000	.415	2.409
Positive Attitude towards stats	.548	.245	.325	2.242	.033	.415	2.410
Sex of participant	−.445	3.686	−.011	−.121	.905	.996	1.004

Figure 13-28:
Interpreting collinearity figures from the coefficients table.

a. Dependent Variable: Statistics exam score

Check for tolerance values less than 0.2 or VIF values greater than 5

Homoscedasticity

The residuals should be equally distributed right along the regression line (*homoscedasticity*). If the residuals aren't equally distributed for example, the residuals increase as the predicted values increase, this suggests there is something strange about the underlying distribution of the data and perhaps a linear regression isn't the appropriate analysis. You sometimes see this assumption called *absence of heteroscedasticity. Heteroscedasticity* simply means the residuals are unequally distributed and the assumption is violated.

To ensure the data meets the homoscedasticity assumption open the regression window as before (Select Analyze, Regression, then Linear) then select the Plots option button. This will open a second Plots window (see Figure 13-29). Draw a scatterplot by moving ZPRED (standardised predicted values) and ZRESID (standardised residual values) to the *y* and *x* axis (it doesn't really matter which way round they go).Then select continue and OK on the regression window.

You expect the residuals to be equally distributed in relation to the predicted value so you therefore expect to see no pattern in the scatterplot. If you see a random cloud of data points this means your data meets the assumption of homoscedasticity (Figure 13-30). If there is a clear pattern in your scatterplot this means your data violates this assumption. For example if your scatterplot was to illustrate a wedge shape this may indicate the residuals increase as the predicted values get increase (Figure 13-31). We realise that this is quite a subjective decision and one that can make students feel uncomfortable. If there is not a clear pattern in the scatterplot it normally means your data is fine and you haven't violated this assumption.

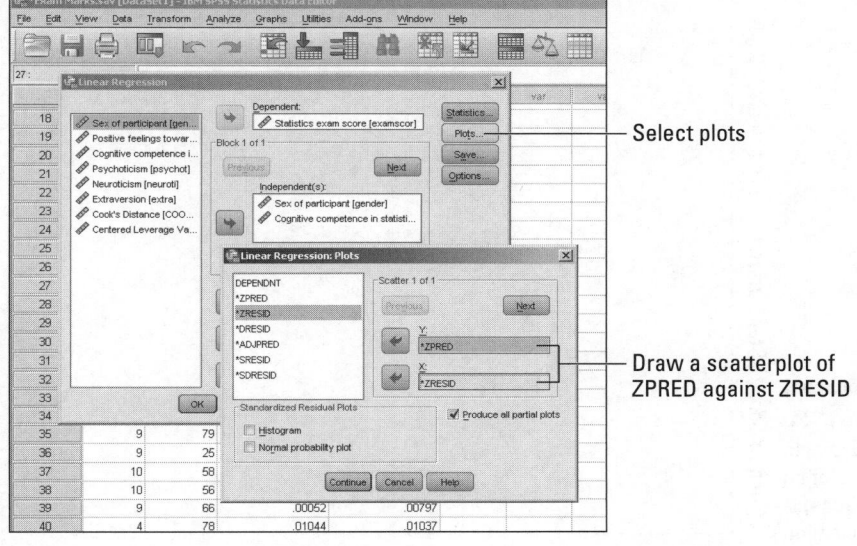

Figure 13-29:
Obtaining
a plot to
assess
homosce-
dasticity

Select plots

Draw a scatterplot of
ZPRED against ZRESID

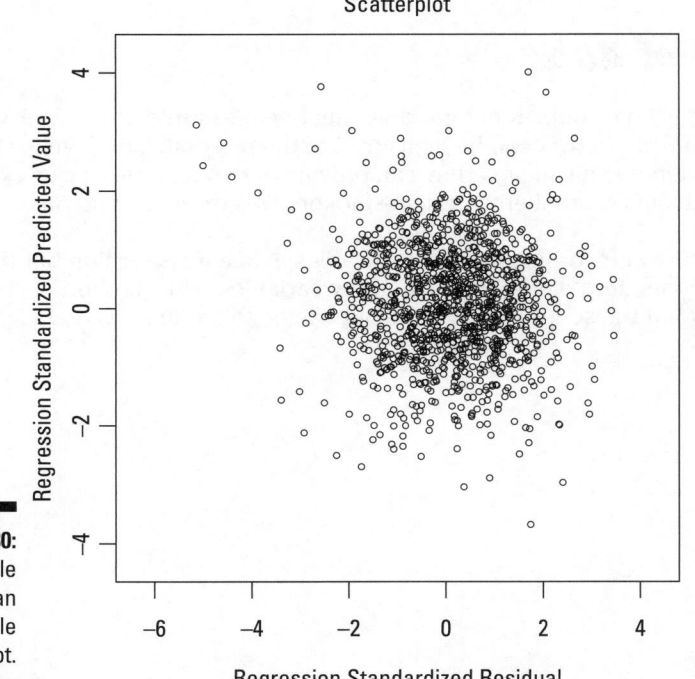

Figure 13-30:
Example
of an
acceptable
plot.

Scatterplot

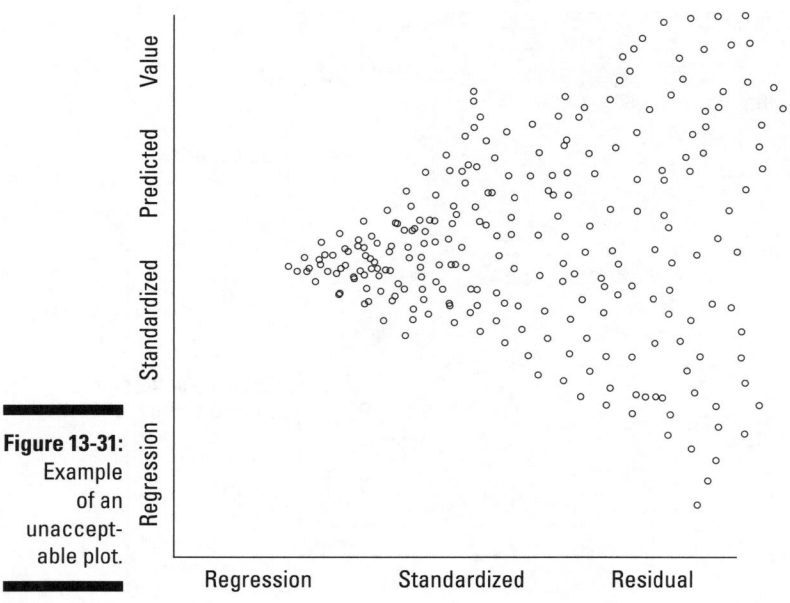

Figure 13-31:
Example of an unacceptable plot.

Type of data

Your criterion or dependent variable must be measured at the interval/ratio level. Your predictors can be measured at the interval/ratio level or they can be *dichotomous* this means they can only have two responses (for example, male and female, smokers and non-smokers, yes or no, and so on).

You can use categorical predictor variables in linear regression but they have to be recoded into dichotomous dummy variables. This method of recoding goes beyond the scope of this book but can be found in most advanced texts.

Chapter 14

Associations between Discrete Variables

. . . .

In This Chapter

▶ Examining associations between categorical variables using contingency tables

▶ Obtaining and interpreting the chi-square statistic

▶ Assessing strength of association between categorical variables using the odds ratio, phi or Cramer's V

▶ Obtaining and interpreting the McNemar test

. . . .

*1*n Chapter 2 we introduce you to *discrete variables*, sometimes called *categorical variables*, which are variables that contain separate and distinct categories. For example, whether or not a person has ever attended a psychologist for therapy is a discrete variable. Either a person has attended a psychologist for therapy or they haven't. Therefore, the variable 'attended a psychologist' has two categories – attended and not attended – so 'attended a psychologist' is a discrete (categorical) variable.

Sometimes you want to examine the association between two discrete variables, and this chapter examines approaches to doing that. We use this example through the chapter: you're conducting a research study to determine whether males or females are better at accurately recalling information – that is, do females have a better memory than males. You're interested in two variables – gender and whether information is recalled accurately. The first variable has two categories (male and female) and the second variable also has two categories (recalled or not).

Summarising Results in a Contingency Table

The simplest way to display the results of a study examining the association between two discrete variables is in the form of a *contingency table*, which presents the number of participants who fall into each category of your discrete variables. An example is provided in Table 14-1.

In your research study on whether males or females are better at accurately recalling information, you ask 150 participants (70 males and 80 females) to listen to a telephone number and then repeat it back to you after 20 minutes has elapsed. You then record whether each participant recalls the number accurately or not. You can use a contingency table to summarise your results.

In this case your contingency table represents the results from a study with two variables, both of which have two categories. We refer to this table as a 2×2 table. If one of the variables had 3 categories and the other variable had 2 categories, we would have a 3×2 table. If both variables had 3 categories we would have a 3×3 table and so on.

Observed frequencies in contingency tables

Table 14-1 shows the contingency table for the 150 participants from the study.

Table 14-1	Contingency Table for Gender and Accurate Recall of Telephone Number		
	Male	*Female*	*Row Totals*
Recalled accurately	39	60	99
Not recalled accurately	31	20	51
Column totals	*70*	*80*	*150*

The numbers in the contingency table are *observed frequencies*: they indicate the number of people that were observed to be in that category. For example, the number 39 at the top left of the table is under the heading 'male' (the column heading) and in line with the heading 'recalled accurately' (the row heading). This means that 39 of the people who recalled the number accurately were male.

The table also contains row and column totals. These provide you with overall information about one of the variables. For example, if you look at the row totals you see that the first value is 99. This is the total number of people in that row – the total number of people who accurately recalled the number. From this information you can see that more people accurately recalled the number than not, but you want to know whether males or females were better at doing this, so you need more information beyond the observed frequencies. One of the things you can do to help with this is to percentage the table, and we show you how in the next section.

Percentaging a contingency table

You can percentage a contingency table in one of two ways:

✔ Percentage based on row totals

✔ Percentage based on column totals

The way you choose to percentage the table affects the interpretations that you make about the information in the table.

The following sections look at an example of each in turn.

Percentages based on the row totals

Table 14-2 illustrates what Table 14-1 looks like when you percentage it based on the row totals. We include the observed frequencies in the table in parentheses.

Table 14-2   Contingency Table Percentaged on the Row Totals

	Male	*Female*	*Row Totals*
Recalled accurately	39.4% (39)	60.6% (60)	100% (99)
Not recalled accurately	60.8% (31)	39.2% (20)	100% (51)
Column totals	*(70)*	*(80)*	*(150)*

Percentaging based on the row total works on the premise that each row total is equivalent to 100 per cent and then you can work out what percentage of this total is in each category within that row. For example, look at the row in Table 14-2 that's headed 'recalled accurately'. There are 99 participants in this row – 39 are male and 60 are female. To convert the numbers of males and females in the row into percentages, you divide the observed frequency by the row total. So, for females, the percentage value is obtained by: 60/99 = 60.6 per cent.

When you percentage a table based on row totals then you can interpret the percentages by comparing between the columns within a row. For example, from the percentages in the first row you can say that of those who recalled the number accurately, 39.4 per cent were male and 60.6 per cent were female. From the percentages in the second row you can say that of those who didn't recall the number accurately 60.8 per cent were male and 39.2 per cent were female.

This might provide you with the information you need, but in this case it doesn't. You want to know whether any difference exists between males and females in terms of accurate recall. Given the way this table is structured, it's probably better to percentage the table based on column totals (see the next section).

Percentages based on the column totals

Table 14-3 illustrates what Table 14-1 looks like when you percentage it based on the column totals. We include the observed frequencies in the table in parentheses.

Table 14-3   Contingency Table Percentaged on the Column Totals

	Male	*Female*	*Row Totals*
Recalled accurately	55.7% (39)	75% (60)	(99)
Not recalled accurately	44.3% (31)	25% (20)	(51)
Column totals	*100% (70)*	*100% (80)*	*(150)*

Percentaging based on the column total works on the premise that each column total is equivalent to 100 per cent and then you can work out what percentage of this total is in each category within that column. For example, look at the column in Table 14-3 which is headed 'male'. There are 70 participants in this row – 39 recalled the number accurately and 31 did not. To convert the numbers in the column into percentages, you divide the observed frequency by the column total. So, for males who recalled the number accurately the percentage value is obtained by: 39/70 = 55.7%.

As with percentaging a table based on row totals, you can interpret the percentages by comparing between the rows within a column. For example, from the percentages in the first column in Table 14-3 you can say that of the males in the study, 55.7 per cent recalled the number accurately and 44.3 per cent didn't. From the percentages in the second column you can say that among the females in the study, 75 per cent recalled the number accurately and 25 per cent didn't.

This information seems to be more directly relevant to the question of interest and illustrates that females performed better on the recall task than males in this study.

The method of percentaging a table to provide the most useful information depends on how the table is constructed: which variable is along the top (columns) and which variable is down the side (rows). Often you want both pieces of information, so you might want to percentage the table based on row totals and then based on column totals and choose which one is most useful, or report both, if both sets of information are useful.

Obtaining contingency tables in SPSS

In SPSS, you create contingency tables through the crosstabulation procedure.

1. **Go to the Analyze menu in SPSS, then choose 'Descriptive Statistics' and then choose 'Crosstabs' (see Figure 14-1).**

2. **In the Crosstabs window, move one of the variables into the box headed 'Row(s)' and the other variable into the box headed 'Column(s)'.**

   It doesn't matter which variable you allocate to the rows and which you allocate to columns – the choice is based on how you want the table to be presented. If you want the table to look like Table 14-1 then you move gender into the columns box and recall into the rows box (see Figure 14-2).

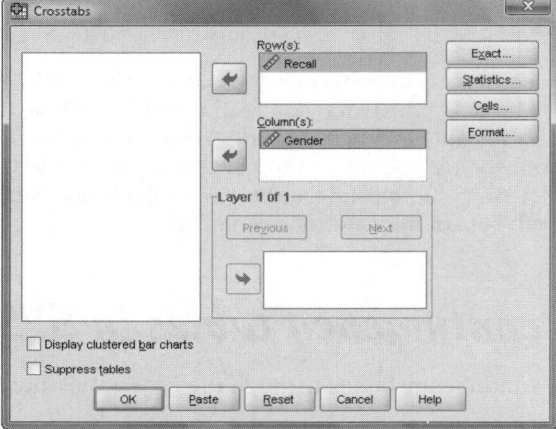

Figure 14-2:
Selecting
the vari-
ables to be
presented
in a contin-
gency table.

3. **To obtain percentages in the contingency table click on the Cells button in the Crosstabs window. This opens another window in which you can choose what information you want presented in the contingency table.**

   When this window opens you notice that observed frequencies are already chosen by default. Below this you notice a list headed 'Percentages'. Under this list you can choose percentages based on row totals, by ticking the box next to the word 'Row', and percentages based on column totals, by ticking the box next to the word 'Column' (see Figure 14-3).

Figure 14-4 shows the output you obtain. You can see that the observed frequencies are referred to as the 'Count', the percentages based on row totals are referred to as '% within Recall', and the percentages based on column totals are referred to as '% within Gender'. They're all presented together – like a combination of Tables 14-1, 14-2 and 14-3.

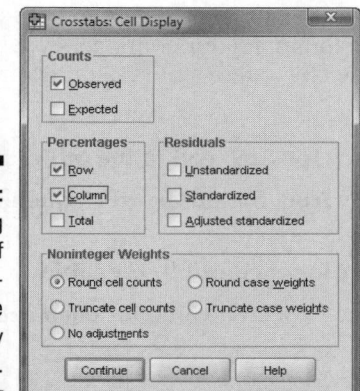

Figure 14-3: Choosing ways of percentaging the contingency table.

Figure 14-4: A contingency table produced by SPSS, with percentages based on row totals and based on column totals.

Recall * Gender Crosstabulation

			Gender		Total
			Male	Female	
Recall	Recalled Accurately	Count	39	60	99
		% within Recall	39.4%	60.6%	100.0%
		% within Gender	55.7%	75.0%	66.0%
	Not Recalled Accurately	Count	31	20	51
		% within Recall	60.8%	39.2%	100.0%
		% within Gender	44.3%	25.0%	34.0%
Total		Count	70	80	150
		% within Recall	46.7%	53.3%	100.0%
		% within Gender	100.0%	100.0%	100.0%

Calculating Chi-Square

Although percentaging a contingency table (which we show you how to do in the previous section) provides you with information about the association between the two variables, it doesn't tell you whether this association is larger than you'd expect by chance. For example, from Table 14-3 you can tell that females performed better on the recall task than males, but is the difference in performance likely to be due to chance or not? If it's simply a chance finding, you conclude that no association exists between the variables gender and recall ability.

The chi-square statistic (χ^2) is a statistic that you calculate to help you determine the likelihood of the association found in your contingency table having occurred by chance. You calculate the chi-square statistic for a contingency table as follows:

1. **Calculate the expected frequency for each cell in the table.**

2. **Subtract the expected frequency from the observed frequency for each cell in the table.**

3. **Square the value found at Step 2 for each cell in the table.**

4. **Divide the result of Step 3 by the expected value for each cell in the table.**

5. **Sum the results of Step 4.**

Expected frequencies

One of the crucial bits of information you need to calculate the chi-square statistic is the expected frequency. The *expected frequencies* are the values that you expect to find in the contingency table if no association exists between the two variables. Table 14-4 presents the expected frequencies for Table 14-1.

Table 14-4	Contingency Table with Expected Frequencies (and Observed Frequencies)		
	Male	*Female*	*Row Totals*
Recalled accurately	46.2 (39)	52.8 (60)	99
Not recalled accurately	23.8 (31)	27.2 (20)	51
Column Totals	*70*	*80*	*150*

You obtain expected frequencies by multiplying the row total that corresponds with a category by the column total that corresponds with this category and then dividing the result by the grand total:

(row total × column total) ÷ grand total

For example, look at the category of males who recalled the number accurately.

1. **Divide row total by grand total.**

   The row total corresponding to this category is 99. The grand total is the number in the bottom right hand corner of the table – it is the total sample size – in this case 150. So the calculation is 99 divided by 150, which equals 0.66. This is the proportion of participants who recalled the number accurately.

2. **Multiply the result by the column total.**

   The column total corresponding to this category is 70. So, 0.66 multiplied by 70 equals 46.2.

Therefore, this category has an expected frequency of 46.2.

Calculating chi-square

Table 14-4 presents the expected frequencies for a contingency table. The next step in calculating chi-square is to subtract these expected frequencies from the observed frequency. If you do this for Table 14-4, you get the results presented in Table 14-5.

Table 14-5	Contingency Table with Observed Minus Expected Frequencies	
	Male	*Female*
Recalled accurately	39 − 46.2 = −7.2	60 − 52.8 = 7.2
Not recalled accurately	31 − 23.8 = 7.2	20 − 27.2 = −7.2

The next step is to square the values obtained in Table 14-5 and then divide the result by the expected value. If you square (multiply the value by itself) the values obtained in Table 14-5, the result in each cell is 51.84. If you divide this number by the expected value in each cell, you get a result as presented in Table 14-6.

Table 14-6	Contingency with Observed Minus Expected Frequencies Squared and Divided by the Expected Frequencies	
	Male	*Female*
Recalled accurately	51.84 / 46.2 = 1.12	51.84 / 52.8 = 0.98
Not recalled accurately	51.84 / 23.8 = 2.18	51.84 / 27.2 = 1.91

Finally, you add up the values obtained in Table 14-6: 1.12 + 0.98 + 2.18 + 1.91 = 6.19. So the chi-square statistic is 6.19.

Obtaining chi-square in SPSS

In SPSS, you get the chi-square statistic for a contingency table through the 'crosstabulation' procedure. Follow the steps in the earlier 'Obtaining contingency tables in SPSS', but in Step 3 click on the 'Statistics' button in the Crosstabs window. This opens another window in which you can obtain the chi-square statistic by ticking the box next to the word 'Chi-Square' (see Figure 14-5).

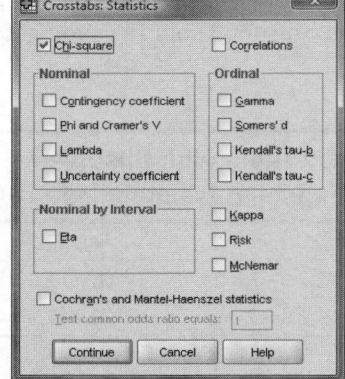

Figure 14-5: Obtaining chi-square for a contingency table.

Figure 14-6 shows the output you obtain.

Figure 14-6: Chi-square results as presented by SPSS.

Chi-Square Tests

	Value	df	Asymp. Sig. (2-sided)	Exact Sig. (2-sided)	Exact Sig. (1-sided)
Pearson Chi-Square	6.188[a]	1	.013		
Continuity Correction[b]	5.358	1	.021		
Likelihood Ratio	6.213	1	.013		
Fisher's Exact Test				.016	.010
Linear-by-Linear Association	6.147	1	.013		
N of Valid Cases	150				

a. 0 cells (.0%) have expected count less than 5. The minimum expected count is 23.80.

b. Computed only for a 2x2 table

Interpreting the output from chi-square in SPSS

Figure 14-6 contains more information than just the chi-square result, so it is worth examining all the information in this figure and trying to make sense of it.

There are two pieces of information in Figure 14-6 which are provided by SPSS only when the contingency table has 2 rows and 2 columns (a 2 × 2 table), that is, when each variable only has 2 categories. These are the Continuity Correction and the Fisher's Exact test. In cases where your contingency table being analysed by chi-square has either more than two rows or more than two columns of data then these bits of information will not be generated because they're not relevant.

Pearson chi-square

This row in the output table in Figure 14-6 contains the chi-square statistic calculated as in the previous section. The value of the chi-square statistic is under the heading 'Value'. From the figure, you can see that SPSS calculated the chi-square statistic to be 6.188. In the section examining the calculation of chi-square in this chapter, we calculated the chi-square statistic to be 6.19 for this table. The results are just about the same, but SPSS is a little more accurate than our calculations.

This row also contains a '*df*' value and an 'Asymp Sig (2-sided)' value:

- **df value:** the degrees of freedom for the chi-square statistic. The degrees of freedom are calculated as follows:

   (number of rows in the table – 1) × (number of columns in the table – 1).

   The degrees of freedom allow you to work out the significance value for the chi-square statistic. However, as SPSS always provides the significance value for you, you don't need to use the degrees of freedom much.

- **Asymp Sig (2-sided):** The significance value for the chi-squared statistic. This stands for asymptotic significance and the 2-sided bit indicates that a two-tailed hypothesis is being tested (see Chapter 8 for a discussion of two-tailed hypotheses). This value tells you the probability of finding this chi-square value if the null hypothesis is true (see Chapter 8 for a discussion of testing the null hypothesis). Basically, if this value is less than 0.05 then you reject the null hypothesis. In other words, if this value is less than 0.05, you conclude that there is a statistically significant association between the two variables. In Figure 14-6 the significance value for the chi-square statistic is 0.013. Therefore, you can conclude that you have a statistically significant association between gender and ability to recall the number accurately.

Continuity correction

Yates's *continuity correction* is a slight adjustment made to the calculation of the chi-square statistic when the chi-square statistic is being calculated for a contingency table with 2 rows and 2 columns only.

In the five steps for calculating chi-square that we provide at the beginning of this section on chi-square, Yates's continuity correction is applied at Step 2. In the continuity correction you change Step 2 slightly to become: Subtract the expected frequency from the observed frequency for each cell in the table and then remove any negative signs from the result and then subtract 0.5 from each result. To calculate chi-square, you then carry on with the remaining steps.

The continuity correction reduces the likelihood of you finding a statistically significant result (compared to the Pearson chi-square result), so it is probably better to use it when it is provided by SPSS, to err on the side of caution. Use the continuity correction instead of the Pearson chi-square result – you don't report both.

Likelihood ratio

The *likelihood ratio* value provided by SPSS in Figure 14-6 is an alternative chi-square statistic. It is a chi-square statistic but calculated using a different formula from the Pearson chi-square statistic. In practice there shouldn't be much difference between the likelihood ratio value and the Pearson chi-square value, and you interpret them in the same way. For contingency tables such as those presented in this chapter, the likelihood ratio test is rarely used.

Fisher's exact test

The *Fisher's exact test* is a slight adjustment made to the significance value accompanying the Pearson chi-square statistic when the chi-square statistic is being calculated for a contingency table with 2 rows and 2 columns only. Fisher's exact test is a more accurate calculation of the level of significance associated with chi-square when there are small sample sizes in any of the cells in the table. Specifically, you use Fisher's exact test when the expected frequency of any cell in the table is less than 5.

As you see in Figure 14-6, SPSS provides a footnote to the output table that tells you the number of cells that have an expected frequency less than 5. If this footnote indicates that any cell in a table with 2 rows and 2 columns has an expected frequency less than 5 then don't report the significance value associated with the Pearson chi-square. Instead, report the Pearson chi-square value but report the significance value provided by the Fisher's exact test. This significance value is interpreted in the same way as the value associated with the Pearson chi-square.

You also notice in Figure 14-6 that the Fisher's exact test provides two significance values – 'Exact Sig (2-sided)' and 'Exact Sig (1-sided)'. These values refer to two-tailed and one-tailed hypotheses respectively (see Chapter 8). For example, you might use this test to test the two-tailed hypothesis 'there will be an association between gender and accurate recall'. Or, you could specify a one-tailed hypothesis: 'Females will perform better on the test of recall than males'. Your knowledge of the literature in the area determines which hypothesis you specify, and the hypothesis you specify determines the significance result you report.

Make sure you specify the hypothesis before you collect the data. Turn to Chapter 8 for more on hypothesis testing.

Linear-by-linear association

A *linear-by-linear association* is generated by SPSS only when both the variables in the analysis are entered as numeric variables (see Chapter 3 for a discussion of labelling variables as numeric in SPSS). When both variables are numeric then SPSS assumes that they could both be measured at the ordinal level (see Chapter 2 for levels of measurement). Of course, this isn't necessarily the case. Both variables can be entered as numeric variables and not be measured at the ordinal level. If your variables are not measured at the ordinal level, then ignore the linear-by-linear association.

Where you have two ordinal variables (or one ordinal variable and one dichotomous variable), then the linear-by-linear association tests whether there is a linear association between the two variables. This is different from the other chi-square values in the table. They simply test whether there is an association between the variables, not a linear one. In other words, the linear-by-linear association asks whether the values in one variable increase in line with values on the other variable. This is a bit like a correlation coefficient for ordinal variables (see Chapter 12).

Writing up the results of a chi-square analysis

When reporting the results of statistical analyses, check whether specific guidelines inform how you should present the statistical findings. For example, if you're preparing a report for your course, check the course guidelines about how information should be presented. Usually, psychologists expect you to report the results of your statistical analyses using the guidelines provided in the American Psychological Association (APA) Publication Manual.

When reporting chi-square results, the APA manual suggests that you report the chi-square value rounded to 2 decimal places, with the sample size and degrees of freedom in parentheses, followed by the significance level. Taking the Pearson chi-square value reported in Figure 14-6, you report the result as follows:

> In the study, there was a statistically significant association between gender and ability to accurately recall the telephone number, $\chi^2(1, N = 150) = 6.19, p = .01$.

Given that the results in Figure 14-6 were obtained from a 2×2 table and given that none of the expected frequencies are less than 5, you're best reporting the chi-square value after the continuity correction has been applied. Therefore, your statement of results becomes:

> In the study, there was a statistically significant association between gender and ability to accurately recall the telephone number, $\chi^2(1, N = 150) = 5.36, p = .02$.

Understanding the assumptions of chi-square analysis

Computers make your life easier because they allow you to do complex calculations very quickly. So, you can calculate the chi-square statistic in a matter of seconds, whereas it takes considerably longer to calculate chi-square manually. The problem with computers, however, is that they give you an answer even when it's nonsensical. So, when conducting statistical analyses, you need to be aware of a number of conditions (or assumptions) that need to be met before you can apply the result produced by the computer.

For chi-square, these are the conditions that must be met before you should be convinced about the result:

- ✔ Both variables should be categorical (see Chapter 2 for a description of categorical variables).
- ✔ The categories should be mutually exclusive (see Chapter 7 for a description of mutually exclusive events).
- ✔ The expected frequency of any cell in the contingency table shouldn't be less than 1.
- ✔ More than 80 per cent of the cells in the contingency table should have an expected frequency of at least 5.

If you find that your data doesn't meet the final condition, and your table has only two rows and two columns of data, then you can use the Fisher's exact test as an alternative to the significance value associated with the chi-square statistic.

Measuring the Strength of Association between Two Variables

The chi-square statistic (which we discuss in the previous section) helps you to determine whether a statistically significant association exists between two categorical variables. However, chi-square doesn't provide you with any information about the strength of this association. In other words, the chi-square statistic simply tells you whether an association exists or not – it doesn't tell you how strong or weak this association is.

Statistics related to chi-square that provide information about the strength of an association between categorical variables are the odds ratio, phi and Cramer's V. These are types of effect size statistics (see Chapter 11 for a discussion of effect size).

Looking at the odds ratio

We discuss the concept of odds in Chapter 7. *Odds* are a way of conveying information about the likelihood of something happening (a bit like probability – see Chapter 7). An *odds ratio* is the likelihood of something happening compared to the likelihood of something else happening. For example, in the previous section we look at the calculation of chi-square for the contingency table presented in Table 14-1. Table 14-7 presents the odds for each column of this contingency table.

Table 14-7	Contingency Table with Odds Based on the Columns	
	Male	*Female*
Recalled accurately	39	60
Not recalled accurately	31	20
Odds	*39 / 31 = 1.26*	*60 / 20 = 3*

Table 14-7 tells you that for males the odds of accurately recalling the telephone number are 1.26, whereas for females the odds of accurately recalling the telephone number are 3. This shows that females are more likely to recall the number accurately than males, but how much more likely?

This is what the odds ratio tells you. The odds ratio is one odds divided by the other. You can decide which way round to divide the odds depending on what conclusions you want to make. For example, if you want to know how much better females are at recalling the number than males then you divide the female odds by the male odds. This gives you $3 \div 1.26 = 2.38$. If you want to know how much better males are at recalling the number than females then you divide the male odds by the female odds. This gives you $1.26 \div 3 = 0.42$.

An odds ratio of 1 means no association exists between the two variables. The farther away from 1 in either direction, the stronger the association.

Odds ratios less than 1 are more difficult to interpret, so when calculating an odds ratio calculate it in such a way that you get a value larger than 1. So, in the example, you would divide the female odds by the male odds rather than the other way round. You might need to calculate the odds both ways, as in the example, and then choose the one that results in an odds ratio greater than one. This choice will influence the way you word your interpretation.

In the example, it's easier to interpret the odds ratio of females compared to males, which is 2.38. This means that if you're female then the odds of you being able to recall the number accurately are 2.38 times greater than if you're male.

An odds ratio is a statistic that is most appropriate for a contingency table with two rows and two columns of data only (a 2×2 table).

Phi and Cramer's V Coefficients

Chi-square (see the earlier section Calculating Chi-square') doesn't provide any information about the strength of an association between two variables because it's influenced by the sample size in the analysis: the larger the sample size, the larger the chi-square statistic. The *phi coefficient* provides a measure of the strength of the association between two variables by using chi-square but taking account of the sample size.

You calculate the phi coefficient by dividing the chi-square value by the sample size and then taking the square root of the result. For example, in the previous section the chi-square result obtained for the contingency table was 6.19, based on a sample size of 150. To obtain the phi coefficient, you divide 6.19 by 150: $6.19 \div 150 = 0.041$. Then take the square root of this result, which is 0.203. This is the phi coefficient.

The phi coefficient ranges from 0 to 1, with 0 indicating no association between the two variables and 1 indicating perfect association. Therefore, the further the phi coefficient is from 0, the stronger the association between the two variables in the contingency table.

A phi coefficient is a statistic that is most appropriate for a contingency table with two rows and two columns of data only (a 2×2 table).

Cramer's V is similar to the phi coefficient, but it can be used for contingency tables which have more than two rows or more than two columns of data. When Cramer's V is used in a 2×2 table, it gives the same value as the phi coefficient. You interpret Cramer's V in the same way as you interpret the phi coefficient.

Obtaining odds ratio, phi coefficient and Cramer's V in SPSS

In SPSS, you find the odds ratio, phi coefficient and Cramer's V statistics through the crosstabulation procedure. Follow the steps in the earlier 'Obtaining chi-square tables in SPSS', but in the Statistics window (see Figure 14-5) tick the box next to 'Phi and Cramer's V' to obtain the phi coefficient and Cramer's V statistics, and tick the box next to 'Cochran's and Mantel-Haenszel statistics' to get the odds ratio.

Figure 14-7 shows the output you obtain for the phi coefficient and Cramer's V. You notice that in Figure 14-7 the phi coefficient is a negative value, which is impossible based on the information already provided about the phi coefficient. This is because in SPSS the phi coefficient is actually provided by calculating a pearson correlation coefficient on the variables (see Chapter 12 for a discussion of correlation coefficients). Although this makes sense, and gives you the same result as the calculation for phi, it allows negative values. You can simply ignore the negative value and report the result of 0.203.

Figure 14-7:
Phi coefficient and Cramer's V results as presented by SPSS.

Symmetric Measures

		Value	Approx. Sig.
Nominal by Nominal	Phi	-.203	.013
	Cramer's V	.203	.013
N of Valid Cases		150	

Figure 14-8 shows the output you obtain for the odds ratio. You get other tables in your output file in addition to the one presented in Figure 14-8, but you can ignore the others. In Figure 14-8 the odds ratio is the first value presented – labelled the 'Estimate'. Notice that this is a value less than 1, which is difficult to interpret as we mention in the earlier section 'Looking at the odds ratio'. This is because SPSS chooses which way to work out the odds ratio and it always takes the odds for the first category and divide by the odds for the second category (in this case the odds for males divided by females). You need to reverse the numbers attributed to males and females in your data sheet to allow SPSS to work out the odds ratio which is easier to interpret (greater than 1).

An alternative, and simpler way of converting the odds ratio provided by SPSS into the one you want is to divide 1 by the odds ratio: 1 ÷ 0.42 = 2.38. This provides you with an odds ratio that's easy to interpret, but you need to remember which category it refers to. This can all be a bit confusing and sometimes it is easier to work out the odds ratio manually, so that you know exactly how the result was obtained!

Mantel-Haenszel Common Odds Ratio Estimate

Estimate			.419
ln(Estimate)			-.869
Std. Error of ln(Estimate)			.353
Asymp. Sig. (2-sided)			.014
Asymp. 95% Confidence Interval	Common Odds Ratio	Lower Bound	.210
		Upper Bound	.838
	ln(Common Odds Ratio)	Lower Bound	-1.561
		Upper Bound	-.177

Figure 14-8: Odds ratio as presented by SPSS.

The Mantel-Haenszel common odds ratio estimate is asymptotically normally distributed under the common odds ratio of 1.000 assumption. So is the natural log of the estimate.

Using the McNemar Test

The McNemar test is a form of a chi-square (see the earlier section 'Calculating the Chi-square') that you use when you have a contingency table with 2 rows and 2 columns of data that represent changes over time. For example, say you conduct a research study to examine the power of advertisements. In the study you ask 100 people whether they would consider buying a particular soft drink within the next 24 hours (they answer yes or no). They watch an advertisement for this drink and you then ask them a second time whether they would consider buying the drink within the next 24 hours. The results of the study can be presented in a contingency table such as Table 14-8.

Table 14-8	Contingency Table Displaying Changes in Intention to Purchase Drink Before and After Watching the Advertisement	
	Before watching the advertisement	
After watching the advertisement	**Yes**	**No**
Yes	60	15
No	5	20

Table 14-8 shows that 80 out of the 100 people didn't change their mind after watching the advertisement (60 said yes at both times and 20 said no at both times). The McNemar test tests whether the proportion of people who change their minds is statistically significant – that is, whether the advertisement has had a statistically significant effect on the decision of the participants.

Calculating the McNemar test

The McNemar test focuses on the people who change between the two time points. You calculate the chi-square value as follows:

1. **Subtract the number of people who change in one direction from the number of people who change in the opposite direction.**

2. **Ignore any negative value obtained in Step 1 and then subtract 1 from this result.**

3. **Square the result from Step 2.**

4. **Divide the result of Step 3 by the total number of people who changed.**

For example, for the data presented in Table 14-8, the calculation of the chi-square value for the McNemar test is:

1. $5 - 15 = -10$
2. $10 - 1 = 9$
3. $9 \times 9 = 81$
4. $81 \div 20 = 4.05$

The chi-square value for the McNemar test in this example is 4.05.

Obtaining a McNemar test in SPSS

In SPSS, you find the McNemar test as follows.

1. **Go to the Analyze menu in SPSS, then choose 'Nonparametric Tests' (in some versions of SPSS you then need to choose 'Legacy Dialogs') and then choose '2 Related Samples' (see Figure 14-9).**

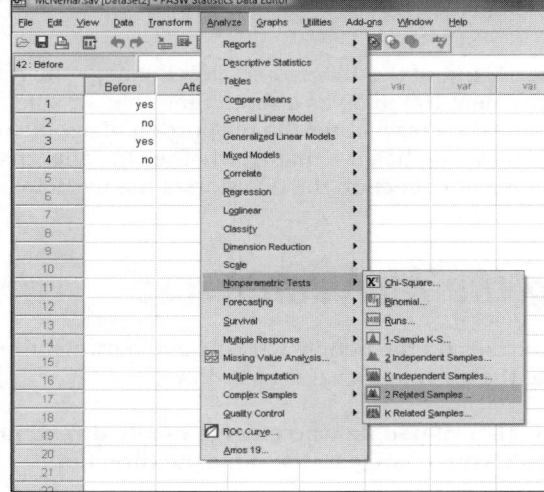

Figure 14-9:
Choosing
the
McNemar
test in
SPSS.

2. **In the two related samples tests window, move the two variables representing the results before the intervention (in this case before the advertisement) and the results after the intervention to the box headed 'Test Pairs'.**

3. **Tick the box next to 'McNemar' under the list headed 'Test Type'(see Figure 14-10).**

Figure 14-11 shows the output you obtain. This output contains a contingency table the same as Table 14-8 and the McNemar test. Notice that SPSS doesn't provide a chi-square value for the McNemar test, only the significance value.

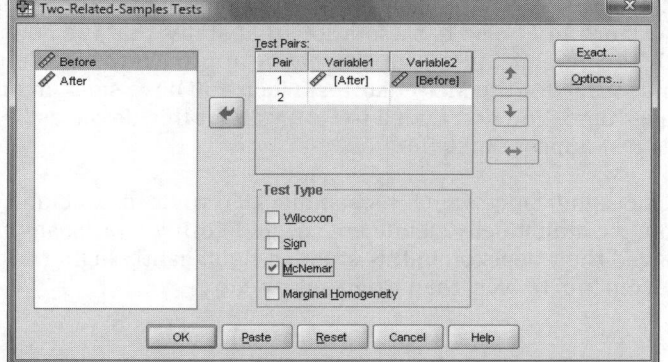

Figure 14-10:
Selecting
the vari-
ables to be
included in
a McNemar
test.

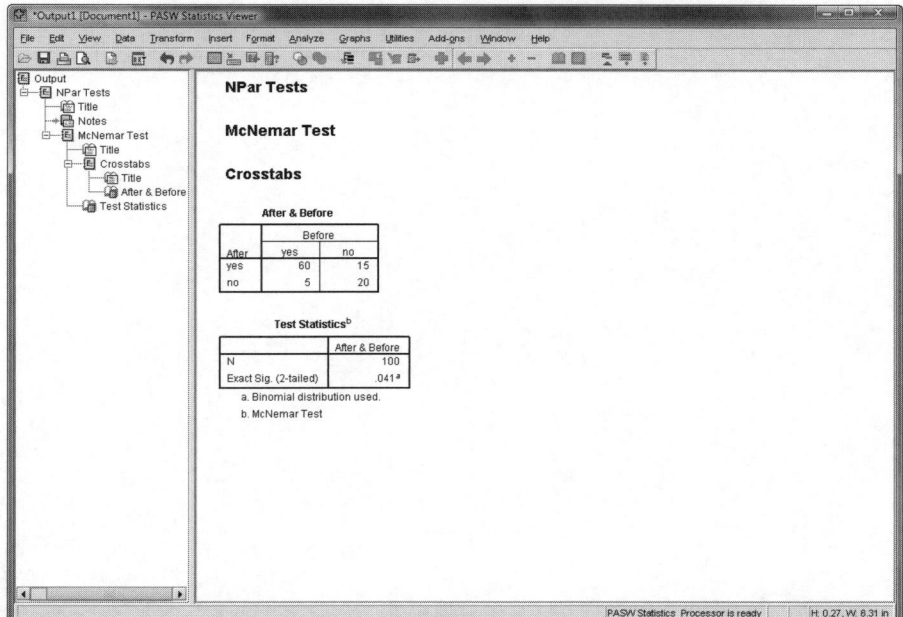

Figure 14-11:
A McNemar
test as pro-
duced by
SPSS.

Figure 14-11 indicates that the significance value is 0.041. The output presented in Figure 14-11 also has a footnote that states that the binomial test was used. The binomial test is an alternative approach to calculating the significance value for the McNemar test when you have small numbers who change over time. You don't need to worry about this detail, as SPSS will apply this test appropriately for you.

Because the significance value is less than 0.05, you can conclude that you've found a statistically significant result. In other words, among those who changed their decision in this study, a significantly higher proportion changed from 'no' to 'yes' than from 'yes' to 'no'.

Part IV
Analysing Independent Groups Research Designs

"I've just found out why I'm bigger than you, dad — It's called Linear Regression."

In this part . . .

Part IV of the book explains the inferential statistics that examine differences between two or more independent groups. We explain what's involved in independent groups design and then go on to address each of the most important statistical tests: Independent *t*-test, Mann–Whitney test and Analysis of Variance (ANOVA). For each technique we offer a clear explanation, followed by instructions on how to perform the analysis in SPSS, how to interpret the subsequent output and how to write up your results coherently.

Chapter 15

Independent *t*-tests and Mann–Whitney Tests

. . . .

In This Chapter

▶ Understanding Independent Groups Design

▶ Obtaining and interpreting an Independent *t*-test

▶ Obtaining and interpreting a Mann–Whitney test

. . . .

*I*ndependent groups design refers to any study where you look for a difference between separate groups of people. For example, if you want to investigate the effect of watching different types of film on positive mood you could test the mood of one group of people after watching a comedy film and then test the mood of a completely separate group of people after they watch a horror film. Your hypothesis is that participants who watched a comedy film would have a significantly higher mood scores than those participants who watched a horror film. In this example there are two levels of the independent variable (and therefore two groups of people) which was type of film watched and the dependent variable is positive mood (we discuss variables in Chapter 2).

If you are comparing the differences between two independent groups then the independent *t*-test or the Mann–Whitney test are the most appropriate statistics to use. The independent *t*-test is a parametric test which means it is a more powerful statistic but is based on certain assumptions that must be met otherwise the results may be inaccurate. The Mann–Whitney test has less stringent assumptions. Both these tests are explained in this chapter. If you are interested in comparing more than two groups, for example separate groups that watched a comedy, a horror and a documentary, then you need to start reading Chapter 16.

Understanding Independent Groups Design

The inferential statistics we discuss in this book are used to analyse data from three types of psychological studies: correlational design, independent groups design and repeated measures design. The first type of study, *correlational design*, is where you examine the relationships between existing variables as they occur naturally; the data from these studies is typically analysed using correlations or regressions and is covered in Part III of the book. The second two types of studies are often called experimental designs as they may involve manipulating the independent variable (see Chapter 2 for a re-cap on independent variables). For example, if you want to see if cognitive behavioural therapy (CBT) was effective in treating depression after bereavement you would manipulate the amount of CBT individuals experienced to see if this influenced depression levels. There are two designs you could use to test this hypothesis. In the first design, one group of bereaved individuals would participate in CBT while another separate group would not have access to CBT and then you compare their depression scores. This example, where you are comparing separate independent groups of people, is known as *independent groups design*. The second design involves measuring the depression levels of all the bereaved participants initially before they have undertaken CBT and again at the end of a CBT course to see if their depression levels have changed. This type of study, where you are interested in changes within the same group of participants, is known as *repeated measures design* and we cover the analyses for this design in Part V of the book.

Part IV of the book deals with analyses for studies that utilise independent groups design. The name *independent groups design* indicates that separate independent groups are tested and no participant can take part in more than one condition (or more than one level of the independent variable). It is also known as a *between-groups design* because you're assessing the difference between different groups of participants. The groups of participants can be manipulated experimentally (for example, you randomly allocate participants to either a group that will be offered CBT or a group that will not be offered CBT) or they can be naturally occurring groups (for example, males and females). Studies that use naturally occurring groups are referred to as *quasi-experimental*.

The Independent t-test

One of the most common analyses performed in psychology looks at the difference between two groups on a particular variable. This could be the difference between the amount of exercise taken by smokers and non-smokers, the differences in post-traumatic stress scores between police and paramedics, or the difference in arrogance between BMW and Audi drivers. The *parametric statistic* you use to assess the difference between two independent groups on an interval/ratio level variable is the *independent t-test* (sometimes called the *student t-test*). This is a statistic very close to our hearts, mainly because it was devised in Dublin's Guinness Brewery. Because this is a parametric test there are certain distributional assumptions that must be checked before we can report the result; we show you how to check these assumptions a little later in this chapter.

When you collect data from two groups it is likely the two means will differ, for example, you may want to examine whether there is a difference between male and female psychology students on statistics anxiety scores. It is very unlikely that the mean score for the sample of males and females will be exactly the same. The *t*-tests assess whether the groups are significantly different or any differences could be due to chance (see Chapter 8).

The independent *t*-test therefore tests the null hypothesis that there is no significant difference between the groups. The alternative hypothesis states that there is a significant difference between the two groups (we explain the null and alternative hypotheses in Chapter 8). The equation for the *t*-test takes into account the differences, variability and sample size of your data set. The answer to the equation gives a value denoted by *t*. The bigger the value of *t*, the more likely you are to find a statistically significant difference.

A perfectly logical question you may be asking is how big a *t*-value has to be to result in a statistically significant difference. This is a good question, and we're glad you asked. As we explain in Chapter 10, the *t*- distribution is based on the sample standard deviation. Consequently, there is no single *t*-value distribution, but there is a different *t*-value distribution for every sample size. Therefore there is no one *t*-value that signifies a statistically significant difference. Instead you need to consider the *t*-value and the degrees of freedom (which reflect sample size).

In the days before computers were readily available you'd conduct the *t*-test by hand, then using the *t*-values and *df* (degrees of freedom) you'd look up a large dusty book to find the appropriate probability value. Thankfully, the SPSS statistical software package conducts the *t*-test for you and reports the relevant *df* and probability values.

Performing the independent t-test in SPSS

Statistics anxiety has been shown to increase procrastination and decrease performance and self-efficacy. We therefore thought it would be interesting to see whether there was a significant difference between males and females on the variable of statistics anxiety. This study is an independent groups design as we are testing the difference in statistics anxiety scores between two separate groups. We now show you how to conduct an independent *t*-test to test this hypothesis.

1. **Select Analyze from the top tool bar, then Compare Means from the drop down menu and finally Independent-Samples T test (Figure 15-1).**

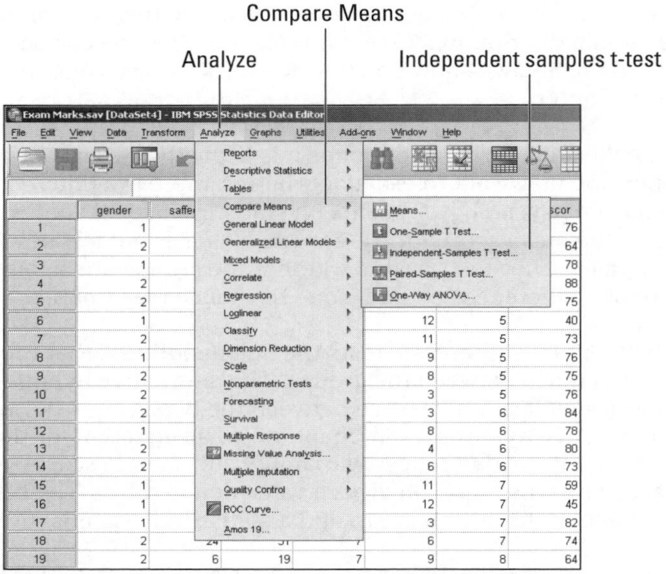

Figure 15-1: Obtaining an independent *t*-test on SPSS.

2. **An independent-Samples *t*-test window opens. Move the dependent variable over to the Test Variable(s) box by using the arrow or drag and drop.**

   Remember this is the variable you hypothesised there would be a difference in. In this example we've selected Statistics Anxiety. You can run several independent *t*-tests at the same time but the output can become confusing; therefore, we recommend that you run them individually.

3. **Move the independent variable into the Grouping Variable box.**

   This is the variable that tells SPSS what the two groups are. If you try to run the test now you notice you can't click on the OK button. That is because you must first specify the two groups your are comparing.

4. **Click on the Define Groups button (see Figure 15-2).**

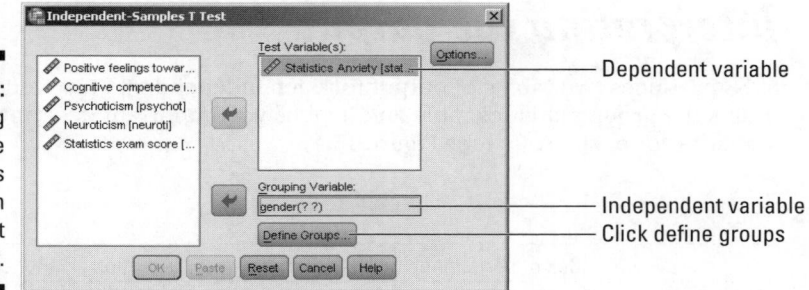

Figure 15-2:
Specifying the variables for an independent *t*-test.

Dependent variable

Independent variable
Click define groups

5. **A Define Groups window opens. Enter the two numbers that were used to code the independent variable.**

   In this example female was coded as 1 and male was coded as 2 so these are the two values. It doesn't really matter which order you enter the numbers. Be sure to check how the independent variable was coded, but it's usually 1 and 2 or 0 and 1 (see Figure 15-3).

   You may question why defining groups was necessary. This step allows you to compare two groups in situations where your independent variable may specify more than two groups. For example, you may wish to compare statistics anxiety between first year students and third year students but your independent variable included first, second and third years. In this case you could directly compare the first and third year groups by entering 1 and 3 into the Define Groups window.

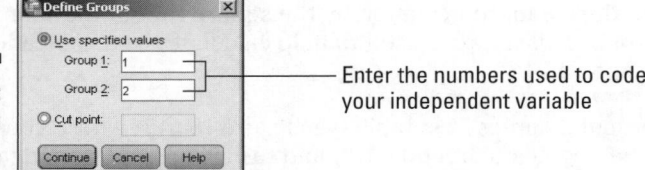

Figure 15-3:
Defining groups.

Enter the numbers used to code
your independent variable

6. **Select Continue, and then OK in the independent sample *t*-test window to run the statistic.**

Interpreting the output

SPSS produces two tables of output for each independent *t*-test you run. The first is the group statistics table and it gives you important descriptive statistics for each group (see Figure 15-4).

Figure 15-4:
Group
Statistics
table.

	Sex of participant	N	Mean	Std. Deviation	Std. Error Mean
Statistics Anxiety	female	45	8.71	1.779	.265
	male	17	6.65	2.029	.492

Here's how to read the table:

 ✔ **N:** The number of participants in each group. In the current example there were 45 females and 17 males.

 ✔ **Mean:** The mean for each group. Females had a mean statistics anxiety score of 8.71 and the male mean statistics anxiety score is 6.65 (for more on the mean, go to Chapter 4).

 ✔ **Std. Deviation:** The standard deviation for each group. The standard deviation for females on statistics anxiety score is 1.78 and the male standard deviation statistics anxiety score is 2.03 (for more on standard deviations see Chapter 5).

 ✔ **Std. Error of the Mean:** The standard error of the mean obtained by dividing the standard deviation by the square root of the sample size for each group. This figure is used to help calculate the significance value (see Chapter 9).

The Independent Samples Test table (see Figure 15-5) is where you find the values of *t*, the degrees of freedom (*df*) and the associated statistical significance. However you will notice there are two *t*-test results produced, one on the top line (called Equal variances assumed) and the second one on the bottom line (called Equal variances not assumed). Which value you interpret depends on the result of Levene's test for equality of variance which, as the name suggests, assesses whether or not your data displays equal variances. We will now explain what the various bits of the table mean and how you should interpret them.

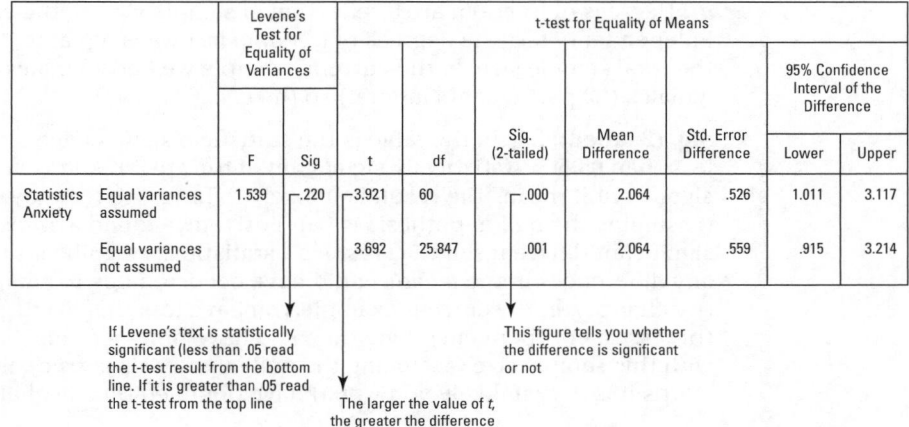

		Levene's Test for Equality of Variances		t-test for Equality of Means						
									95% Confidence Interval of the Difference	
		F	Sig	t	df	Sig. (2-tailed)	Mean Difference	Std. Error Difference	Lower	Upper
Statistics Anxiety	Equal variances assumed	1.539	.220	3.921	60	.000	2.064	.526	1.011	3.117
	Equal variances not assumed			3.692	25.847	.001	2.064	.559	.915	3.214

Figure 15-5: Independent Samples Test table.

If Levene's text is statistically significant (less than .05 read the t-test result from the bottom line. If it is greater than .05 read the t-test from the top line

The larger the value of *t*, the greater the difference between the two groups

This figure tells you whether the difference is significant or not

---

- **Levene's Test for Equality of Variances:** This is a test for *homogeneity of variance* which is one of the assumptions of the independent *t*-test (you can read more about this in the 'Considering assumptions' section, later in this chapter). For interpretation purposes all you need to know is whether the test is significant. If the test isn't significant (sig. is greater than 0.05) the assumption isn't violated and you can read the remaining figures from the top line called Equal variances assumed (see Figure 15-5). If Levene's test indicates a significant result (sig. is less than 0.05) this means the assumption is violated and you should read the remaining values from the bottom line of the table called equal variances not assumed. In this example Levene's test for equality of variances indicates the assumption isn't violated (*p* = .220) so you report the values from the top line of the table (see Figure 15-5).

- **t:** This is the t statistic and is used to test if there is a significant difference between the two means. The larger the *t*-value is (irrespective of sign) the greater the difference between the groups.

t can be positive or negative. This simply reflects which way round the variables were coded. In the current example we coded females as 1 and males as 2 and we have a *t*-value of 3.92. This simply reflects that the females had higher mean scores. If we reverse the coding (males as 1 and females as 2) we get a negative value of *t* of –3.92. As the decision of how to code the variables is arbitrary the *t* statistic is normally reported as a positive number.

✔ *df:* Degrees of freedom are a reflection of sample size. In the case of an independent *t*-test the degrees of freedom is always equal to 2 less than the total sample size. In the current example we had 45 males and 17 females (62 participants in total) so the *df* is 62 – 2=60.

✔ **Sig. (2-tailed):** Sig. in the table is the statistical significance. Any value less than 0.05 is statistically significant. If the *t*-test result is statistically significant it means the result is unlikely to have occurred by chance (assuming the null hypothesis is true) or you've found a statistically significant difference. If the *t*-test isn't statistically significant it means any differences in the means could have occurred due to sampling error (by chance). In the current example you have less than 0.001 probability (or less than .1 per cent) that you could have obtained this difference with this sample size (assuming the null hypothesis is true); in other words it is very unlikely you would have obtained this by chance.

As denoted this is the statistical significance for a two-tailed hypothesis. To obtain a significance value for a one-tailed hypothesis simply divide the two-tailed significance value by 2 (see Chapter 8 for a discussion of the difference between a one-tailed and two-tailed hypothesis).

Your statistical significance or probability is never equal to zero. SPSS only reports to 3 decimal places so it looks like the value is 0; it's not! If you don't believe us, double click on any probability value that looks like zero and SPSS gives you a more accurate figure (in this case it is .00022 895668). Therefore, you never report that $p = 0$ but $p < .001$.

✔ **Mean Difference:** This is the difference between mean of group 1 and the mean of group 2. In the current example females had a mean score of 8.71 and the male was 6.65 resulting in a mean difference of 2.06 (8.71 – 6.65).

✔ **Std. Error Difference:** This is the standard error of the difference obtained by dividing the mean difference by the *t*-value. You use the standard error in calculating the confidence interval of the difference (see Chapter 8).

✔ **95 per cent Confidence Interval of the Difference**: This is the range in which we are 95 per cent confident that the true population mean difference falls. In the current example the sample mean difference is 2.06 but we're 95 per cent confident that the estimated population mean difference is between 1.01 and 3.12 (see Chapter 8 for a discussion of confidence intervals).

Writing up the results

When reporting *t*-test results, the APA manual suggests that you should report the *t*-value rounded to 2 decimal places, with the degrees of freedom in parentheses, followed by the significance level. Taking the independent *t*-test result reported in Figure 15-5, you report the result as follows:

> In this study there was a statistically significant difference between males and females on statistics anxiety score, *t* (60) = 3.92, *p* < .001.

Anyone reading your report now realises there is a significant difference between the groups, but doesn't know which group had the higher score. You should always therefore also report the means and standard deviations of each group:

> Females had a higher mean statistics anxiety score of 8.71 (*SD* = 1.78) compared to the mean male score of 6.65 (*SD* = 2.03).

We also recommend reporting the effect size for the difference as we outline in Chapter 11.

Considering assumptions

The independent *t*-test is a parametric statistic and has similar assumptions to other parametric statistics.

Normal distribution

The independent *t*-test assumes that the sampling distribution is normally distributed (see Chapter 8 for a discussion of the sampling distribution). You can't examine the sampling distribution directly to check this assumption, but you can check whether this assumption is likely to be met by looking at a histogram of scores.

If it turns out that the histogram of scores doesn't approximate a normal distribution, consider performing a Mann–Whitney test instead (see the following section). However, this check is only necessary for small sample sizes. For large sample sizes (that is, around 30 or more) you can assume that the sampling distribution is normal (see Chapter 8).

Homogeneity of variance

Homogeneity of variance simply refers to the fact that the variances of the dependent variable should be similar for both groups (for more on variance see Chapter 5). The *t*-statistic calculates the ratio of the difference between the groups compared to the difference within the groups, therefore if the two groups differ substantially in variance (as illustrated in Figures 15-6 and 15-7), the *t*-test is difficult to interpret.

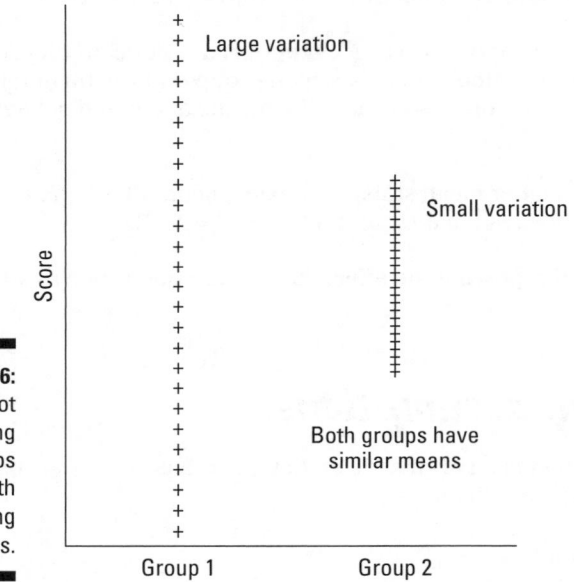

Figure 15-6: Scatterplot illustrating two groups with differing variances.

Helpfully, SPSS has a built-in test for this assumption. Levene's test for equality of variances (that appears in the Independent Samples Test table) is a test for homogeneity of variance. If the F ratio and associated significance test for Levene's test isn't statistically significant then that means the variance in the two groups doesn't differ substantially. This means the assumption isn't violated and you can report the *t*-test result from the top line called *equal variances assumed* (see Figure 15-5).

If the variance in the groups do vary substantially Levene's test indicates a statistically significant effect which means the *t*-test result may not be accurate. Luckily, SPSS has pre-empted this scenario and has produced a modified *t*-test that takes into account the fact that the groups have unequal variances; this result is produced in the bottom line of the Independent Samples Test table called equal variances not assumed (see Figure 15-5).

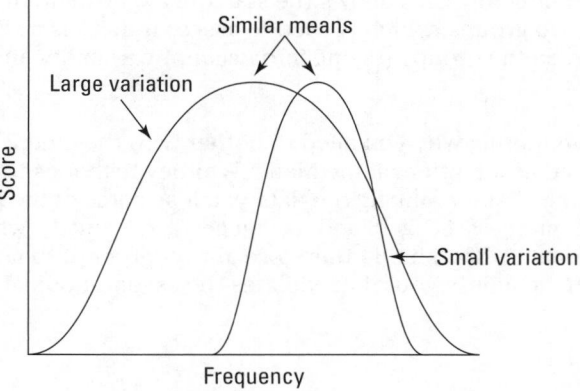

Figure 15-7:
Differing
variations
means the
t-test
cannot be
meaningfully
interpreted.

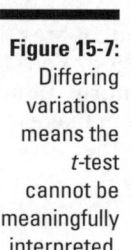

Therefore if Levene's test produces a non-significant result you should interpret the top set of *t*-test figures called equal variance assumed (see Figure 15-5), and if Levene's test produces a significant result interpret the bottom set of *t*-test figures called equal variance not assumed (see Figure 15-5). If you have large sample sizes (that is, 30 or more) and equal numbers in each group you can assume homogeneity of variance and therefore you do not need to refer to Levene's test.

Type of data

The independent variable must contain two separate mutually exclusive groups. The dependent variable should be measured at the interval or ratio level. If the dependent variable is measured at the ordinal level you can consider using the Mann–Whitney test instead (see the next section).

Mann–Whitney test

The *Mann–Whitney test* (sometimes called the *Mann–Whitney U test* or the *Wilcoxon–Mann–Whitney test*) is the non-parametric equivalent of the independent *t*-test (see the earlier section on the *t*-test). You use the Mann–Whitney test to test the null hypothesis that there is no significant difference between two independent groups, just like the independent *t*-test, but it is subject to less stringent assumptions (for the lowdown on null hypotheses, head to Chapter 8). You can use this statistic when your dependent variable is measured at the ordinal level (see Chapter 2). When calculating the Mann–Whitney test all the data is ranked (the lowest score becomes 1, the second lowest score becomes 2, and so on) and then the ranks for each group are added up. This allows the statistic to calculate the mean rank for each of the two groups, which is used to assess if there is a significant difference between the groups (taking into account variability and sample size).

You might be wondering why you need to bother with the independent *t*-test and its associated assumptions if the Mann–Whitney test does the job. You need to remember that by ranking the data you lose some of the information (if you rank the numbers 4, 15, 16 and 27 you get 1, 2, 3 and 4), which makes the test less powerful. You should therefore always attempt to use the parametric statistic unless your data violates the assumptions of the independent *t*-test.

Performing the Mann–Whitney test in SPSS

Vegetotherapy is a form of psychotherapy which involves the client breathing deeply while being tickled by the therapist. A student wanted to see whether professionals thought this was a suitable technique to treat personality disorders, so asked a range of psychologists and psychiatrists to rate the effectiveness of Vegetotherapy on a scale from zero (indicating that it's completely rubbish) to 7 (meaning it's the best form of therapy for all conditions). She now wants to see whether there is a significant difference between the psychologists' and psychiatrists' ratings. As the rating scales were measured at the ordinal level she must conduct a Mann–Whitney test.

To perform a Mann–Whitney test:

1. **Select Analyze from the top toolbar, Nonparametric Tests from the drop-down menu (Mann–Whitney is a nonparametric statistic) then Independent Samples (the design of the study is independent groups design) (see Figure 15-8).**

2. **A new Nonparametric test window opens and asks you to define your objective because there are several non-parametric tests you could conduct (see Figure 15-9). The default option is to automatically compare distributions across groups, and this is what you want to do. Helpfully, SPSS has described each of the options and if you look at the bottom of the window it confirms this is the correct option for conducting a Mann–Whitney (or a Kruskal–Wallis) test. Therefore you can click the Fields tab at the top left hand corner (or click the run button).**

   If you're having problems defining the variables, ensure the correct measurement levels have been specified in the variable view window. See Chapter 3 for more details.

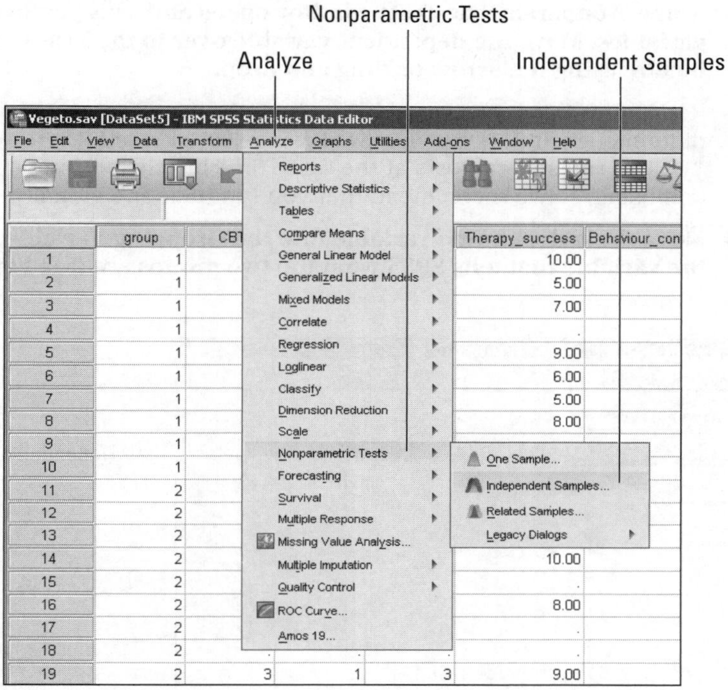

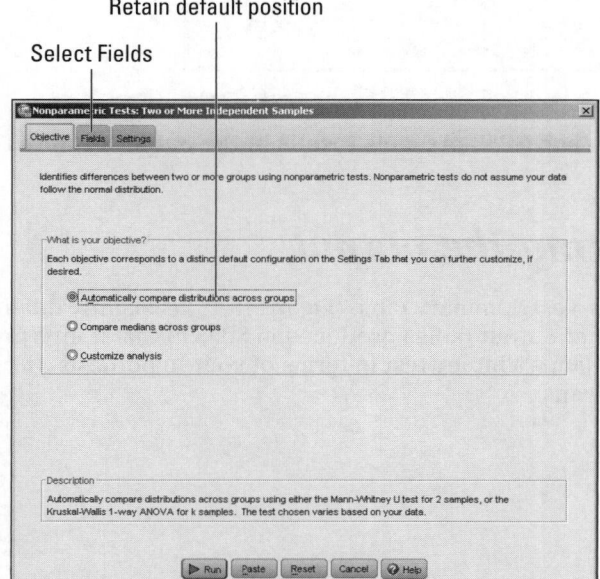

Figure 15-8: Obtaining a Mann–Whitney test in SPSS.

Figure 15-9: Obtaining a Mann–Whitney test in SPSS.

3. **A new Nonparametric Tests window opens and asks you to specify the variables. Move the dependent variable over to the Test Variable(s) box by using the arrow or drag and drop.**

Remember this is the variable you hypothesised there would be a difference in. In this example we have selected Vegetotherapy rating. You can run several tests at the same time but the output can become confusing, so we recommend that you run them individually.

4. **Move the independent variable into the Grouping Variable box; this is the variable that tells SPSS what the two groups are (see Figure 15-10).**

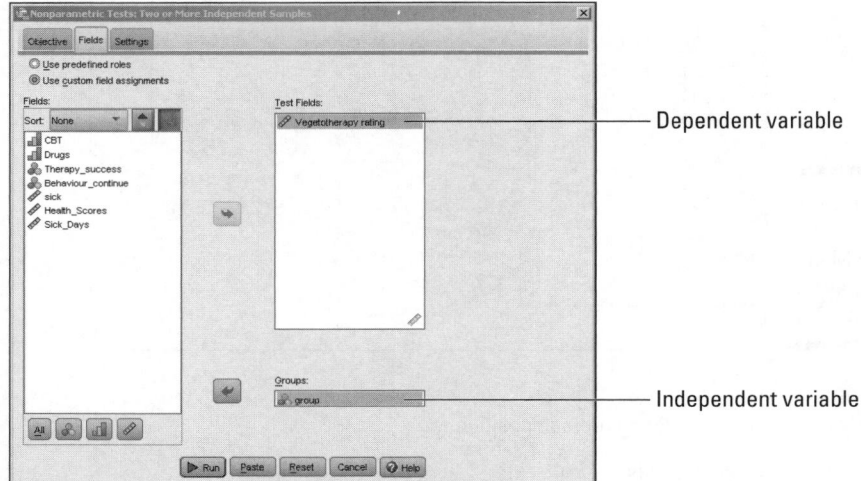

Figure 15-10: Specifying the variables for an Mann–Whitney test.

5. **Select Run and SPSS presents results in the output window.**

Interpreting the output

The Hypothesis Test Summary table (Figure 15-11) is slightly different from many of the other output tables produced in SPSS in that it interprets the result of your Mann–Whitney test in terms of your hypothesis. Here's what each section means:

✔ **Sig.:** The statistical significance. Remember, any statistical significance figure less than 0.05 means there is a less than 5 per cent probability that you could have achieved this result if the null hypothesis is true; in other words, if the value is less than 0.05 it means you have a significant difference between the two groups. If the significance value is greater than 0.05 any difference could have occurred by chance and therefore there is no statistically significant difference between the groups. In the current example $p = .525$ which indicates that no statistically significant difference exists in rating scores between psychologists and psychiatrists.

✔ **Null Hypothesis:** The Null Hypothesis simply states the null hypothesis! In the case of the Mann–Whitney test it is that there is no significant difference between the groups.

✔ **Test:** This is just a quick reminder that the statistic you just conducted was the Mann–Whitney test.

✔ **Decision:** SPSS has tried to help you here by telling you whether to retain or reject the null hypothesis. If the significance value is less than .05 SPSS advises you to reject the null hypothesis. If the significance value is greater than .05 (as it is in the current example) you are advised to retain the null hypothesis.

Check this figure to see if there was a significant
difference between the 2 groups.

Figure 15-11:
Hypothesis
Test
Summary
table.

Hypothesis Test Summary			
Null Hypothesis	**Test**	**Sig.**	**Decision**
1 The distribution of Vegetotherapy rating is the same across categories of group.	Independent-Samples Mann-Whitney U Test	.525[1]	Retain the null hypothesis.
Asymptotic significances are displayed. The significance level is .05.			
[1]Exact significance is displayed for this test.			

You now know that there was no significant difference between the two groups, but you still don't have the Mann–Whitney statistic that must be reported. Has SPSS let you down? Not at all! If you double click on Hypothesis Test Summary table in the ouput window SPSS opens another window with more detailed information (see Figure 15-12). It first provides a frequency chart which displays the distribution of the data. In this example you can see the most common rating response for the psychiatrist group was 3 and one psychologist rated the therapy as 5. In the table below SPSS provides several values but the only one you're interested in is the Mann–Whitney U value, which in this example is 66.

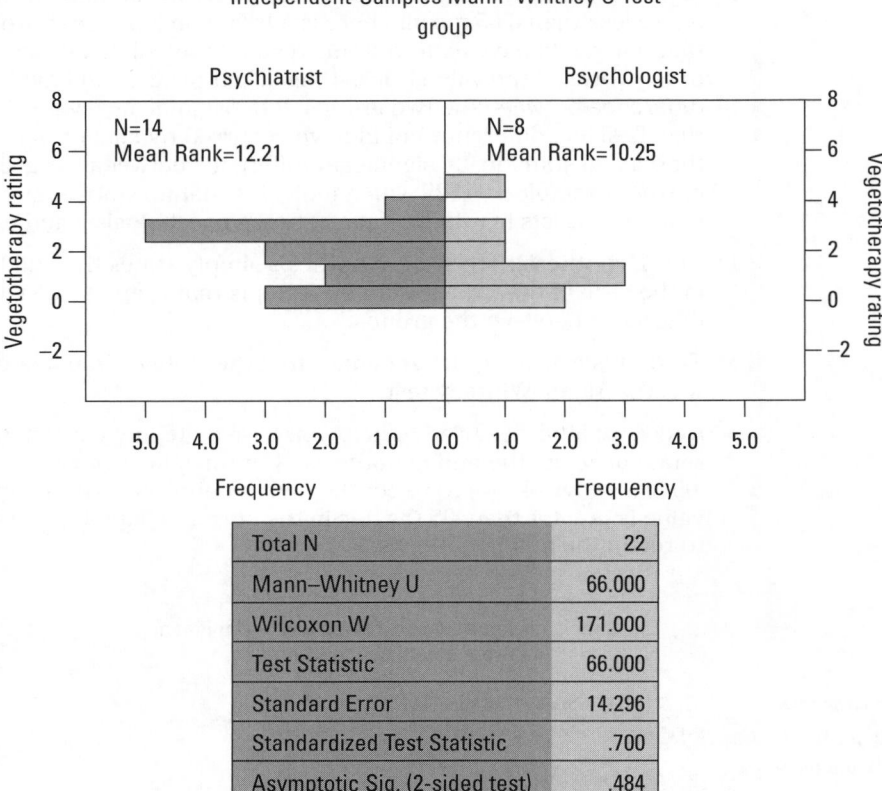

Total N	22
Mann–Whitney U	66.000
Wilcoxon W	171.000
Test Statistic	66.000
Standard Error	14.296
Standardized Test Statistic	.700
Asymptotic Sig. (2-sided test)	.484
Exact Sig. (2-sided test)	.525

Figure 15-12: Frequency chart and Mann–Whitney U result.

Writing up the results

When reporting the result of your Mann–Whitney test you include the U value rounded to 2 decimal places followed by the significance level. In the current example the format would look like this:

$U = 66, p = .53$

As always, describe the results in words:

There was no statistically significant difference between psychologists and psychiatrists on the rating scores for vegetotherapy, $U = 66, p = .48$.

We have shown you how to report a Mann–Whitney test, but anyone reading your report wants some indication of the scores of the two groups. This is especially important if you're reporting a statistically significant result. When describing ordinal data the most appropriate measure of central tendency is the median (see Chapter 4), and the most appropriate measure of dispersion is the interquartile range (see Chapter 5). For example:

> The psychologist group reported a median rating of 1.00 (interquartile range = 2.5) and the psychiatrists had a higher median rating of Vegetotherapy of 2 (interquartile range = 2).

Considering assumptions

As the Mann–Whitney test is a non-parametric statistic it's free from the stringent assumptions of the independent *t*-test. However, the independent variable must form two separate mutually exclusive groups and the dependent variable should be measured at least at the ordinal level.

Chapter 16

Between-Groups ANOVA

. . . .

In This Chapter

▶ Obtaining and interpreting a one-way between-groups ANOVA

▶ Obtaining and interpreting a two-way between-groups ANOVA

▶ Obtaining and interpreting a Kruskal–Wallis test

. . . .

A set of analyses commonly used in psychology and other disciplines is the analysis of variance tests, or ANOVA tests for short. We refer to a *set* of tests on purpose, to highlight that the ANOVA isn't a single test. In fact, there are different forms of the ANOVA and although they're all based on the same principle, the different ANOVA tests are used for different purposes. Basically, your choice of ANOVA test depends on the type of research design you have and the number of variables you want to analyse.

In this chapter, we focus on ANOVA tests for independent groups research designs (which we explain in Chapter 15). In this case, the ANOVA tests are used to examine differences between groups. For example, you might want to examine the difference between psychology students, medical students and history students on their knowledge of statistics. In this example, the type of student is the independent variable and knowledge of statistics is the dependent variable (Chapter 2 explains variables). Because the independent variable contains independent groups, this design is known as an independent groups research design. *Independent groups* means that the groups are separate and distinct: psychology students are separate and distinct from medical and history students and medical students are separate and distinct from history students.

In Chapter 19 we discuss ANOVA tests for research that involves repeated measurements, also known as within-groups research designs, and in Chapter 21 we examine ANOVA tests for research designs that include independent groups and repeated measurements (mixed ANOVA).

In an ANOVA, you always have only one dependent variable. When you also have only one independent variable then you conduct a one-way ANOVA; when you have two independent variables, you can conduct a two-way ANOVA; when you have three independent variables, you can conduct a three-way ANOVA, and so on. In this book we examine the one-way and two-way ANOVA tests only. If you understand these tests, then you will be able to understand the principle behind more complex ANOVA tests.

One-Way Between-Groups ANOVA

A one-way between-groups ANOVA is sometimes called a one-way independent-groups ANOVA or simply a one-way ANOVA. You use a *one-way between-groups ANOVA* to examine the differences between two or more independent groups; usually, to examine the difference between three or more groups, because you can use an independent *t*-test to examine the difference between two groups (see Chapter 15). In fact, an independent *t*-test and a one-way between-groups ANOVA conducted to examine the difference between two groups result in exactly the same conclusions. So, think of the one-way between-groups ANOVA as an extension to the independent *t*-test when you have more than two groups.

For example, imagine you have conducted a research study to examine the difference in intelligence between people who think John Wayne was the best cowboy, people who think Clint Eastwood was the best cowboy, and people who don't watch cowboy movies. You recruit three groups: 10 people who prefer John Wayne, 10 people who prefer Clint Eastwood, and 10 people who don't watch cowboy movies. You then administer an intelligence test to each person (scored from 0 to 100, with higher scores indicating higher intelligence). Your hypothesis is (understandably) that people who prefer John Wayne score highest in intelligence. You obtain the data in Table 16-1.

Table 16-1	Intelligence Test Scores
Type of Cowboy Preferred	*Intelligence Score*
John Wayne	66
John Wayne	64
John Wayne	66
John Wayne	47
John Wayne	66
John Wayne	71

Type of Cowboy Preferred	Intelligence Score
John Wayne	76
John Wayne	84
John Wayne	72
John Wayne	68
Clint Eastwood	65
Clint Eastwood	53
Clint Eastwood	73
Clint Eastwood	80
Clint Eastwood	70
Clint Eastwood	81
Clint Eastwood	46
Clint Eastwood	88
Clint Eastwood	72
Clint Eastwood	53
None	72
None	81
None	69
None	75
None	55
None	60
None	61
None	73
None	54
None	65

Seeing how ANOVA works

A one-way between-groups ANOVA tests the null hypothesis that the mean scores for all groups are equal (see Chapter 8 for a discussion of the null hypothesis).

To test the null hypothesis that these means are equal, you analyse the variance (see Chapter 5), which might seem a bit strange – why analyse variance when we want to analyse the means (see Chapter 4)? The rationale for this is as follows. The scores that you obtain from individuals vary: not everyone will get the same score on a test. Therefore, the scores from individuals within each group in our research study will vary. When you want to examine differences between groups you need to examine whether the mean scores from each group vary more than the variation that occurs between individuals. In other words, do the scores between people in different groups vary more than the scores of people within each group? If the mean scores for each group vary more than the scores of individuals then you can conclude that there is something about being in the different groups that affects the scores on the test – that is, you wouldn't expect people in the different groups to get the same scores on the test.

If this logic makes sense, then the only thing you need to calculate is a measure of variation for the mean scores and a measure of variation for the individual scores and then compare these measures of variation (see the next section).

Calculating a one-way between-groups ANOVA

It is useful to examine the calculation of a one-way between-groups ANOVA, to help you understand how an ANOVA works. Take the data presented in Table 16-1. To measure variation in the scores you can use a statistic called the variance (see Chapter 5). This is, obviously, where the analysis of variance gets its name.

Calculating sums of squares

The first thing you need to do is to calculate the variance for the individual scores within each group. The first step in doing this is to calculate the sum of the squared deviations of each individual score from its group mean. To do this, you subtract the group mean from each score within that group and then square the result. Then you add up the values obtained (see Chapter 5). This is known as the *sum of squared deviations* (or *sum of squares*).

The mean intelligence score for each group in Table 16-1 is as follows (see Chapter 4 for information about calculating the mean score):

Group who prefer John Wayne = 68.0

Group who prefer Clint Eastwood = 68.1

Group who don't watch cowboy movies = 66.5

Table 16-2 provides the squared deviations from the group mean. For example, the person on line 1 of the table prefers John Wayne and obtained an intelligence score of 66. The mean score for this group is 68.0. If you subtract 68.0 from 66, you get –2 (the value in the deviation column in Table 16-2). If you square this value, you get 4 (the value in the final column in Table 16-2). The sum of squares for the individual scores is the sum of the final column in Table 16-2, which is 3239.40. This is known as the *sum of squares within groups*.

Table 16-2	Squared Deviations from the Group Mean		
Type of Cowboy Preferred	*Intelligence Score*	*Deviation*	*Squared Deviation*
John Wayne	66	–2	4
John Wayne	64	–4	16
John Wayne	66	–2	4
John Wayne	47	–21	441
John Wayne	66	–2	4
John Wayne	71	3	9
John Wayne	76	8	64
John Wayne	84	16	256
John Wayne	72	4	16
John Wayne	68	0	0
Clint Eastwood	65	–3.1	9.61
Clint Eastwood	53	–15.1	228.01
Clint Eastwood	73	4.9	24.01
Clint Eastwood	80	11.9	141.61
Clint Eastwood	70	1.9	3.61
Clint Eastwood	81	12.9	166.41
Clint Eastwood	46	–22.1	488.41
Clint Eastwood	88	19.9	396.01
Clint Eastwood	72	3.9	15.21
Clint Eastwood	53	–15.1	228.01
None	72	5.5	30.25
None	81	14.5	210.25
None	69	2.5	6.25
None	75	8.5	72.25

(continued)

Table 16-2 *(continued)*

Type of Cowboy Preferred	Intelligence Score	Deviation	Squared Deviation
None	55	−11.5	132.25
None	60	−6.5	42.25
None	61	−5.5	30.25
None	73	6.5	42.25
None	54	−12.5	156.25
None	65	−1.5	2.25

You can then follow the same principle to calculate the sum of squared deviations of each group mean from the grand mean. The *grand mean* is the mean for all scores in the analysis. In the example, the grand mean is 67.53.

For this calculation you replace each individual score with its group mean score and then work out the deviation of this score from the grand mean. For example, the first person in Table 16-2 has a group mean score of 68.0. If you subtract the grand mean from this score you get: 68.0 − 67.53 = 0.47. If you then square this deviation, you get approximately 0.218.

If you follow this procedure for everyone in the data set, and then add up the squared deviations, you get a sum of squared deviations of 16.07. This is the sum of squares between groups.

Calculating mean square

The sum of squares values (see the preceding section) provides a sense of the amount of variation between groups and within groups. However, this isn't the variance, because the variance also takes account of the number of values that contributed to the calculation of the sums of squares (see Chapter 5). In a normal calculation of the variance, you divide the sum of squares by $n - 1$, where n is the number of values used to calculate the sum of squares (see Chapter 5). However, in the context of an ANOVA, your calculation is a little more complicated.

In an ANOVA, you divide the sum of squares by its degrees of freedom (*df*). For the between-groups sum of squares, the *df* is the number of groups minus 1. In the example there are 3 groups. Therefore the *df* for the between-groups sum of squares is 2. The mean square is the sum of squares divided by the *df*, so the between-groups mean square is 16.07 ÷ 2 = 8.035.

For the within groups sum of squares, the df is the number of individuals in the analysis minus the number of groups. In the example there are 30 people and 3 groups. Therefore, the within groups df is $30 - 3 = 27$. As the mean square is the sum of squares divided by the df, then the within-groups mean square is $3239.40 \div 27 = 119.98$.

Calculating the F ratio

The goal of the ANOVA is to compare the variability between groups to the variability within groups. You do this by dividing the between-groups mean square by the within-groups mean square (the figures you calculate in the previous two sections). The result is known as the *F ratio*:

F ratio = Between-groups mean square / within-groups mean square

In the example the *F* ratio is $8.035 \div 119.98 = 0.067$.

If the *F* ratio is 1, this indicates that there is no effect on the dependent variable of being in the different groups. In other words, there is no difference between the groups. If the *F* ratio is greater than 1, this indicates that there is a difference between the groups. The *p* value that accompanies the *F* ratio then tells you whether or not this difference is statistically significant.

In the example the *F* ratio is less than 1, suggesting that there is more variability between individuals than there is between groups, that is, the groups have no association with the scores on the dependent variable.

Obtaining a one-way between-groups ANOVA in SPSS

You can obtain a one-way between-groups ANOVA in SPSS in several ways. One method is as follows.

1. **Go to the Analyze menu and choose General Linear Model. Then choose Univariate (see Figure 16-1).**

2. **In the new window move your dependent variable (in this case 'intelligence') into the box headed 'Dependent Variable' and move your independent variable (in this case 'cowboy') into the box headed 'Fixed Factor(s)' (see Figure 16-2).**

General Linear Model

Analyze

Univariate

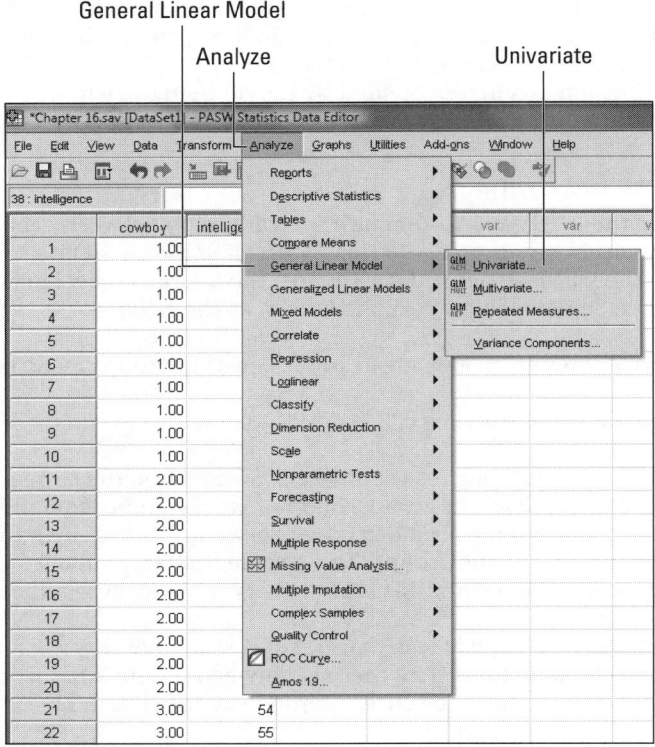

Independent
variable

Dependent
variable

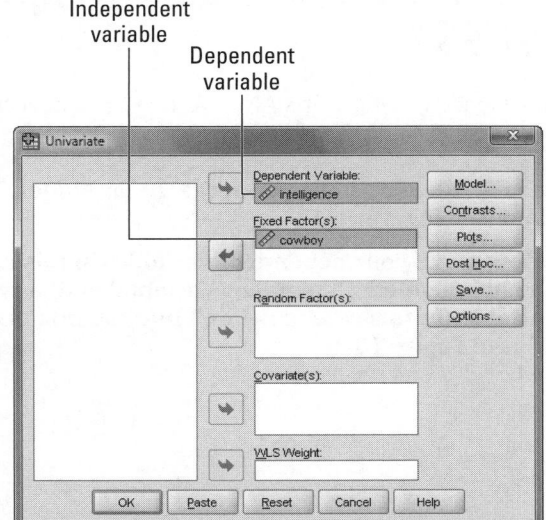

3. **Select Options. In the window that opens tick the box beside the words 'Descriptive statistics', in the list headed 'Display' (see Figure 16-3).**

4. **Tick the box next to the 'Homogeneity tests' for homogeneity of variance (see the section 'Considering assumptions of a one-way between-groups ANOVA' in this chapter).**

5. **Select Continue.**

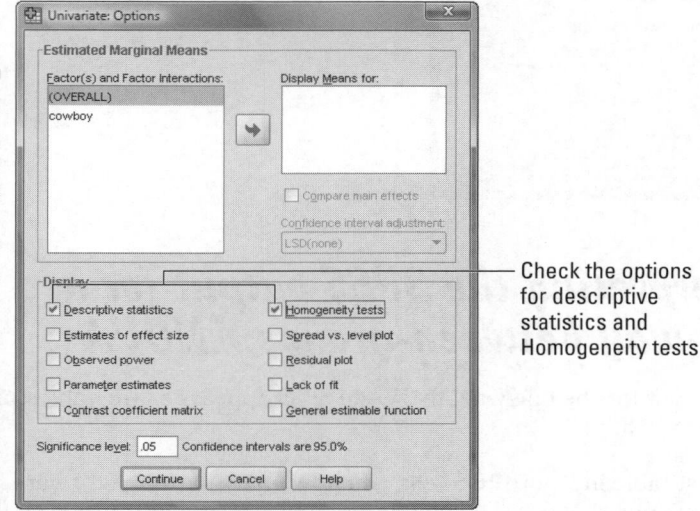

Figure 16-3: Obtaining descriptive statistics and a homogeneity of variance test as part of the between-groups ANOVA procedure in SPSS.

Check the options for descriptive statistics and Homogeneity tests

6. **Select Save. This allows you to save the residual scores for this analysis that are useful for checking the assumptions of the between-groups ANOVA (see the section 'Considering assumptions of a one-way between-groups ANOVA' in this chapter).**

7. **In the window that opens, tick the box beside the word 'Unstandardized' in the list headed 'Residuals' (see Figure 16-4).**

8. **Select Continue and then OK to run the procedure.**

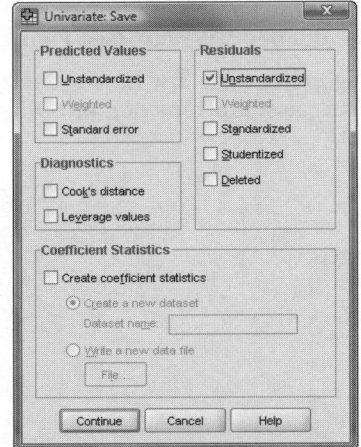

Figure 16-4:
Obtaining
residuals for
a between-
groups
ANOVA in
SPSS.

Interpreting the SPSS output for a one-way between-groups ANOVA

The output for the one-way ANOVA in SPSS appears as the tables presented in Figure 16-5.

The first table in Figure 16-5 tells you how many participants were in each group in your analysis. The next table presents the descriptive statistics for each group and for the overall sample. These are important because if your ANOVA shows a significant difference between group means then you need the descriptive statistics in order to see where these differences are.

The Levene's test in Figure 16-5, tests whether the variances of each group in the independent variable are approximately equal. If the significance value for this test is 0.05 or greater, then the variances can be considered to be sufficiently similar to meet the assumption of the one-way ANOVA (see the later section 'Considering assumptions of a one-way between-groups ANOVA'). In this case the sig value is 0.217 and therefore our variables do meet this assumption.

Finally, Figure 16-5 presents the ANOVA table. It contains the sum of squares, *df*, mean square and *F* ratio values that we describe in the earlier section 'Calculating a one-way between-groups ANOVA'.

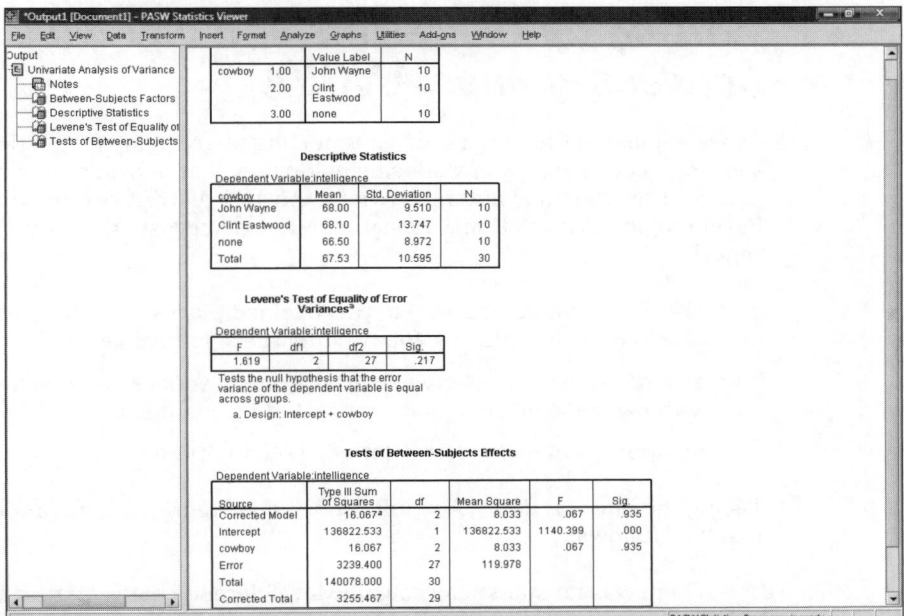

Figure 16-5:
One-way
ANOVA out-
put in SPSS.

Notice that there are several rows of information in the ANOVA table in Figure 16-5. The most important row is the row that corresponds with the name of your independent variable (labelled 'cowboy' in the example). The other important row in the table is the one labelled 'error'. This is the term used for the within-groups information that we referred to in the section on Calculating a one-way between-groups ANOVA. So, the error mean square is the value used as the denominator in the F ratio calculations. At this stage you can ignore the other information in the ANOVA table.

The final column in the ANOVA table is the probability (p or sig.) value associated with the F ratio. As with all inferential statistics, if this value is less than 0.05, then you can reject the null hypothesis. In this example, the p value is 0.935, which means you fail to reject the null hypothesis that the mean scores for all groups are equal. In other words, there is no statistically significant difference between the mean scores of the three groups.

Writing up the results of a one-way between-groups ANOVA

As we explain in Chapter 14, when reporting the results of statistical analyses, you need to follow any specific guidelines that inform how you should present the statistical findings. When reporting ANOVA results, the American Psychological Association Publication Manual suggests that you should report:

✔ The *F* ratio value rounded to two decimal places, with the degrees of freedom in parentheses, followed by the significance level.

✔ Two *df* – one for the between-groups mean square and one for the within-groups mean square, separated by a comma.

✔ An appropriate effect size statistic (see Chapter 11).

Taking the one-way ANOVA result reported in Figure 16-5, you report the result as follows:

> There was no statistically significant difference between the three groups in terms of their intelligence scores, *F*(2,27) = 0.07, *p* = .94.'

It is also important to report the mean and standard deviation values for each group. This is particularly important when the ANOVA indicates a statistically significant finding. In this case, the mean scores allow the reader to understand the nature of the difference.

The ANOVA only indicates whether there is a statistically significant difference between groups. It doesn't indicate the nature of the difference and it doesn't tell you where the significant difference lies. For example, if you find a significant difference between three groups it might be the case that all three groups differ significantly from each other or that one group differs from the other two. To uncover this detail you need to conduct post hoc tests or planned comparisons between the groups (see Chapter 17).

Considering assumptions of a one-way between-groups ANOVA

Calculating an ANOVA test has been made considerably easier with the design of computer packages that allow you to do this quickly. However, you always have the risk that the computer sometimes gives you an answer when the information you input isn't appropriate for the analysis you've chosen.

Therefore, you need to spend some time thinking about the conditions (or assumptions) that need to be met before you can apply the result produced by the computer.

For a one-way ANOVA, these are the conditions that must be met before you should interpret the result:

- ✔ The independent variable should be categorical (see Chapter 2 for a description of categorical variables).
- ✔ The dependent variable should be measured at the interval/ratio level (see Chapter 2).
- ✔ The groups have approximately equal variances. This is sometimes called *homogeneity of variances* (see the following section 'Testing homogeneity of variances').
- ✔ The residual scores should follow an approximately normal distribution (see the following section 'Testing normality of residuals').

When the assumptions for a one-way between-groups ANOVA aren't met, then you should consider conducting a Kruskal–Wallis test (see the later section in this chapter).

Testing homogeneity of variances

To examine the homogeneity of variance assumption, you can ask SPSS to conduct a Levene's test (see Figure 16-3 for choosing a homogeneity of variance test). The Levene's test provides a significance value, and if this value is 0.05 or greater then you can conclude that the variances of the groups are similar (see Figure 16-5).

The good news is that when you have equal sample sizes in your groups and when the groups are reasonably large (around 20 cases in each group) then this assumption isn't important.

Testing normality of residuals

In technical terms, a *residual score* is the difference between a score and its expected value. In the case of a one-way between-groups ANOVA, a *residual* is the difference between a score and its group mean. We've already calculated residual scores – they're the deviation scores in Table 16-2.

SPSS can calculate these scores for you (see Figure 16-4). Running this procedure results in a new variable being added to your data window in SPSS. The new variable will be called 'RES_1' and contains the residual scores for this analysis.

A one-way between-groups ANOVA assumes that these residual, or deviation, scores are normally distributed (see Chapter 9 for a description of the normal distribution). You can test this by plotting the deviation scores on a graph, such as a histogram (see Chapter 6), and by conducting a test, such as the Kolmogorov-Smirnov test to examine the departure of this graph from normality (see Chapter 9).

Two-Way Between-Groups ANOVA

A two-way between-groups ANOVA is sometimes called a two-way independent-groups ANOVA or a factorial ANOVA. You use a *two-way between-groups ANOVA* to examine the differences between two or more independent groups on two independent variables. Therefore a two-way ANOVA always has two independent variables and one dependent variable.

Two-way ANOVAs are often described by the number of levels of the two independent variables. For example, a two-way ANOVA where each independent variable has 3 levels will be known as a 3×3 ANOVA; a two-way ANOVA where one independent variable has 3 levels and the other independent variable has 4 levels will be known as a 3×4 ANOVA and so on.

As an example, we can use the research study in the earlier section 'Using One-Way Between-Groups ANOVA' that examines the difference in intelligence between people who prefer different cowboys, but add in looking at whether gender influences intelligence scores. So you recruit three groups: 10 people who prefer John Wayne; 10 people who prefer Clint Eastwood; and 10 people who do not watch cowboy movies. Half of the people in each group are male and half are female. You then administer an intelligence test to each person.

In this research design you have two independent variables (cowboy and gender) and one dependent variable (intelligence scores). The independent variable 'gender' has two levels – male or female. The independent variable 'cowboy' has 3 levels – preference for John Wayne, Clint Eastwood, or none. Therefore an appropriate analysis would be a 2×3 between-groups ANOVA.

Your hypotheses are that:

- ✔ People who prefer John Wayne will have higher intelligence than people who prefer Clint Eastwood or people who do not watch cowboy movies.

- ✔ There will be a difference between the intelligence scores of males and females.

- ✔ The effect of cowboy preference on intelligence will only be found for males.

The first two hypotheses here are known as *main effects* and the final hypothesis is known as an *interaction*.

Understanding main effects and interactions

In a two-way ANOVA you can obtain two main effects and an interaction. The *main effects* are the effects of each independent variable on the dependent variable. The result that you get from a one-way ANOVA is also known as a main effect. So, the main effects in a two-way ANOVA are a bit like conducting two separate one-way ANOVAs – one for each independent variable (but see the nearby sidebar 'One plus one doesn't always equal two').

The *interaction effect* in a two-way ANOVA is the effect of the combination of the two independent variables on the dependent variable. Interaction effects are useful when you think that the effect of an independent variable on a dependent variable isn't simple but is influenced by another variable. In statistical terms you describe the effect of one independent variable on the dependent variable being moderated by another variable.

For example, the third hypothesis in the introduction to this section suggests that the effect of cowboy preference on intelligence will be influenced by gender. This is an interaction. It is a slightly more complex relationship but that's more like real life, so that's why two-way ANOVAs are useful – they allow you to examine more complex, real-life situations.

Usually, when you conduct a two-way ANOVA the interaction is the result that you are most interested in and you should pay close attention to it. If the interaction result is statistically significant then this overrides the main effects. In other words, the interaction result provides more information than any single main effect result. So, in the light of the added information from the interaction result, the results of the main effects might become obsolete.

For example, if you found that the two-way ANOVA supported the interaction hypothesis (that the effect of cowboy preference on intelligence was only found for males), it wouldn't make sense to draw conclusions about the other two hypotheses – it wouldn't make sense to talk about the effect of cowboy preference on intelligence when you know from the interaction result that this effect only exists for a subgroup of people – males.

Of course, when the interaction effect isn't significant then the main effects are important.

One plus one doesn't always equal two

When you conduct a two-way ANOVA you get an analysis for two main effects (in addition to the interaction). Each main effect is a test of the effect of each independent variable on the dependent variable. So, the two main effects that you obtain in a two-way ANOVA are a bit like conducting two separate one-way ANOVAs. But the results you obtain for the main effects in a two-way ANOVA are not the same as the results you would get if you conducted two one-way ANOVAs.

For example, compare the main effect of the independent variable 'cowboy' in a one-way ANOVA (see Figure 16-5) with the main effect of the same independent variable in the context of a two-way ANOVA (see Figure 16-8). The scores on the dependent variable are exactly the same for both analyses and you notice that the sum of squares, df and mean square values are exactly the same on both ANOVA tables; however, the F ratio and significance value obtained are different. Why?

The answer is quite technical but the difference is because of the error (or within-subjects or sometimes called the residual) sums of squares. Remember that the F ratio is the mean square for the effect divided by the error mean square. The error mean square for the two-way ANOVA is different from the one-way ANOVA. Hence the different F ratio and associated significance value.

The error mean square is different because there is more information in a two-way ANOVA. A one-way ANOVA only contains one independent variable. A two-way ANOVA contains two independent variables, which results in three terms – two main effects and an interaction. The addition of this information to the ANOVA means that you can explain more of the variance in the dependent variable. In other words, there will be less error variance – variance that is not explained by the independent variables.

Obtaining a two-way between-groups ANOVA in SPSS

You get a two-way between-groups ANOVA in SPSS using the same procedure as that outlined for obtaining the one-way ANOVA (see Figures 16-1 to 16-4). However, when choosing your variables for analysis (see Figure 16-2), be sure to move both independent variables (in this case 'cowboy' and 'gender') into the box headed 'Fixed Factor(s)'.

If you need to examine the interaction further, one of the useful pieces of information that you can get in SPSS is the interaction plot (see the next section). You obtain an interaction plot in SPSS by adding the following steps to the steps completed in Figures 16-1 to 16-4.

1. Click on the 'Plots' button. In the new window move one of the variables from the box on the left headed 'Variables' to the box on the right headed 'Horizontal axis'. Move the other variable from the box on the left to the box on the right headed 'Separate lines' (see Figure 16-6).

2. Press Add. The name of the requested graph will then appear in the box at the bottom of the window headed 'Plots'.

3. Select Continue and then OK to run the procedure.

Figure 16-6: Obtaining an interaction plot for a two-way between-groups ANOVA in SPSS.

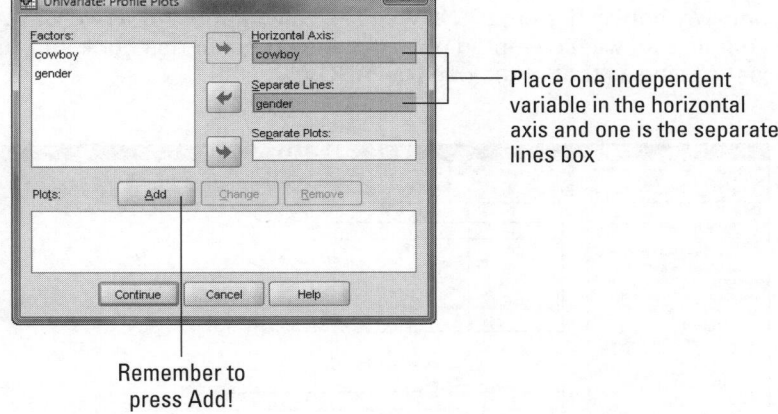

Place one independent variable in the horizontal axis and one is the separate lines box

Remember to press Add!

It doesn't matter which variable is on the horizontal axis and which is attributed to the separate lines. However, changing the variables around might make the plot easier to interpret, so it's useful to get two plots – one with the variables presented as in Figure 16-6 and then one where the variables swap positions. You can ask for these at the same time in SPSS. Remember – both plots contain the same information, so you only need to present one in your report, but having both might help you better understand the nature of the interaction.

Interpreting the SPSS output for a two-way between-groups ANOVA

The output for the two-way ANOVA in SPSS appears as the tables presented in Figures 16-7 and 16-8, and the plot in Figure 16-9.

Figure 16-7 presents the number of participants in each group, the descriptive statistics for each group and for the overall sample, and the Levene's test for homogeneity of variances. The Levene's test tests whether the variances across the groups of the independent variables are approximately equal. If the significance value for this test is 0.05 or greater, then the variances can be considered to be sufficiently similar to meet the assumption of the two-way ANOVA (see the later section 'Considering assumptions of a two-way between-groups ANOVA' in this chapter).

Interpreting the ANOVA table for a two-way between-groups ANOVA

Figure 16-8 is the ANOVA table. It contains the sum of squares, df, mean square and F ratio values that we describe in the earlier section 'Calculating a one-way between-groups ANOVA'. The calculations for a two-way ANOVA are complex, so we have opted not to include them in this book, but the principle is the same as that of the one-way ANOVA.

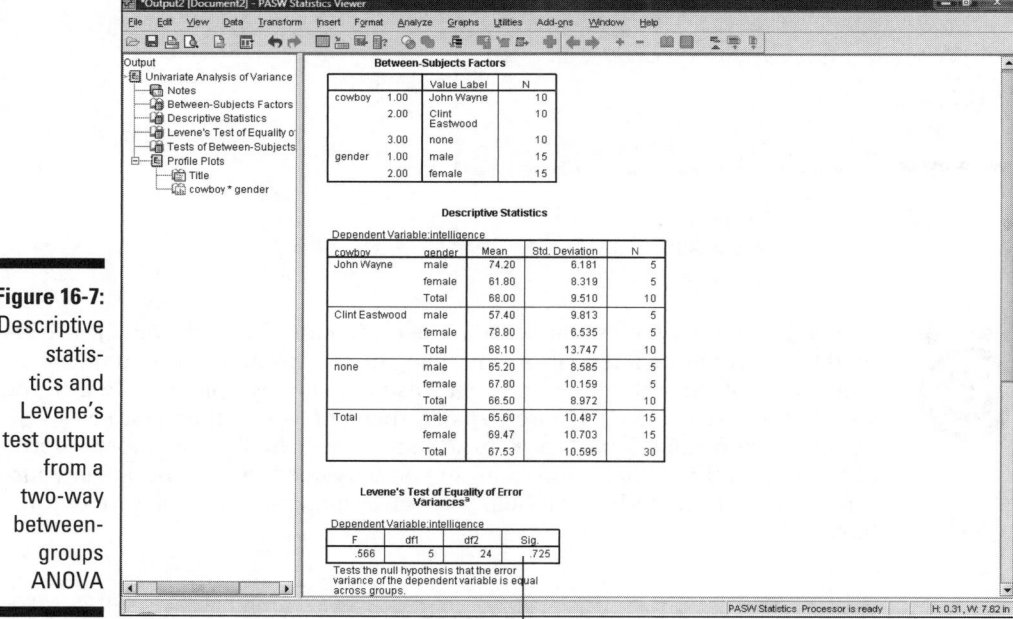

Figure 16-7: Descriptive statistics and Levene's test output from a two-way between-groups ANOVA

If this value is greater than 0.05 it means the assumption is not violated.

Notice that there are several rows of information in the ANOVA table in Figure 16-14. The most important rows are those that correspond with the names of your variables. So, the information for the main effect for cowboy preference can be found along the row labelled 'cowboy' and the main effect for gender can be found along the row labelled 'gender'. The interaction effect can be found along the row which is labelled with the product of both variables: 'cowboy * gender'. The other important row in the table is the one labelled 'error'. This is like the row in the one-way ANOVA table that referred to the within-groups information. So, the error mean square is the value used as the denominator in the F ratio calculations. At this stage you can ignore the other information in the ANOVA table.

The final column in the ANOVA table is the probability (p or sig.) value associated with the F ratio. As with all inferential statistics (see Chapter 7 for an explanation of inferential statistics), if this value is less than 0.05, then you can reject the null hypothesis. In a two-way ANOVA, there are three important significance values – one for each of the two main effects and one for the interaction result.

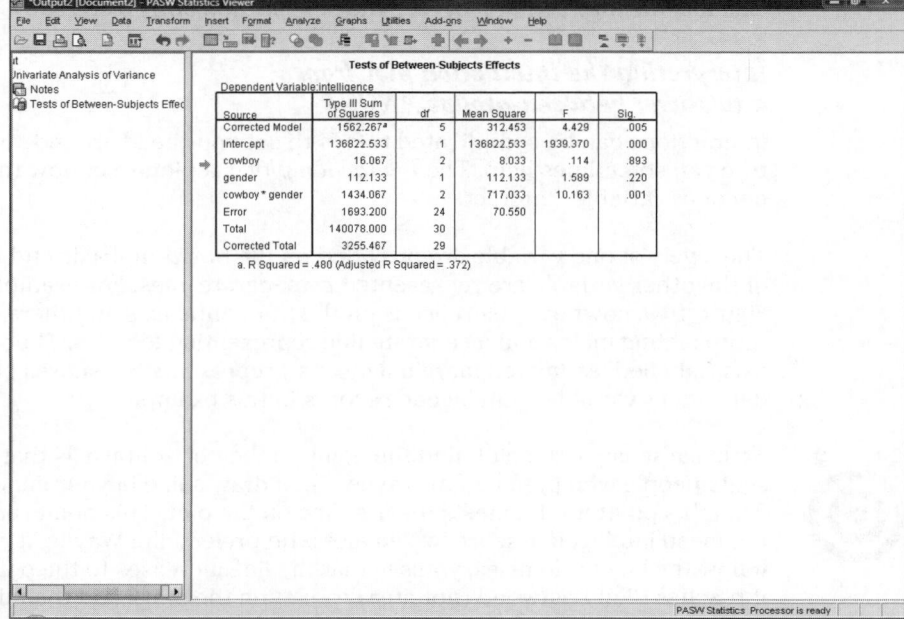

Tests of Between-Subjects Effects

Dependent Variable:intelligence

Source	Type III Sum of Squares	df	Mean Square	F	Sig.
Corrected Model	1562.267ᵃ	5	312.453	4.429	.005
Intercept	136822.533	1	136822.533	1939.370	.000
cowboy	16.067	2	8.033	.114	.893
gender	112.133	1	112.133	1.589	.220
cowboy * gender	1434.067	2	717.033	10.163	.001
Error	1693.200	24	70.550		
Total	140078.000	30			
Corrected Total	3255.467	29			

a. R Squared = .480 (Adjusted R Squared = .372)

Figure 16-8:
ANOVA output from the two-way ANOVA procedure in SPSS.

In this example, the *p* value for the main effect of 'cowboy' is 0.893, which means you fail to reject the null hypothesis that the mean scores for all groups are equal. In other words, there is no statistically significant difference between the mean scores of the three groups.

The *p* value for the main effect of 'gender' is 0.220, which means you fail to reject the null hypothesis that the mean scores for both groups is equal. In other words, there is no statistically significant difference between the mean scores of the two groups.

Finally, the *p* value for the interaction term is 0.001, which means that there is a statistically significant interaction. In other words, the effect of cowboy preference on intelligence is influenced by gender.

It is also possible to say that the effect of gender on intelligence is influenced by cowboy preference. Your hypothesis about the interaction determines which way round you present the results. The interaction result in the ANOVA table doesn't provide you with any information about the nature or direction of the interaction, only that it exists. To examine the nature of the interaction you need to look at the interaction in more detail. The best way to do this is to examine the interaction plot (see the next section and Figure 16-9).

Interpreting the interaction plot from a two-way between-groups ANOVA

Interactions can be complicated things to get your head around, and a picture can sometimes help. The *interaction plot* is a picture of how the two independent variables interact.

The levels of one variable are provided on the horizontal axis and the levels of the other variable are represented by separate lines. For example, in Figure 16-9, cowboy preference is on the horizontal axis and there is a line representing males and a separate line representing females. The vertical axis (labelled 'estimated marginal means') represents the scores on the dependent variable – intelligence scores in this example.

To make sense of the plot, find the point on the horizontal axis that represents people who prefer John Wayne. Then draw a line in your mind upwards from this point until it meets the first line on the plot. This point represents the mean intelligence score for females who prefer John Wayne. If you now follow the line for females, you see that the line increases to the point where it reaches Clint Eastwood (not literally, just on the plot), and then decreases to the point where it meets the people who don't watch cowboy movies. For females, then, the plot suggests that females who prefer Clint Eastwood have higher intelligence scores than other females in the sample.

Females who prefer Clint have a higher mean score!

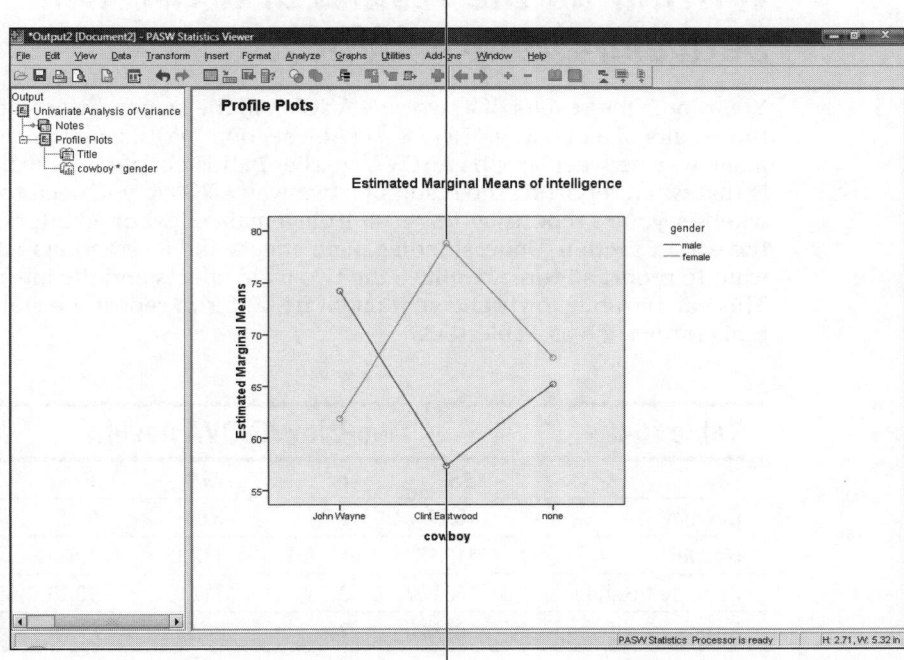

Figure 16-9:
An interaction plot for a two-way between-groups ANOVA.

Males who prefer Clint have the lowest mean score!

You can follow the same procedure to follow the line for males. In this case, the plot suggests that males who prefer John Wayne have higher intelligence scores than the other males in the sample.

There are several ways of interpreting this plot, but you should focus your interpretation around your hypothesis. So, the nature of the interaction seems to be that cowboy preference has an important influence on intelligence depending on whether you are male or female. This may explain why there is no mean effect found for cowboy preference overall, because the effect is different for the two genders and therefore overall no effect is seen. The graph shows that when the subjects don't watch cowboy films then there is no real difference in intelligence between genders. However, for females intelligence is higher for those who like Clint Eastwood, but for males it is higher for those who prefer John Wayne.

Writing up the results of a two-way between-groups ANOVA

You report the results of a two-way ANOVA in the same way as you report the results of a one-way ANOVA (see the section 'Writing up the results of a one-way between-groups ANOVA', earlier in this chapter). The difference is that when reporting the result of a two-way ANOVA, you need to clarify whether you're reporting the result from a main effect or an interaction (see the earlier section 'Understanding main effects and interactions'). Often you want to report all three results – the two main effects and the interaction. This can be a bit wordy and so it might be better to report the statistics in table form, such as Table 16-3.

Table 16-3	Two-Way ANOVA Results				
	SS	*df*	*MS*	*F*	*p*
Cowboy	16.07	2	8.03	0.11	.89
Gender	112.13	1	112.13	1.59	.22
Cowboy * Gender	1434.07	2	717.03	10.16	.001
Error	1693.20	24	70.55		

Taking the two-way ANOVA result reported in Table 16-3, you report the result in the text as follows:

> A 3×2 ANOVA with cowboy preference (John Wayne, Clint Eastwood, none) and gender (male, female) as between-subjects factors revealed no main effect for cowboy preference, $F(2,24) = 0.11$, $p = .89$, or gender, $F(1,24) = 1.59$, $p = .22$. However, there was an interaction effect, $F(2,24) = 10.16$, $p = .001$. The interaction plot suggested that among males, intelligence scores are higher for those who prefer John Wayne compared to the other cowboy preferences and among females, intelligence scores are higher for those who prefer Clint Eastwood compared to other cowboy preferences.

Present ANOVA results in a table or in the text. There is no need to present both.

We also recommended that you report an appropriate effect size statistic (see Chapter 11) and the mean and standard deviation values for each group. This is particularly important when the ANOVA indicates a statistically significant finding. In this case, the mean scores allow the reader to understand the nature of the difference.

If you report statistically significant main effects, where the independent variable has more than 2 groups then you might need to conduct post hoc tests or planned comparisons between the groups to unravel the nature of this main effect (see Chapter 17). This is because all the significance tells you is whether there is a difference somewhere between the groups, in this case cowboy preference. If this had been significant it still doesn't inform you whether this difference is between all 3 groups and in which directions the differences are.

Considering assumptions of a two-way between-groups ANOVA

The assumptions listed for a one-way between-groups ANOVA in this chapter also hold for a two-way between-groups ANOVA, so read 'Considering assumptions of a one-way between-groups ANOVA', earlier in this chapter.

In the case of a two-way between-groups ANOVA, if your data doesn't meet the assumption of normality of residual scores then you need to either abandon your plans to conduct a two-way ANOVA, or get some help to look at ways of transforming your data. This type of work is outside the scope of this book.

Kruskal–Wallis Test

You use the Kruskal–Wallis test in similar situations to when you would use a one-way between-groups ANOVA. The only difference between the two tests is in the nature of the dependent variable (see the section 'Considering assumptions of a Kruskal–Wallis test' in this chapter for more information).

You use a *Kruskal–Wallis* test to examine the differences between two or more independent groups – usually three or more groups, because you can use a Mann–Whitney U test to examine the difference between two groups (see Chapter 15). In fact, a Mann–Whitney U test and a Kruskal–Wallis test conducted to examine the difference between two groups result in exactly the same conclusions. So, think of the Kruskal–Wallis test as an extension to the Mann–Whitney U test when you have more than two groups.

For example, imagine you have conducted a research study to examine the difference in speech development between children who watch different television programs. You recruit three groups of children – 10 children who mostly watch children's television; 10 children who mostly watch reality shows; and 10 children who don't watch television. You then rate the level of speech development of each child into one of five categories using a 1 to 5 scale where 1 indicates very poor speech development, with higher numbers representing better speech development up to a score of 5 which represents very good speech development. Your hypothesis is that children who mostly watch reality shows have poorer speech development than other children.

Obtaining a Kruskal–Wallis test in SPSS

The simplest method of obtaining a Kruskal–Wallis test in SPSS is as follows.

1. **Go to the Analyze menu and choose 'Nonparametric Tests' (depending on your version of SPSS you might need to then choose 'Legacy Dialogs') and then 'K independent samples' (see Figure 16-10).**

2. **In the new window make sure that the box is ticked beside 'Kruskal–Wallis H' in the list of tests headed 'Test Type'.**

3. **Move your dependent variable (in this case 'speech') into the box headed 'Test Variable List' and move your independent variable (in this case 'television') into the box headed 'Grouping Variable' (see Figure 16-11). This will highlight the 'Define Range' button below this box. Press this button.**

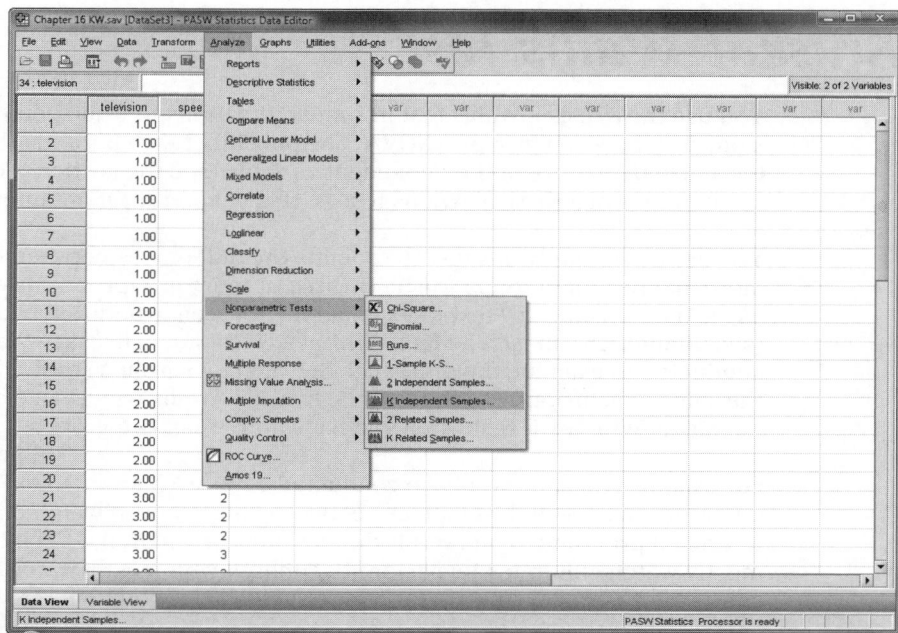

Figure 16-10: Choosing a Kruskal–Wallis test on SPSS.

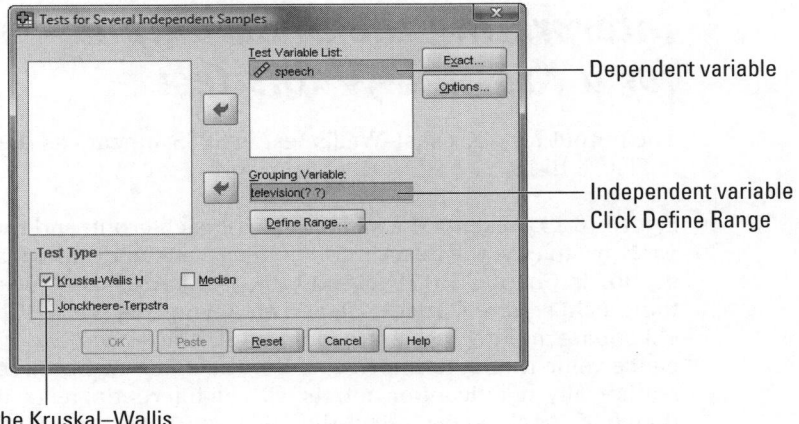

— Dependent variable

— Independent variable
— Click Define Range

Figure 16-11:
Selecting
variables for
a Kruskal–
Wallis test.

Ensure the Kruskal–Wallis
test is selected.

4. **In the new window that opens, you need to tell SPSS the numbers you have used to indicate the categories in your independent variable. The independent variable in the example has 3 categories, numbered 1, 2 and 3. Therefore, type a 1 in the box beside 'Minimum' and a 3 in the box beside 'Maximum' (see Figure 16-12).**

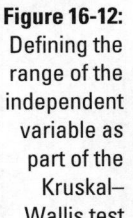

Figure 16-12:
Defining the
range of the
independent
variable as
part of the
Kruskal–
Wallis test
procedure
in SPSS.

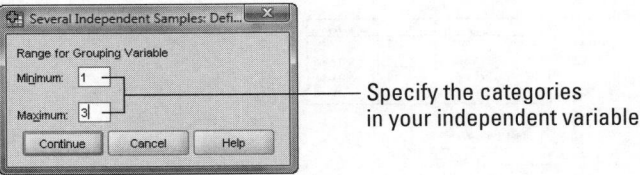

Specify the categories
in your independent variable

5. **Select Continue and then OK.**

Interpreting the SPSS output for a Kruskal–Wallis test

The output for a Kruskal–Wallis test in SPSS appears as the tables presented in Figure 16-13.

Figure 16-13 presents the sample size of each group and the mean rank for each group (see the description of mean rank under the Mann–Whitney test section in Chapter 15). The next table is the Kruskal–Wallis test result. It contains a chi-square statistic, df, and an Asymp. Sig. Value. Chapter 14 explains chi-square and degrees of freedom or df. The *Asymp. Sig. value* is the significance value that determines whether the difference between the groups is statistically significant or not. As with all inferential tests, if this value is less than 0.05 then you can reject the null hypothesis that there is no difference between the speech development score distributions of the groups.

In this example, the *p* value for the main effect of 'television' is 0.935, which means you fail to reject the null hypothesis. In other words, there is no statistically significant difference between the scores of the three groups.

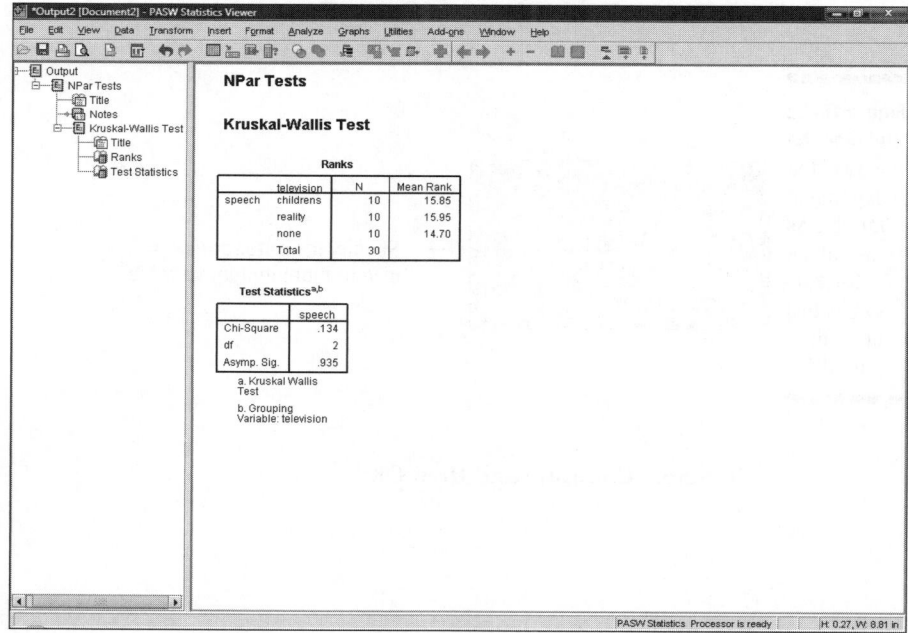

Figure 16-13: Kruskal–Wallis test output from SPSS.

Writing up the results of a Kruskal–Wallis test

When reporting Kruskal–Wallis test results, the American Psychological Association Manual suggests that you should report the Kruskal–Wallis H value rounded to 2 decimal places, with the degrees of freedom in parentheses, followed by the significance level (the *H value* is the chi-square value presented in Figure 16-13). Taking the result reported in Figure 16-13, you report the result as follows:

> There was a statistically significant difference between the three groups of children in terms of their speech development, $H(2) = 0.07$, $p = .04$.'

You also need to report some descriptive information about each group to help the reader to understand the nature of the difference. Often you report the median value (see Chapter 4) and the interquartile range (see Chapter 5) for each group. You also report an effect size measure that is similar to the eta-squared value calculated for a one-way ANOVA (see Chapter 11) and is related to the Cramer's V statistic calculated for chi-square analysis (see Chapter 14). This value is obtained by dividing the chi-square value from the Kruskal–Wallis test by the sample size minus one.

The Kruskal–Wallis test only indicates whether there is a statistically significant difference between groups. It doesn't indicate the nature of the difference, nor where the significant difference lies. For example, if you find a significant difference between three groups it might be the case that all 3 groups differ significantly from each other or that one group differs from the other two. To uncover this detail you need to compare the different pairs of groups in post hoc tests or planned comparisons (see Chapter 17 for a discussion of the differences) using Mann–Whitney U tests (see Chapter 15).

Considering assumptions of a Kruskal–Wallis test

The Kruskal–Wallis test is used in similar situations to when you would use a one-way between-groups ANOVA. You might hear it referred to as the nonparametric equivalent of a one-way ANOVA. *Non-parametric* means that the test makes no assumptions about the data. As you see in the section 'Considering assumptions of a one-way between-groups ANOVA', there are various assumptions that need to be met before the results of this test are considered valid. The Kruskal–Wallis test doesn't have many of these assumptions and so it is considered to be free from assumptions, or non-parametric.

Actually, the Kruskal–Wallis isn't free from assumptions, because there are some conditions that need to be met by your data before a Kruskal–Wallis test can be used validly. These conditions are:

- The independent variables should be categorical (see Chapter 2 for a description of categorical variables).

- The dependent variable should be measured at the ordinal level. It also might be the case that the dependent variable is measured at the interval/ratio level (see Chapter 2) but the assumptions of normality and/or homogeneity of variance that are required by a one-way ANOVA are not met.

Chapter 17

Post Hoc Tests and Planned Comparisons for Independent Groups Designs

. . . .

In This Chapter

▶ Obtaining and interpreting a Tukey post hoc test

▶ Obtaining and interpreting a Dunnett planned comparison

. . . .

*W*hen you find a significant difference between two independent groups, using an independent *t*-test or a Mann–Whitney U test (see Chapter 15) then you can easily determine which group is scoring higher than the other group by looking at the mean or median scores of the groups. When you find a significant difference between 3 or more independent groups, using a between-groups ANOVA or a Kruskal–Wallis test (see Chapter 16) then working out where this significant difference lies can be more difficult.

This is because the ANOVA or Kruskal–Wallis test only indicates whether there is a statistically significant difference between groups. They do not tell you where the significant difference lies. For example, if you find a significant difference between three groups it might be the case that all three groups differ significantly from each other or that one group differs from the other two. Of course, examining the mean or median scores (see Chapter 4) of each group gives you an indication of where the significant difference is likely to be. This might be sufficient in some circumstances but often you want to have more evidence about the nature of the significant difference. This is where post hoc tests and planned comparisons are useful.

The difference between a post hoc test and a planned comparison is that *post hoc tests* compare every possible pair of groups whereas *planned comparisons* only make specific comparisons between groups which have been decided in advance of conducting the analysis. Therefore, planned comparisons are usually driven by theory, whereas post hoc tests simply trawl the data looking for any significant findings. As a result post hoc tests are less sensitive than planned comparisons: post hoc tests are less likely to find significant differences than planned comparisons.

Before conducting any analyses, decide whether there are planned comparisons that you want to examine. If there are then build these into your plan of analysis. If not then this leaves the opportunity of conducting post hoc tests. It's inappropriate to conduct both planned comparisons and post hoc tests on the same data – so choose one or the other.

Post Hoc Tests for Independent Groups Designs

One way of examining the differences between three or more groups to determine which are significantly different is to test the difference between all possible pairs of groups. For example, if you have three groups in your analysis and a between-groups ANOVA indicates that there is a significant difference between these three groups then you could compare each pair of groups by conducting an independent *t*-test to compare Group 1 with Group 2, another *t*-test to compare Group 1 with Group 3, and another *t*-test to compare Group 2 with Group 3.

Imagine you conduct a research study to examine the difference between psychologists, physicists and historians on a scale of sociability. You collect sociability scores from 30 psychologists, 30 physicists and 30 historians and conduct a one-way between-groups ANOVA (see Chapter 16). The ANOVA indicates that there is a statistically significant difference between these three groups on the measure of sociability. But how do you know whether psychologists are significantly more sociable than historians or whether physicists are significantly more sociable than psychologists? You could conduct three separate independent *t*-tests – one to compare historians with psychologists, one to compare historians with physicists and one to compare psychologists with physicists. If any of these *t*-tests are significant then you could examine the mean scores to see who's most sociable.

The principle here is sound (although the analyses can become cumbersome if your independent variable has many levels), but in practice it creates a problem which statisticians refer to as multiplicity, which we explore in the next section. And to manage the issue of multiplicity, you need to use a post hoc test.

Multiplicity

Multiplicity occurs when you conduct several significance tests to test a single hypothesis. In the example from the introduction to this section the ANOVA tested your hypothesis that the three groups would differ on sociability. To determine where this significant difference lies you then conducted three *t*-tests (three more significance tests) – so you have conducted three tests for one hypothesis.

Our students often find it difficult to understand why multiplicity is a problem. It relates to the concept of probability, so it's not an obvious problem in your analysis. Also, there is a lack of consensus among statisticians about when multiplicity is a problem, so not everyone reacts in the same way to this situation. Therefore, we try to keep our advice as simple and uncontroversial as possible.

Basically, the problem here relates to the concept of the Type I error (see Chapter 8 for a discussion of the Type I error). Usually, when you conduct a significance test, there is a 5 per cent chance that you will make a Type I error; so, a 5 per cent chance that you will find a significant difference when you shouldn't have. This isn't an error that you make in your analysis; it's an error that relates to the fact that all significance tests are based on probability. In other words, you can never be certain about the conclusions of a significance test; you can only state your conclusions with a high degree of probability. This means that there is a small chance that your conclusions are wrong.

This 5 per cent chance of making a Type I error is the maximum that's acceptable, which is why you use the 0.05 cut-off point to determine whether a result is statistically significant or not. However, multiplicity suggests that when you conduct more than one significance test under the same hypothesis, you're increasing your overall chances of making a Type I error. For example, if you conduct three *t*-tests as a result of finding a significant ANOVA result then you have a 5 per cent Type I error rate associated with each *t*-test. In simple terms this means that you have a 5 per cent + 5 per cent + 5 per cent = 15 per cent error rate for this set of three tests. Actually, it doesn't add up to exactly 15 per cent because the calculation is a little more complex, but this is the principle behind multiplicity.

The solution to this problem is to use a post hoc test that has been designed to manage the issue of multiplicity (see the next section).

Choosing a post hoc test

Many post hoc tests exist, designed to examine differences between groups without raising the multiplicity problem. The most commonly used post hoc tests in psychology are the Scheffé test and the Tukey Honestly Significant Difference (HSD) test, which is often simply referred to as the Tukey test.

These tests differ in the way that they adjust the Type I error rate for the analyses. Without going into a mathematical explanation, the Scheffé test tends to have less power than the Tukey test. In other words, you're more likely to find statistically significant differences between pairs of groups using the Tukey test than when using the Scheffé test. Therefore, the Tukey test is often the best option.

It's worth noting that there might be situations when your ANOVA provides a statistically significant result but the post hoc tests suggest that there are no significant differences between groups. This might seem a bit odd but it happens because when you examine comparisons between pairs of groups you are leaving other groups out of your analysis. This reduces your sample size – so, the sample size in a comparison between two groups is less than the sample size in the ANOVA, which has more than two groups. With a reduced sample size comes reduced power (see Chapter 11), which means that you might find it's more difficult to detect differences between groups.

In the case where you have conducted a Kruskal–Wallis test and you want to examine differences between pairs of groups, the only option available is to conduct Mann–Whitney tests (see Chapter 15) on all pairs of groups, because no post hoc test exists for situations when the dependent variable is measured at the ordinal level.

To control for the multiplicity problem in this case, you need to adjust your conclusions about the Mann–Whitney tests by adjusting the cut-off point for determining whether a finding is statistically significant or not.

A simple way of doing this is to divide the normal cut-off point (0.05) by the number of Mann–Whitney tests conducted. So, if you conduct three Mann–Whitney tests to examine the difference between groups after a Kruskal–Wallis test, then the cut-off point for determining statistical significance would be $0.05 \div 3 = 0.0167$. Therefore, a Mann–Whitney test would need to have a significance value less than 0.0167 in this specific case before the difference between the two groups would be considered to be statistically significant. This is known as applying a *Bonferroni correction*.

Obtaining a Tukey HSD post hoc test in SPSS

You perform post hoc tests for independent groups designs via the between-groups ANOVA procedure.

1. **Go to the Analyze menu and choose General Linear Model. Then choose Univariate (see Figure 17-1).**

2. **In the new window move your dependent variable (in this case 'sociability') into the box headed Dependent Variable and move your independent variable (in this case 'profession') into the box headed Fixed Factor(s) (see Figure 17-2).**

3. **Click on the 'Post Hoc' button. This opens a new window with a range of post hoc test options. The independent variable appears on the left-hand side in a box headed 'Factor(s)'. Move this variable into the box on the right-hand side headed 'Post Hoc Tests for'.**

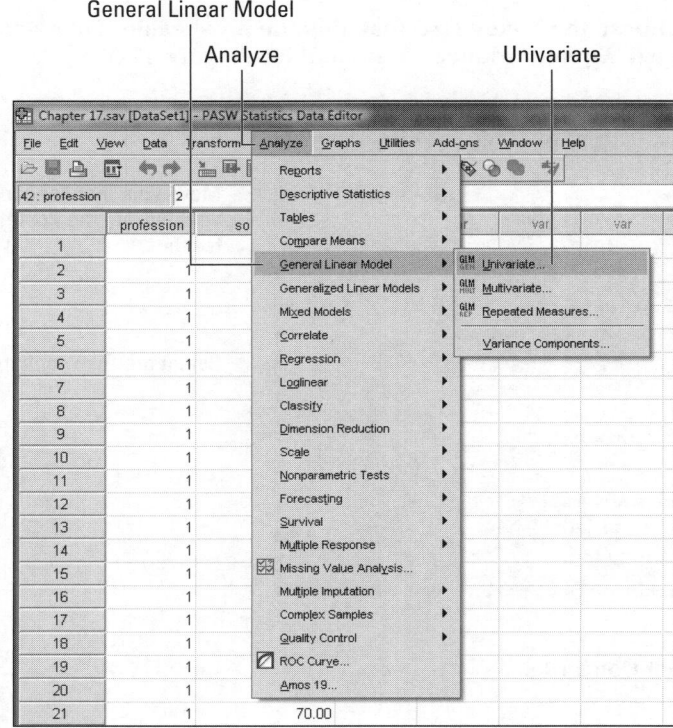

Figure 17-1: Choosing the between-groups ANOVA procedure on SPSS.

Dependent
variable

Independent
variable

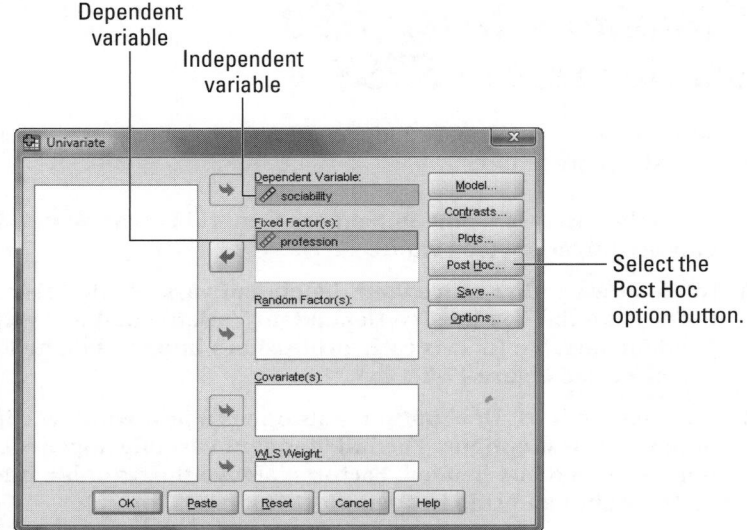

Select the
Post Hoc
option button.

Figure 17-2:
Selecting
variables for
a between-
groups
ANOVA.

4. **To choose the Tukey HSD test, tick the box beside 'Tukey' in the list headed 'Equal Variances Assumed' (see Figure 17-3).**

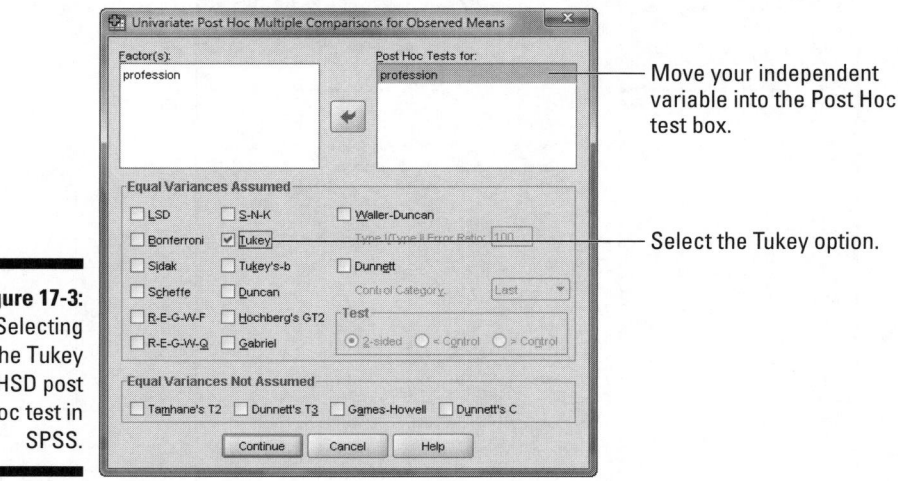

Move your independent
variable into the Post Hoc
test box.

Select the Tukey option.

Figure 17-3:
Selecting
the Tukey
HSD post
hoc test in
SPSS.

5. **Select Continue.**

6. **Click on the Options button and in the window that opens tick the box beside the words 'Descriptive statistics', in the list headed 'Display' (see Figure 17-4).**

Select
Descriptive statistics

7. **Select Continue and then OK.**

Interpreting the SPSS output for a Tukey HSD post hoc test

The output for the post hoc test in SPSS appears as the tables presented in Figures 17-5 and 17-6.

Figure 17-5 presents the output from the one-way between-groups ANOVA (see Chapter 16 for a discussion of how to interpret this output). The ANOVA table confirms that there is a statistically significant difference between the three groups.

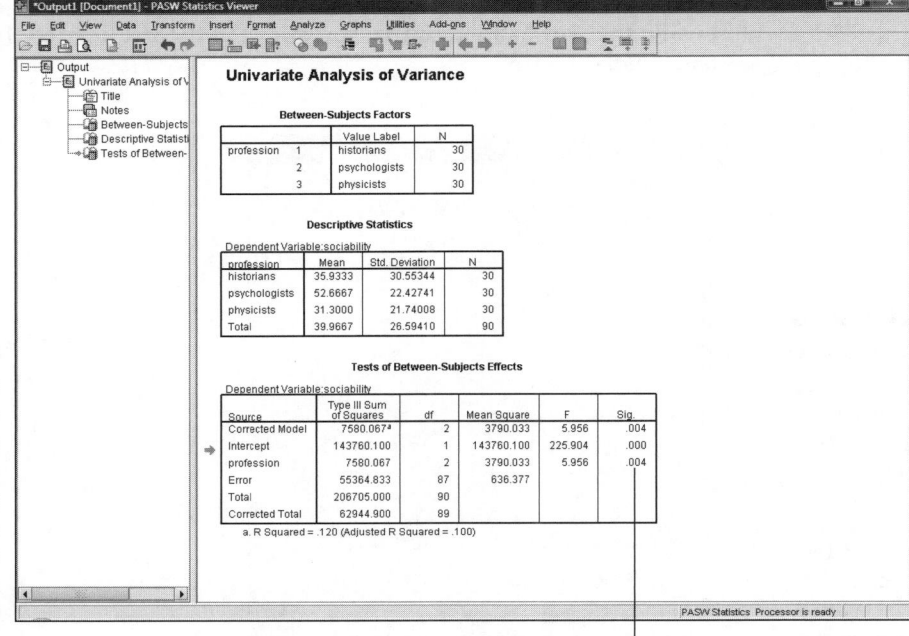

Figure 17-5:
ANOVA output from the between-groups ANOVA procedure in SPSS.

The ANOVA results tells you if
there is a significant difference
between the groups

Figure 17-6 presents the results of the post hoc Tukey test. From these results you can see a significant difference between the psychologists and the physicists and between the psychologists and the historians. For example, the first line in the table compares the sociability scores of historians with the scores of psychologists. If you read across this line to the column headed 'sig.', you see that the significance value is 0.032, which indicates that these two groups differ significantly (the sig. value is less than 0.05).

The second line of the table compares the sociability scores of historians with the scores of physicists. If you read across this line to the column headed 'sig.', you see that the significance value is 0.757, which indicates that these two groups don't differ significantly (the sig. value is greater than 0.05).

You interpret the remainder of the table in the same way.

You might also notice that the table in Figure 17-6 repeats information. For example, compare the first line (historians versus psychologists) with the third line (psychologists versus historians). The information provided in these two lines is almost the same. This is because the same two groups are being compared, just the other way round. The significance values for the difference between two groups is always the same no matter which group comes first, so one of these lines of information is redundant. In fact, there are six significance values in the table in Figure 17-6, even though you have only conducted three significance tests. This is because every test is repeated, so you can ignore the repetition of the same information.

There is also a table headed 'Homogenous subsets' which is provided by SPSS. You can ignore this table for now.

The Tukey test indicates that there is a significant difference between psychologists and the other two groups but you can't easily discern whether the psychologists score significantly higher than the other groups. To obtain this information you can examine the descriptive statistics (see Figure 17-5).

The Descriptive Statistics table in Figure 17-5 indicates that the psychologists have a higher mean sociability score than the other groups. Therefore you can conclude that psychologists are significantly more sociable than historians or physicists (the result was never in doubt!).

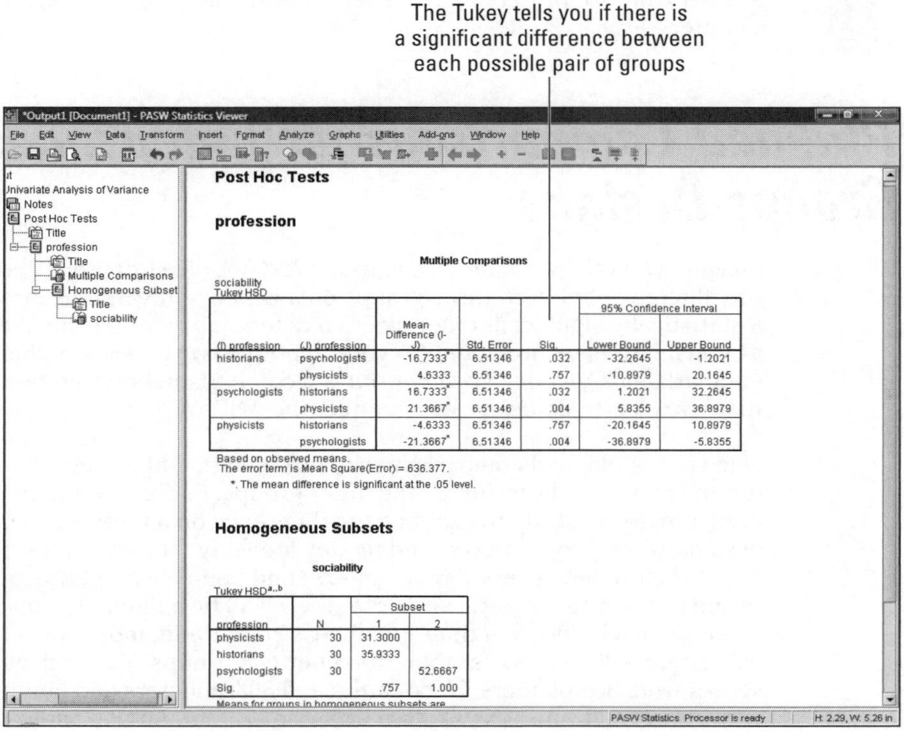

The Tukey tells you if there is
a significant difference between
each possible pair of groups

Figure 17-6:
Tukey post hoc test as presented by SPSS.

Writing up the results of a post hoc Tukey HSD test

As we explain in Chapter 14, when reporting the results of statistical analyses, you need to follow any specific guidelines that inform how you should present the statistical findings. You present the results of a post hoc test in conjunction with the results of the ANOVA and along with the mean and standard deviation scores for each group in the analysis. Taking the analyses reported in Figures 17-5 and 17-6, you report the result as follows:

> There was a statistically significant difference between the three professions in terms of their sociability scores, $F(2,87) = 5.96$, $p = .004$. Post hoc Tukey HSD tests indicated that psychologists ($M = 52.67$, $SD = 22.43$) had significantly ($p = .03$) higher sociability scores than historians ($M = 35.93$, $SD = 30.55$) and significantly ($p = .004$) higher sociability scores than physicists ($M = 31.30$, $SD = 21.74$). There was no significant difference found between physicists and historians ($p = .757$).

It is also important to report an effect size for the ANOVA result (see Chapter 11).

Planned Comparisons for Independent Groups Designs

Imagine you conduct a between-groups ANOVA (see Chapter 16) to examine the difference between three groups on a dependent variable and you find a statistically significant difference. To determine whether this difference is as you might have predicted (in your hypothesis) you can conduct planned comparisons. A *planned comparison* is a comparison between two groups that you plan to do *before* you conduct the ANOVA.

One type of planned comparison is to examine the difference between one group in your analysis and all the other groups. For example, say you conduct a research study to examine the difference on a measure of greediness between people who spend money foolishly (spenders), people who count their money every day (counters) and people who photocopy money (fraudsters). Your hypothesis is that there will be a difference between the three groups in terms of their greediness scores and, more specifically, that fraudsters will be greedier than the other two groups. You collect greediness scores from 30 spenders, 30 counters and 30 fraudsters and conduct a one-way between-groups ANOVA (see Chapter 16). The ANOVA indicates that a statistically significant difference exists between these three groups on the measure of greediness. You also conduct a follow-up planned comparison to examine the difference in greediness scores between fraudsters and the other two groups.

Choosing a planned comparison

To compare a group with all other groups in the analysis, you can use the Dunnett test. This test allows you to run a one-tailed test or a two-tailed test (see Chapter 8 for a discussion of the difference). A one-tailed test is more powerful and so you should choose it if possible. The group to which all other groups is compared (fraudsters in the example) is referred to as the *control group* by the Dunnett test. Your hypothesis states that fraudsters will be more greedy than the other two groups and therefore you can choose a one-tailed Dunnett test.

In the case where you have conducted a Kruskal–Wallis test and you wish to examine differences between pairs of groups in planned comparisons, the only option available is to conduct Mann–Whitney tests on the pairs of groups for which you want planned comparisons, as there is no planned comparison test developed for situations when the dependent variable is measured at the ordinal level. In this case you need to adjust your conclusions about the significance value as discussed in the earlier section 'Choosing a post hoc test'.

Obtaining a Dunnett test in SPSS

Post hoc tests for independent groups designs are obtained via the between-groups ANOVA procedure. Follow all the steps we outline in the earlier section 'Obtaining a Tukey HSD post hoc test in SPSS', but in Step 4 choose the Dunnett test (see Figure 17-3).

When you select the Dunnett test you then need to indicate which category is the control category – that is, the category that you want to compare the others against (in this case the fraudsters group). SPSS only allows this category to be the first or the last category and you need to choose which one from the drop-down menu. The groups in your independent variable are numbered, so the first category means the group with the lowest number and the last category means the group with the highest number. In this example, the groups are numbered 1, 2 and 3, with fraudsters as group 1. Therefore the 'control' category is the first.

The Dunnett test also requires you to specify whether your hypothesis is that the 'control' group will score higher than the other groups in the analysis (< Control), lower than all the other groups in the analysis (> Control) or whether you cannot say (two-sided). Choose the most appropriate option, based on your hypothesis. In the example, you hypothesised that the fraudsters would score higher on the greediness scale than the other two groups, so you choose '< Control'.

Interpreting the SPSS output for a Dunnett test

The output for the Dunnett test in SPSS will appear as the tables presented in Figures 17-7 and 17-8.

Figure 17-7 presents the results of a one-way between-groups ANOVA (see Chapter 16 for a discussion of how to interpret this output). The ANOVA table in Figure 17-7 confirms that there is a significant difference between the 3 groups.

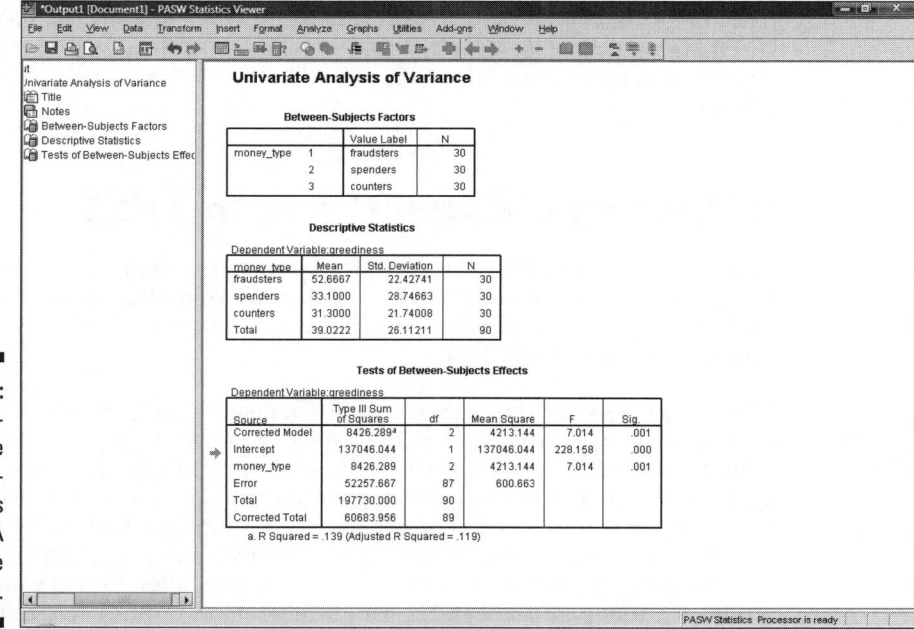

Figure 17-7: ANOVA output from the between-groups ANOVA procedure in SPSS.

Figure 17-8 presents the results of the Dunnett test. From these results you can see a significant difference between the fraudsters and the other two groups, in accordance with the hypothesis. For example, the first line in the table compares the greediness scores of spenders with the scores of fraudsters. If you read across this line to the column headed 'sig.', you see that the significance value is 0.003, which indicates that these two groups differ significantly (the sig value is less than 0.05).

The second line of the table compares the greediness scores of counters with the scores of fraudsters. If you read across this line to the column headed 'sig.', you see that the significance value is 0.001, which indicates that these two groups differ significantly (the sig value is less than 0.05).

The Dunnett test indicates that a significant difference exists between the fraudsters and the other two groups, but you can't easily discern whether the fraudsters score significantly higher than the other groups, as hypothesised. To obtain this information you look at the descriptive statistics (see Figure 17-7).

The Descriptive Statistics table in Figure 17-7 indicates that the fraudsters have a higher mean greediness score than the other groups. Therefore you can conclude that fraudsters are significantly more greedy than spenders or counters.

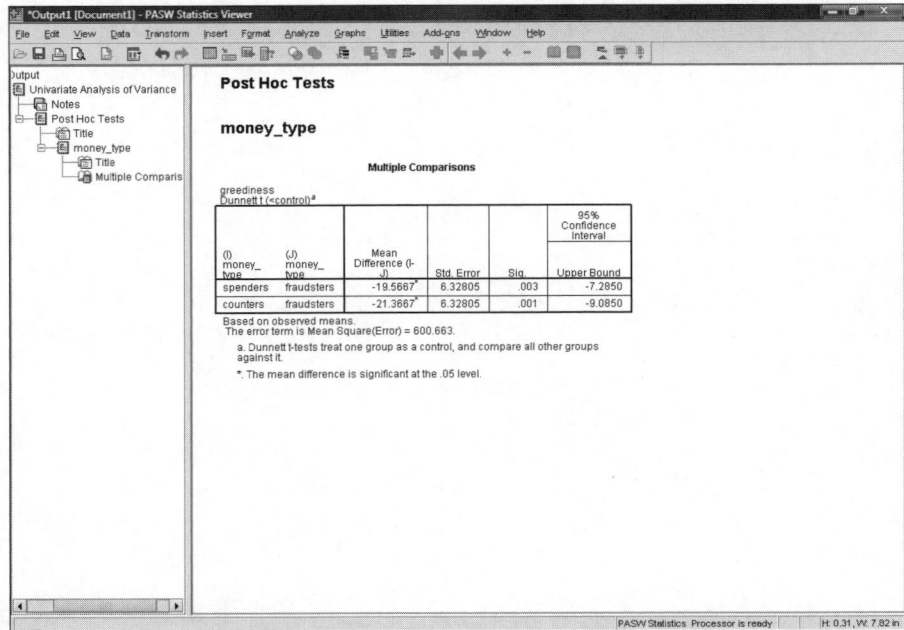

Figure 17-8:
Dunnett test as presented by SPSS.

Writing up the results of a Dunnett test

You present the results of a planned comparison in conjunction with the results of the ANOVA and along with the mean and standard deviation scores for each group in the analysis. Taking the analyses reported in Figures 17-7 and 17-8, you report the result as follows:

> There was a statistically significant difference between the three groups in terms of their greediness scores, $F(2,87) = 7.01$, $p = .001$. Planned comparisons using a Dunnett test, to test the hypothesis that the fraudsters would score significantly higher than the other two groups in the analysis, indicated that fraudsters ($M = 52.67$, $SD = 22.43$) had significantly ($p = .003$) higher greediness scores than spenders ($M = 33.10$, $SD = 28.75$) and significantly ($p = .001$) higher greediness scores than counters ($M = 31.30$, $SD = 21.74$).

And also report an effect size for the ANOVA result (see Chapter 11).

If you have a specific hypothesis you want to test it may be more appropriate to conduct a planned contrast. You have the option of six pre-set planned comparisons if you conduct your between-groups ANOVA through the General Linear Model option instead of the Compare Means option. We explain all six planned contrasts in Chapter 20.

Part V
Analysing Repeated Measures Research Designs

"It's our patron saint."

In this part . . .

Here we come to the inferential statistics that examine differences between two or more repeated measurements. This part covers the Paired *t*-test, the Wilcoxon test and Analysis of Variance (ANOVA) and how they can be used to bring statistical meaning to your research data. We also focus on analysis of research designs that include both independent groups and repeated measurements: the Mixed ANOVA. Not as intimidating as it all sounds, we promise.

Chapter 18

Paired *t*-tests and Wilcoxon Tests

Part V of this book deals with analyses that are appropriate for experimental studies that employ repeated measures design, in other words, studies that investigate how variables change within the same group of people. This means you test the same participants more than once, for example, if you wanted to see the change in spelling ability between 7- and 8-year-old children you would test the children when they were aged 7 and again when they were 8 years old. Here your dependent variable is spelling ability and the independent variable is age; because you tested age twice you say the independent variable has two levels. In these studies where you have tested your participants twice (or your independent variable has two levels) you can use the parametric paired *t*-test or the non-parametric Wilcoxon test to see if the difference in scores is statistically significant. If you have tested the same group of participants more than twice (that is, your independent variable has more than two levels) then the within-groups ANOVA or the non-parametric Friedman test that we cover in Chapter 19 is most appropriate. In this chapter we cover the paired *t*-test and the Wilcoxon test.

Understanding Repeated Measures Design

Repeated measures design is an experimental design where participants take part in all experimental conditions or all levels of an independent variable. For example, if you want to see whether alcohol has an effect on dancing performance then you give a person several shots of whiskey and score her dancing *and* at a later date you score her dancing when she's completely sober. This differs from an independent groups design where you have two separate independent groups, one that consumes alcohol and a different group that consumes no alcohol. (We discuss independent groups design in

Part IV.) The name *repeated measures* indicates that you repeat your measurements with the same group. This design is also called a *within-subjects design* because you're looking for changes within the same participants.

In repeated measures designs the independent variable has at least two levels, for example, alcohol or no alcohol. But you can have more than two levels of your independent variable in the case of longitudinal or developmental studies; for example, you may wish to study the development of metacognition in children and test the same children each month for three years (see Chapter 19).

The advantage of the repeated measures design is that you're controlling for individual differences. If you have two independent groups, the individuals in those groups vary in personality, honesty, attitudes, experiences and dancing ability among other things. This variation between groups that you get in independent groups designs can be problematic. For example, it is possible that you could detect an effect on dancing ability that was nothing to do with alcohol if one group happened to contain mainly keen amateur dancers and all members of the other group had two left feet! When you employ a repeated measures design, you're controlling for many of these differences because you're looking for changes within the same people. Any changes in dancing scores can be attributed to the effect of the alcohol (and not pre-existing differences between groups) as the only thing that varies is alcohol consumption. Less variability exists, so significant differences are easier to detect – which makes this design powerful. (See Chapter 11 for more information on power.)

Paired t-test

The *paired t-test* (also called the related-samples or dependent *t*-test) is appropriate when you want to test whether scores (on a variable measured at the interval/ratio level) from the same participants have changed between two time points. For example, the scores could be anxiety before and after therapy, children's ethical judgements at the start and end of the year or boredom before and after watching a political party broadcast. The paired *t*-test looks at the mean differences between scores at the two testing sessions (or the two levels of your independent variable). This entails calculating the difference between the scores for each participant (their score at time 1 minus score at time 2). You're likely to find that some scores increase and some decrease; however, you're interested in seeing whether the overall mean difference is substantial enough to say a *significant* difference exists. So the paired *t*-test tests the null hypothesis that no significant mean difference exists and therefore any differences that exist are due to sampling error (chance). We explain null hypotheses in Chapter 8.

The *t*-test provides a *t* value. The larger the value of *t*, the greater the mean difference in scores between the two time points. The *t* distribution is based on the sample standard deviation, and consequently a *t*-value distribution exists for every sample size (head over to Chapter 10 for the low-down on the *t* distribution). This means no one cut-off value exists that signifies a significant difference between the two points. Therefore, you always need to report the *t*-value, the degrees of freedom (which reflect sample size) and the statistical significance.

You could run an independent *t*-test on the same data (we explain independent *t*-tests in Chapter 14). But (as explained in the preceding section) the fact that you're looking at changes within the same people means that the paired *t*-test is a more powerful statistic.

An independent *t*-test in used to assess difference on a variable between two separate groups of people on a variable (independent groups design), A paired *t*-test is used to assess difference or change on a variable when the same people have been tested twice (repeated measure design).

Performing a paired t-test in SPSS

Statistics anxiety is a bad thing. Students with high levels of statistics anxiety think they don't like statistics (we know you'd never think like that), and the anxiety impacts on their self-confidence and means they hand in their reports late. We hypothesised that we'd find a significant difference in statistics anxiety scores at the start of the term (time 1) compared to the statistics anxiety scores at the end of the term (time 2). We tested the same students at the start of term and at the end of term, meaning the study followed a repeated measures design. The paired *t*-test was the appropriate statistic to analyse the data because we have a repeated measures design where the independent variable (time) has two levels and we wish to see whether there is a significant difference or change on the dependent variable (statistics anxiety).

Here's how you perform a paired *t*-test in SPSS:

1. **Select Analyze from the top toolbar, and then Compare Means from the drop-down menu and finally Paired-Samples T Test (Figure 18-1).**

2. **A Paired-Samples *t*-test window opens. Move the two variables of interest into the Paired Variables box starting with the variable that was measured at time 1. Put the time 1 variable in the Variable1 column and, you guessed it, the time 2 variable in the Variable2 column (see Figure 18-2).**

Compare Means

Analyze | Paired-Samples T Test

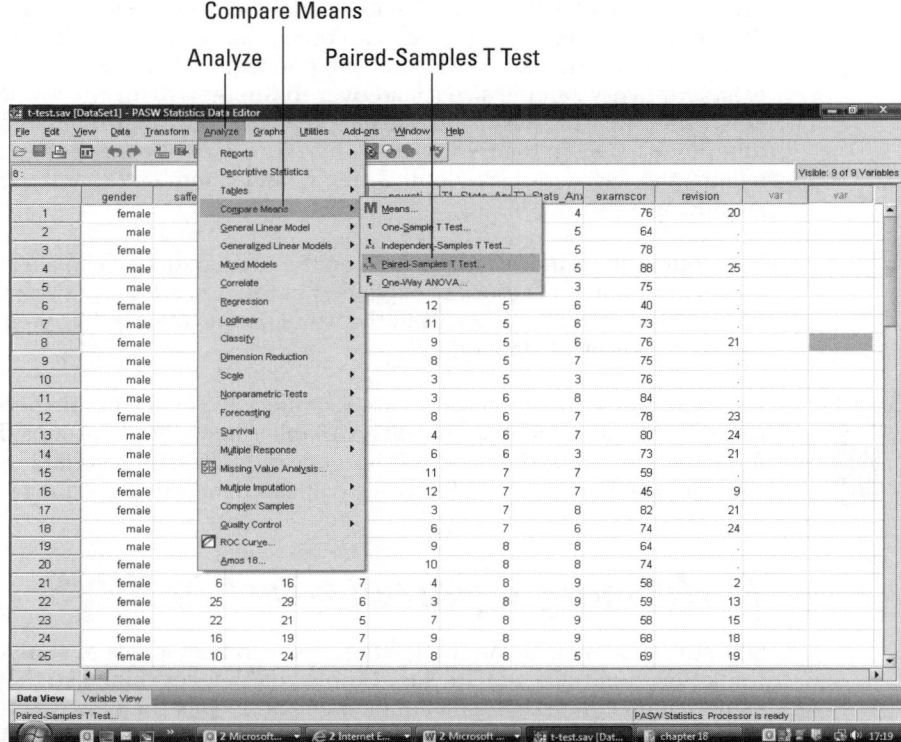

Figure 18-1:
Obtaining a
paired *t*-test
on SPSS.

Enter the 2 variables of interest

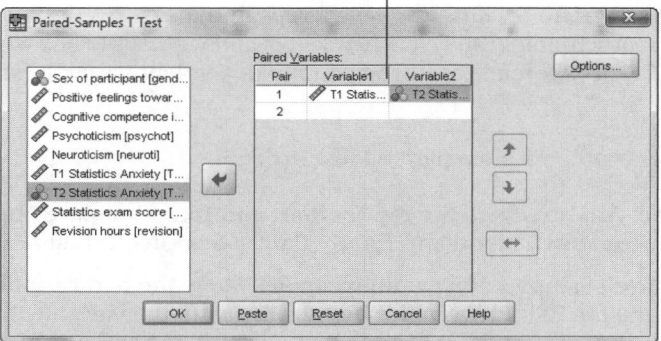

Figure 18-2:
Specifying
the vari-
ables for an
independent
t-test.

3. **Click OK to run the statistic.**

You can run several paired *t*-tests at the same time but the output can become confusing. So we recommend that you run them individually.

Interpreting the output

SPSS produces three tables of output for each paired *t*-test you run: a table of descriptive statistics, a correlation and the paired samples test table.

The first table (Figure 18-3) presents descriptive statistics for your analysis.

Figure 18-3: Paired Samples Statistics table.

		Mean	N	Std. Deviation	Std. Error Mean
Pair 1	T1 Statistics Anxiety	8.15	62	2.055	.261
	T2 Statistics Anxiety	8.56	62	2.480	.315

Here's how to understand the table:

✔ **Mean:** The mean at each testing session. The mean statistics anxiety score at time 1 was 8.15 and this increased slightly to a mean of 8.56 at time 2.

✔ **N:** The number of participants. In the current example 62 students were tested both at time 1 at time 2.

If you tested 62 students at time 1 but only tested 55 students at time 2 then the analysis would only be conducted on the 55 students that had scores at both testing sessions (at both levels of the independent variable).

✔ **Std. Deviation:** The standard deviation for each testing session. The standard deviation at time 1 was 2.06 and 2.48 at time 2.

✔ **Std. Error of the Mean:** The standard error of the mean (or the standard deviation of the sampling distribution of means – see Chapter 8). You obtain the standard error of the mean by dividing the standard deviation by the square root of the sample size. You don't need to report this figure.

TIP

Make sure the two variables are appropriately labelled so you easily tell which relates to time 1 and time 2. You can label variables in the variable view window of SPSS – flick to Chapter 3 for details.

The next table (see Figure 18-4) is a Pearson's correlation of time 1 scores and time 2 scores. In the current example a strong, positive statistically significant correlation exists between statistics anxiety scores at time 1 and time 2; $r(62) = .85$, $p < .001$. This indicates that high scores at time 1 were related to high scores at time 2 (see Chapter 12 for more information on correlations). In many cases you're not interested in the correlation between the testing sessions and can ignore it. The t-test and correlation describe two complementary (and not opposing) trends within your data; if you want to find out more about relationships and differences check out the entry in Chapter 22.

Figure 18-4: Paired Samples Correlations table.

		N	Correlation	Sig.
Pair 1	T1 Statistics Anxiety & T2 Statistics Anxiety	62	.846	.000

Paired samples table

The paired samples test table (Figure 18-5) provides your t-test result.

Figure 18-5: Paired Samples Test table.

		Paired Differences							
					95% Confidence Interval of the Difference				
		Mean	Std. Deviation	Std. Error Mean	Lower	Upper	t	df	Sig. (2-tailed)
Pair 1	T1 Statistics Anxiety - T2 Statistics Anxiety	-.419	1.325	.168	-.756	-.083	-2.492	61	.015

This value tells if the difference between the two testing sessions is significant or not

Here's how to understand the table:

- **Mean:** The mean difference between time 1 and 2. You can check this by looking at the means from time1 and time 2 in Figure 18-3. It can be a positive or negative number. A positive number indicates the score at time 1 was greater than time 2. A negative number, as in this example, means the score at time 2 is greater than time 1.

- **Std. Deviation:** The standard deviation of the differences. If you calculate the difference in scores (time 1 – time 2) for each person, this value is the standard deviation of those difference scores.

- **Std. Error Mean:** The standard error of the mean is the standard deviation of the difference scores divided by the square root of the sample size. You use the standard error of the mean to calculate the significance value and confidence interval (see Chapter 8). You don't need to report the figure.

- **95% Confidence Interval of the Difference:** The range in which you're 95 per cent confident the true population mean difference falls. In the current example the sample mean difference is –0.42 but we're 95 per cent confident that the estimated population mean difference is between –0.76 and –0.08 (see Chapter 8 for further information about the confidence interval).

- ***t:*** The *t* statistic, which you use to test whether a significant mean difference exists between the testing sessions. The larger the t-value is (irrespective of sign), the greater the difference between the groups. A positive *t*-value indicates the score at time 1 was greater than time 2. A negative *t*-value, as in this example ($t = -2.49$) means the score at time 2 is greater than time 1.

- ***df:*** Degrees of freedom are a reflection of sample size. In the case of a paired *t*-test the degrees of freedom are always equal to 1 less than the *sample size* (the number of participants who took part in study at time 1 and time 2). In the current example we had 62 participants in total, so the *df* is $62 - 1 = 61$.

- **Sig. (2-tailed):** Sig. in the table is the statistical significance. You usually regard any value less than .05 as statistically significant. If the *t*-test result is statistically significant, it indicates that the mean difference between the testing sessions is unlikely to have occurred by chance (assuming the null hypothesis is true) or you've found a statistically significant difference. If the *t*-test isn't statistically significant, it means that any differences in the means could have occurred due to sampling error (by chance). In the current example we have a .015 probability (1.5 per cent chance) that we'd have obtained this difference between the testing sessions with this sample size (assuming the null hypothesis is true); in other words, it's very unlikely we'd have obtained this difference by chance.

As denoted the statistical significance in Figure 18-5 is for a two-tailed hypothesis. To obtain a significance value for a one-tailed hypothesis simply divide the two-tailed significance value by 2.

Writing up the results

The guidelines provided in the American Psychological Association Publication Manual state that you should report the t-value rounded to 2 decimal places, with the degrees of freedom in parentheses, followed by the significance level. Taking the paired *t*-test result reported in Figure 18-5, we would report the result as follows:

> In this study there was a statistically significant difference on mean statistics anxiety scores between the start of term and the end of the term, t (61) = 2.29, p = .015.

You don't need to report the minus sign in front of your *t*-value. Whether the *t*-value is positive or negative simply reflects the order in which you entered the variables into SPSS.

Anyone who now reads your report now realises that a significant difference exists, but the reader doesn't know whether the scores increased or decreased over time. So you always report the means and standard deviations of each group as well:

> The mean statistics anxiety score at the start of term was 8.15 (SD = 2.06) and this demonstrated an increase to 8.56 (SD = 2.48) at the end of the term.

Oh dear! It therefore looks like statistics anxiety seems to increase during term, but at least this effect is only small. Obviously, the solution is to read this book, which alleviates all anxiety and makes your life better in every way . . .

Also you must report the effect size for the difference – we explain how to do so in Chapter 11.

Assumptions

The paired *t*-test is a parametric statistic which means it is only suitable to test certain types of data; specifically it is only appropriate if the data follows a specific distribution and the data is measured in a particular way. If the data conforms to these assumptions the test can be powerful and accurate. If the data does not meet these assumptions the results may be incorrect therefore it is important that you check both these assumptions.

Normal distribution

The paired *t*-test assumes that the sampling distribution of the difference scores is normally distributed (see Chapter 8 for a discussion of the sampling distribution). You can't examine the sampling distribution directly to check this assumption, but you can check whether this assumption is likely to be met by looking at a histogram of the difference scores. Of course you won't automatically have a variable representing difference scores in your data set, but it's very easy to get in SPSS:

1. **Select Transform from the top toolbar and then Compute Variable (see Figure 18-6).**

Transform Compute variable

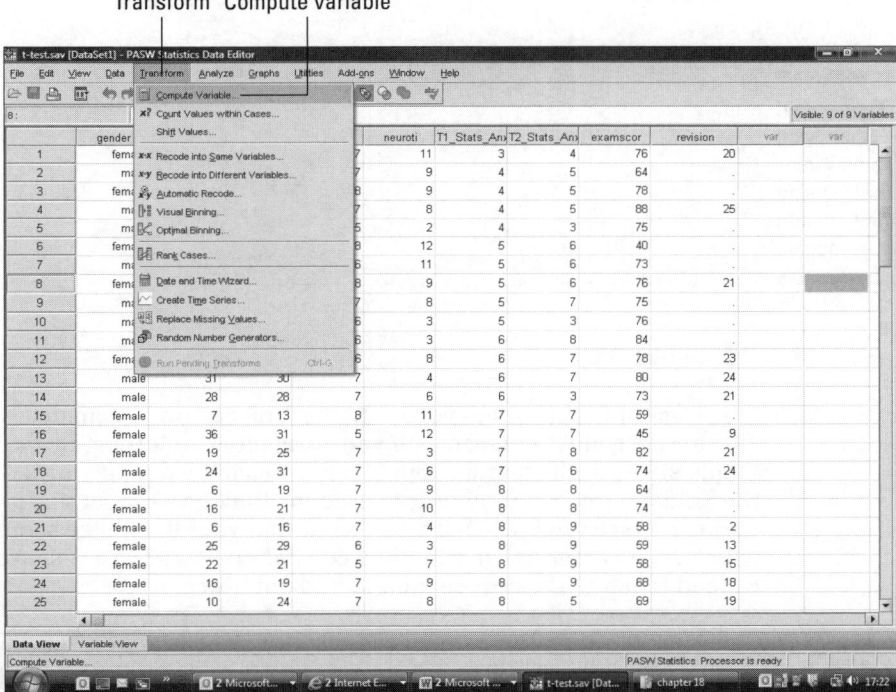

Figure 18-6: Computing a new variable in SPSS.

2. **A new Compute Variable window opens. SPSS asks you what you wish to call your new variable. In this example we've named it difference.**

3. **Move your time one variable from the left-hand list over to the Numeric Expression box.**

4. **Select the minus sign (from the little keypad below or just type in the sign).**

5. **Move over your time two variable to complete the expression. You've just completed the simple equation: time1 minus time 2 (see Figure 18-7).**

Enter a name for
the new variable   Variable 1 – Variable 2

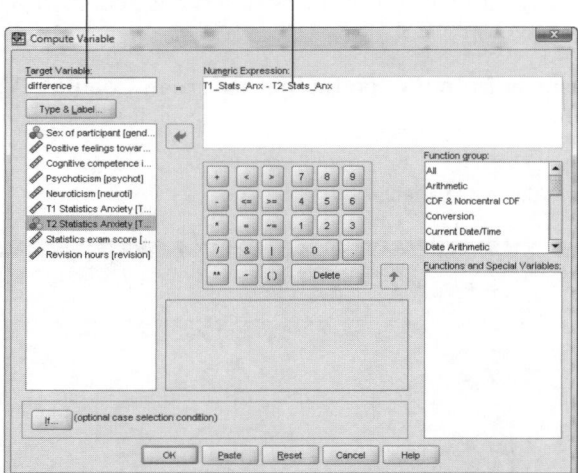

Figure 18-7:
Specifying
a new vari-
able using
the Compute
function.

6. **Select OK.**

A new variable appears in your data file. You can now examine this variable for normality. You can estimate normality by plotting the variable on a graph, such as a histogram (see Chapter 6) and by conducting a test, such as the Kolmogorov–Smirnov test, to examine the departure of this graph from normality (see Chapter 9). If it turns out that your difference scores don't approximate a normal distribution, consider performing a Wilcoxon test instead (head to the next section to find out how).

Checking for normality is only necessary for small sample sizes. For large sample sizes (around 30 or more) you can assume that the sampling distribution is normal (see Chapter 8).

Type of data

The dependent variable should be measured at the interval or ratio level (more on levels in Chapter 2). If the dependent variable is measured at the ordinal level, you can consider using the Wilcoxon test instead.

The Wilcoxon Test

The *Wilcoxon signed-rank test* is the non-parametric equivalent of the paired *t*-test (turn to Chapter 1 to recap on parametric and non-parametric tests). Like the paired *t*-test you use it to assess the difference in scores between two time points in a repeated measures design. Unlike the paired *t*-test the Wilcoxon test can be used when the dependent variable is measured at the ordinal level or when the data does not approximate a normal distribution.

In a Wilcoxon test, the data for time 1 is ranked (the lowest score becomes 1, the second lowest score becomes 2, and so on) and then the data for time 2 is ranked. You can calculate the difference in ranks for each person; if the person scores lower at time 2 then she has a positive score $(10 - 8 = 2)$; if she scores higher at time 2 then she has a negative score $(10 - 12 = -2)$; and if she scores the same then the difference is zero.

By ranking the data you lose some of the information (if you rank the numbers 4, 15, 16 and 27, you get 1, 2, 3 and 4). Therefore always attempt to use the parametric statistics unless the data violates the parametric assumptions.

Performing the Wilcoxon test in SPSS

A student, Jo, wants to assess the effect of beauty magazines on her classmates' body image. She asks 37 female psychology students to rate how happy they are with their body shape between 1 and 10. Jo then asks the students to read beauty magazines for 30 minutes, after which they re-rate how happy they are with their body shape. Jo hypothesises that a significant difference in ratings will exist before and after reading the beauty magazines. To test this hypothesis, she conducts a Wilcoxon test as she has a repeated measures design where participants were tested twice (the independent variable has two levels) and the dependent variable was measured at the ordinal level.

Here's how you perform a Wilcoxon test:

1. **Select Analyze from the top toolbar, Nonparametric Tests from the drop-down menu (because Wilcoxon is a nonparametric statistic) and then Related Samples (because the design of the study is repeated measures) (see Figure 18-8).**

Analyze   Nonparametric   Related
                  tests   Samples

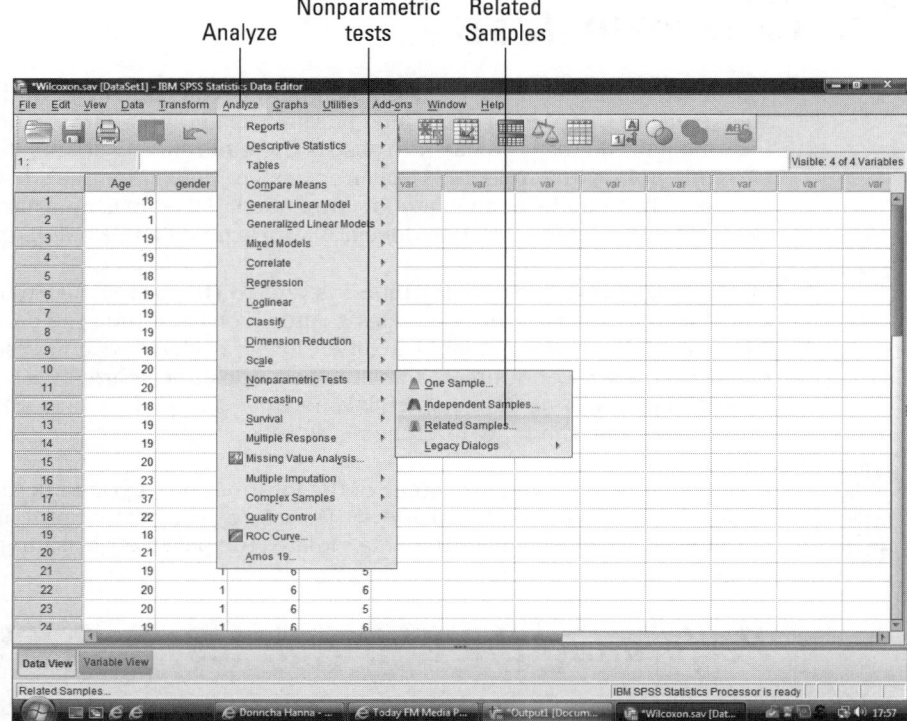

Figure 18-8:
Obtaining
the
Wilcoxon
test in
SPSS 1.

2. **A new Nonparametric test window opens and asks your objective (because you can conduct several non-parametric tests). The default option is to automatically compare observed data to hypothesized, and this is what you want to do (see Figure 18-9).**

3. **Click the Fields tab at the top left-hand corner (or click the Run button).**

If you're having problems defining the variables, ensure that you've specified the correct measurement levels in the Variable View window. If the analysis still refuses to run, try specifying both variables at the scale level. See Chapter 3 for more detail.

4. **A new Nonparametric Tests window asks you to specify the variables you want to test. Move the two variables representing the scores and time 1 and time 2 into the Test Field box by using the arrow or drag and drop (see Figure 18-10). In this example we've selected Pre_rating (body image scores before reading the magazines) and Post_rating (body image scores after reading the magazines). Don't move any other variables.**

5. Click Run and SPSS presents results in the output window.

Select Fields   Retain default option

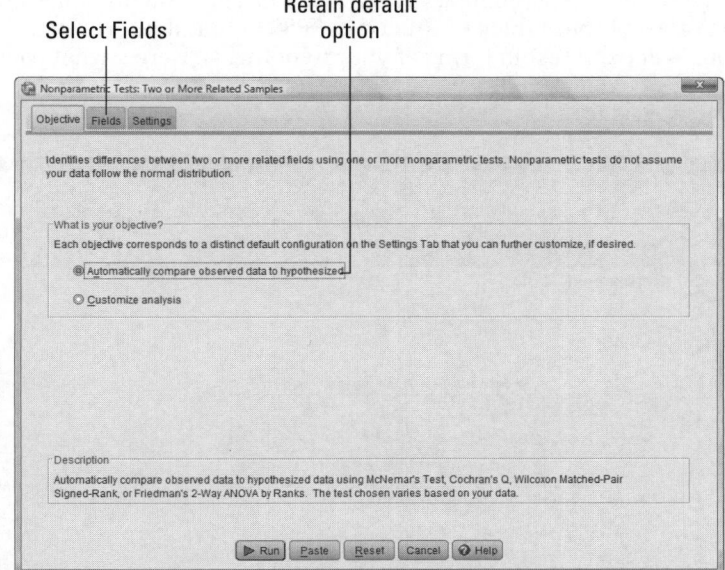

Figure 18-9:
Obtaining
the
Wilcoxon
test in
SPSS 2.

Move the 2 variables of
interest into the Test Fields box

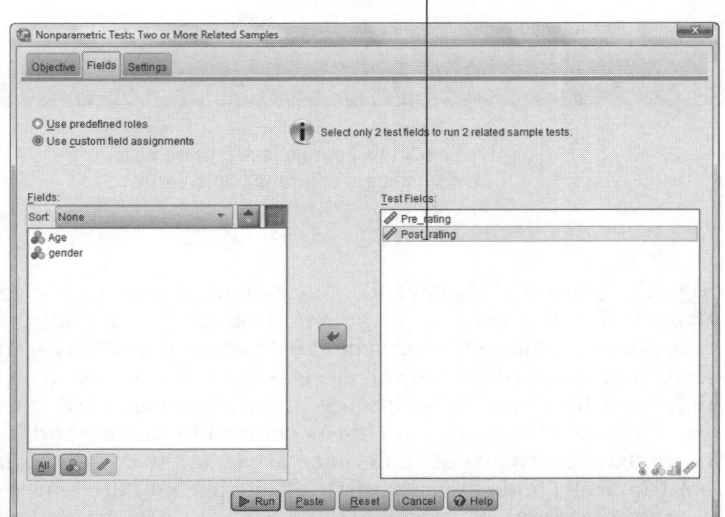

Figure 18-10:
Specifying
the vari-
ables for an
independent
t-test.

Interpreting the output

The Hypothesis Test Summary (see Figure 18-11) is slightly different to many of the other output tables produced in SPSS in that it interprets the result of your Wilcoxon test in terms of your hypothesis. Here's what each section means:

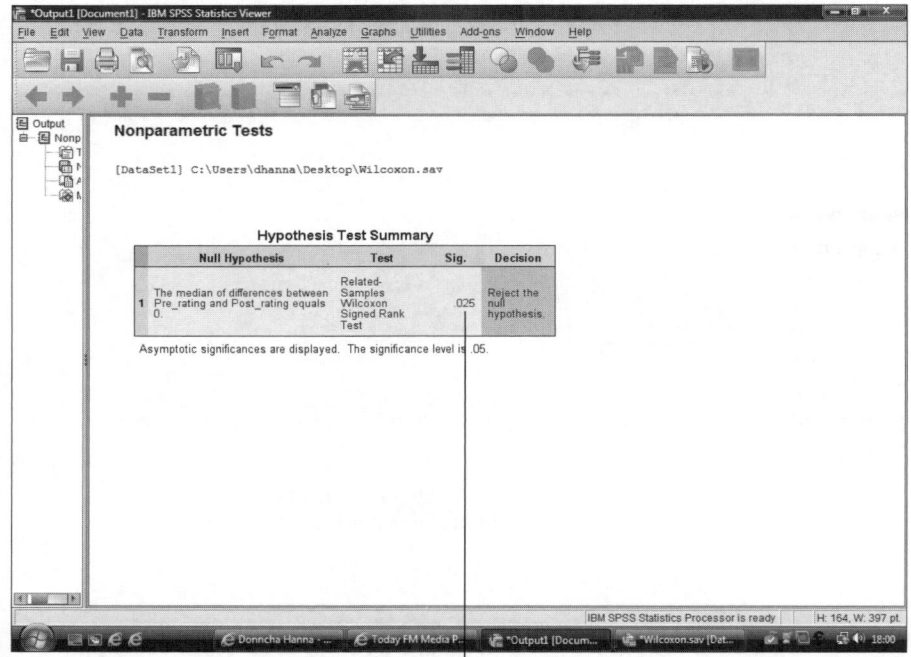

Figure 18-11:
Hypothesis
Test
Summary
table.

Check this figure to see if there was
a significant difference between
the 2 testing sessions

✔ **Sig.:** The statistical significance. Any statistical significance value less than .05 means a less than 5 per cent probability that you could have achieved this difference between the groups if the null hypothesis is true; in other words, if the value is less than .05 you have a significant difference between the two groups. If the significance value is greater than .05 any difference could have occurred by chance and therefore no statistically significant difference exists. In the current example $p = .025$, which indicates a statistically significant difference in rating scores before and after reading the magazines. There is only a 2.5 per cent probability that you could have achieved these scores assuming the null hypothesis is true.

To obtain a significance value for a one-tailed hypothesis, simply halve the two-tailed significance.

✔ **Null Hypothesis:** The Null Hypothesis simply states the null hypothesis. In the case of the Wilcoxon test it states that no significant median difference exists between ratings at time 1 and time 2 (or the difference is zero). The alternative hypothesis states that a significant difference in scores exists between the two time points.

The median is referred to because it is the most appropriate measure of central tendency when dealing with data measured at the ordinal level. Head to Chapter 4 for more on measures of central tendency.

✔ **Test:** Just a quick reminder that the statistic you just conducted was the Wilcoxon signed-rank test.

✔ **Decision:** SPSS has tried to help you here by telling you whether to retain or reject the null hypothesis. If the significance value is greater than .05 SPSS advises you to retain the null hypothesis. If the significance value is less than.05 (as it is in this example), SPSS advises you to reject the null hypothesis.

You know whether or not a significant difference exists between the testing sessions, but you still need to report a figure for the Wilcoxon statistic. If you double click on Hypothesis Test Summary table, SPSS opens another window with more detailed information (see Figure 18-12).

First, you see a frequency chart, which displays the distribution of the data. In this example you can see there were 6 positive differences (individuals where scores increased), 14 negative differences (individuals where scores decreased) and 17 ties (individual scores remained the same).

In the table below SPSS displays the total sample size (Total *N*), the Wilcoxon statistic (Test Statistic), the standard error, the Wilcoxon Z-score (Standardized Test Statistic) and the statistical significance value (Asymptotic Sig. 2-sided test). The value you need to report from this table is Standardized Test Statistic, which in this example is –2.24. A negative score indicates a decrease between testing sessions and a positive score indicates an increase between testing sessions.

Writing up the results

People seldom report the Wilcoxon statistic because SPSS standardises the figure to produce a Z score (we take you through Z scores in Chapter 10). The Z score is presented in 18-12 as the Standardized Test Statistic. Therefore, you report the standardized test statistic value (denoted by *Z*) rounded to 2 decimal places followed by the significance level. In the current example the format looks like this:

$Z = 2.24, p = .025.$

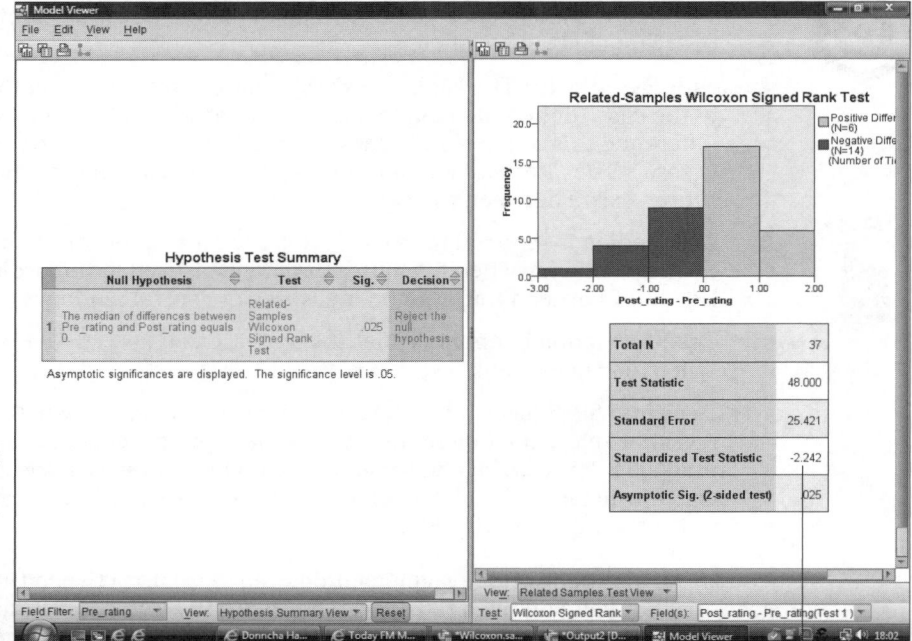

Figure 18-12:
Frequency
chart and
Wilcoxon
test result.

This is the Z Score

You don't need to report the minus sign in front of your Z score. Whether the Z score is positive or negative simply reflects the order in which you entered the variables into SPSS.

As always, describe the results in words:

> There was a statistically significant difference on body image scores from before to after reading the beauty magazines; $Z = 2.24$, $p = .025$.

You have stated that a significant difference exists between the two time points, but anyone reading your report wants to know whether the scores increased or decreased over time. So you must also use descriptive statistics to describe the changes between time 1 and time 2. If you have data measured at the ordinal level, the most appropriate measure of central tendency is the median (see Chapter 4) and the most appropriate measure of dispersion is the interquartile range (see Chapter 5).

The median body image rating was 6 (interquartile range = 1) before participants were exposed to the beauty magazines and this decreased to 5 (interquartile range = 1.5) after participants were exposed to the beauty magazines. There were 14 participants who demonstrated decreased ratings, 6 participants increased their rating and 17 participants had no change in their scores from before to after being exposed to the beauty magazines.

Because the Wilcoxon test is a non-parametric statistic, it's free from many of the stringent assumptions of the paired *t*-test. However, you need to measure your dependent variable at least at the ordinal level of measurement.

Chapter 19

Within-Groups ANOVA

● ●

In This Chapter

▶ Obtaining and interpreting a one-way within-groups ANOVA

▶ Obtaining and interpreting a two-way within-groups ANOVA

▶ Obtaining and interpreting a Friedman test

● ●

*1*n this chapter, we focus on analysis of variance tests (ANOVA tests) for repeated measures research designs. In this case, you use the ANOVA tests to examine differences within the same group of participants. For example, say you want to examine how statistical knowledge of students increases through the first, second and third year of their university course. In this example, the year of study is the independent variable and knowledge of statistics is the dependent variable (for more on variables, see Chapter 2). In this repeated measures design you test the same group of participants three times, a year apart, so you're repeating your measurements. This is also known as a *within groups design* because you're looking for changes within the same group of participants.

In an ANOVA, you always have only one dependent variable. When you also have only one independent variable then you conduct a one-way ANOVA; when you have two independent variables then you conduct a two-way ANOVA; when you have three independent variables you conduct a three-way ANOVA; and so on. In this chapter, we examine the one-way and two-way within-groups ANOVA tests only, but you can obtain and interpret all within-groups ANOVA models using the framework we outline in this chapter. We also explain the Friedman test which is the non-parametric equivalent of the one-way within-groups ANOVA.

One-Way Within-Groups ANOVA

You use a *one-way within-groups ANOVA* (sometimes called a one-way repeated-measures ANOVA) to analyse data from a repeated measures study where the same people have participated in three or more testing sessions; another way of saying this is that the independent variable has three or more levels. In this type of study you are interested in how one dependent variable changes over the testing sessions. You can think of the one-way within-groups ANOVA as an extension of the paired *t*-test: a paired *t*-test is used to assess difference or change on a variable when the same people have been tested twice, while an ANOVA is used to assess difference or change on a variable when the same people have been tested three times or more.

In this section we use an example to explain how to calculate one-way within-groups ANOVA and then use the same example to demonstrate how to obtain and interpret the ANOVA on SPSS. It is important to realise that when you are analysing your data you won't actually calculate ANOVA by hand (unless you're weird) but use SPSS which is faster and less error-prone! The reason we are showing you how to calculate the statistic by hand is that it helps you understand how ANOVA works, and many courses require you to have knowledge of what the various parts of the ANOVA table mean and how they are calculated.

Within-groups ANOVA models have an advantage over between-groups ANOVA (see Chapter 16) because you're not comparing different groups of people. Repeated measures design studies tend to be more powerful than independent groups design and subsequently require smaller sizes to detect a significant effect, if one exists.

Knowing how ANOVA works

A one-way within-groups ANOVA tests the null hypothesis that the mean scores for all conditions are equal (see Chapter 8 for a discussion of the null hypothesis). To test the null hypothesis that these means are equal, you analyse the variance (we explain the variance in Chapter 5). Strange, you may be thinking, 'Why analyse variance when you want to analyse the means?' The rationale is as follows: The scores from individuals within each testing session (or level of the independent variable) of your research study will vary. You want to ascertain how much of this variance is due to the different levels of the independent variable (the *experimental effect*) and how much is due to random factors not included in the study (which is called *error variance* in ANOVA terminology). This is what the ANOVA actually does; the result of the ANOVA, called the *F* ratio, simply compares how much of the variability in the data is due to the experimental effect and how much is due to error or random effects.

The example

Imagine you conduct a research study to examine the difference in pain relief ratings between three different drugs: ibuprofen, aspirin and a *placebo* (a pill with no active ingredients). You recruit ten participants who have chronic back pain. Over three days each participant tries each of the drugs (they were called drugs so participants would not be aware one was a placebo) and rates how effective the drug is in reducing pain. A score of 1 means the drug is very effective in reducing pain and a score of 10 means it's very ineffective in reducing pain. Your hypothesis is that the placebo will be less effective in reducing pain than ibuprofen or the aspirin. You obtain the data in Table 19-1. This is the data we will use to calculate the ANOVA.

Table 19-1	Pain Relief Scores for Each of the Three Conditions		
	Session A	*Session B*	*Session C*
Participant	*Ibuprofen*	*Aspirin*	*Placebo*
1	4	5	8
2	5	5	9
3	7	6	7
4	5	7	8
5	4	3	7
6	5	6	7
7	6	5	7
8	6	7	6
9	4	5	7
10	4	4	5

Calculating a one-way within-groups ANOVA

To get to the *F* ratio there are a number of steps. First you have to calculate a measure of total variation within your data set, a measure of variation due to the experimental effect and a measure of the variation due to error or random effects; these measures of variation are called the *sum of squares* (for reasons that will become apparent). The next step is to convert the measures of variation into actual variances; the variances in ANOVA terminology are called *mean squares*. The *F* ratio is then simply the experimental effect mean square divided by the error variance mean square.

Calculating sums of squares

The first step in calculating the F ratio is getting a measure of the variation (called sum of squares) in your data. You have to calculate three separate sum of squares.

The first represents the total amount of variation within your participants (remember, as you do not have separate groups to compare you do not need to worry about between-groups variation) and this is called the *within-groups or within participants sum of squares*.

Next is the variation due to the experimental effect and this is known as the *model sum of squares*. Finally, you calculate the error sum of squares. We show you how to calculate these in the following steps.

Step 1: Calculating the within-groups sum of squares

To do this you calculate the sum of the squared deviations (or sum of squares) of each individual score from the individual's mean for all their scores across all conditions:

1. **Subtract each individual's mean score from each individual score.**

2. **Square the result.**

3. **Add up the values obtained.**

Chapter 5 explains the sum of squares and deviations in more detail.

Table 19-2 shows the squared deviations from the individuals' means. For example, participant 1 has an individual mean of 5.67, if you add his three effectiveness rating scores together and divide by 3. In session A he had an effectiveness score of 4. If you subtract the individual mean of 5.67 from 4, you obtain −1.67 (the value in the deviation column for participant 1 at session A in table 19-2). If you square this value, you get 2.78. If you add all 30 squared deviations, you obtain a value of 43.31, which is the within-groups sum of squares.

Table 19-2		**Squared Deviations from the Individual Mean**					
		Session A		Session B		Session C	
Participant	Individual Mean	Deviation	Squared Deviation	Deviation	Squared Deviation	Deviation	Squared Deviation
1	5.67	−1.67	2.78	−.67	.44	2.33	5.44
2	6.33	−1.33	1.78	−1.33	1.78	2.67	7.11
3	6.67	.33	.11	−.67	.44	.33	.11

		Session A		Session B		Session C	
Participant	Individual Mean	Deviation	Squared Deviation	Deviation	Squared Deviation	Deviation	Squared Deviation
4	6.67	−1.67	2.78	.33	.11	1.33	1.78
5	4.67	−.67	.44	−1.67	2.78	2.33	5.44
6	6.00	−1.00	1.00	.00	.00	1.00	1.00
7	6.00	.00	.00	−1.00	1.00	1.00	1.00
8	6.33	−.33	.11	.67	.44	−.33	.11
9	5.33	−1.33	1.78	−.33	.11	1.67	2.78
10	4.33	−.33	.11	−.33	.11	.67	.44

Step 2: Calculating the model sum of squares

The within-groups sum of squares reflects the amount of variance across the testing sessions within the participants. To calculate how much of the variation is due the experimental effect you calculate the model sum of squares.

Calculating the model sum of squares follows the same principle except this time you obtain the deviation by taking the grand mean away from the mean of each testing session. The _grand mean_ is the mean for all scores in the analysis. The deviations are then squared and added up.

1. **Subtract the grand mean from the session mean for each testing session (or level of the independent variable).**

2. **Square each result.**

3. **Add up the values obtained.**

4. **Multiply by the number of participants.**

In the example, the grand mean is 5.8. The mean score for session A is 5, for session B it is 5.3 and for session C it is 7.1. You can check this figure by calculating the grand mean or session means from Table 19-1. Therefore the deviation for session A is the session mean minus the grand mean, which gives you a value of −0.8 (5-5.8). If you then square this deviation, you get 0.64. The squared deviation for session B is 0.25 and 1.69 for session C. If you then add up the squared deviations you get 2.58. This accounts for 3 sessions but doesn't include the fact there were 10 participants so we must multiply this figure by 10. This gives you a model sum of squares of 25.8, which reflects the amount of variation due to the experimental effect.

Step 3: Calculating the error sum of squares

The error sum of squares reflects variation not due to the experimental effect. This one is easy! If you know the total amount of variation and the amount of variance due to the experimental effect then the error variation (or random effects) must be the total amount of within-groups variation minus the experimental effect variation. Any variation that is not due to the experimental effect must be variation due to error (or random effects). To phrase it differently your error sum of squares will be the within-groups sum of squares minus the model sum of squares. So, in this example:

Error sum of squares = Within-groups sum of squares – Model sum of squares

Error sum of squares = 43.31 – 25.8

Error sum of squares = 17.51

Calculating mean square

The sum of squares values provides a sense of the amount of variation within groups. However, the sum of squares isn't the variance, because the variance also takes account of the number of values that contributed to the calculation of the sums of squares. Therefore, you need to divide the sum of squares by their degrees of freedom (*df*). This will result in the variances or the mean squares you require. So you now must work out the degrees of freedom (*df*) for the experimental effect and the error or random effect.

Step 4: Calculating the df for the model sum of squares

For the model sum of squares, the df is the number of testing sessions minus 1. In the example there are 3 testing sessions. Therefore the *df* for the error sum of squares is 2.

Step 5: Calculating the model mean square

To convert the measure of experimental effect variation into a variance we need to take into account the number of testing sessions so we divide the model sum of squares by its *df*. Therefore the mean square is the sum of squares divided by its *df*, and so the model mean square is 25.8 / 2 = 12.9.

Step 6: Calculating the df for the error sum of squares

For the error sum of squares, the df is the number of individuals minus 1 multiplied by the number of testing sessions minus 1. In the example there are 10 participants and 3 testing sessions. Therefore, the df is $(10 - 1) \times (3 - 1) = 18$.

Step 7: Calculating the error mean square

In order to convert the variation due to error (or random effects) into a variance you simply divide by its df value. The mean square is therefore the sum of squares divided by its df, so in this example the error mean square is 17.51 / 18 = 0.97.

You needed to calculate a measure of total variation (within-groups sum of squares) in order to obtain the error variation as outlined in Step 3. You do not require a df or mean square for the total variation as the aim of the ANOVA is to compare experimental effect variance with error (random effects) variance

Calculating the F ratio

The goal of the ANOVA is to compare the variability due to the experimental effect to the variability due to error (variations due to unexplained factors). You do this by dividing the model mean square by the error mean square. The result is known as the *F* ratio.

Step 8: Calculating the F ratio

F ratio = model mean square / error mean square

In the example the *F* ratio is 12.9 / 0.97 = 13.30.

If the *F* ratio is 1, this indicates that there is no effect on the dependent variable of the different testing sessions. In other words, there is no difference between testing sessions. If the *F* ratio is greater than 1, this indicates that there is a difference between the groups. The *p* value (significance value; see Chapter 8) that accompanies the *F* ratio then tells you whether or not this difference is statistically significant. If you calculate your *F* ratio by hand you will need to consult a book that contains tables of critical values for ANOVA models; you can look up the value of the *F* ratio and dfs to see if the value indicates a statistically significant effect. The alternative is to use SPSS to conduct your ANOVA and it will provide you with the relevant *p* value for your result.

Obtaining a one-way within-groups ANOVA in SPSS

Here's how to conduct a one-way within-groups ANOVA in SPSS:

1. **Go to the Analyze menu, choose General Linear Model and then select Repeated Measures (see Figure 19-1).**

2. **A new Repeated Measures Define Factor(s) window opens (see Figure 19-2). Specify a short label for your independent variable and state the number of levels or conditions measured.** In the current example, we have called the independent variable drug and as we have 3 different types of drugs, then the independent variable had 3 levels or each participant participates in 3 testing sessions.

3. **Click Add and then Define.**

General Linear
Model   Analyze   Repeated Measures

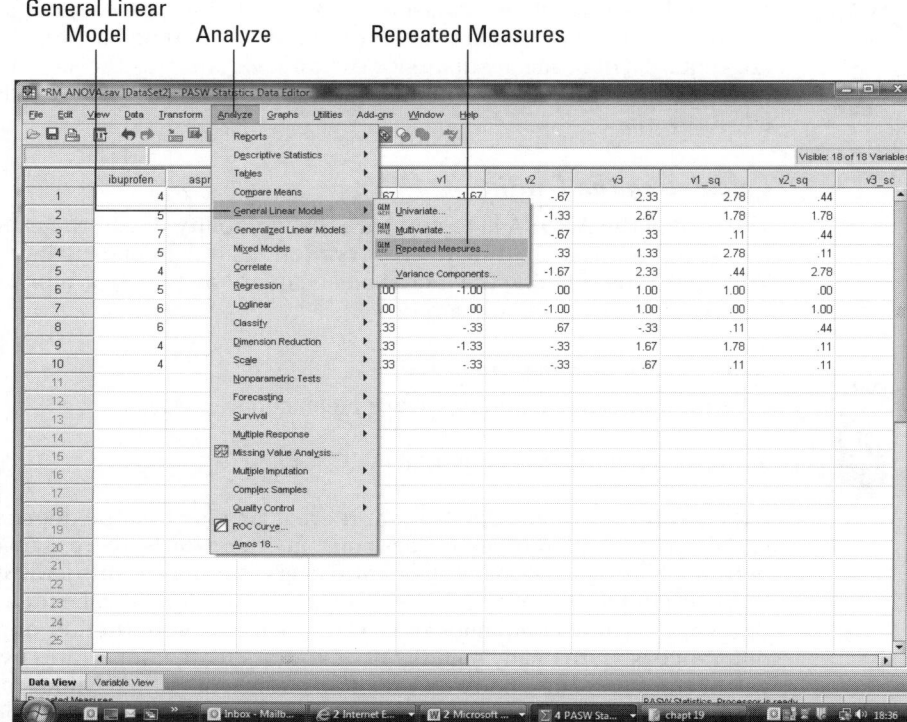

Figure 19-1:
Choosing
a one-way
within-
groups
ANOVA on
SPSS.

State the number of   Specify a name
levels of your   for your independent
independent variable   variable

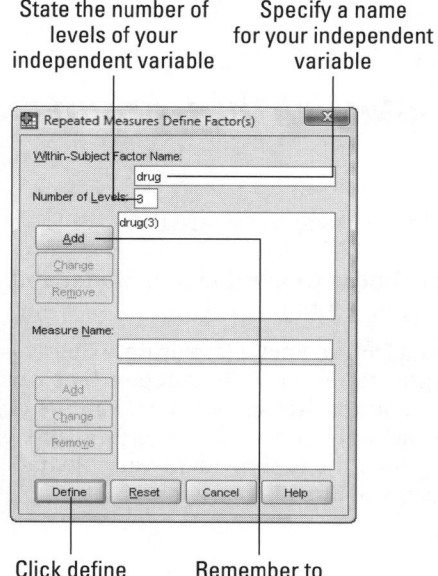

Figure 19-2:
Defining
your inde-
pendent
variable.

Click define   Remember to
press Add

4. **In the new Repeated Measures window move the columns representing each level of the independent variable into the Within-Subjects Variables box.** In the example we specified there were three levels of the independent variable so we can only select three variables (see Figure 19-3).

Select the variables representing each level of your independent variable (or each testing session)

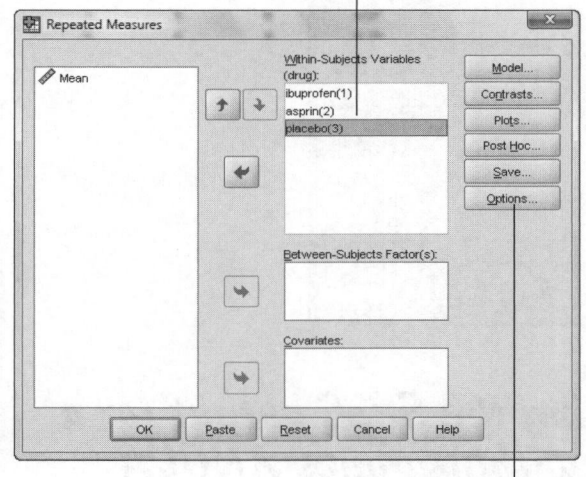

Select options to obtain descriptive statistics

Figure 19-3: Selecting variables for a within-groups ANOVA.

5. **At this stage it is also useful to ask for some descriptive statistics, so click on the options button and, in the window that opens, tick the box beside the word Descriptive statistics, in the list headed Display (see Figure 19-4).**

6. **Select Continue and then OK to run the procedure.**

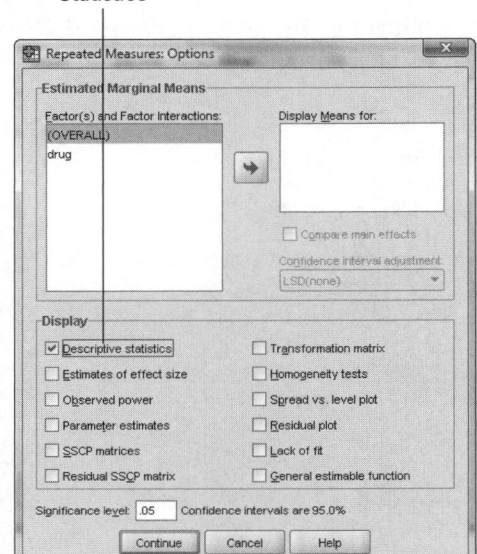

Check Descriptive Statistics

Figure 19-4: Obtaining descriptive statistics as part of the repeated measures ANOVA procedure in SPSS.

Interpreting the SPSS output for a one-way within-groups ANOVA

The output for the one-way within-groups ANOVA in SPSS appears as seven tables (presented in Figures 19-5 to 19-11). It seems like you've got a lot of information here, but don't worry, you only need to interpret certain tables.

The Within-Subject Factor table (Figure 19-5) is a reminder of how each dependent variable was coded.

Figure 19-5: Within-Subject Factor table as produced in SPSS output.

drug	Dependent Variable
1	ibuprofen
2	asprin
3	placebo

Figure 19-6 presents the descriptive statistics for the dependent variable at each level of the independent variable.

Figure 19-6:
Descriptive
Statistics
table as
produced
in SPSS
output.

	Mean	Std. Deviation	N
ibuprofen	5.00	1.054	10
asprin	5.30	1.252	10
placebo	7.10	1.101	10

Multivariate tests are a different way to calculate repeated measure differences (Figure 19-7). The advantage of these tests is they're not dependent on the assumption of sphericity (see 'Assumptions of a one-way within-groups ANOVA', later in the chapter). The disadvantage is that they're often not as powerful as the ANOVA and they're not suitable for analysing small sample sizes. We therefore recommend you don't interpret this table.

Figure 19-7:
Multivariate
Tests table
as produced
in SPSS
output.

Effect		Value	F	Hypothesis df	Error df	Sig.
drug	Pillai's Trace	.682	8.571[a]	2.000	8.000	.010
	Wilks' Lambda	.318	8.571[a]	2.000	8.000	.010
	Hotelling's Trace	2.143	8.571[a]	2.000	8.000	.010
	Roy's Largest Root	2.143	8.571[a]	2.000	8.000	.010

Mauchly's test (see Figure 19-8) examines the assumption of sphericity, which is that the differences between each testing session have approximately equal variances (see 'Assumptions of a one-way within-groups ANOVA', later in the chapter). If Mauchly's test isn't significant then it means the assumption isn't violated and you can interpret the ANOVA results from the Sphericity Assumed values (see Figure 19-9). If Mauchly's test is significant then the assumption is violated and you should interpret the ANOVA results from the Greenhouse-Geisser values (see Figure19-9). The three epsilon figures are estimates of the degree of sphericity. Because your interpretation of Mauchly's test relies on the significance value, you don't need to worry about the epsilon values.

Figure 19-8:
Mauchly's
Test of
Sphericity
table as
produced
in SPSS
output.

Within Subjects Effect	Mauchly's W	Approx. Chi-Square	df	Sig.	Epsilon [a]		
					Greenhouse - Geisser	Huynh - Feldt	Lower - bound
drug	.820	1.590	2	.452	.847	1.000	.500

Check if Mauchly's test indicates a significant result

Figure 19-9 is the ANOVA table. It contains the sum of squares, df, mean square and F ratio values described in the section 'Calculating a one-way within-groups ANOVA', earlier in the chapter. The final column in the ANOVA table is the probability (p or Sig.) value associated with the F ratio. As with all inferential tests, if this value is less than .05 then you can reject the null hypothesis.

Notice that four separate versions of the ANOVA are reported. Which one you interpret depends on the results of Mauchly's test in the table above. If Mauchly's test isn't significant, you can interpret the ANOVA results from the Sphericity Assumed values. If Mauchly's test is significant, interpret the ANOVA results from the Greenhouse-Geisser values. In this example Mauchly's test wasn't significant (see Figure 19-8) so you can interpret the Sphericity Assumed values. The p value is less than .001, which means you reject the null hypothesis that the mean scores for all groups are equal. In other words, a statistically significant difference exists between the mean scores of the three testing sessions.

Figure 19-10 tests trends within the data. A linear trend suggests a linear trend between the variables. A quadratic trend suggests the trend is a U (or inverted U shape) relationship. Looking at the means or plots to examine trends is more appropriate, and therefore you don't need to interpret this table.

Figure 19-11 is a test for a between subject effect. Because this is a one-way repeated measures ANOVA you have no between-subjects variables so you don't need to interpret this table.

Source		Type III Sum of Squares	df	Mean Square	F	Sig.
drug	Sphericity Assumed	25.800	2	12.900	13.243	.000
	Greenhouse-Geisser	25.800	1.695	15.225	13.243	.001
	Huynh - Feldt	25.800	2.000	12.900	13.243	.000
	Lower - bound	25.800	1.000	25.800	13.243	.005
Error (drug)	Sphericity Assumed	17.533	18	.974		
	Greenhouse-Geisser	17.533	15.251	1.150		
	Huynh - Feldt	17.533	18.000	.974		
	Lower - bound	17.533	9.000	1.948		

Figure 19-9: Tests of Within-Subjects Effects table as produced in SPSS output.

If Mauchly's test is not significant, interpret the Sphericity Assumed figures.

If Mauchly's test is significant, interpret the Greenhouse - Geisser figures.

Figure 19-10: Tests of Within-Subjects Contrasts table as produced in SPSS output.

Source	drug	Type III Sum of Squares	df	Mean Square	F	Sig.
drug	Linear	22.050	1	22.050	18.990	.002
	Quadratic	3.750	1	3.750	4.765	.057
Error (drug)	Linear	10.450	9	1.161		
	Quadratic	7.083	9	.787		

Figure 19-11: Tests of Between-Subjects Effects table as produced in SPSS output.

Source	Type III Sum of Squares	df	Mean Square	F	Sig.
Intercept	1009.200	1	1009.200	520.008	.000
Error	17.467	9	1.941		

Writing up the results of a one-way within-groups ANOVA

As we explain in Chapter 14, when reporting the results of statistical analyses, follow any specific guidelines that inform how you should present the statistical findings. When reporting ANOVA results, the American Psychological Association manual suggests that you should report:

- ✔ The *F* ratio value rounded to 2 decimal places, with the degrees of freedom in parentheses, followed by the significance level

- ✔ Two *df* – one for the model mean square and one for the error mean square, separated by a comma.

Taking the one-way ANOVA result reported in Figure 19-9, you report the result as follows:

> There was a statistically significant difference between the three drugs on pain relief ratings: $F(2,18) = 13.24$, $p < .001$.

You also need to report the mean and standard deviation values for each group (more on these in Chapters 4 and 5, respectively), and an appropriate effect size (see Chapter 11).

The ANOVA only indicates whether a statistically significant difference exists between the testing sessions. The ANOVA doesn't indicate the nature of the difference, nor where the significant difference lies. For example, all three drugs may have significantly different pain rating scores or one drug may have a different pain rating scores from the other two. To uncover this detail you need to conduct post hoc tests or planned comparisons between the groups (see Chapter 20).

Assumptions of a one-way within-groups ANOVA

The ANOVA is a parametric statistic which means it is only appropriate for certain types of data (see Chapter 1 for a recap). It is important that you spend some time checking the underlying assumptions because if you have conducted an ANOVA with inappropriate data you run the risk of producing a result that is incorrect. If your data does not meet the assumption of the one-way within-groups ANOVA you can consider using the non-parametric Friedman test instead.

For a one-way within-groups ANOVA, the conditions that must be met before you should interpret the result are:

✔ The independent variable should be categorical (see Chapter 2 for a description of categorical variables).

✔ The dependent variable should be measured at the interval/ratio level (see Chapter 2).

✔ The residual scores should follow an approximately normal distribution (see Chapter 9 for a description of the normal distribution). You can estimate normality by plotting the variables (within-groups ANOVA plots of the residuals and raw scores are equivalent) on a graph, such as a histogram (see Chapter 6) and by conducting a test, such as the Kolmogorov-Smirnov test, to examine the departure of this graph from normality (see Chapter 9).

✔ The differences between each testing session (or each level of the independent variable) have approximately equal variances. This is known as *sphericity*. SPSS automatically provides Mauchly's test (if you have three or more testing sessions), which tests the null hypothesis that the variances of the differences are equal:

- If Mauchly's test produces a *non-significant* result (see Figure 19-8), this indicates that the variances of the differences between each testing session are approximately equal. So the assumption isn't violated, and when interpreting your ANOVA results you report the sphericity assumed figures (see Figure 19-9).

- If Mauchly's test produces a *significant* result, it suggests that the variances between the differences aren't equal and the assumption of sphericity is violated. If this assumption is violated you can interpret the Greenhouse-Geisser values; this applies a correction to the degrees of freedom to account for the variation in differences producing a more conservative test. If you look at figure 19.9 you will notice SPSS actually provides you with two other alternative corrected versions of the ANOVA result. The Huynh-Feldt and Lower-bound are similar to the Greenhouse-Geisser correction in that they account for the violation of sphericity and produce results that are which are less and more conservative respectively. These versions are not commonly reported.

When the assumptions for a one-way within-groups ANOVA aren't met then consider conducting a Friedman test (see the later section in this chapter).

Two-Way Within-Groups ANOVA

You use a *two-way within-groups ANOVA* (sometimes called a two-way repeated measures ANOVA) when you have two independent variables that are both measured with a repeated measures design.

You often describe two-way ANOVAs by the number of levels of the two independent variables. For example, a two-way ANOVA where each independent variable has 3 levels is a *3 × 3 ANOVA* (which would mean 9 testing sessions); a two-way ANOVA where one independent variable has 3 levels and the other independent variable has 4 levels is a *3 × 4 ANOVA* and so on.

In this section we use the example of a research study to examine the effect of caffeine and of background music on performance on an IQ test. You recruit 17 participants to take part in the study and each participant must take the IQ test four times: once after consuming caffeine and with music in the background; once with caffeine and no music; once with no caffeine and music in the background; and finally with no caffeine and no music.

In this research design you have two independent variables (caffeine and background music) and one dependent variable (IQ scores). The independent variable caffeine has two levels – caffeine (participants consume a strong cup of coffee) and having no caffeine (no caffeine consumed in 24 hours). The independent variable background music has 2 levels – music in the background or no music. Therefore an appropriate analysis is a 2 × 2 within-groups ANOVA.

Your hypotheses are that:

✔ When participants have consumed caffeine they will have higher IQ scores

✔ When there is no music in the background participants will have higher IQ scores

✔ The effect of caffeine on IQ scores will only be found when there is no music in the background.

The first two hypotheses here are main effects and the final hypothesis is known as an interaction.

Main effects and interactions

In a two-way ANOVA you can obtain two main effects and an interaction.

The *main effects* are the effects of each independent variable on the dependent variable. The result that you get from a one-way ANOVA is also known as a main effect. So, the main effects in a two-way ANOVA are a bit like conducting two separate one-way ANOVAs – one for each independent variable (but see the 'one plus one doesn't always equal two' sidebar in Chapter 16).

The *interaction effect* in a two-way ANOVA is the effect of the combination of the two independent variables on the dependent variable. Interaction effects are useful when you think that the effect of an independent variable on a dependent variable isn't simple but is influenced by another variable. In statistical terms you describe the effect of one independent variable on the dependent variable being moderated by another variable.

For example, in the hypotheses, the third hypothesis suggests that the effect of caffeine on IQ scores will be influenced by music in the background. This is an interaction. It is a slightly more complex relationship, but that's more like real life, and that's why two-way ANOVAs are useful – they allow you to examine more complex, real-life situations.

Usually, when you conduct a two-way ANOVA the interaction is the result that you're most interested in and you should pay close attention to it. If the interaction result is statistically significant then this overrides the main effects. In other words, the interaction result provides more information than any single main effect result. So, in the light of the added information from the interaction result, the results of the main effects might become obsolete.

In the example, if you found that the two-way ANOVA supported the interaction hypothesis (that the effect of caffeine on IQ scores was only found when there was no music in the background) then it would not make sense to draw conclusions about the other two hypotheses. That is, it would not make sense to talk about the effect of caffeine on intelligence when you know from the interaction result that this effect only exists in certain conditions – when there is no background music.

Of course, when the interaction effect isn't significant then the main effects will be important.

Obtaining a two-way within-groups ANOVA in SPSS

You obtain a two-way within-groups ANOVA in SPSS as follows. Go to the Analyze menu, choose General Linear Model and then select Repeated Measures (see Figure 19-12).

A new window will open where you define your factors (Figure 19-13). In this example of a 2×2 repeated measures ANOVA there are two independent variables (caffeine and music) and each independent variable has two levels (caffeine and no caffeine, music and no music). Enter the name and number of levels for each variable. It is important to remember which way round you define the variables so that you enter them correctly. We recommend that you fill out a quick table to enable you to code the variables correctly (see Table 19-3).

General Linear
Model   Analyze   Repeated Measures

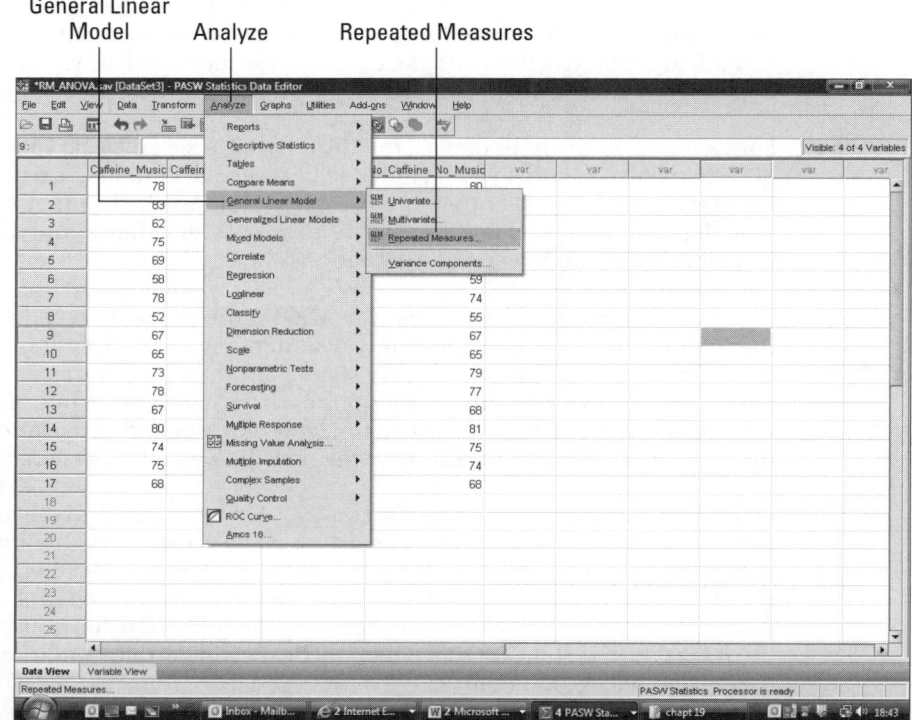

Figure 19-12:
Selecting
variables
for a within-
groups
ANOVA in
SPSS

Table 19-3   Noting the Order in Which the Variables Were Named

First Variable	*Caffeine (1)*		*No Caffeine (2)*	
Second variable	Music (1)	No Music (2)	Music (1)	No Music (2)
Code	(1,1)	(1,2)	(2,1)	(2,2)

In the new Repeated Measures window (Figure 19-14) move the columns representing each level of the independent variable into the Within-Subjects Variables box. In this example we specified there were 2 independent variables each with 2 levels, therefore SPSS asks us to select $(2 \times 2) = 4$ variables. You can use Table 19-3 to help ensure you entered the variables in the correct order. Remember caffeine was the first variable entered (Figure 19-13), so it will treat caffeine as the first variable (if we entered music first it would be the first variable). Enter all relevant variables then double check your diagram (Table 19-3) to confirm the variables have been entered correctly.

Remember to press
Add after entering
each independent
variable

Name each
independent
variable

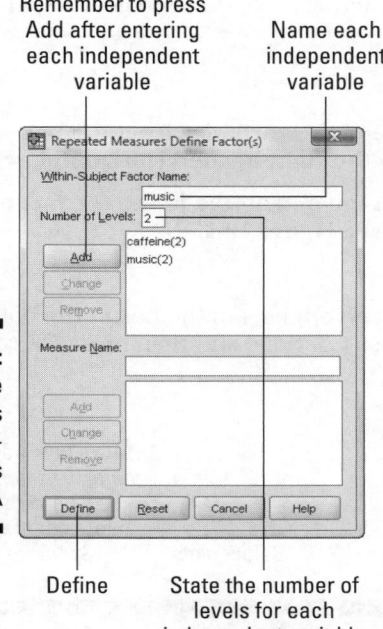

Figure 19-13:
Defining the
variables
in a within-
groups
ANOVA

Define

State the number of
levels for each
independent variable

At this stage it is also useful to ask for some descriptive statistics, so click
on the Options button and, in the window that opens, tick the box beside
Descriptive statistics, in the list headed Display (see Figure 19-4). Then click
continue.

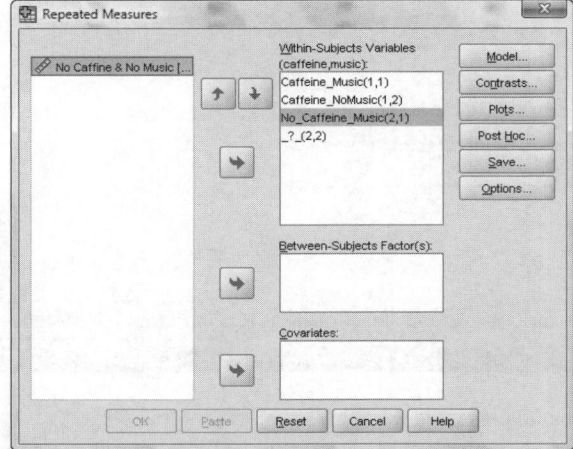

Figure 19-14:
Selecting
variables for
a two-way
within-
groups
ANOVA.

It is important to examine the interaction so get SPSS to generate the interaction plot:

1. **Click on the Plots button.**
2. **In the new window move one of the variables from the box on the left headed Factors to the box on the right headed Horizontal axis.**
3. **Move the other variable from the box on the left to the box on the right headed Separate lines (see Figure 19-15).**
4. **Click Add.**

   The name of the requested graph appears in the box at the bottom of the window headed Plots. Press Continue and then press OK to run the procedure.

Move one independent variable to the horizontal axis and the other independent variable to Separate Lines

Select plots

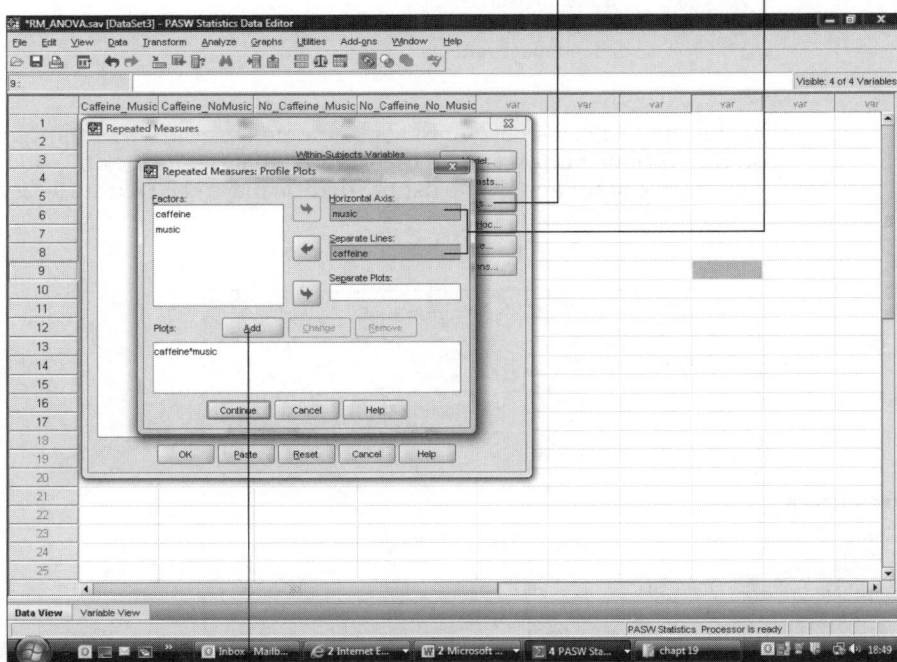

Figure 19-15: Obtaining an interaction plot for a two-way within-groups ANOVA in SPSS.

Remember to press Add

It doesn't matter which variable is on the horizontal axis and which is attributed to the separate lines. However, changing the variables around might make the plot easier to interpret, so it's useful to get two plots. Just swap the variable on the horizontal axis with the variable on the separate lines option. You can ask for these at the same time in SPSS. Remember, both plots contain the same information, so you only need to present one in your report, but having both might help you better understand the nature of the interaction.

The later section 'Interpreting the interaction plot from a two-way within-groups ANOVA' helps you understand the plot.

Interpreting the SPSS output for a two-way within-groups ANOVA

The output for the two-way within-groups ANOVA in SPSS appears as seven tables (presented in Figures 19-16 to 19-23 below). It seems like there is a lot of information here but you only need to interpret certain tables.

Figure 19-16: Within-Subjects Factors table as produced in SPSS output

Caffeine	Music	Dependent Variable
1	1	Caffeine_Music
	2	Caffeine_NoMusic
2	1	No_Caffeine_Music
	2	No_Caffeine_No_Music

The Within-Subject Factor table is a reminder of how each dependent variable was coded. You should check this with the notes you made to ensure the variables have been coded correctly.

Figure 19-17 presents the descriptive statistics for the dependent variable at each level of the independent variable or for the dependent variable at each testing session.

Figure 19-17: Descriptive Statistics table as produced in SPSS output

	Mean	Std. Deviation	N
Caffeine & Music	70.71	8.320	17
Caffeine & No Music	72.59	7.746	17
No Caffeine & Music	71.06	7.750	17
No Caffeine & No Music	70.82	8.141	17

Effect		Value	F	Hypothesis df	Error df	Sig.
Caffeine	Pillai's Trace	.160	3.044[a]	1.000	16.000	.100
	Wilks' Lambda	.840	3.044[a]	1.000	16.000	.100
	Hotelling's Trace	.190	3.044[a]	1.000	16.000	.100
	Roy's Largest Root	.190	3.044[a]	1.000	16.000	.100
Music	Pillai's Trace	.085	1.494[a]	1.000	16.000	.239
	Wilks' Lambda	.915	1.494[a]	1.000	16.000	.239
	Hotelling's Trace	.093	1.494[a]	1.000	16.000	.239
	Roy's Largest Root	.093	1.494[a]	1.000	16.000	.239
Caffeine * Music	Pillai's Trace	.265	5.760[a]	1.000	16.000	.029
	Wilks' Lambda	.735	5.760[a]	1.000	16.000	.029
	Hotelling's Trace	.360	5.760[a]	1.000	16.000	.029
	Roy's Largest Root	.360	5.760[a]	1.000	16.000	.029

Figure 19-18: Multivariate Tests table as produced in SPSS output

Multivariate tests are a different way to calculate repeated measure differences (See Figure 19-18). The advantage of these tests is they are not dependent on the assumption of sphericity. The disadvantage is that they are often not as powerful as the ANOVA and they are not suitable to analyse small sample sizes. We therefore recommend you do not interpret this table.

Figure 19-19: Mauchly's Test of Sphericity table as produced in SPSS output

Within Subjects Effect	Mauchly's W	Approx. Chi - Square	df	Sig.	Epsilon[a]		
					Greenhouse - Geisser	Huynh - Feldt	Lower - bound
Caffeine	1.000	.000	0	.	1.000	1.000	1.000
Music	1.000	.000	0	.	1.000	1.000	1.000
Caffeine * Music	1.000	.000	0	.	1.000	1.000	1.000

Mauchly's test examines the assumption of sphericity. If Mauchly's test is not significant it means the assumption is not violated and you can interpret the ANOVA results from the Sphericity Assumed values (see Figure 19-19). If Mauchly's test is significant it means the assumption is violated and you should interpret the ANOVA results from the Greenhouse-Geisser values (see Figure 19-20). In this example Mauchly's test has not been conducted as sphericity is only a consideration if you have three or more levels in your independent variables. The variables caffeine and music only had two levels each, therefore we do not need to consider sphericity assumption and can interpret the ANOVA results from the Sphericity Assumed values, although when a Mauchly's test is not possible to calculate, then sphericity isn't an issue and so all the lines in the ANOVA table will provide the same information (see Figure 19-20).

Source		Type III Sum of Squares	df	Mean Square	F	Sig.
Caffeine	Sphericity Assumed	8.471	1	8.471	3.044	.100
	Greenhouse - Geisser	8.471	1.000	8.471	3.044	.100
	Huynh - Feldt	8.471	1.000	8.471	3.044	.100
	Lower - bound	8.471	1.000	8.471	3.044	.100
Error (Caffeine)	Sphericity Assumed	44.529	16	2.783		
	Greenhouse - Geisser	44.529	16.000	2.783		
	Huynh - Feldt	44.529	16.000	2.783		
	Lower - bound	44.529	16.000	2.783		
Music	Sphericity Assumed	11.529	1	11.529	1.494	.239
	Greenhouse - Geisser	11.529	1.000	11.529	1.494	.239
	Huynh - Feldt	11.529	1.000	11.529	1.494	.239
	Lower - bound	11.529	1.000	11.529	1.494	.239
Error (Music)	Sphericity Assumed	123.471	16	7.717		
	Greenhouse - Geisser	123.471	16.000	7.717		
	Huynh - Feldt	123.471	16.000	7.717		
	Lower - bound	123.471	16.000	7.717		
Caffeine * Music	Sphericity Assumed	19.059	1	19.059	5.760	.029
	Greenhouse - Geisser	19.059	1.000	19.059	5.760	.029
	Huynh - Feldt	19.059	1.000	19.059	5.760	.029
	Lower - bound	19.059	1.000	19.059	5.760	.029
Error (Caffeine * Music)	Sphericity Assumed	52.941	16	3.309		
	Greenhouse - Geisser	52.941	16.000	3.309		
	Huynh - Feldt	52.941	16.000	3.309		
	Lower - bound	52.941	16.000	3.309		

Figure 19-20: Tests of Within-Subjects Effects as produced in SPSS output

There is lots of information in Figure 19-20. The most important rows are those that correspond with the names of your variables (which represents the main effects), and the interaction effect (which is denoted by both variable names separated by an asterisk). So, the information for the main effect for caffeine can be found along the row labelled caffeine and the main effect for background music can be found along the row labelled music. The interaction effect can be found along the row which is labelled with the product of both variables: caffeine*music.

The final column in the ANOVA table is the probability (*p* or sig.) value associated with the *F* ratio. As with all inferential tests, if this value is less than .05, then you can reject the null hypothesis. In a two-way ANOVA, there are three important significance values – one for each of the two main effects and one for the interaction result.

In this example, the *p* value main effect of caffeine is .10, which means you fail to reject the null hypothesis that the mean scores for all groups are equal. In other words, there is no statistically significant difference between the mean scores of the caffeine and no caffeine conditions.

The *p* value for the main effect of music is .24, which means you fail to reject the null hypothesis that the mean scores for both groups are equal. In other words, there is no statistically significant difference between the mean scores of the music and no music conditions.

Finally, the *p* value for the interaction term is .029 which is less than .05, and that means there is a statistically significant interaction. In other words, the effect of caffeine on IQ score is influenced by whether there was background music.

It is also possible to say that the effect of background music on IQ scores is influenced by caffeine consumption. The interaction result in the ANOVA table does not provide you with any information about the nature or direction of the interaction, only that it exists. To examine the nature of the interaction you need to look at the interaction in more detail. The best way to do this is to examine the interaction plot (see Figure 19-23).

Figure 19-21:
Tests of Within-Subjects Contrast table as produced in SPSS output

Source		Music	Type III Sum of Squares	df	Mean Square	F	Sig.
Caffeine	Linear		8.471	1	8.471	3.044	.100
Error (Caffeine)	Linear		44.529	16	2.783		
Music		Linear	11.529	1	11.529	1.494	.239
Error (Music)		Linear	123.471	16	7.717		
Caffeine * Music	Linear	Linear	19.059	1	19.059	5.760	.029
Error (Caffeine * Music) Linear		Linear	52.941	16	3.309		

Figure 19-21 tests trends within the data. It is more appropriate to look at the means or plots to examine trends and therefore you do not need to interpret this table.

Figure 19-22:
Tests of
Between-
Subjects
Effects as
produced in
SPSS output

Source	Type III Sum of Squares	df	Mean Square	F	Sig.
Intercept	345633.882	1	345633.882	1429.673	.000
Error	3868.118	16	241.757		

Figure 19-22 provides a test for between-subject effects. As this is a two-way within-groups ANOVA you have no between-subjects variables so you do not need to interpret this table.

Interpreting the interaction plot from a two-way within-groups ANOVA

Interactions can be complicated things to get your head around, so a picture can help. The interaction plot is a picture of how the two independent variables interact.

The levels of one variable are on the horizontal axis and the levels of the other variable are represented by separate lines. For example, in Figure 19-23, caffeine consumption is on the horizontal axis and there is a line representing music being played in the background and a separate line representing no music. It can help to have Table 19-3 or Figure 19-16 close by when you're trying to interpret the plot. The vertical axis represents the scores on the dependent variable, which is IQ in this example.

To make sense of the plot, find the point on the horizontal axis that represents caffeine having being consumed (this is denoted by 1 on the *x*-axis). Then draw a line in your mind straight up from this point until it crosses the two lines. The point at which it crosses the first line represents the mean IQ score when participants consumed coffee and there was background music present. The point at which you cross the second line represents the mean score for IQ score when participants consumed coffee and there was no music. From this you can see that when caffeine had been consumed IQ scores were higher in the no music condition compared to when background music was present.

The mean score for this condition
is higher than the other 3 conditions

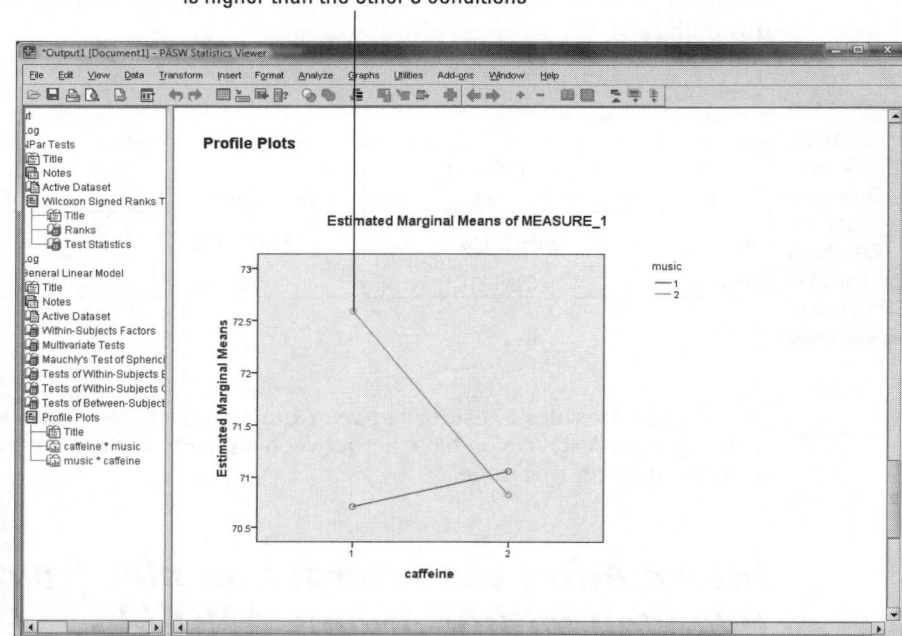

Figure 19-23:
Interaction
plot as
produced in
SPSS output

If you now look to the point on the horizontal axis that represents no caffeine consumed (denoted by 2 on the *x*-axis) you see that mean IQ scores are very similar when music was and wasn't present. The no caffeine consumed mean scores are also similar to the point on the plot representing the mean score of the caffeine consumed and background music present condition. So, the nature of the interaction seems to be that caffeine has an important influence on IQ scores only when there is no background music.

Writing up the results of a two-way within-groups ANOVA

You report the results of a two-way ANOVA in the same way as you report the results of a one-way ANOVA (see the section 'Writing up the results of a one-way within-groups ANOVA' in this chapter). The difference is that when reporting the result of a two-way ANOVA, you need to clarify whether you're reporting the result from a main effect or an interaction. Often you want to report all three results – the two main effects and the interaction. This can be a bit wordy, so you can report it in table form, as in Table 19-4.

Table 19-4	Reporting Your Two-Way ANOVA Result				
	SS	*df*	*MS*	*F*	*p*
Caffeine	8.47	1	8.47	3.04	.10
Error (caffeine)	44.53	16	2.78		
Music	11.53	1	11.53	1.49	.24
Error (music)	123.47	16	7.72		
Caffeine x Music	10.06	1	19.06	5.76	.029
Error (caffeine x music)	52.94	16	3.31		

Taking the two-way ANOVA result reported in Table 19-4, you report the result in the text as follows:

> There was no statistically significant main effect on IQ scores due to caffeine consumption; $F(1,16) = 3.04$, $p = .10$. There was no statistically significant main effect on IQ scores due to background music; $F(1,16) = 1.49$, $p = .24$. There was a significant interaction between caffeine consumption and background music on IQ scores; $F(1,16) = 5.76$, $p = .029$. The highest mean scores occurred in the condition when participants had consumed caffeine and there was no background music.

The same advice from the section 'Writing up the results of a one-way within-groups ANOVA' applies here: report an appropriate effect size statistic and the mean and standard deviation values for each group. This is particularly important when the ANOVA indicates a statistically significant finding.

If you report statistically significant main effects where the independent variable has more than two groups, then consider post hoc tests or planned comparisons between the groups to unravel the nature of this main effect (see Chapter 20).

Assumptions of a two-way within-groups ANOVA

The assumptions for a one-way within-groups ANOVA in this chapter also hold for a two-way within-groups ANOVA, so take a look at the section 'Assumptions of a one-way within-groups ANOVA'.

For a two-way ANOVA, the assumptions that must be met before you should interpret the result are:

- ✓ The independent variables should be categorical (see Chapter 2 for a description of variables).
- ✓ The dependent variable should be measured at the interval/ratio level (see Chapter 2).
- ✓ The differences between each session have approximately equal variances. This is known as sphericity.
- ✓ The residual scores should follow an approximately normal distribution.

The Friedman Test

The Friedman's analysis of variance test is the non-parametric equivalent of the one-way within-groups ANOVA. You use the test to assess the difference in scores between two or more conditions in repeated measures design. As the Friedman test is non-parametric it is subject to less stringent assumptions than the parametric within-groups ANOVA, which means you can use Friedman with ordinal data or when your data doesn't approximate a normal distribution (check out Chapter 1 to differentiate between parametric and non-parametric tests).

You can test the difference between two conditions in a repeated measures design using the Wilcoxon test (see Chapter 18), so you normally employ the Freidman test when you have three or more levels of your independent variable. Think of the Friedman test as an extension of the Wilcoxon test when you have more than two conditions. In common with the Wilcoxon test, it ranks scores instead of using the raw data.

For example, you may want to examine the effect of different genres of movies on mood. You recruit 35 participants and ask them to watch three movies; each participant watches a documentary, a horror film and a comedy. Immediately after each movie you ask the participants to rate their mood on a 1 to 5 scale where 1 represents a very negative mood and 5 represents a very positive mood. Your hypothesis is that comedy movies will result in more positive mood ratings than documentary or horror movies.

Obtaining a Friedman test in SPSS

You obtain a Friedman test in SPSS as follows:

1. **Go to the Analyze menu, choose Nonparametric Tests, then select Legacy Dialogs and then K related samples (see Figure 19-24).**

2. **In the new window (Figure 19-25) make sure that the default option is ticked beside Friedman in the list of tests headed 'Test Type'.** Also tick the box next to the Kendall's W option.

3. **Move the levels of your independent variables into the box headed Test Variable.** In this case we had three levels of the independent variable or three testing sessions: Documentary, Horror and Comedy.

4. **Select OK to run the analysis.**

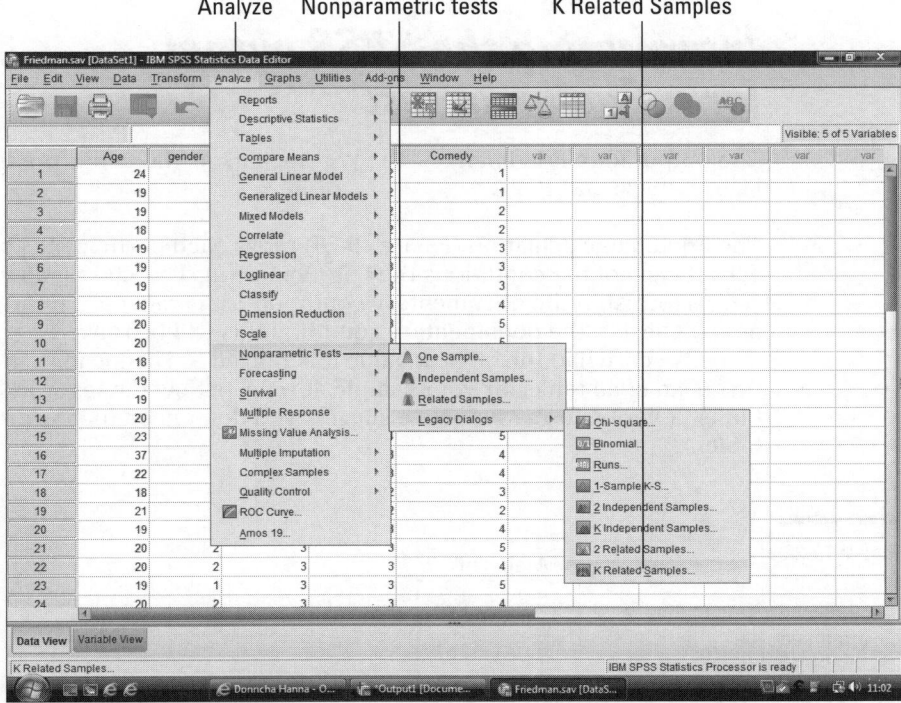

Figure 19-24: Choosing a Friedman test on SPSS.

Check Friedman
and Kendall's W

Have each level of your
independent variable
into the Test Variable box

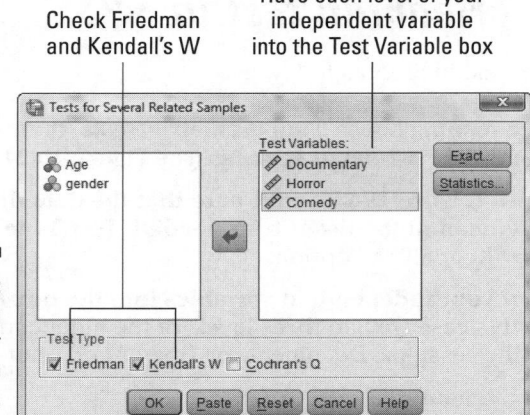

Figure 19-25:
Selecting
variables for
a Friedman
test.

Interpreting the SPSS output for a Friedman test

The output for a Friedman test in SPSS appears as the tables presented in Figures 19-26 and 19-27.

The Friedman calculation (Figure 19-26) ranks each participant's scores across each of the conditions they participate in. Therefore if an individual scores lowest in the documentary condition 1 it is ranked 1, if they score next highest in the documentary condition this will be ranked 2 and if their comedy score had the highest value it is ranked 3. The mean rank is simply the mean of all ranks for your sample. It reflects how the test was calculated but isn't very informative so we suggest you don't need to interpret this table.

Figure 19-26:
Mean Ranks
table as
produced
by SPSS
output.

	Mean Rank
Documentary	1.89
Horror	1.57
Comedy	2.54

Figure 19-27 presents the Freidman test result. It contains a chi-square statistic, df, and an Asymp. Sig. value. The *Asymp. Sig. value* is the significance value that determines whether the difference between the groups is statistically significant or not. As with all inferential tests, if this value is less than .05 then you can reject the null hypothesis that there is no difference between the groups.

Figure 19-27:
Test Statistics table as produced by SPSS.

N	35
Kendall's W[a]	.282
Chi-Square	19.738
df	2
Asymp. Sig.	.000

In this example, the *p* value is less than .001, which means you reject the null hypothesis. In other words, a statistically significant difference exists between the mean scores of the three conditions.

Additionally, this table provides Kendall's Coefficient of Concordance, which is an estimate of effect size and is denoted by *W*. Kendall's *W* ranges between 0 and 1, with higher scores indicating a larger effect.

Writing up the results of a Friedman test

Report the Friedman Chi-Square value rounded to two decimal places, with the degrees of freedom and sample size in parentheses, followed by the significance level. Taking the result reported in Figure 19-27, you report the result as follows:

> There was a statistically significant difference between the three genres of movies in terms of mood ratings, $\chi^2(2, n = 35) = 19.74$, $p < .001$

Report some descriptive information about each group to help the reader to understand the nature of the difference. Report the median value (see Chapter 4) and the interquartile range (see Chapter 5) for each group, and the Kendall's Coefficient of Concordance as an estimate of effect size.

The Friedman test doesn't tell you where the significant difference lies. For example, if you find a significant difference between three conditions it might be the case that all three groups differ significantly from each other or that one condition differs from the other two. To uncover this detail you need to compare the different pairs of groups using Wilcoxon tests (see Chapter 18). In this example there were three conditions so you'd need three Wilcoxon tests (documentary versus horror, documentary versus comedy and horror versus comedy).

Assumptions of the Friedman test

Your data must meet these conditions before you can use a Friedman test validly:

- ✔ The independent variables should be categorical (see Chapter 2 for a description of variables).
- ✔ The dependent variable should be measured at least at the ordinal level.

Chapter 20

Post Hoc Tests and Planned Comparisons for Repeated Measures Designs

*I*f you conduct a within-groups ANOVA (see Chapter 19) you might find a statistically significant difference or a significant main effect (which are the same thing – the difference depends on the terminology you are using). This tells you that differences exist between the conditions, levels of the independent variable or scores obtained at different testing sessions. While this is an interesting finding it doesn't tell you *where* a difference actually exists; it could be between only one pair of conditions, or perhaps every condition is significantly different from every other condition. For example, if a within-groups ANOVA suggests that anxiety significantly differs over repeated sessions with a therapist, we do not know whether anxiety only decreases after the first session and then remains constant or if anxiety levels continue to decrease after every visit to the therapist. To explore where the significant differences actually are, you must conduct post hoc tests or planned comparisons.

In this chapter we explain why you need to use post hoc tests and planned comparisons (and shouldn't use *t*-tests) and how these two sets of tests differ. Then taking post hoc tests and planned comparisons separately, we explain the different types of tests available in SPSS, how to conduct and interpret the relevant tests and then how to report the results. You should only conduct post hoc tests or planned comparisons if you obtain a statistically significant difference in an ANOVA. If you have conducted a non-parametric Friedman test and want to explore where the differences lie, you will need to perform Wilcoxon tests with Bonferroni corrections; we explain how to do this at the end of the chapter.

Why do you need to use post hoc tests and planned comparisons?

When you find a significant difference between two conditions (or two levels of your independent variable) in a repeated measures design using a paired *t*-test or a Wilcoxon test, you can easily determine which group is scoring significantly higher than the other group by looking at the mean or median scores of the groups (see Chapter 18). But when you find a significant difference between three or more conditions using a within-groups ANOVA or a Friedman test (see Chapter 19), working out where this significant difference lies can be more difficult. This is because the ANOVA or Friedman test only indicates that a statistically significant difference exists between conditions. It doesn't tell you *where* the significant difference lies. For example, if you find a significant difference between three conditions, all three conditions may differ significantly from each other, or only one condition may differ from the other two. Of course, examining the mean or median scores of each condition gives you an indication of where the significant difference is likely to be. This might be sufficient in some circumstances, but usually you want to have more firm evidence about the nature of the significant difference. This is where post hoc tests and planned comparisons are useful; they tell you where exactly the significant differences actually exist.

Why should you not use t-tests?

One way of examining the differences between three or more conditions (or three or more levels of your independent variable) is to test the difference between all possible pairs of conditions. For example, if you have three conditions in your analysis and a within-groups ANOVA indicates that a significant difference exists between these three conditions, then you could compare each pair of conditions by conducting a paired *t*-test to compare condition 1 with condition 2, another *t*-test to compare condition 1 with condition 3, and another *t*-test to compare condition 2 with condition 3. (We discuss within-groups ANOVA in Chapter 19 and paired *t*-tests in Chapter 18.) The principle here is sound, but in practice you encounter a problem which statisticians refer to as *multiplicity* (see Chapter 17 for a discussion of multiplicity).

Remember that when you conduct any statistical test there is a 5 per cent chance of making a Type I error. Making a Type I error means you conclude there is a statistically significant effect in the population but there really isn't (see Chapter 8 for a recap on Type I errors).

This means that if you conduct three separate *t*-tests you are increasing the chances of making a Type I error and reporting an incorrect result. This increased chance of making a Type I error due to performing multiple inferential statistics is known as multiplicity. Post hoc tests and planned comparisons are designed to examine where significant differences exist but also to control for the potential influence of multiplicity.

What is the difference between post hoc tests and planned comparisons?

The difference between a post hoc test and a planned comparison is that post hoc tests compare every possible pair of conditions, whereas planned comparisons only make specific comparisons between conditions you decided upon in advance of conducting the analysis (we outline these specific comparisons later, in the section on planned comparisons). Therefore, planned comparisons are usually driven by theory, whereas post hoc tests simply trawl the data looking for any significant findings. As a result post hoc tests are less sensitive than planned comparisons, so post hoc tests are less likely to find significant differences than planned comparisons. Whether you use post hoc tests or planned comparisons depends on your hypothesis. If you need to explore your data by comparing every possible pair of conditions, you should use post hoc tests. If you have a very specific experimental hypothesis, for example, comparing each condition (or level of the independent variable) with only the first condition, then planned comparisons are more appropriate.

Before conducting any analyses, decide whether planned comparisons exist that you want to examine. If you find planned comparisons then build these into your plan of analysis. If not, you can conduct post hoc tests. But don't conduct planned comparisons and post hoc tests on the same data – choose one or the other.

Post Hoc Tests for Repeated Measures Designs

You use post hoc tests when you obtain a statistically significant ANOVA result and want to find out where the differences are. Post hoc tests achieve this by comparing every possible pair of conditions. In this section we outline the three different types of post hoc test that are available in SPSS, then we explain how to obtain and interpret your chosen post hoc test in SPSS. Finally we show how to write up the results of your post hoc test in conjunction with your ANOVA result.

The example

In Chapter 19, we introduce the example of a research study to examine the difference in pain relief ratings between three different tablets: ibuprofen, aspirin and a *placebo* (a tablet with no active ingredients). The study had ten participants who tried the three drugs (they were all called drugs so that the participants would not know one was a placebo) over three days, and rated how effective the drug was in reducing pain on a 1 to 10 scale (1 is very effective; 10 is very ineffective). In Chapter 19 we conduct a one-way within-groups ANOVA and concluded that there was a significant difference (or significant main effect) between the three drugs on ratings of pain relief: $F(2,18)$ = 13.24, $p < .001$. However this ANOVA result simply tells you that there is a difference: You don't know whether ibuprofen is significantly more effective than aspirin or whether the placebo is significantly less effective than the other two drugs. As you want to compare the difference between each possible pair of conditions (ibuprofen versus aspirin, ibuprofen versus placebo, and aspirin versus placebo) post hoc tests are most appropriate.

Choosing a post hoc test

SPSS offers three post hoc tests when you're conducting within-groups ANOVA. Each method compares the difference between every possible pair of conditions but does it in a slightly different way. You need to select the test that suits your data best; this is normally the Bonferroni test unless you have lots of conditions, in which case the Sidak test is most appropriate. The three post hoc tests available in SPSS are:

- ✔ **Least Significant Difference test (LSD):** This test is available, but doesn't correct for multiplicity, so we advise you not to use this method.

- ✔ **Bonferroni test:** Effectively multiplies each p-value (significance value; see Chapter 8) by the number of comparisons made. For example, if you have three conditions then three comparisons are made so to control for multiplicity the p-value for each test is multiplied by 3. This is known as a *conservative correction* because it reduces the power of the test; you are less likely to obtain a significant result but you are also less likely to obtain a Type I error. This is the most commonly used post hoc test.

✔ **Sidak test:** Makes an adjustment to the Bonferroni correction so it's not as conservative or has slightly more power (Chapter 11 explains power). The Sidak test is most appropriate if you have lots of conditions in your study and therefore have lots of comparisons to make.

Obtaining a post-hoc test for a within-groups ANOVA in SPSS

For the purposes of the illustration, in this section we conduct a Bonferroni post hoc test. If you want to obtain and interpret a Sidak test you follow the same general procedure.

To obtain post-hoc tests run your within-groups ANOVA again (as outlined in steps 1 to 3) and then select the relevant post hoc options (as explained in steps 4 to 8). If you need a reminder on how to obtain a within-groups ANOVA you can turn to chapter 18.

1. **Go to the Analyze menu, choose General Linear Model and then select Repeated Measures.**

2. **Define the independent variable and the number of levels or conditions.**

3. **In the new Repeated Measures window move the columns representing each level of the independent variable into the Within-Subjects Variables box.**

4. **Select the Options button on the right-hand side of the Repeated Measures Window.** This opens a new window (see Figure 20-1).

5. **Move your independent variable from the left-hand side Factor(s) box to the Display Means For box.** In the example we've moved the independent variable 'drug'.

6. **Check the box under your independent variable entitled 'Compare main effects'.** This allows you to choose one of three post-hoc methods. We have selected Bonferroni.

7. **Select continue to close the window.**

8. **Select OK on the Repeated Measures window to run the analyses.**

Move the independent variable
of interest into the Display Means box

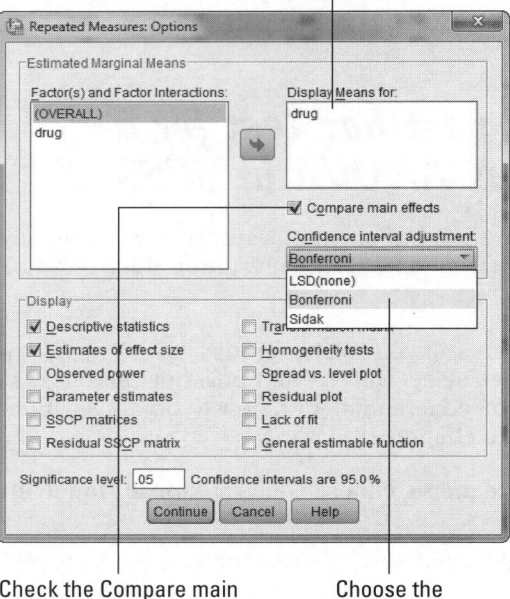

Figure 20-1:
Obtaining
post-hoc
test as
part of the
within-
groups
ANOVA
procedure
in SPSS

Check the Compare main
effects option

Choose the
appropriate test

Interpreting the SPSS output for a post-hoc test

You get quite a lot of output for a within-groups ANOVA. We've attempted to explain each part of output to you in Chapter 19. Because you requested post-hoc tests, you now have additional tables to interpret.

The pairwise comparison table (Figure 20-2) presents the results of your post-hoc tests. Each condition is compared with every other condition.

		Mean			95% Confidence Interval for Difference[a]	
(I) drug	(J) drug	Difference (I – J)	Std. Error	Sig.[a]	Lower – Bound	Upper – Bound
1	2	−.300	.335	1.000	−1.283	.683
	3	−2.100*	.482	.005	−3.514	−.686
2	1	.300	.335	1.000	−.683	1.283
	3	−1.800*	.490	.015	−3.237	−.363
3	1	2.100*	.482	.005	.686	3.514
	2	1.800*	.490	.015	.363	3.237

Figure 20-2: The Pairwise Comparisons table: post-hoc tests as presented by SPSS

The sig values tell you if there is a significant difference between each possible pair of conditions

Look at the first row to compare condition 1 with condition 2. Condition 1 relates to ibuprofen and condition 2 relates to aspirin. The order in which the conditions are coded is based on the order they were entered; the very first table in the SPSS output also gives you this information (see Figure 20-3). The mean difference in pain relief rating between the ibuprofen condition and the aspirin condition is −0.3. If you check the third Sig. column you can see that the *p*-value (which is approximately equal to 1) is greater than 0.05 indicating that no significant difference exists in mean scores between the two conditions.

Figure 20-3: The Within-Subjects Factors table as presented by SPSS

drug	Dependent Variable
1	ibuprofen
2	asprin
3	placebo

If you look at the second row you can see a mean difference between the ibuprofen condition (1) and the placebo condition (3) of −2.1, and this represents a significant difference (*p*=.005).

Following this logic you can interpret Figure 20-2 as illustrated in Table 20-1.

Table 20-1 Interpretation of the Pairwise Comparison Table

Comparison	Mean difference	Conclusion
Ibuprofen v Aspirin	−0.30	No significant difference ($p \approx 1$)
Ibuprofen v Placebo	−2.10	Significant difference ($p.005$)
Aspirin v Ibuprofen	0.30	No significant difference ($p \approx 1$)
Aspirin v Placebo	−1.80	Significant difference ($p = .015$)
Placebo v Ibuprofen	2.10	Significant difference ($p = .005$)
Placebo v Aspirin	1.80	Significant difference ($p = .015$)

You might notice that the table in Figure 20-2 and Table 20-1 repeat information. For example, compare the first line (ibuprofen v. aspirin) with the third line (aspirin v. ibuprofen). The information provided in these two lines is the same. This is because you're comparing the same two conditions, just the other way round. The significance values for the difference between two conditions will always be the same no matter which condition comes first, so one of these lines of information is redundant. In fact, there are six significance values in the table in Figure 20-2, even though you've only conducted three significance tests. This is because every test is repeated, so you can ignore the repetition of the same information.

The post hoc tests indicate that a significant difference exists between the placebo and the other two conditions. You must also report means (and standard deviations) of each condition to see whether pain relief scores increase or decrease between the conditions.

Writing up the results of a post hoc test

As we explain in Chapter 14, when reporting the results of statistical analyses, you need to follow any specific guidelines that inform how you should present the statistical findings.

As you only conduct post hoc tests when you have obtained a statistically significant ANOVA result you should present the results of a post hoc test in conjunction with the results of the ANOVA and along with the mean and standard deviation scores for each group in the analysis. Taking the analyses reported in Figure 20-2, you would report the results in conjunction with the ANOVA result and descriptive statistics (which can be found in Figures 19-16 and 19-19) as follows:

> There was a statistically significant difference between the three drugs on pain relief ratings: $F(2,18) = 13.24$, $p < .001$. Post hoc Bonferroni tests indicated that the ibuprofen condition ($M = 5$, $SD = 1.05$) had significantly ($p = .005$) lower pain relief scores than the placebo condition ($M = 7.1$, $SD = 1.1$). Post hoc Bonferroni tests also indicated that the aspirin condition ($M = 5.3$, $SD = 1.25$) had significantly ($p = .015$) lower pain relief scores than the placebo condition ($M = 7.1$, $SD = 1.1$). There was no significant difference found between ibuprofen and aspirin scores ($p \approx 1$).

Also report an effect size for the ANOVA result (see Chapter 11).

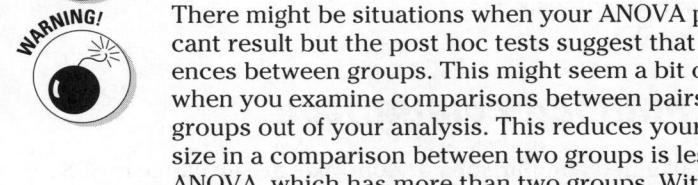

There might be situations when your ANOVA provides a statistically significant result but the post hoc tests suggest that there are no significant differences between groups. This might seem a bit odd but it happens, because when you examine comparisons between pairs of groups you are leaving other groups out of your analysis. This reduces your sample size – so, the sample size in a comparison between two groups is less than the sample size in the ANOVA, which has more than two groups. With a reduced sample size comes reduced power (see Chapter 11), which means that you might find it's more difficult to detect differences between groups.

Planned Comparisons for Within Groups Designs

Post hoc tests examine every possible combination of conditions (or levels of the independent variable). The alternative is to conduct a planned comparison, which makes specific comparisons (which we will outline shortly). The advantage of planned comparisons is that they tend to be more powerful than post hoc tests (Chapter 11 explains power) which means they are more likely to detect a significant result if one exists. The disadvantage is that they don't compare every possible pair of conditions. You have to decide whether you're interested in a planned comparison or a post hoc test when you're designing your study. In this section we explain the specific comparisons that planned comparisons allow you to make, then we show you how to obtain, interpret and report planned comparisons using SPSS.

The example

We employ the same example as we used in 'Post Hoc Tests for Repeated Measures Designs' earlier in this chapter. A repeated measures research study examined the difference in pain relief ratings between three different tablets (ibuprofen, aspirin and a placebo) and the subsequent one-way within-groups ANOVA concluded that there was a significant difference (or significant main effect) between the three tablets on ratings of pain relief: $F(2,18) = 13.24$, $p < .001$ (see Chapter 19 for more detail). This time your hypothesis is slightly different, in that you want to test if the placebo condition resulted in significantly different pain rating scores than the other two drugs. This means you do not need to compare every possible combination of conditions (you are not interested in comparing aspirin v ibuprofen) and therefore planned comparisons are the appropriate analysis. There are several types of planned comparisons available on SPSS so you must choose the one that addresses your hypothesis.

Choosing a planned comparison

Six different types of planned comparisons or contrasts are available in SPSS. The most commonly used types of planned comparisons in psychology are *simple contrasts* and *repeated contrasts*.

✔ **Simple contrasts:** Compares each condition to *either* the first or the last condition. (Whether a condition is first or last simply reflects the order the conditions were entered when specifying the variables when you were requesting a within-groups ANOVA in SPSS). If you wish to compare each condition to the first condition then you specify the reference category as the first condition in SPSS and if you want to compare each condition with the last condition then you specify the reference category as the last condition (see Figure 20-4). For example, if you employed a simple contrast with the first condition as the reference category in the example results would compare ibuprofen (the first condition – see Figure 20-3) with aspirin and ibuprofen with the placebo. Note that simple contrast makes only two comparisons and doesn't compare the aspirin and placebo conditions. If you run a simple contrast with the reference category as the last condition, it compares the placebo and ibuprofen conditions, and the placebo and aspirin conditions (as placebo was the last condition entered – see Figure 20-3). The simple contrast is most useful if you have a baseline or control condition you want to compare with subsequent conditions or inventions.

The group to which all other groups is compared (placebo in the example) is referred to as the *reference category* by the simple contrast.

✔ **Repeated contrasts:** Compares each condition to the previous condition. For instance, if you have three conditions in your study, repeated contrasts compares condition 1 with condition 2, and then condition 2 with condition 3. In the current example, repeated contrasts would compare ibuprofen (1) with aspirin (2), and aspirin (2) and placebo (3). Notice that repeated contrasts only makes two comparisons and doesn't compare the ibuprofen (1) and aspirin (3) conditions. Repeated contrasts are most useful if you're interested in change over time and the three conditions in your analysis represent different points in time.

✔ **Deviation contrasts:** Compares each condition (except one) with the grand mean. Deviation contrasts don't compare the first condition with the grand mean if the reference category is set to first; nor does the technique compare the last condition with the grand mean if the reference category is set to last. For example, if the reference category is set to last and you have three conditions, contrasts would compare condition 1 with the grand mean and condition 2 with the grand mean.

✔ **Helmert contrasts:** Compares each condition (except the last) to the mean of the subsequent conditions. If you have four conditions in your study, this method compares condition 1 with the mean of conditions 2, 3 and 4; compares condition 2 with the mean of conditions 3 and 4; and compares condition 3 with condition 4.

✔ **Difference contrasts:** Similar to the Helmert condition, but in reverse! In this method each condition (except the first) is compared with the mean of the preceding conditions. If you have four conditions in your study, this method compares condition 4 with the mean of condition 3, 2 and 1; condition 3 with the mean of conditions 2 and 1; and condition 2 with condition 1.

✔ **Polynomial contrasts:** Looks for a significant trend between the conditions. These trends may be linear, quadratic, cubic or more complex polynomial functions. Polynomial contrasts are only useful when you have hypothesized a particular polynomial trend between your conditions (for example, a linear trend suggests a straight line relationship between conditions whereas a quadratic trend suggests an inverted-U shaped relationship).

Obtaining a simple planned contrast in SPSS

For the purposes of the illustration we will conduct a simple planned contrast to investigate the hypothesis that the placebo will be less effective in reducing pain than ibuprofen or the aspirin. If you want to obtain and interpret other contrasts you follow the same procedure.

To obtain planned comparisons (called *contrasts* in SPSS) run your within-groups ANOVA again (as outlined in steps 1 to 3) and then select the relevant options (as explained in steps 4 to 9). If you need a reminder on how to obtain a within-groups ANOVA you can turn to Chapter 19.

1. **Go to the Analyze menu, choose General Linear Model and then select Repeated Measures.**

2. **Define each the independent variable and the number of levels or conditions.**

3. **In the new Repeated Measures window move the columns representing the each level of the independent variable into the Within-Subjects Variables box.**

4. **Choose your variable.** The top of the box contains your independent variable(s). If you have more than one variable highlight the one of interest.

5. **Choose the contrast.** Move down to the contrast options under Change Contrast and click the option list (polynomial will be the default option). A drop-down list offers you six different types of contrasts; choose the most appropriate contrast, which in this case is Simple.

6. **Choose your reference category.** This is whether you want to compare your conditions against the first or last condition. In this example we want to compare our conditions against the placebo, which is the third condition or last reference category (see Figure 20-3), so ensure the last option is selected (see Figure 20-5); this will compare placebo with aspirin and placebo with ibuprofen. If you selected the first condition as the reference section you would compare the first condition with other conditions (which in this example would be ibuprofen with placebo and ibuprofen with aspirin).

Highlight the independent
variable of interest

Figure 20-4:
Obtaining
a simple
planned
contrast
as part of
the within-
groups
ANOVA
procedure
in SPSS 1.

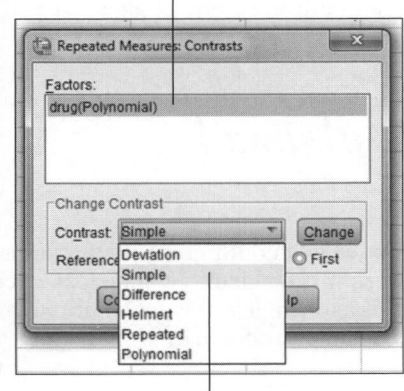

Select the appropriate contrast

Which condition is first or last simply reflects the ordered they were entered into SPSS. Helpfully in the ANOVA output a within-subjects factors table reminds you the order you entered the conditions (or levels of the independent variable) (see Figure 20-3).

Figure 20-5:
Obtaining a simple planned contrast as part of the within-groups ANOVA procedure in SPSS 2.

Ensure correct contrast has been selected

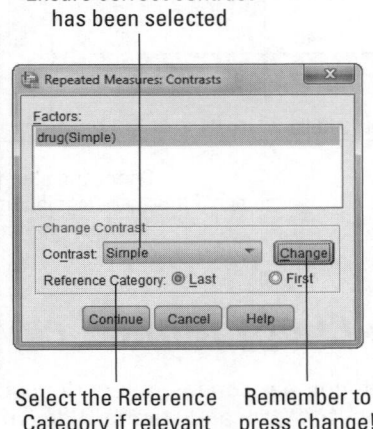

Select the Reference Category if relevant

Remember to press change!

7. **Click the Change button.** If you forget to click Change button the correct contrast won't run.

8. **Select Continue to close the Contrasts window.**

9. **Select OK on the Repeated Measures window to run the analyses.**

Interpreting the SPSS output for planned comparison tests

Chapter 19 explains the output for a within-groups ANOVA. When you conduct planned comparison tests you obtain an extra table; the Tests of Within-Subjects Contrasts table (Figure 20-6) which displays the result of your planned contrasts.

SPSS presents only two tests. The first compares level 1 (ibuprofen) with level 3 (placebo) and the second compares level 2 (aspirin) with level 3 (placebo). If you read across to the Sig. column you can see a significant difference between ibuprofen and placebo score ($p = .002$) and a significant difference between aspirin and placebo score ($p = .005$) because the Sig. values are less than .05.

Source	drug	Type III Sum of Squares	df	Mean Square	F	Sig.
drug	Level 1 vs. Level 3	44.100	1	44.100	18.990	.002
	Level 2 vs. Level 3	32.400	1	32.400	13.500	.005
Error (drug)	Level 1 vs. Level 3	20.900	9	2.322		
	Level 2 vs. Level 3	21.600	9	2.400		

Check the planned contrasts
to see if there are significant differences
between specific conditions

Writing up the results of planned contrasts

You present the results of a planned comparison in conjunction with the results of the ANOVA and along with the mean and standard deviation scores for each group in the analysis. Taking the analyses reported in Figure 20-6 and the results of the ANOVA that was obtained in Chapter 19 you report the result as follows:

There was a statistically significant difference between the three drugs on pain relief ratings: $F(2,18) = 13.24$, $p < .001$. Planned comparisons revealed that there was a significant difference on pain relief rating between the ibuprofen condition and the placebo condition ($F(1,9) = 18.99$, $p = .002$); the ibuprofen condition ($M = 5$, $SD = 1.05$) had lower pain relief scores than the placebo condition ($M = 7.1$, $SD = 1.1$). Additionally there was a significant difference on pain relief rating between the aspirin condition and the placebo condition ($F(1,9) = 32.40$, $p = .005$); the aspirin condition ($M = 5.3$, $SD = 1.25$) had lower pain relief scores than the placebo condition ($M = 7.1$, $SD = 1.1$).

It also important to report an effect size for the ANOVA result (see Chapter 11).

Examining Differences between Conditions: The Bonferroni Correction

In the case where you've conducted a Friedman test and you want to examine differences between conditions, the only option available is to conduct several Wilcoxon tests (see Chapter 18), because no post hoc test exists for situations when the dependent variable is measured at the ordinal level (Chapter 2 explains variables and levels).

To control for the multiplicity problem in this case, you need to adjust your conclusions about the Wilcoxon tests by adjusting the cut-off point for determining whether a finding is statistically significant or not. One simple way of doing this is to perform a *Bonferroni correction*. To do this, divide the normal cut-off point (.05) by the number of Wilcoxon tests conducted. So, if you conduct three Wilcoxon tests to examine the difference between conditions after a Friedman test then the cut-off point for determining statistical significance is .05/3 = .0167. Therefore, a Wilcoxon test needs to have a significance value less than .0167 (instead of .05) in this specific case before the difference would be considered to be statistically significant.

Chapter 21

Mixed ANOVA

- -

In This Chapter

▶ Obtaining a mixed ANOVA in SPSS

▶ Interpreting your results

- -

This chapter focuses on mixed ANOVA (the standard abbreviation for *analysis of variance*). Chapter 16 deals with ANOVA models you use to analyse your data when your study follows the independent groups (or between-groups) research design, and Chapter 19 explains the ANOVA models that are relevant when the study employs repeated measures (or within-groups) design. There may be times where your study has elements of both designs; one of your independent variables may be a between-groups variable and another independent variable may a within-groups variable. In these cases a mixed ANOVA may be the most appropriate statistical analysis.

Getting to Grips with Mixed ANOVA

A typical study in which a mixed ANOVA would be useful might be as follows. Say you're interested in how therapy affects quality of life scores in clients with severe Obsessive Compulsive Disorder (OCD). You could design an independent groups study where you looked at quality of life scores in participants where each separate group had experienced a different type of therapy. However, differences in quality of life may already have existed between the separate groups before they received the therapy and therefore have nothing to do with the type of therapy that they undertook. Therefore, it would be useful to additionally measure clients' quality of life scores before, during and after each type of therapy. In this case you are using a mixed design. You have two independent variables: a between-groups variable that allows you to compare differences between separate groups that experienced different types of therapy and a within-groups variable that allows you to see how scores changed over time. You would then analyse this type of study with a mixed ANOVA.

A mixed ANOVA is sometimes called a *split-plot* ANOVA or a *mixed factorial* ANOVA. The factorial bit just refers to any ANOVA with more than one independent variable.

Don't get a mixed ANOVA confused with a MANOVA; this is an advanced multivariate technique where several dependent variables are analysed together. We don't cover it in this book.

A mixed ANOVA will always have at least two independent variables and one dependent variable. One of the independent variables will be an independent groups (or between-groups) variable and one of the independent variables will be a repeated measures (or within-groups) variable.

Mixed ANOVAs are often described by the number of levels of the independent variables. For example, a two-way mixed ANOVA (*two-way* meaning there are two independent variables – see Chapter 16 for a recap on what a two-way ANOVA refers to) where each independent variable has three levels will be known as a 3×3 ANOVA; a two-way ANOVA where the between-groups variable has three levels and the within-groups variable has four levels will be known as a 3×4 ANOVA and so on. Sometimes (but not always!) you see the number representing the within-groups variable in parentheses so the previous example would be reported as a $3 \times (4)$ ANOVA. This convention lets you know it is a mixed ANOVA and the within-groups variable has four levels.

The example

For example, imagine you have conducted a research study to examine critical thinking in university students. You wanted to see how critical thinking develops during an individual's time at university so you measured critical thinking in 20 students in their first, second and third years of study. In this example the year of study is a within-groups (or repeated measures) variable as you are looking at changes within the same students over their years of study. You may also want to investigate whether students from different courses had different levels of critical thinking, so 10 of the students you recruited were psychology students and the other 10 were drama students. Course of study is a between-groups (or independent groups) variable, because you are looking at difference between separate groups.

In this research design you have two independent variables:

- **Year:** A within-groups variable
- **Course:** A between-groups variable

You also have one dependent variable – critical thinking scores. The variable *year* has three levels – first, second and third year of university. The variable *course* has two levels – psychology or drama. Therefore an appropriate analysis would be a $(3) \times 2$ mixed ANOVA.

Your null hypotheses are that:

- ✔ Critical thinking scores do not significantly change over the three years of university degree.
- ✔ There will be no significant difference between the critical thinking scores of psychology and drama students.
- ✔ The two groups of students will not significantly differ in how their critical thinking skills change over the three years.

The first two hypotheses here are known as *main effects* and the final hypothesis is known as an *interaction*.

Main Effects and Interactions

In any two-way ANOVA you can obtain two main effects and an interaction. The main effects are the effects of each independent variable on the dependent variable. The result that you get from a one-way ANOVA is also known as a main effect. So, the main effects in a two-way ANOVA are a bit like conducting two separate one-way ANOVAs; in this case it would be one within-groups ANOVA and one between-groups ANOVA.

Conducting a two-way ANOVA and two one-way ANOVAs isn't exactly the same. In the two-way ANOVA you are accounting for more of the variance because you are getting an extra interaction effect. See the side bar 'One plus one doesn't always equal two' in Chapter 16 for more on this. Things are a little more complex in a mixed ANOVA as there are two separate error terms; one for the within-groups variable and the interaction and another for the between-groups ANOVA.

The two-way ANOVA gives you an interaction effect that you don't get with one-way ANOVAs. The interaction effect in a two-way ANOVA is the effect of the combination of the two independent variables on the dependent variable. Interactions are often the most interesting result in your analysis!

In the example, a significant main effect of the year or study would suggest that critical thinking skills change over the three years of attending university; you would expect university to influence critical thinking skills so this result should not be that shocking! A significant main effect of the student's course would suggest that psychology students and drama students had different critical thinking scores; again, different courses may attract or foster different skills, so this finding might be expected. A significant interaction would be much more interesting. It would suggest one group of students (psychology or drama) could have critical thinking scores that increased and the other group of students might demonstrate a decrease or no change in their critical thinking scores over the three years.

Usually when you conduct a two-way ANOVA the interaction is the result that you are most interested in and you should pay close attention to it. If the interaction result is statistically significant, then this overrides the main effects. In other words, the interaction result provides more information than any single main effect result. So, in the light of the added information from the interaction result, the results of the main effects might become obsolete. Of course, when the interaction effect is not significant, then the main effects will be important.

Performing the ANOVA in SPSS

Go to the Analyze menu, choose General Linear Model and then select Repeated Measures (see Figure 21-1).

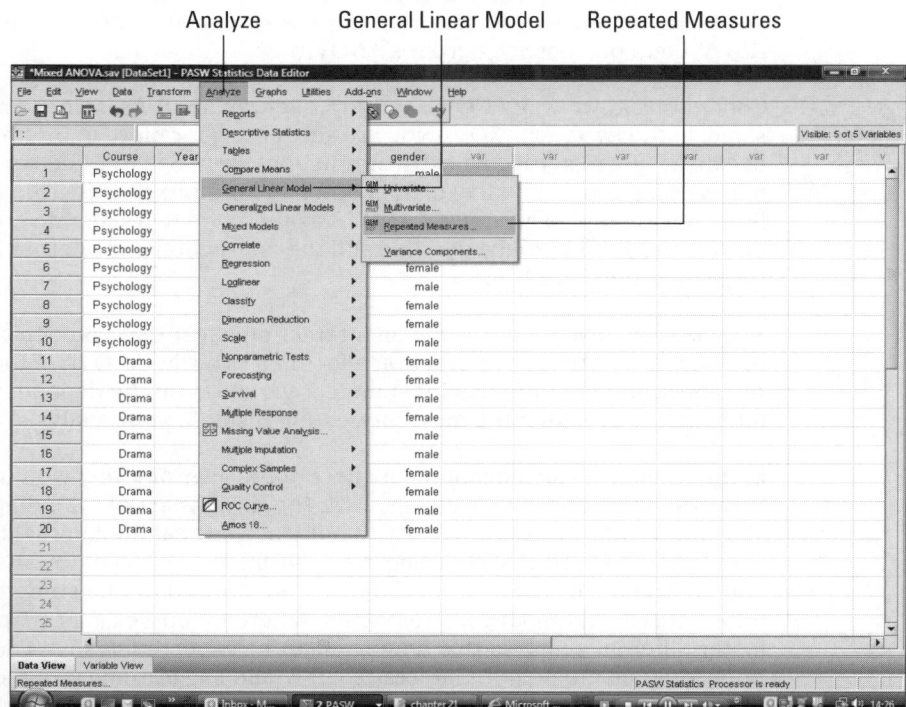

Figure 21-1: Choosing a mixed ANOVA in SPSS.

A new Repeated Measures Define Factor(s) window will open. Here you must specify a short label for your within-groups (or repeated measures) variable. In this example the within-groups variable is the year of study so we have entered 'year' in the Within-Subject Factor Name box. Secondly you need to state the number of levels or conditions that were measured. In the current example, we have collected data from the students when they were in first, second and third year so we have three levels. When you have entered your factor name and the number of levels remember to click Add and then Define to progress. See Figure 21-2.

Enter a name for your within-groups variable

Enter the number of levels (or testing session) for the variable

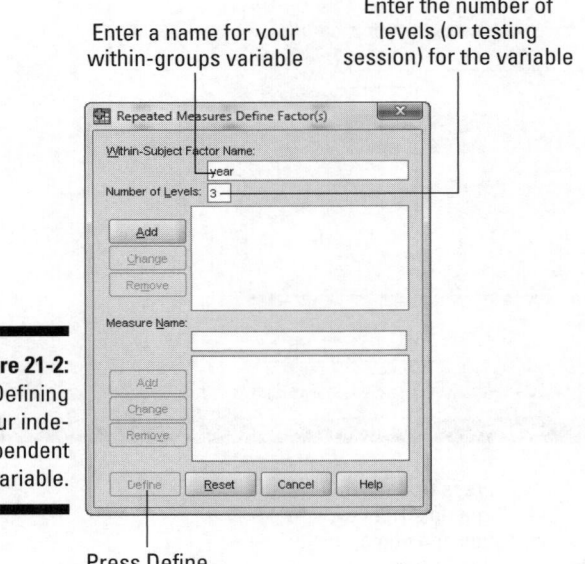

Figure 21-2: Defining your independent variable.

Press Define

In the new Repeated Measures window move the columns representing each level of the within-groups variable into the 'Within-Subjects Variables' box. In this example we specified there were three levels so we can only select three variables (see Figure 21-3). You can then select your between-groups variable by moving it into the relevant box as shown; for this example we have moved the within-groups (or independent group) variable of 'Course' into the 'Between-Subjects Factor(s)' box (see Figure 21-3).

Select the variables
representing each level
of groups within-groups variable

Select the Between-groups
variable

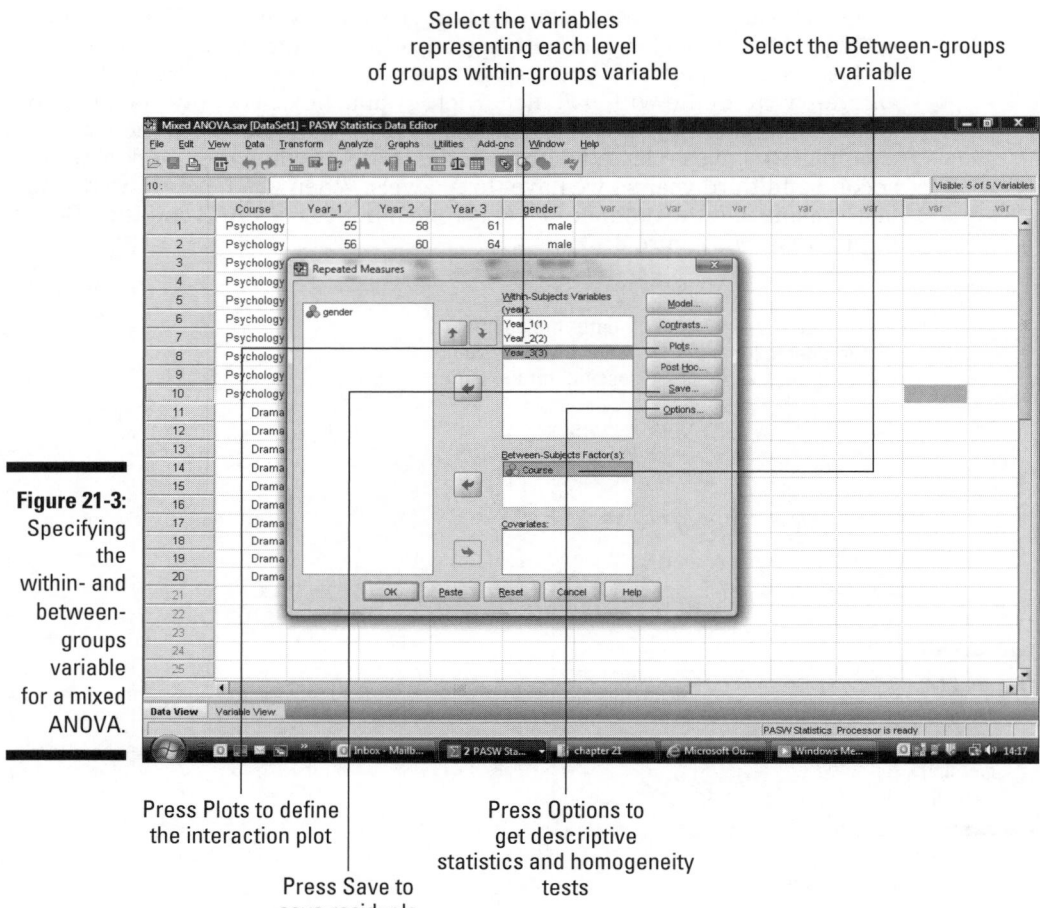

Figure 21-3:
Specifying
the
within- and
between-
groups
variable
for a mixed
ANOVA.

Press Plots to define
the interaction plot

Press Options to
get descriptive
statistics and homogeneity
tests

Press Save to
save residuals

At this stage it is also useful to ask SPSS to generate some extra output; specifically it would be convenient to have descriptive statistics for the variables, tests of homogeneity and standard residuals to check assumptions (which are covered a little later in this chapter) and finally interaction plots to examine the interaction between the two variables.

For descriptive statistics and tests of homogeneity you need to click on the 'Options' button in the Repeated Measures window. When the new Repeated Measures:Option window opens tick the box beside the words 'Descriptive statistics', in the list headed 'Display' (see Figure 21-4). In this window you can also obtain homogeneity tests (see the section on assumptions of a mixed ANOVA in this chapter), by ticking the box helpfully called 'Homogeneity tests' (see Figure 21-4). Click continue.

Select the Descriptive   Select the Homogeneity
Statistics option   tests option

Figure 21-4:
Obtaining
descriptive
statistics
and homo-
geneity test
as part of
the mixed
ANOVA
procedure.

Then press continue

To generate residuals you need to click on the 'Save' button in the Repeated Measures window. When the new Repeated Measures:Save window opens tick the box beside the words 'Standardized ', in the list headed 'Residuals' (see Figure 21-5). Click continue.

You may wonder why you can't see any information regarding the residuals in your SPSS output; this is because the residuals are saved as new columns in your data file. We will tell you what to do with this new information when we address the assumptions later in this chapter.

The final piece of output that you should request SPSS to produce is the interaction plots. In order to obtain an interaction plot in SPSS, click on the Plots button in the Repeated Measures window. In the new window move one of the variables from the box on the left headed 'Factors' to the box on the right headed 'Horizontal axis'. Move the other variable from the box on the left to the box on the right headed 'Separate lines' (see Figure 21-6). Then press Add. The name of the requested graph will then appear in the box at the bottom of the window headed 'Plots'. Press 'Continue' on the plots window and then press 'OK' in the Repeated Measures window to run the procedure.

Select Standardized Residuals

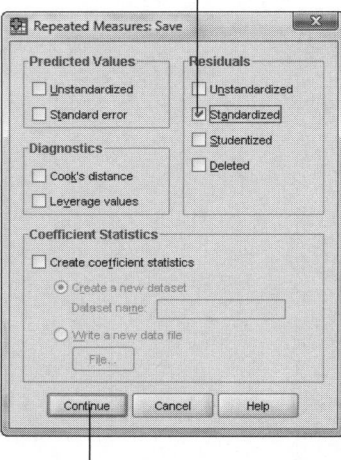

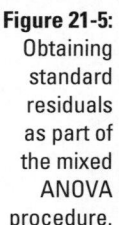

Figure 21-5:
Obtaining
standard
residuals
as part of
the mixed
ANOVA
procedure.

Then press Continue

Select the within-groups
variable on the
Horizontal Axis

Remember to
press Add

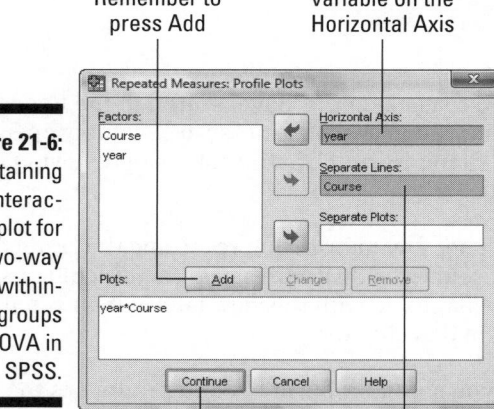

Figure 21-6:
Obtaining
an interac-
tion plot for
a two-way
within-
groups
ANOVA in
SPSS.

Then press Continue   Select the between-
groups variable as
Separate Lines

When it comes to interpreting Mixed ANOVA interaction plots we find having
the within-groups variable on the horizontal axis and the between-groups variable presented as separate lines usually makes most sense.

Interpreting the SPSS output for a two-way mixed ANOVA

The output for the two-way mixed ANOVA in SPSS will appear as 10 tables (presented in Figures 21-7 to 21-16 below). It seems like there is a lot of information here, but you only need to interpret certain tables.

Figure 21-7:
Within-Subjects Factors table as produced in SPSS output.

year	Dependent Variable
1	Year_1
2	Year_2
3	Year_3

The Within-Subject Factor table is a reminder of how each level of the within-groups variable was coded (see Figure 21-7). Have a quick check to ensure you entered the levels in the right order.

Figure 21-8:
Between-Subjects Factors table as produced in SPSS output.

		Value Label	N
Course	1	Psychology	10
	2	Drama	10

The Between-Subject Factor table states how each level of the between-groups variable was coded (see Figure 21-8). In this example psychology students were coded as 1 and drama students were coded as 2. You can also see there were 10 participants in each group.

	Course	Mean	Std. Deviation	N
1st year critical thinking mark	Psychology	61.30	5.165	10
	Drama	53.90	9.327	10
	Total	57.60	8.262	20
2nd year critical thinking mark	Psychology	65.90	6.008	10
	Drama	55.90	9.422	10
	Total	60.90	9.245	20
3rd year critical thinking mark	Psychology	69.00	6.464	10
	Drama	59.70	10.209	10
	Total	64.35	9.588	20

Figure 21-9: Descriptive statistics obtained from the mixed ANOVA procedure in SPSS.

Figure 21-9 presents the descriptive statistics for each group at each level of the within-groups variable. For example, you can see the mean critical thinking score for first year psychology students was 61.30, for drama students it was 53.90 and the mean critical thinking score for all the first year students combined was 57.60. You can also see that there were 10 participants in each cell, that is, there were 10 psychology students and 10 drama students and they all took part in each of the 3 testing sessions.

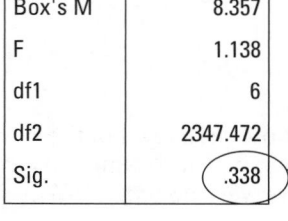

Figure 21-10: Box's Test of Equality of Covariance Matrices.

Box's M	8.357
F	1.138
df1	6
df2	2347.472
Sig.	.338

If the *p*-value for Box's test is less than .001 and you have unequal sample sizes it means you have violated the *assumption* of homogeneity of variance – covariance matrices.

Box's test (see Figure 21-10) examines the assumption that the dependent variable has approximately equal (or homogenous) variance–covariance matrices; this is explained in more detail later in the section when we deal with assumptions. You only need to interpret this table if you have unequal sample sizes. If you have equal sample sizes in each group at each testing you can assume homogeneity of variance–covariance matrices. If you have unequal cell sizes (that is, your sample sizes vary between groups or testing sessions) then you need to interpret this table. To interpret the test look at the sig. (or *p*-) value. If this value is greater than .001 then this assumption is not violated and you should interpret the ANOVA result as normal. If the *p*-value for Box's test is less than .001 it may indicate you do not have homogeneity of variance–covariance matrices and you shouldn't use a mixed ANOVA to analyse your data as this assumption has been violated. The current example has equal cell sizes (there were 10 psychology students and 10 drama students and they all took part in each of the 3 testing sessions as shown in Figure 21-9) therefore we can assume homogeneity of variance–covariance matrices and do not need to check Box's test.

Effect		Value	F	Hypothesis df	Error df	Sig.
year	Pillai's Trace	.789	31.699[a]	2.000	17.000	.000
	Wilks' Lambda	.211	31.699[a]	2.000	17.000	.000
	Hotelling's Trace	3.729	31.699[a]	2.000	17.000	.000
	Roy's Largest Root	3.729	31.699[a]	2.000	17.000	.000
year * Course	Pillai's Trace	.340	4.377[a]	2.000	17.000	.029
	Wilks' Lambda	.660	4.377[a]	2.000	17.000	.029
	Hotelling's Trace	.515	4.377[a]	2.000	17.000	.029
	Roy's Largest Root	.515	4.377[a]	2.000	17.000	.029

Figure 21-11: Multivariate tests table as produced in SPSS output.

Multivariate tests are a different way to calculate repeated measure differences (Figure 21-11). While these tests have some advantages, they are often not as powerful as the ANOVA statistic and they are not suitable to analyse small sample sizes. We therefore recommend you do not interpret this table.

Figure 21-12:
Mauchly's
Test of
Sphericity
table as
produced
in SPSS
output.

Within Subjects Effect	Mauchly's W	Approx. Chi - Square	df	Sig.	Epsilon^a		
					Greenhouse - Geisser	Huynh - Feldt	Lower - bound
year	.425	14.542	2	.001	.635	.699	.500

If Mauchly's test is not significant, interpret the sphericity assumed values from table 21-14.
If Mauchly's test is significant, interpret the Greenhouse–Geisser value from table 21-14.

Mauchly's test (see Figure 21-12). examines the assumption of sphericity (this was covered in Chapter 19 if you want a refresher). If Mauchly's test is not significant it means the assumption is not violated and you can interpret the ANOVA results from the Sphericity Assumed values (see Figure 21-14). If Mauchly's test is significant it means the assumption is violated and you should interpret the ANOVA results from the Greenhouse–Geisser values (see Figure 21-14). In this example Mauchly's test is statistically significant as the Sig or *p*-value of .001 is less than .05 (see Figure 21-12). This means the assumption of sphericity is violated and therefore the Greenhouse–Geisser figures in Within-Subjects Effects table should be interpreted (see section on assumptions in this chapter).

Figure 21-13:
The
Levene's
test for
assessing
homogeneity
of variances
in a mixed
ANOVA.

	F	df1	df2	Sig.
1st year critical thinking mark	4.287	1	18	.053
2nd year critical thinking mark	2.945	1	18	.103
3rd year critical thinking mark	2.723	1	18	.116

A significant Levene's test indicates the assumption of homogeneity of variances has been violated.

Figure 21-13 presents the results of the Levene's test, which tests whether the variances across the groups of the between-groups variables are approximately equal (which is known as the *homogeneity of variances assumption* and is covered in more detail in Chapter 16). If the significance value or *p*-value for this test is .05 or greater, then the variances can be considered to be sufficiently similar to meet this assumption of the mixed ANOVA (see section on assumptions in this chapter) and you can interpret the ANOVA result as normal. If any of the *p*-values for Levene's test is less than .05 it indicates that you do not have homogeneity of variance and this assumption has been violated. In the current example all the *p*-values are greater than .05 (just!) so this assumption is not violated and you can interpret the results of the ANOVA.

This is the mean effect for your within-groups variable

Check Mauchly's test to determine the correct figures to interpret

Source		Type III Sum of Squares	df	Mean Square	F	Sig.
year	Sphericity Assumed	455.700	2	227.850	56.105	.000
	Greenhouse-Geisser	455.700	1.270	358.842	56.105	.000
	Huynh-Feldt	455.700	1.399	325.830	56.105	.000
	Lower-bound	455.700	1.000	455.700	56.105	.000
year * Course	Sphericity Assumed	18.100	2	9.050	2.228	.122
	Greenhouse-Geisser	18.100	1.270	14.253	2.228	.145
	Huynh-Feldt	18.100	1.399	12.942	2.228	.141
	Lower-bound	18.100	1.000	18.100	2.228	.153
Error (year)	Sphericity Assumed	146.200	36	4.061		
	Greenhouse-Geisser	146.200	22.859	6.396		
	Huynh-Feldt	146.200	25.174	5.807		
	Lower-bound	146.200	18.000	8.122		

Figure 21-14: Tests of Within-Subjects Effects as produced in SPSS output.

This is the interaction effect

When you conduct a mixed ANOVA, the table of Tests of Within-Subjects Effects (see Figure 21-14) presents two important pieces of information. First, it gives you the main effect for your within-groups variable. This is in the first row denoted by the name of your within-subjects variable, which in this example was year. The second is your interaction effect (which is denoted by both variable names separated by an asterisk).

In this example information for the main effect for year of study can be found along the row labelled 'year' and the interaction effect can be found along the row which is labelled with the product of both variables: 'year*Course'.

Just like the within-groups ANOVA from Chapter 19, there are four separate versions of each result reported. Which one you should interpret depends on the results of Mauchly's test in Figure 21-14. If Mauchly's test is not significant you can interpret the ANOVA results from the Sphericity Assumed values. If Mauchly's test is significant, interpret the ANOVA results from the Greenhouse–Geisser values. In this example Mauchly's test was significant (see Figure 21-12), so we can interpret the Greenhouse–Geisser values. (This is explained in the assumptions section later in this chapter.)

The last column in the ANOVA table is the probability (p or sig.) value associated with the F ratio. As with all inferential tests, if this value is less than 0.05, then you can reject the null hypothesis. In this example, the p-value main effect of year is $< .001$, which means you can reject the null hypothesis that the mean scores for all groups are equal. In other words, there is a statistically significant difference in the mean scores of the critical thinking between the three years of study. Finally, as the p-value for the interaction term is 0.145, which is greater than 0.05, that means there is no statistically significant interaction. In other words, the effect year of study on critical thinking scores is not influenced by the course of study.

Figure 21-15:
Tests of Within-Subjects Contrast table as produced in SPSS output.

Source	year	Type III Sum of Squares	df	Mean Square	F	Sig.
year	Linear	455.625	1	455.625	64.147	.000
	Quadratic	.075	1	.075	.074	.789
year * Course	Linear	9.025	1	9.025	1.271	.274
	Quadratic	9.075	1	9.075	8.902	.008
Error (year)	Linear	127.850	18	7.103		
	Quadratic	18.350	18	1.019		

Figure 21-15 tests trends within the data. It is more appropriate to look at the means or plots to examine trends and therefore you do not need to interpret this table.

In a mixed ANOVA the table of Tests of Between-Subjects Effects presents the main effect for your between-groups variable (see Figure 21-16). This is in the row denoted by the name of your between-subjects variable which in this example was 'Course'.

Figure 21-16:
Tests of
Between-
Subjects
Contrast
table as
produced
in SPSS
output.

Source	Type III Sum of Squares	df	Mean Square	F	Sig.
Intercept	222894.150	1	222894.150	1210.395	.000
Course	1188.150	1	1188.150	6.452	.021
Error	3314.700	18	184.150		

This is the between-subjects main effect.

The final column in the ANOVA table is the probability (*p* or *sig.*) value associated with the *F* ratio. As with all inferential tests, if this value is less than 0.05, then you can reject the null hypothesis. In this example, the *p*-value for the main effect of year is .021, which means you can reject the null hypothesis that the mean scores for all courses are equal. In other words, there is a statistically significant difference in the mean scores of critical thinking between psychology students and drama students.

When you conduct a mixed ANOVA you can find the main effect for your within-groups variable and interaction effect in the table of Tests of Within-Subjects Effects. You can find the main effect for your between-groups variable in the table of Tests of Between-Subjects Effects.

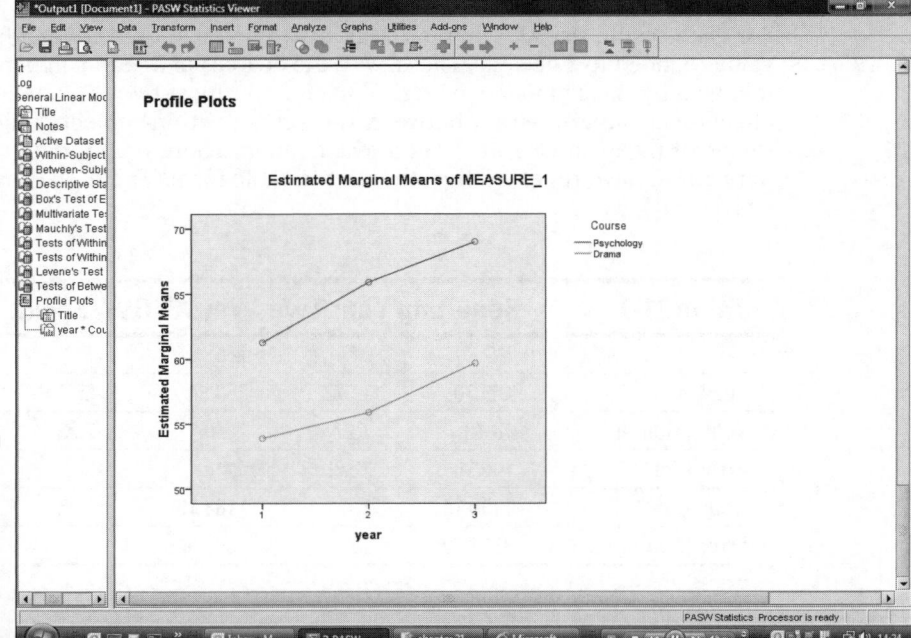

Figure 21-17:
The interaction plot as produced in SPSS output.

It is always important to spend some time looking at your interaction plot to figure out what is happening in your data. In Figure 21-17 the *y*-axis displays the critical thinking scores and the *x*-axis denotes the first, second and third year of study at university. There are two separate lines in the plot; one represents the psychology student group and the other the drama student group. If you look at the top line, which represents the psychology students' mean scores you can see they demonstrated an increase each year. The drama students' mean scores, represented by the lower line, demonstrated a similar pattern. You should also note the drama students have lower mean scores than psychology students in year one and this difference is maintained in years two and three. So it appears the critical thinking scores of both psychology and drama students increase during their courses but drama students have lower scores at each time point.

Writing up the results of a two-way mixed ANOVA

When reporting the results of a mixed ANOVA there are three important pieces of information you must include:

- ✔ The between-subjects main effect
- ✔ The within-subjects main effect
- ✔ The interaction effect

For each result, the APA manual suggests that you should report the F ratio value rounded to 2 decimal places, with the degrees of freedom in parentheses, followed by the significance level. You should report two *df* – one for the effect mean square (either between-subjects or within-subjects) and one for the error mean square, separated by a comma. There is a lot of information here so we have reported the statistics in table form (Table 21-1) as well as in words.

Table 21-1	Reporting Your Two-Way ANOVA Result				
	SS	*df*	*MS*	*F*	*p*
Year	455.70	1.27	358.84	56.10	<.001
Year x Course	18.10	1.27	14.25	2.23	.145
Error (Year)	146.20	22.86	6.40		
Course	1188.15	1	1188.15	6.45	.021
Error (Course)	3314.70	18	184.15		

Taking the two-way ANOVA result reported in Table 21-1, you report the result in the text as follows:

> The critical thinking scores were analysed using a (3) × 2 mixed-ANOVA with the within-subjects factor of year of study (first, second and third year of study) and the between-subjects factor of course studied (psychology or drama). Mauchly's test indicated that the assumption of sphericity had been violated so the Greenhouse–Geisser correction was employed. There were statistically significant main effects for the year of study; $F(1.27,22.86) = 56.10$, $p < .001$, and for course of study; $F(1,18) = 6.45$, $p = .021$. There was no significant interaction between year of study and course; $F(1.27,22.86) = 2.23$, $p = .145$.

Just like when you report any inferential statistic, you should report an appropriate effect size statistic (see Chapter 11) and the relevant descriptive statistics (which in this case are the mean and standard deviation values that are presented in Figure 21-9). The plot of the interaction should be included and described in words; this is particularly important when the ANOVA indicates a statistically significant interaction.

If you report statistically significant main effects where the independent variable has more than two levels (to unravel where the differences actually exist) then you will need to consider the relevant post hoc tests or planned comparisons. If you need to conduct post hoc tests or planned comparisons for the main effect of the between-groups variable refer to Chapter 17 and for the main effect of a within-group variable see Chapter 20. In this example you know there is a statistically significant main effect of year of study but to find out where these differences actually exist you need to conduct the appropriate follow-up tests. There is no need to conduct follow-up tests for the statistically significant main effect of course, as it only has two levels.

Assumptions

The mixed ANOVA is a parametric statistic which means it is based on certain assumptions about the distribution of the data. It is therefore important that you spend some time checking the underlying assumptions, because if you have conducted an ANOVA with inappropriate data you run the risk of performing inappropriate analyses, which means your results, and therefore your conclusions, may be incorrect. Unfortunately there is no non-parametric equivalent of the mixed ANOVA, so if you find your data violates the assumptions outlined, we suggest you contact a statistical advisor. For a mixed ANOVA, the conditions that must be met before you should interpret the result are covered in the following sections.

Type of data

The independent variables should be categorical and the dependent variable should be measured at the interval/ratio level (see Chapter 2 for more on levels of measurement).

Residuals approximate a normal distribution

The residual scores should follow an approximately normal distribution (see Chapter 9 for a description of the normal distribution). You have saved the standardised residual when you conducted the analysis by ticking the relevant box as illustrated in Figure 21-5. This means there are residuals saved in your data file. You can estimate normality by plotting these residuals on a graph, such as a histogram (see Chapter 6) and by conducting a test, such as the Kolmogorov–Smirnov test, to examine the departure of this graph from normality (see Chapter 9). There is more information on this assumption in Chapter 16 if you want a recap.

Homogeneity of variances

Homogeneity of variances refers to the assumption that each level of the between-groups variable (or the different groups) should have approximately equal variances. You assess this via Levene's test see Figure 21-13.

If the significance value or *p*-value for Levene's test is .05 or greater, then you can conclude that the variances of the groups are similar and the results can be interpreted as usual.

If the significance value or *p*-value for Levene's test is less than .05 the variances of the groups may not be similar and this assumption has been violated.

If you have equal sample sizes in your groups and when the groups are reasonably large (around 20 cases in each group) then you can assume homogeneity of variances; this means you do not have to check Levene's test and interpret the results as usual.

Sphericity

The differences between each level of the within-groups variable (or differences between testing sessions) should have approximately equal variances. This is known as *sphericity*. SPSS automatically provides Mauchly's test (if you have three or more testing sessions), which tests the null hypothesis that the variances of the differences are equal.

If Mauchly's test produces a non-significant result (see Figure 21-12), this indicates that the variances of the differences between each testing session are approximately equal. So the assumption isn't violated, and when interpreting your ANOVA results you report the sphericity assumed figures (see Figure 21-14).

If Mauchly's test produces a significant result (see Figure 21-12), it suggests that the variances between the differences aren't equal and the assumption of sphericity is violated. If this assumption is violated you can interpret the Greenhouse–Geisser values (see Figure 21-14); this applies a correction to the degrees of freedom to account for the variation in differences, producing a more conservative test.

You only need to check Mauchly's test if your within-groups variables have more than two levels (or you had more than two testing sessions).

If you look at Figure 21-14 you will notice SPSS actually provides you with two other alternative corrected versions of the ANOVA result. The Huynh-Feldt and Lower-bound are similar to the Greenhouse–Geisser correction in that they account for the violation of sphericity and produce results which are less and more conservative respectively. These versions are not normally reported.

Homogeneity of variance–covariance matrices

Mixed ANOVAs have an additional assumption you will not see elsewhere in this book. As well as variances being approximately equal (checked via the homogeneity of variances and sphericity assumptions) you now have the covariances or the relationships between the variables to consider. This is known as the homogeneity of variance–covariance matrices assumption and it is assessed by Box's M test.

If you have equal cell sizes (that is, your sample size is the same for each group and testing session) then you can assume homogeneity of variance-covariance matrices. This means you do not need to consult Box's M test and can interpret the rest of the results as usual.

If you have unequal cell sizes and the *p*-value for Box's M test is greater than .001, then this assumption is not violated and can interpret the rest of the results as usual (see Figure 21-10).

If you have unequal cell sizes and the *p*-value for Box's test is less than .001 it may indicate you do not have homogeneity of variance-covariance matrices and this assumption is violated (see Figure 21-10).

The explanation of homogeneity of variance–covariance matrices gets complicated very quickly, as it involves matrix algebra which is beyond the scope of this book. This is not helped by the fact that Box's M test is generally regarded as too sensitive in detecting violations of this assumption, especially when dealing with large sample sizes. This is why we suggest you adopt a more conservative interpretation of the result and only assume the assumption is violated if the *p*-value is less than .001 rather than the usual .05.

Part VI
The Part of Tens

In this part . . .

Every *For Dummies* book has a Part of Tens, and this one is no exception. This part provides you with hints and tips on how to avoid mistakes and write up your results in the most appropriate way. These pointers can save you from the pitfalls often suffered by inexperienced researchers, and contribute to you producing a better results section. We outline some of the common mistakes and misunderstandings students make when performing statistical analyses and how you can avoid them, and we provide quick and useful tips for writing your results section.

Chapter 22

Ten Pieces of Good Advice for Inferential Testing

• •

In This Chapter

▶ Avoiding common statistical pitfalls

▶ Knowing which tests you need to perform – and which you don't

▶ Getting help with your statistics

• •

*T*his chapter outlines some of the best ways to avoid common mistakes in performing statistical analysis. We tend to see these mistakes a lot so please take the time to read through this chapter. We outline the confusion between statistical significance and practical significance or clinical relevance, we briefly explain how Type I and Type II errors occur and the other common misunderstandings that often occur in students' (and colleagues') reports! More importantly, we tell you what to do to avoid them.

Statistical Significance Is Not the Same as Practical Significance

Statistical significance has a very specific meaning. It tells you whether or not your result could have occurred by chance (assuming the null hypothesis is true). It does not tell you anything about the importance or size of the effect. If you were to find a correlation of magnitude 0.07 between two variables in a sample of 1000 participants you would correctly report this is as statistically significant; $r(998) = .07$, $p = .01$. This simply means you are confident that this is the relationship that exists in the data. If you actually look at the correlation coefficient you can see the actual effect size of relationship is very small indeed. If you square the correlation coefficient to get the shared variance you can see there is approximately 0.5 per cent of shared variance between the variables. We would argue that this has little practical, applied or clinical significance. Always check your effect size in conjunction with statistical significance.

Fail to Prepare, Prepare to Fail

Failure to recruit an appropriate sample size may mean you will fail to detect a significant effect (that is, make a Type II error). For example, imagine you wish to investigate the relationship between eccentricity and the number of years spent lecturing. If you recruited ten professors from your university you might conclude there was no statistical relationship; $r(8) = .5$, $p = .07$. If you had recruited two more professors you may have had exactly the same effect size but concluded that there was a significant relationship between eccentricity and the number of years spent lecturing; $r(10) = .5$, $p = .049$. Always conduct appropriate sample size calculations before commencing any study.

Don't Go Fishing for a Significant Result

Remember that when you conduct any statistical test there is a 5 per cent chance of making a Type I error, which means you conclude that there is a statistically significant effect in the population but there really isn't. If you conduct 100 correlations desperately trying to find something to report it is likely you will find a significant effect, but you have massively increased your chances of making Type I errors. When you design your study you should have a specific hypothesis in mind, so you should limit your analysis to this research question.

Check Your Assumptions

Before reporting any statistical test, make sure you check the relevant assumptions for that statistic. For example, if you are conducting linear regression then the relationship between your predictor variables and the criterion should be linear! If you neglect to ensure your data meets the assumptions for the analysis you are conducting, you may fail to find a significant result or, worse, report a significant effect when it is not appropriate. Remember to state in your write up which assumptions you checked.

My p Is Bigger Than Your p

Do not be tempted to compare p-values between different statistical tests as it doesn't make any sense! Remember the statistical significance tells you about chance while effect sizes tell you about the magnitude of the effect you are looking at. If you wish to compare effects it is more appropriate to contrast effect sizes.

Differences and Relationships Are Not Opposing Trends

It is possible to obtain both a significant correlation and significant difference between the same two variables. Differences and relationships are not opposing trends. For example, let's imagine you measured self-confidence in a group of 20 participants before and after a successful intervention and everyone's score increased 50 per cent after the intervention. In this case you would have a very strong positive significant correlation, as those people who had the highest self-confidence before the intervention still would have the highest self-confidence scores and the people with the lowest self-confidence would still have the lowest scores. The relationship between the variables reflects consistency, as they have all increased by the same factor. You will also have a statistically significant difference between the groups as each participant's score has increased by 50 per cent.

Where Did My Post-hoc Tests Go?

When you conduct an ANOVA and find a significant effect, post-hoc tests and planned contrasts are appropriate if your independent variable has more than two levels. If you only have two comparisons to make, these statistics are not necessary. If you find a significant difference, for example, between smokers and non-smokers on halitosis ($F(2,29 = 7.28, p < .001$) then smokers and non-smokers significantly differ on halitosis! Similarly if you are conducting a within-groups ANOVA and your independent variable only has two levels the assumption of sphericity is not relevant and Mauchly's test of sphericity will not be produced.

Categorising Continuous Data

Sometimes students feel the need to categorise interval and ratio data. For example, they may decide to categorise extraversion scores into introverts and extroverts groups. By doing this you are losing lots information in your data set. You also may be forcing participants into categories that may not be appropriate. Let's look at an example where extroversion scores range from 10 to 50 and you decide than anyone who scores less than 20 is an introvert and anyone who scores 20 or more will be categorised as an extrovert. For example, if we have 3 extroversion scores of 19, 21 and 47. This will mean the person who scored 21 will be in the same group as the participant who scored 47 when they may have more in common with the person who scored 19. Always select the analysis to suit your data instead of trying to fit your data to a particular analysis.

Be Consistent

Ensure you treat variables in the same way throughout your analyses. For example, you may correctly decide to conduct a Spearman's correlation between participants' rating of their own attractiveness and rating of their own self-confidence; both variables are measured at the ordinal level: So far, so good! Then you wish to see if there is a difference in self-rated attractiveness between males and females so conduct an independent *t*-test. This is a problem as the *t*-test assumes your dependent variable is measured at the interval/ratio level. Ensure all variables are treated consistently when conducting descriptive and inferential statistics.

Get Help!

Hopefully the information contained in this book will help you conduct useful statistical analyses, but this is only the beginning. There are other, more complex statistical tests that exist for more complex research questions. If you find that this book does not appear to contain the analyses necessary to answer your research question, then you might need to get help from a statistics advisor, but we strongly encourage you to involve a statistics advisor in your research from the outset. This person will provide useful advice about sample size calculations and the type of data that you should collect in order to answer your research questions. If you do not approach the statistics advisor until after you have collected your data, the statistics advisor can only provide limited help.

The guiding principle is that the statistics advisor should be there to provide advice, not to conduct your statistical analysis for you! It is therefore imperative you ask the right questions. You should approach the statistics advisor with a rationale of your project and ask them if your plan for analysis is appropriate to address your hypotheses. If you simply show up with the data and ask what analyses you should do, you are expecting too much!

Chapter 23

Ten Tips for Writing Your Results Section

▶ Reporting what you need to report

▶ Steering clear of unnecessary stats

▶ Being clear on what your stats really show

*T*his chapter provides quick and useful tips for writing your results section. Even if you have written a few reports we hope that by using these top ten tips you can improve the results section of your report. We offer advice on how to report values, reminders to include important information and the structure you should adopt.

Reporting the p-value

The American Psychological Association (APA) manual states you should always report the exact *p*-value (the statistical significance level) when you are writing up your results, unless the value is less than .001. Report your *p*-value to three decimal places (that is, three numbers after the decimal place) when the number is very small, and two decimal places for larger *p*-values, and remember that there is no need to include a zero before the decimal point. Some students and journals only report that the *p*-value is greater than .05 ($p > .05$) or less than .05 ($p < .05$). While you do use these criteria to judge you have if a statistically significant effect, using this format in your written response limits the amount of information you present to the reader. For example, $t(9) = 1.79$, $p = .053$ lets the reader know that this is approaching statistical significance and suggests an increased sample size may have led to a different conclusion. When the *p*-value is less than .001 you should report that $p < .001$. Remember *p* is never equal to zero. If the *p*-value appears as .000 in the SPSS output it simply means that the value is very small and should be reported as $p < .001$.

Reporting Other Figures

When reporting your results you should round off all figures (means, standard deviations, *t*-values, *F*-ratios, and so on) to 2 decimal places. This means there should be only 2 numbers after the decimal point. The rule for rounding off is that if the figure at the third decimal place is 4 or less, then you round down (or leave the numbers as it is). For example:

$$12.764729 \rightarrow 12.76$$

If the figure at the third decimal place is 5 or greater then round up (that is, increase the figure at the second decimal place by 1). For example:

$$37.23871 \rightarrow 37.24$$

Also bear in mind that the APA manual states that any statistical symbols must be italicised. This includes symbols used for means (*M*), standard deviation, (*SD*), correlations (*r*), *t*-values (*t*), probabilities (*p*), *F*-ratios (*F*), and so on.

Don't Forget About the Descriptive Statistics

The descriptive statistics will help the reader to form a picture of the sample (in terms of demographic characteristics and the key variables in the study) and should be included at the start of your results section. This will be useful in determining whether the research findings are likely to be applicable to the reader's own situation. Descriptive statistics are also useful in making sense of further analyses. For example, it might be the case that you find a small correlation between two variables in your study that you would expect to be correlated more strongly. Such a discrepancy might be explained by an examination of the descriptive statistics – if these variables have very low estimates of variance (for example, very low standard deviation values), then this lack of variation could be the reason for the lower than expected correlation coefficient.

Do Not Overuse the Mean

The mean is a very useful measure of central tendency to describe your data. There are many occasions when it is not appropriate and is misleading to report the mean. It is inappropriate to use the mean to summarise nominal or categorical data. Statements like 'The mean gender was 1.27' or 'The mean nationality was 3.72' clearly don't make sense! In these cases it is most appropriate to use the mode or percentages to describe the data; for example, 'The most frequently occurring nationality was Monegasque (53 per cent), followed by Sammarinese (37 per cent) and finally Liechtensteiner (10 per cent)'. It is also inappropriate to use the mean when your interval or ratio level data is highly skewed or has large outliers. For example, imagine a small manufacturing company with 20 employees who all earn £30,000 a year. The average wage is therefore £30,000. If we include the owner-manager of the company, who pays himself a generous £600,000, the mean jumps up to £57,143 which is clearly not reflective of most the employees. Always use the measure of central tendency and dispersion that is most suited to your data.

Report Effect Sizes and Direction of Effects

After getting your head around inferential statistics and learning what statistical significance actually means there can be a tendency to focus on the *p* value of your result. For example, if you only report that 'There is a statistically significant difference in IQ between those people who watch soap operas compared to those who not watch soap operas; $t(367) = 1.66$, $p = .049$' this sounds like a very interesting result but this only means that you are confident your result did not occur by chance (assuming the null hypothesis is true). You have not said anything about the direction of the relationship or the strength of the effect. You have not told us which group had a higher IQ and which had the lower IQ (although in this example we could guess!). Furthermore, we need some indication of the effect size. We may be very interested if the effect size is large, but if there is a really tiny effect (0.1 per cent difference between the groups) it becomes less interesting. Always report the direction of the effect and the effect size.

The Case of the Missing Participants

Although you should include your sample size when writing up your report, you should also specify whether you had missing participants, and consider whether this could have any effect on your analysis. For example, if you were examining exercise and health with school children in the classroom, several of your potential participants may choose to withdraw from the study. You may not get parental consent, or the students may not be able to physically participate in your study. There may be other children off sick or who are not in the class the day you conducted your testing. This may raise questions about how easily your results can be generalised if you are testing only those children who are physically fit and healthy. Always report the total sample approached and the final sample size used for analysis, and account for any missing participants.

Be Careful with Your Language

Make sure to use language that is appropriate to the analysis you have conducted. When conducting correlations you are describing relationships, a chi-square assesses associations, *t*-tests evaluate differences, and you should use predictions or relationships when discussing regression. When you are describing ANOVAs you can talk about differences, main effects and interactions.

Beware Correlations and Causality

Correlations do not imply causality! Correlations only indicate the strength and direction of a relationship between two variables. Correlations, irrespective of size, do not imply that one variable causes a change in the other variable. For example, you may find a very large correlation between the head sizes within a sample of children and their mathematical ability. This does not mean that big heads make bright kids or mathematical knowledge causes children's heads to expand (in this case it may be due to another variable such as age). Of course sometimes you may get a significant correlation because there is an underlying cause and effect relationship (for example, revision hours and exam mark). So causality can't be implied from a correlation coefficient but it also shouldn't necessarily be written off as a possibility.

Make Sure to Answer Your Own Question

If you are formulating a hypothesis make sure your analysis addresses it specifically. For example, did your analysis test for a significant difference between males and females on depression or did you test for a significant difference between male and female psychology students on scores of the Beck Depression Inventory? Also remember to check if your hypotheses are one or two-tailed and ensure you report the appropriate one- or two-tailed *p*-value.

Add Some Structure

A good results section will be structured and focused. This will usually start with a presentation of your descriptive results. Next you should present the analyses that address your hypotheses. If, for example, you have two hypotheses you should have two clear, separate analyses. Do not be tempted to adopt a shotgun approach where you run every analysis that you possibly can! Concentrate on those analyses that directly address your hypotheses only.

Index

• D •

● **L** ●

FOR DUMMIES®

Making Everything Easier!™

GADGETS

978-1-1180-2444-7

978-1-1180-3671-6

978-1-1180-2445-4

MAC OS X LION

978-1-1180-2205-4

978-1-1180-2206-1

978-1-1180-2772-1

PROGRAMMING LANGUAGES

978-0-470-37173-2

978-0-470-92996-4

978-0-470-52275-2

Amazing Android Apps For Dummies
978-0-470-93629-0

AutoCAD 2012 For Dummies
978-1-118-02440-9

BlackBerry PlayBook For Dummies
978-1-118-01698-5

Blender For Dummies, 2nd Edition
978-0-470-58446-0

Creating Web Pages All-in-One For Dummies, 4th Edition
978-0-470-64032-6

Digital SLR Cameras and Photography For Dummies, 4th Edition
978-1-118-14489-3

Facebook For Dummies, 4th Edition
978-1-118-09562-1

HTML, XHTML & CSS For Dummies, 7th Edition
978-0-470-91659-9

iPad 2 For Dummies, 3rd Edition
978-1-118-17679-5

Laptops and Tablets For Seniors For Dummies, 2nd Edition
978-1-118-09596-6

Mac Application Development For Dummies
978-1-118-03222-0

Macs For Dummies, 11th Edition
978-0-470-87868-2

Nikon D5100 For Dummies
978-1-118-11819-1

QuickBooks 2012 For Dummies
978-1-118-09120-3

Samsung Galaxy Tab 10.1 For Dummies
978-1-118-22833-3

Twitter Marketing For Dummies, 2nd Edition
978-0-470-93057-1

WordPress Web Design For Dummies
978-0-470-93503-3

Windows Phone 7 Application Development For Dummies
978-1-118-02175-0

Available wherever books are sold. For more information or to order direct go to www.wiley.com or call +44 (0) 1243 843291

FOR DUMMIES®

Making Everything Easier! ™

WEB DEVELOPMENT

978-1-1180-7342-1

978-0-470-64032-6

978-0-470-91659-9

MOBILE DEVELOPMENT

978-1-1180-9134-0

978-1-1180-9623-9

978-1-1180-2175-0

SOCIAL MEDIA

978-1-1180-9562-1

978-0-470-58468-2

978-0-470-76879-2

Android 3 SDK Programming For Dummies
978-1-118-00825-6

BlackBerry For Dummies, 5th Edition
978-1-118-10035-6

Canon EOS Rebel T3/1100D For Dummies
978-1-118-09497-6

E-Mail Marketing For Dummies, 2nd Edition
978-0-470-94767-8

Facebook Application Development For Dummies
978-0-470-76873-0

Google AdWords For Dummies, 3rd Edition
978-1-118-11561-9

iPhone 4S For Dummies, 5th Edition
978-1-118-03671-6

Mac OS X Lion For Dummies
978-1-118-02205-4

Java For Dummies, 5th Edition
978-0-470-37173-2

PCs All-in-One For Dummies, 6th Edition
978-1-118-28035-5

R For Dummies
978-1-119-96284-7

Search Engine Optimization All-in-One For Dummies, 2nd Edition
978-1-118-02441-6

Spotify For Dummies
978-1-119-95234-3

Switching to a Mac For Dummies, Mac OS X Lion Edition
978-1-118-02446-1

VMware vSphere For Dummies
978-0-470-76872-3

QuickBooks For Dummies, UK Edition
978-1-119-96894-8